FOUR PLAYS BY
ARISTOPHANES

The Clouds

The Birds

Lysistrata

The Frogs

TRANSLATIONS BY
WILLIAM ARROWSMITH,
RICHMOND LATTIMORE,
AND DOUGLASS PARKER

A MERIDIAN BOOK

MERIDIAN
Published by the Penguin Group
Penguin Books USA Inc., 375 Hudson Street,
New York, New York 10014, U.S.A.
Penguin Books Ltd, 27 Wrights Lane,
London W8 5TZ, England
Penguin Books Australia Ltd, Ringwood,
Victoria, Australia
Penguin Books Canada Ltd, 10 Alcorn Avenue,
Toronto, Ontario, Canada M4V 3B2
Penguin Books (N.Z.) Ltd, 182–190 Wairau Road,
Auckland 10, New Zealand

Penguin Books Ltd, Registered Offices:
Harmondsworth, Middlesex, England

Published by Meridian, an imprint of Dutton Signet, a division of Penguin
Books USA Inc. Previously appeared in a Meridian Classic edition. These
plays were previously published by New American Library in separate
volumes.

First Meridian Printing, May, 1994

30 29 28 27 26 25 24 23 22 21

REGISTERED TRADEMARK—MARCA REGISTRADA

LIBRARY OF CONGRESS CATALOG CARD NUMBER: 84–61181

Printed in the United States of America

FOUR PLAYS BY
ARISTOPHANES

THE CLOUDS: The most controversial of Aristophanes' plays, it is a brilliant caricature of the philosopher Socrates, seen as a wily sophist who teaches men to cheat through cunning argument....

THE BIRDS: This portrayal of a flawed utopia called Cloudcuckooland is an enchanting escape into the world of free-flying fantasy that explores the eternal dilemmas of man on earth....

LYSISTRATA: In the twenty-first year of the Peloponnesian War, the women of Athens and Sparta, tired of the incessant fighting between their men, resolve to withhold sex from their husbands until peace is settled....

THE FROGS: Visiting the underworld, the god Dionysus seeks the counsel of the dead tragedians Aeschylus and Euripides on how to bring good writing back to Athens. A fierce debate—full of scathing insults and literary satire—ensues between the two dramatists....

WILLIAM ARROWSMITH has been a Rhodes Scholar and Woodrow Wilson Fellow and has won numerous other distinguished awards. Recognized as one of the world's foremost classical teachers, scholars, and translators, he has been a prime mover and shaper of the dramatic resurgence of the art of translation in recent years.

RICHMOND LATTIMORE has been a Fulbright Fellow in Greece and a Fulbright Lecturer at Oxford and has received awards from the National Institute of Arts and Letters and the American Council of Learned Societies.

DOUGLASS PARKER was a Junior Fellow at the Center for Hellenistic Studies in Washington, D.C. He has also translated works of Terence, Aeschylus, and Socrates.

CONTENTS

The
Clouds

CONTENTS

For
John K. Colby
who first taught me Greek

Introduction

The Play

The original version of *The Clouds* was presented in March, 423 B.C at the Great Dionysia, where it disappointed Aristophanes' hopes by being placed third. The First Prize was awarded to the aging Kratinos for his final comedy, *Pytine* (or *The Wineflask*) and the runner-up was Ameipsias with his *Konnos*.[1] After the success of both *Acharnians* and *Knights*, this defeat must have been a bitter blow for Aristophanes. In *Knights* of the year before he had twitted Kratinos with being a doddering drunkard whose comic talents had decayed, and the drunkard had replied by confessing his drunkenness in a play of such comic verve and gaiety—accusing Aristophanes, for instance, of being a mere "Euripidaristophanizing" plagiarist—that he completely defeated his brash young critic Worse yet, Ameipsias' *Konnos* was, like *The Clouds*, an attack on the sophistic movement, containing a Chorus of Sophists and, evidently, satirizing Sokrates by name. All this might not have mattered had *The Clouds* been a less ambi-

---

[1]Konnos was the name of Sokrates' music teacher, and it is likely that the play attacked the "New Music."

tious play, but Aristophanes regarded it as by far the finest comedy of his career to date.[2]

Probably in the hope of getting a second hearing—if only from readers—he revised the play, and the version of *The Clouds* which we now possess is not the original of 423 B.C. but a revision carried out some three or four years later. According to the Scholiast, the revision was thorough and extensive changes were made, but the chief alterations affected three sections in particular: the *parabasis*, the *agon* between the two *Logoi*, and the finale, the burning of the Thinkery. The full extent of these changes cannot be ascertained. In the *parabasis*, the original choral anapests were replaced by a passage whose meter is unique in a *parabasis* (a probable indication that the poet had no expectation of seeing the play restaged) and in which Aristophanes takes off the customary choral mask and speaks to his readers directly in the first person. To the *agon* was added the famous, passionate defense of the Old Education, a speech clearly designed, through its power of conviction and moral seriousness, to show Aristophanes' critics that what was at stake in his play was nothing less than the fate and future of civilized Athens. About the finale no such certainty is possible, though there is some small reason to believe that in the original version it was the god Hermes, rather than Strepsiades, who fired the Thinkery.

Even in its present form, revised for readers rather than for the stage, *The Clouds* is visibly a masterpiece, a play of wonderful, ragging satire, tilted so expertly toward the preposterous and the absurd that its effect is wholly and unmistakably comic. We have, in fact, almost a *reductio ad absurdum* of the satirical intent, satire become so *buffa* and burlesque that its characters and targets, by sheer exaggeration and incongruity, survive as directly comic. In short, a splendid play, beautifully sustained and shaped, and everywhere guided by Aristophanes' genius for comic distortion and his cunning of absurdity. If not the funniest play he ever wrote, it is certainly the cleverest: clever in construction and plot, clever

---

[2]*The Clouds*, 522: "convinced . . . that this play was the finest of my comedies .   ."

in its exploitation of incongruities, clever in polemic and wit. Almost, perhaps, too clever for its own good. But for Aristophanes these very qualities of cleverness and wit were precisely what made *The Clouds* superior to his own previous work and that of his "cheap and vulgar rivals": for their slapstick of situation and crude horseplay he here substitutes the ludicrous slapstick of the intellect and the better horseplay of poetry and imagination. In its structure too *The Clouds* is an improvement. Unusually tight and coherent,[3] at least by Aristophanic standards, its action is all of a piece, a continuously unfolding plot, written to be performed by a small cast, and singlemindedly devoted to the pursuit of its quarry. If it lacks the miraculous violence and vigor of *The Knights* or the exuberance of *The Acharnians*, it makes up for those qualities by the greater clarity and economy of its design and the pure lyricism of its poetry. Until *The Birds*, there is nothing in Aristophanes to match the loveliness of the poetry here assigned to the Chorus of Clouds as it enters. In this play, for the first time, we catch a glimpse of that exquisite tension between slapstick and poetry, the obscene and sublime, which was Aristophanes' major individual contribution to comedy and which lies at the heart of his two greatest lyrical comedies, *The Birds* and *The Frogs*.

At first blush the improbable victim of *The Clouds* seems to be the philosopher Sokrates. But actually Aristophanes is deliberately exploiting Sokrates here as a convenient comic representative of the sophistic corruption which is the play's real subject. In the illustration of that corruption, Sokrates is nothing more than the poet's cipher, a curious catchpaw of those enormous cultural polarities (Old and New, Tradition and Innovation, Country and City, Peace and War, Poetry and Prose, Custom and Logic, etc.) which Aristophanes loved to elaborate and which he presented in play after play as locked in a life-and-death struggle for the soul of Athens. Whether Aristophanes privately believed that Sokrates was a

---

[3]In my opinion the only major structural flaw in the play is the abrupt change in the role of the Chorus. At least I find a jar when the Clouds suddenly reveal that they are actually celestial *agents provocateurs* masking as the patrons of the Sophists.

Sophist or presented him that way for its comic and preposterous effect, we shall never know. But for the purposes of the play, Sokrates is merely a genial polemical emblem of the sophistic movement—if that extraordinary simultaneous flowering of individual genius, crankery, "educationalism," and fraud can be called a movement at all. For Aristophanes such distinctions are academic, and to his mind the Sophists are a movement only because they are something worse, a conspiracy of charlatans and humbugs. Distinctions of doctrine and belief are totally disregarded. Jumbled together in ludicrous proximity and then stuffed into the mouth of Sokrates are the doctrines of Protagoras, the pre-Socratics generally, Anaxagoras, Diagoras, Gorgias, Prodikos, and perhaps Thrasymachos. It is grotesque—and hilarious. It is polemic on the grand scale, contemptuous of niceties, careless of reputations, unfair, Procrustean, and passionately loyal to its central perception. Addressed to, and exploiting, the average man's ridiculous stereotype of philosophy and science, it remains an honest and uncompromising play.

Grant Aristophanes his premises, and his logic is ruthlessly consistent. If Sokrates is a symbol of intellectual corruption and fraud, Strepsiades represents the Old Tradition in its corruption. Far from presenting Sokrates as the indispensable corrupter, Aristophanes shows that Strepsiades can be hoodwinked only because he had been corrupted *prior* to his enrollment in the Thinkery. All Sokrates does is to complete the process—or at least he tries to. But for Aristophanes the Sophists are merely symptoms of the general corruption, not its causes; they stand to education and the life of the mind exactly as Kleon stands to politics and Euripides to tragedy. If the Sophists are strong in being unprincipled, Strepsiades is weak because he is stupid and because the principles and values that might have protected him from his own stupidity have deteriorated. He is essentially only a denser Dikaiopolis become citified and decadent; in another context he might have been a peasant hero. But transplanted to Athens from the country, cursed with an expensive aristocratic marriage and a playboy son, he is an Awful Warning on the Perils of the City and the Evils of Imperialism. According to Aristophanes, the process of corruption began with Athenian imperialism and the war fought to maintain the empire. If imperialism brought with it tyranny, luxury, litigation, and the domination of political life by demagogic rhetoric, the war was destroying the very fabric of Athenian life by ravaging the countryside and forcing the evacuation of the country population into the city. There, cut off from the earth and uprooted from the context that gave it life and value, the Old Order had decayed, and with it were being destroyed all those traditions and virtues and decencies, which, for a conservative countryman like Aristophanes, were synonymous with Athenian civilization itself. Strepsiades is his comic image of this corruption and Sokrates its aggravating symptom. If the causes were irremediable, he could at least struggle with the symptoms. And no quarter asked or given.

Aristophanes and Sokrates

Why did Aristophanes select Sokrates as his spokesman for the Sophists, and was he guilty of malicious slander and moral irresponsibility in so doing?

By now these two questions have become inextricably bound up with the fortunes of the play which is, ironically, more commonly read as a perverse adjunct to The Socratic Problem than for its satire of the Sophists. No definite answer is possible in the poor state of our evidence, but the questions cannot be shrugged off, and I offer the following considerations for what they may be worth.

1. Plato's charge against Aristophanes is the serious charge of moral irresponsibility. By circulating a distorted image of Sokrates, Aristophanes created, or abetted, those slanders which Plato believed led to Sokrates' death. The official indictment read: "Sokrates is a malefactor who meddles in the matters of the heavens and the earth below, who makes the Worse Argument appear the Better and teaches others to follow his example." And the Platonic Sokrates comments to the jury: "You yourselves have seen these very things in Aristophanes' comedy—a Sokrates who is carried around in a basket and asserts that he walks upon the air and a great many other absurdities, of which I am completely ignorant." We

may, if we wish, doubt Plato's interpretation, but presumably the charges are accurately reported, and the implication is clear: the slanders of *The Clouds*, directly or indirectly, created the formal accusation brought against Sokrates in 399 B.C

2. But the evidence is partisan and polemical. Plato's account is that of a devoted disciple, not a reporter, and the prejudice of Platonists is almost religious [4]

3. Sokrates' own reaction, if Plutarch can be trusted,[5] was not that he had been slandered but that he had been teased: "I am twisted in the theater as I would be at a drinking-party."

4. Nonetheless, judging from the available evidence, the caricature of Sokrates in *The Clouds* is so distorted that it cannot be called a caricature at all. Thus Sokrates refused payment, was not an atheist, had no Thinkery, and never held the doctrines which are here put into his mouth. Worse, he consistently attacked the Sophists and their doctrines. He does, however, admit in the *Apology* that in his earlier days he had dabbled in "scientific" research.

5. That Aristophanes could not have foretold the consequence of his "slanders" is irrelevant. Slander is slander.

6. Aristophanes' private opinion of Sokrates is also irrelevant. In Plato's *Symposium*, the two men are presented as being on friendly terms, but this does not entitle us to suppose that Aristophanes really admired Sokrates or thought his views anything but pernicious. If it does, then Aristophanes was a hypocrite as well as morally irresponsible.

7. If Aristophanes was really ignorant of Sokrates' beliefs, he is equally culpable. Ignorance is no excuse for slander. But Aristophanes was anything but an ignorant man, and his refusal to allow his Sokrates to make one statement that is recognizably Sokratic seems to me to indicate strategy rather than stupidity.

8. The distortions practiced upon Sokrates are typical and

---

[4]It has even been suggested that *The Clouds* failed to win First Prize because the audience recognized—and disliked—the distorted image of Sokrates. Given what happened to Sokrates, this seems excessively naive.

[5]*De educatione puerorum* xiv.

not exceptional. They are, for instance, completely of a piece with Aristophanes' systematic distortion of Euripides; if Euripides' words are quoted against him, they are invariably taken from their context and parodied by willfull misunderstanding. But those who are angered by the spectacle of Sokrates mocked have never lifted a finger in defense of Euripides.[6]

9. In any case, the treatment of Sokrates is *not*, by Aristophanic standards, harsh or "pitiless satire," as Platonists claim. It is, in fact, surprisingly mild and impersonal. (The savage attack upon Kleon in *The Knights* is an instructive comparison.) Thus, apart from a couple of gibes at Sokrates' gait and general bathlessness, his personal life is strictly avoided. We hear nothing of the shrewish Xanthippe, nothing of the fashionable pederasty of the Socratic circle (or at least nothing that implicates Sokrates), nothing about Sokrates' midwife-mother (*cf.* the treatment meted out of Euripides' mother), etc. The charges are wholly professional: Sokrates is a humbug and a charlatan.

10. Aristophanes' "slanders" are, in some real sense, dictated by convention. Comedy is the heir of the early *komos*, and the *komos* was a convention whose essential attributes were invective and abuse. Which is to say merely that the Athenian comedian was not merely given license to be abusive, but that abuse was *expected* of him. And precisely because it was conventional, was expected, it could be discounted as conventional; and presumably those who were ragged were expected to take their ragging in good part—as Sokrates did, though Kleon (and Plato) did not. Needless to say, such a convention makes the notion of "moral irresponsibility" extremely hard to assess.

11. Sokrates is presented as preposterous and this strikes me as cool and deliberate strategy—doubtless sustained by malice and even a little contempt. There is, after all, a kind of humor—the kind of humor of the *komos*, I suspect—which contrives its fun out of a total inversion of the truth. Because the humor is conventional, the exaggeration is understood *as*

---

[6] As Speaker of the House Rayburn said in a different context: "It all depends on *whose* ox is gettin' gored."

exaggeration and the humorist's success consists in the very size and absurdity of the distortion The comedy lies in the disparity between the known truth and the degree of distortion achieved. This explanation might be less acceptable if it were not for the fact that Aristophanes is, of all comedians, the master of the incongruous, and that the stunning distortion is everywhere his stock-in-trade

12. If Aristophanes has not made Sokrates preposterous because the preposterousness was funny, he has done so out of dislike and the conviction that Sokrates was dangerous. In this he was probably mistaken, but Aristophanes was a man in the livery of an Idea, and if Sokrates is distorted or satirized in the service of that Idea, it is regrettable but not culpable. Ideas distort the world and those who serve them. Platonists should understand

Text and Acknowledgments

The texts which I have used as a basis of this translation are primarily those of Cantarella and Coulon. and I am, like every other translator of Aristophanes, indebted to B. B. Rogers' splendid notes and commentaries on individual passages. To both the University of California at Riverside and the University of Texas I owe my thanks for generous grants for the preparation of the manuscript. For help and encouragement and criticism, I am indebted to a great many people, but particularly to Douglass Parker and to my wife.

WILLIAM ARROWSMITH

Characters of the Play

STREPSIADES. *father of Pheidippides*
PHEIDIPPIDES. *a playboy*
XANTHIAS. *a slave*
STUDENTS OF SOKRATES
SOKRATES
CHORUS OF CLOUDS
KORYPHAIOS. *or Chorus Leader*
ARISTOPHANES
PHILOSOPHY
SOPHISTRY
PASIAS. *creditor of Strepsiades*
AMYNIAS. *creditor of Strepsiades*
CHAIREPHON. *disciple of Sokrates*

SLAVES. STUDENTS. WITNESSES. etc.

SCENE: *A street in Athens. On the left, the house of Strepsiades,** *an old farmer compelled by the war to leave the country and take up residence in Athens; on the right, the tiny, grubby, ramshackle hovel which houses Sokrates' Thinkery. On the extreme left, a statue of Poseideon. Before Strepsiades' house* *stands a Herm, a bust of the god Hermes supported by a square pillar; in front of Sokrates' house, balancing the Herm, stands a potbellied stove with a long tapering flue and a placard which reads:*

MODEL OF THE UNIVERSE
ACCORDING TO THE CONVECTION
PRINCIPLE.

Two cots are placed before Strepsiades' house, one occupied by Strepsiades himself, the other by Pheidippides. Huddled on the ground nearby lie several loudly snoring slaves. The time is just before dawn.

STREPSIADES

Thrashing restlessly, then throwing off his blankets and sitting bolt upright. He yawns.

Yaaaahhuuuuu.
Great Zeus Almighty, what an endless monster
of a night it's been! Won't the daylight *ever* come?
I could have sworn I heard the roosters crowing hours
ago.
And listen to those slaves. Still snoring away!
By god, things around here were a long sight different
in the good old days before this war! Drat
this stinking war anyway! It's ruined Athens.
Why, you can't even whip your own slaves any more
or they'll desert to the Spartans.*
                                        Bah.

Pointing to Pheidippides.

                                        And as for *him*,
that precious playboy son of mine, he's worse yet.
Look at him, stretched out there sleeping like a log
under five fat blankets, farting away.
                                        —All right,
if that's the way you want it, boy, I'll snuggle down
and fart you back a burst or two.

He burrows under the blankets for a moment, then throws them off and sits up again.

DAMN!
I'm so bitten up by all these blasted bedbuggering debts
and bills and stables-fees, I can't catch a wink.

Turning on Pheidippides.

And all because of YOU!
Yes, you and your damned horses!
Gigs, rigs, nags, ponytails*. . . . Hell,
horses everywhere! Horses in your dreams!
But *me?*
I'm bankrupt, broke, ruined, waiting for the end of the
month when all these debts come due.

Savagely kicking Xanthias awake.

—You. You there,
light me a lamp and bring me my ledger.

*The slave rises, lights a flickering lamp, and brings him the
ledger.*

Now then.
I'll just run over this account of my debts and see
how much I owe.
Hmmmm.

Reading aloud.

TO PASIAS: *THE SUM OF
THREE HUNDRED—*
Three hundred to Pasias? What in god's name for?
Of course. I remember. That gelding I bought from him. Idiot!
Better I should have gelded myself.

PHEIDIPPIDES

Shouting in his sleep.

PHILO,
YOU FOULED ME! KEEP IN YOUR OWN
LANE!

STREPSIADES

That's it.
That's the horsey blight that has blasted me dead.
Even in his dreams he thinks he's winning the derby.

PHEIDIPPIDES

In his sleep.

HOW MANY LAPS FOR THE STEEPLE-
CHASE?

STREPSIADES

Laps, is it?
A fat lot of laps you've driven your poor old man!

Resuming his accounting.

Let's see now. What's the next entry after Pasias?

Reading aloud.

TO AMYNIAS: FOR GIG, BODY AND WHEELS
INCLUDED, THE SUM OF—

PHEIDIPPIDES

In his sleep.

ROLL THE HORSE IN
THE DUST, TRAINER, AND THEN STABLE HIM.

STREPSIADES

You've rolled *me* out of house and
home, damn you!
I've lost two or three lawsuits on your account and now
the other creditors are clamoring for confiscation.

PHEIDIPPIDES

Waking up crossly.

Damn it,

Dad, why do you have to thrash around like this all night
long?

STREPSIADES

Because there's a bumbailiff* in the mattress biting me,
that's why.

PHEIDIPPIDES

      Oh, for god's sake, let me sleep, will you?

STREPSIADES

Go on, damn you, sleep! But I give you warning, boy.
Someday these debts will land on *your* head.

Pheidippides' only answer is a snore.

                                        By god,
I hope that meddling matchmaker who prodded me on
to marry your mother dies a nasty death!
I used to be a farmer—the sweetest life on earth,
a lovely, moldy, unspruce, litter-jumbled life,
bursting with honeybees, bloated with sheep and olives.
And then, poor hick, what did I do but marry
your mother, a city girl, and niece of that Megakles
who was son and heir of old Blueblood Megakles* himself?
She was a pretty piece: Miss Megakles-de-luxe
Well, so we go married and we clambered into bed—
me, a stink of wine-lees, fig-boxes, and wool-fat;
she, the whiff of spices, pure saffron, tonguekisses,
Luxury, High Prices, gourmandizing, goddess Lechery,
and every little elf, imp, and sprite of Intercourse.
But I'll say this for your mother: she was a worker.
Nothing slow about *her*. All day long she'd sit there
working away at her loom and shoving in the wool.
and then in bed at night she'd work on me
for more.
           Expense meant nothing.
                      Clipped?
                          I was *shorn*.

"Madam," I said, "what do you think I am? A man
or a goat?"

Suddenly the oil lamp sputters and goes out.

XANTHIAS

   There's no oil left in the lamp.

STREPSIADES

          Jackass!
And why in god's name did you light that guzzler of a lamp?
Come here and be whipped.

XANTHIAS

       But why? What have *I* done?

STREPSIADES

Because you put in potbellied wicks, that's why.

*He lunges at Xanthias who ducks away and disappears into
the house.*

Anyway, when that darling brat of ours was born
to the missus and me, we immediately started squabbling
over his name. She, of course, wanted something fancy,
some upperclass, high-horse handle with *hippos** in it—
Xanth*ippos* or Char*ippos* or Kall*ippi*des—while I naturally
wanted to give him the fine old name of Pheidonides*
in honor of his thrifty grandfather. Well, we haggled
and at last agreed on a compromise name: Pheidippides.*
She used to gush over the baby: "Just imagine. Some day
he'll be an important man, just like his Uncle Megakles,
and drive in his purple robes up to the Akropolis."
And I'd put in: "Ha, drive his goats from the hills,
you mean, dressed like his dad in a filthy smock."
Well, needless to say, he paid no heed to me
and now he's ended up by squirting his dirty horse-pox

all over my money.

                Anyway, after beating my brains
all night long, I think I've finally found a way,
the *only* way out, a wonderful little chink of a loophole.
Now if I can only shove him through it, I'm saved.
But first I've got to find some way of waking him up.
I wonder what's the nicest way to wake up.

                            Hmmmm.

Cooing in Pheidippides' ear.

Pheidippides.
            Little Pheidippides.

PHEIDIPPIDES

Waking angrily.

Damn it, Dad, what *now?*

STREPSIADES

Give your Old Man a kiss. There, now your hand, son.

PHEIDIPPIDES

Look here, what's this all about?

STREPSIADES

                      Tell me, my boy,
are you *really* fond of your poor old father?

PHEIDIPPIDES

                    Sure, Dad.
I swear it. So help me Poseidon.

STREPSIADES

                  No, NOT THAT!
For god's sake, none of those horse-god oaths* of yours!
Poseidon indeed! That god's the cause of all my troubles.

But if you *really* love me, my boy, I beg you, implore you,
do what I ask.
                    Please.

PHEIDIPPIDES

Suspiciously.

                              Depends. What are you asking?

STREPSIADES

Reform yourself, boy. Change your whole way of life
Follow my advice and make a new man of yourself
A fresh Pheidippides.

PHEIDIPPIDES

                    But how?

STREPSIADES

                              First promise.

PHEIDIPPIDES

Reluctantly.

                                        I promise.
So help me—Dionysos.

STREPSIADES

                    Good. Now then, look over there.
Do you see that dirty little hovel with the dinky door?

PHEIDIPPIDES

Yes. But what are you driving at, Dad?

STREPSIADES

Awesomely.

                         My boy,
that little hovel is the Thinkery Intellectuals live there,

professors who will teach you—and what's more, *prove* it—
that the whole atmosphere is actually a Cosmical Oven*
and we're not really people but little bits of charcoal
blazing away. What's more—for a fee,* of course—
they offer a course called *The Technique of Winning
Lawsuits.* Honest or dishonest, it's all one.

PHEIDIPPIDES

Who are they?

STREPSIADES

Great Scholars. Scientists.

PHEIDIPPIDES

Fine. Who are they?

STREPSIADES

Er

Gentlemen. Men of Learning.

PHEIDIPPIDES

Yes, but what are their *names?*

STREPSIADES

Why . . .

PHEIDIPPIDES

Oh lord, I know those filthy charlatans you mean—
those frauds, those barefoot pedants with the look of death.
Chairephon and that humbug, Sokrates.

STREPSIADES

Scandalized.

Here, here, boy.
Hush. For shame. Don't ever let me hear you talking

so disrespectfully. What's more, if you don't want
your poor Old Man to starve, you'd better go study there
and ditch your damn horses.

PHEIDIPPIDES

By Dionysos, I *won't!*
Not on your life. I wouldn't go there if you bribed me
with every racehorse in Leogoras' stable!

STREPSIADES

My dearest boy,
I implore you. *Please* go and study at the Thinkery.

PHEIDIPPIDES

Study *what?*

STREPSIADES

I've heard that they teach two kinds of Logic.*
One of them is called Philosophical, or Moral, Logic—
whatever *that* may be. The other one is called
Sophistic, or Sokratic, Logic. Now, if you could learn
this second Logic, I wouldn't have to pay a penny
of all those debts you've saddled me with.

PHEIDIPPIDES

Count me out.
I'd rather die. Why, those vampires would suck me dry.
They'd scrape the tan right off my face. How could I
face the fellows down at the track?

STREPSIADES

Then, by Demeter,
you've had your last meal on me. Take your critturs
and pack out of this house and be damned to you!

PHEIDIPPIDES

> Uncle Megakles
won't let me go horseless for long. I'll go to him.
The hell with you.

Exit Pheidippides.

STREPSIADES

> I'm down, but not for long.
First I'll say a little prayer to the gods, and then
I'll go and enroll at the Thinkery myself.

> But whoa:
at my age the memory is bad, the intellect dull.
How could I ever master that hair-splitting logic?
Still, I have to go, so why am I dawdling here
instead of banging on the door?

He walks over to Sokrates' house and kicks at the door.

> —Hey, porter!

STUDENT

From within.

Go bang yourself.

Opening the door

> Who are you to kick our door?

STREPSIADES

Strepsiades, son of Pheidon. From Kikynna.

STUDENT

By god, the way you come here and kick in our door
I think your name should damn well be Stupidities.
Do you realize that you've just caused the miscarriage*
of a great scientific discovery?

STREPSIADES

Humbly apologetic.

Oh, please excuse me.
I didn't realize. You see, I come from the country.
But tell me, what discovery miscarried?

STUDENT

It's top secret.
Classified information. Access only to students.

STREPSIADES

You can tell *me* then. That's why I've come here,
to be a student at the Thinkery.

STUDENT

In that case, very well.
But remember, our researches are solemn mysteries.

Whispering.

Listen.
Just a minute ago Sokrates was questioning Chairephon
about the number of fleafeet a flea could broadjump.
You see, a flea happened to bite Chairephon on the eyebrow
and then vaulted across and landed on Sokrates' head.

STREPSIADES

How did he measure it?

STUDENT

A stroke of absolute genius.
First he melted some wax. Then he caught the flea,
dipped its tiny feet in the melted wax,
let it cool, and lo! little Persian bootees.
He slipped the bootees off and measured the distance.

STREPSIADES

Lord Zeus, what exquisite finesse of mind!

STUDENT

Elementary really. You haven't heard *anything* yet.
Would you like another sample?

STREPSIADES

                    Oh, I'd *like* that. Go on.

STUDENT

Well, it seems that Chairephon was asking Sokrates
which of two theories he held: that gnats tootled
through their mouths or, in reverse, through their tails.

STREPSIADES

Eagerly.

Gosh. Go on. What was his theory about the gnat?

STUDENT

                                        Attend.
According to him, the intestinal tract of the gnat
is of puny proportions, and through this diminutive duct
the gastric gas of the gnat is forced under pressure
down to the rump. At that point the compressed gases,
as through a narrow valve, escape with a whoosh,
thereby causing the characteristic tootle or cry
of the flatulent gnat.

STREPSIADES

                    So the gnat has a bugle up its ass!
O thrice-blessèd mortals! What bowel-wisdom!
Why, the man who has mastered the ass of the gnat
could win an acquittal from any court!

STUDENT

And you know,
just the other day he was cheated of an immense discovery
because of a lizard.

STREPSIADES

Cheated by a *lizard?* But how?

STUDENT

It happened at night, during the course of his researches on
the orbit of the moon. There he stood, gaping wide-mouthed
at the sky, when a lizard on the roof let loose on him.

STREPSIADES

Ha! A lizard crapping on Sokrates! That's rich.

STUDENT

And last night there was nothing in school to eat.

STREPSIADES

Goodness,
how did he ever manage your supper?

STUDENT

A combination
of science and legerdemain.
He quickly sprinkled the table
with a fine film of powderlike ashes. Then,
deftly bending a skewer in the shape of a compass
he drew a vast arc along whose perimeter
the hook of his compass encountered somebody's cloak.
Quickly flicking his hand, he pulled back compass
and catch. He pawned the cloak; we ate the proceeds.

STREPSIADES

Why, Thales himself was an amateur compared to this!

Throw open the Thinkery! Unbolt the door
and let me see this wizard Sokrates in person.
Open up! I'm MAD for education!

*The ekkyklema is wheeled about to show the whole interior
court of Sokrates' Thinkery. High overhead the crane supports.
Sokrates in his basket busily scanning the heavens. Hanging
on the walls of the Thinkery are various charts, maps,
instruments, etc. In the center of the courtyard stand a number of utterly pale, emaciated students deeply engaged in a
rapt contemplation of the ground.*

                                    Great Herakles,
what kind of zoo is this?

STUDENT

                        What's so strange about it?
What do you take them for?

STREPSIADES

                        Spartan prisoners
from Pylos.* But why are they all staring at the ground?

STUDENT

They're engaged in geological research:* a survey
of the earth's strata.

STREPSIADES

                    Of course. Looking for truffles.

To one of the students.

—You there, don't strain yourself looking. I know
where they grow big and beautiful.

Pointing to other students who are bent completely double.

                            Hey, and look there:
what are those fellows doing bent over like that?

STUDENT

Those are graduate students doing research on Hades.

STREPSIADES

On Hades? Then why are their asses scanning the skies?

STUDENT

Taking a minor in Astronomy.

To the students.

—Quick, inside with you.
Hurry, before the Master catches you.

STREPSIADES

No, wait.
Let them stay a little longer. I want to speak to them
on a *private* matter.

STUDENT

Impossible. The statutes clearly forbid
overexposure to fresh air.

*The students disappear through a door at the rear. Strepsiades
meanwhile is staring at the various maps and instruments on
the walls.*

STREPSIADES

Pointing to a chart.

In the name of heaven,
what's *that?*

STUDENT

That's for astronomy.

STREPSIADES

Pointing to surveying instruments.

And what are those?

STUDENT

They're for geometry.

STREPSIADES

Geometry? And what's that good for?

STUDENT

Surveying, of course.

STREPSIADES

Surveying what? Lots?

STUDENT

No. The whole world.

STREPSIADES

What a clever gadget!
And as patriotic as it is useful.*

STUDENT

Pointing to a map.

Now then, over here
we have a map of the entire world. You see there?
That's Athens.

STREPSIADES

That, Athens? Don't be ridiculous.
Why, I can't see even a single lawcourt in session.*

STUDENT

Nonetheless, it's quite true. It really is Athens.

STREPSIADES

Then where are my neighbors of Kikynna?

STUDENT

Here they are
And you see this island squeezed along the coast?
That's Euboia.

STREPSIADES

I know that place well enough.
Perikles squeezed it dry.* But where's Sparta?

STUDENT

Sparta? Right over here.

STREPSIADES

That's MUCH TO CLOSE!
You'd be well advised to move it further away.

STUDENT

But that's utterly impossible.

STREPSIADES

You'll be sorry you didn't.
by god.

*For the first time Strepsiades catches sight of Sokrates in his
basket overhead.*

Look: who's that dangling up there in the basket?

STUDENT

Himself.

STREPSIADES

Who's Himself?

STUDENT

Sokrates.

STREPSIADES

SOKRATES!
Then call him down. Go on. Give a great big shout.

STUDENT

Hastily and apprehensively taking his leave.

Er . . . *you* call him. I'm a busy man.

Exit Student.

STREPSIADES

O Sokrates!

No answer from the basket.

Yoohoo. Sokrates!

SOKRATES

From a vast philosophical height.

Well, creature of a day?

STREPSIADES

What in the world are you doing up there?

SOKRATES

Ah, sir,
I walk upon the air and look down upon the sun
from a superior standpoint.

STREPSIADES

Well, I suppose it's better
that you sneer at the gods from a basket up in the air
than do it down here on the ground.

SOKRATES

Precisely. You see,
only by being suspended aloft, by dangling
my mind in the heavens and mingling my rare thought
with the ethereal air, could I ever achieve strict
scientific accuracy in my survey of the vast empyrean.
Had I pursued my inquiries from down there on the ground,
my data would be worthless. The earth, you see, pulls down
the delicate essence of thought to its own gross level.

As an afterthought.

Much the same thing happens with watercress.

STREPSIADES

Ecstatically bewildered.

You don't say?
Thought draws down . . . delicate essence . . . into
watercress. O dear little Sokrates, please come down.
Lower away, and teach me what I need to know!

Sokrates is slowly lowered earthwards.

SOKRATES

What subject?

STREPSIADES

Your course on public speaking and debating techniques.
You see, my creditors have become absolutely ferocious.
You should see how they're hounding me. What's more,
Sokrates, they're about to seize my belongings.

SOKRATES

How in the
world could you fall so deeply in debt without realizing it?

STREPSIADES

How? A great, greedy horse-pox ate me up, that's how.
But that's why I want instruction in your second Logic,
you know the one—the get-away-without-paying argument.
I'll pay you *any* price you ask. I swear it.
By the gods.

SOKRATES

By the gods? The gods, my dear simple fellow,
are a mere expression coined by vulgar superstition.
We frown upon such coinage here.

STREPSIADES

What do *you* swear by?
Bars of iron, like the Byzantines?*

SOKRATES

Tell me, old man,
would you honestly like to learn the truth, the *real* truth,
about the gods?

STREPSIADES

By Zeus, I sure would. The *real* truth.

SOKRATES

And also be admitted to intercourse with their Serene
Highnesses, our goddesses, the Clouds?

STREPSIADES

Intercourse with *real*
goddesses? Oh yes, I'd *like* that.

SOKRATES

                                  Very well. First, however,
you must take your seat upon the mystical couch.*

STREPSIADES

                                            I'm sitting.

SOKRATES

And now we place this sacrificial wreath on your head.

STREPSIADES

A *sacrificial* wreath?
                        Hey, NO!
                              Please, Sokrates,
don't murder me like poor Athamas* in Sophokles' play!

SOKRATES

Athamas was saved. You must mean Phrixos.

STREPSIADES

                                        Athamas.
Phrixos—so who's the critic? Dead is dead.

SOKRATES

Courage, gaffer. This is normal procedure, required
of all our initiates alike.

STREPSIADES

                        Yeah? What's in it for me?

SOKRATES

Sprinkling Strepsiades from head to toe with ritual flour

You shall be reborn, sir, as the perfect flower of orators.
a consummate. blathering, tinkling rascal

STREPSIADES

> That's no joke
> I'll be all flour the way you're powdering me.

SOKRATES

> Silence!
> Holy hush command your tongue. Listen to my
> prayer.

He stretches out his hands to heaven and prays.

> *O Lord God Immeasurable Ether, You who envelop the*
> *world! O Translucent Ozone!*
> *And you, O lightningthundered*
> *holy Clouds!*
> *Great Majesties, arise!*
> *Reveal yourselves to your Sophist's*
> *eyes.*

STREPSIADES

> Whoa, ladies, don't rain yet. Don't get me wet. Let me wrap
> up.

He wraps his head in his tunic.

> What a damned fool! Coming without a hat.

SOKRATES

> *Come forth,*
> *be manifest, majestic Clouds! Reveal your forms to me.*
> *And whether on Olympos' snow your brooding eyrie lies,*
> *or on the waves you weave the dance with Ocean's lovely*
> *daughters,*
> *or dip your golden pitchers in the waters of the Nile,*
> *or hover on Mount Mimas' snows, or over Lake Maiotis—*
> *come forth, great Clouds!*
> *Accept our prayers!*
> *O hear us!*
> Amen.

From far off in the distance the Clouds are heard singing. As they slowly approach Athens, the singing increases steadily in volume as it rises in pitch.

CHORUS

> Rise and soar
> eternal Clouds!
> Lift your loveliness of rain,
> in sodden splendor come!
> Soar from ocean's sullen swell,
> rise higher to the peaks,
> to the tall cliffs and trees!
> Rise and soar,
> while far below,
> earth and shining harvest lie.
> sound of god in river water.
> blessèd ocean at its roar
> Arise!
> For Ether's sleepless eye
> now breaks with blazoned light!
> Shake loose the rain,
> immortal forms,
> and walk upon the world!

A sustained burst of thunder is heard.

SOKRATES

O Clouds consummately blest, how clearly thy answer rumbles!

To Strepsiades.

—Did you hear that thunder crack. that *basso profundo* peal?

STREPSIADES

And how!
All hail your holyships! What a nasty jolt you gave me!
What a ratatat! You scared me so I've got to thunder too.

He breaks wind.

Sacrilege or not, I'VE GOT TO CRAP!

SOKRATES

                                 Silence, boor!
No more of your smut. Leave filth like that to the comic
stagè.

A short low growl of thunder is heard.

Shhh.
       Quiet.
              The goddess swarm is stirring to its song.

CHORUS

                 Virgins of rain,
                 look on Pallas' shining earth,
                 this oil-anointed land,
                 country of Kekrops'
                 hero-breeding plain!
                 Holiness is here,
                 home of the mysteries,
                 whose unrevealable rites
                 sanctify the soul.
                 And here the gods have gifts.
                 Below the splendid gables go
                 processions of the blest,
                 and every season sees
                 its festivals, its crowns.
                 And early every Spring
                 Dionysos brings his joy,
                 the weaving of the dance,
                 the Muses and the flutes.

STREPSIADES

Holy Zeus, Sokrates, who were those ladies that sang
that solemn hymn? Were they heroines of mythology?

SOKRATES

No, old man.
Those were the Clouds of heaven, goddesses of men of
leisure and philosophers. To them we owe our repertoire of
verbal talents: our eloquence, intellect, fustian, casuistry,
force, wit, prodigious vocabulary, circumlocutory skill—

STREPSIADES

Suddenly carried away in cloudy inspiration.

Then that's why
I suddenly tingled all over—as though I were carried up,
buoyant, exalted, swollen somehow with the flatus of
philosophy: a mist of verbal fluff, a sudden unsubstantial
swelling, a tumid bubble of wrangling words, a windbag of
debate! I seemed rent by lightning speech, ah, the thrust
and parry of opinion, of minds massively meeting . . .
In short, Sokrates,
if I could see those ladies in person, I'd LOVE to.

SOKRATES

Then look over toward Parnes. I can see them settling down
ever so gently.

STREPSIADES

Where?

SOKRATES

There, a vast drifting swarm
nuzzling along through woods and valleys.

STREPSIADES

Rubbing his eyes.

I wonder what's wrong.
I can't see them.

SOKRATES

Look: just offstage.

STREPSIADES

Now I see them!

SOKRATES

You've got cataracts, friend, if you can't see them now.

Slowly and majestically, the Chorus of Clouds files in and takes up its position in the orchestra.

STREPSIADES

Ooh, what venerable ladies! They take up all the space.

SOKRATES

And you actually mean to say that it's never occurred to you that the Clouds of heaven were goddesses?

STREPSIADES

By Zeus, it's news to me. I always used to think they were just fog and drizzle and mist.

SOKRATES

Clearly then you must also be ignorant of the fact that the Clouds are also patrons of a varied group of gentlemen, comprising: chiropractors, prophets, longhairs, quacks, fops, charlatans, fairies, dithyrambic poets, scientists, dandies, astrologers, and other men of leisure. And because all alike, without exception, walk with their heads among the clouds and base their inspiration on the murky Muse, the Clouds support them and feed them.

STREPSIADES

I see. That's why they write*—

> O downblow, dazed, of the sodden skies!

and

> Ho, tresses of the Typho-headed gale! Ho, puffcheek squalls!

or

> Spongy humus of the hyaline!

and

> Hail ye heaven-scudders, sudden ospreys of the winds!

and

> Come ye wheeling cumuli, ye clammy condensations, come!

And in return, these poets gorge themselves on the flesh of the mullet and eat of the breast of the thrush?

SOKRATES

And why not?

STREPSIADES

But what I want to know is this. why if these ladies are really Clouds, they look like women? For honest clouds aren't women.

SOKRATES

Then what *do* they look like?

STREPSIADES

I don't know for sure. Well, they look like mashed-up fluff, not at all like women. No, by Zeus. Women have . . . noses.

SOKRATES

Would you mind if I asked you a question or two?

STREPSIADES

Go right ahead.

SOKRATES

Haven't you sometimes seen a cloud that looked like a
centaur? Or a leopard perhaps? Or a wolf? Or a bull?

STREPSIADES

Often. So what?

SOKRATES

Well, the Clouds assume whatever shape they wish. Now
suppose they happened to meet some shaggy, hairy beast of
a man—Hieronymos, for instance; instantly they turn into
wild centaurs as a caricature of his lust.

STREPSIADES

I see. But what if they
run into Simon, that swindler of government funds?

SOKRATES

Presto, they turn into wolves
and catch his likeness to a T.

STREPSIADES

Oh, I see. And yesterday
because they met the coward Kleonymos, they turned into
deer?

SOKRATES

Precisely. And just now, when they saw Kleisthenes in the
audience, they suddenly turned into women.

STREPSIADES

Welcome then, august Ladies!
Welcome, queens of heaven!
If ever you spoke to mortal man,
I implore you, speak to me!

A great burst of thunder. Strepsiades cowers with fright.

KORYPHAIOS

      Hail, superannuated man!
Hail, old birddog of culture!

To Sokrates.

     And hail to you, O Sokrates,
high priest of poppycock!
      Inform us what your wishes are.
For of all the polymaths on earth, it's you we most prefer—
you and Prodikos. Him we love for wisdom's sake, but you,
sir, for your swivel-eyes, your barefoot swagger down the
street, because you're poor on our account and terribly
affected.

STREPSIADES

Name of Earth, what a voice! Solemn and holy and awful!

SOKRATES

These are the only gods there are. The rest are but figments.

STREPSIADES

Holy name of Earth! Olympian Zeus is a figment?

SOKRATES

Zeus?
  What Zeus?
    Nonsense.
      There is no Zeus.

STREPSIADES

        No Zeus?
Then *who* makes it rain? Answer me that.

SOKRATES

Why, the Clouds.
of course.
What's more, the proof is incontrovertible.
For instance.
have you ever yet seen rain when you didn't see a cloud?
But if your hypothesis were correct, Zeus could drizzle
  from an empty sky
while the clouds were on vacation.

STREPSIADES

By Apollo, you're right. A pretty
  proof.
And to think I always used to believe the rain was just Zeus
pissing through a sieve.
All right, *who* makes it thunder?
Brrr. I get goosebumps just saying it.

SOKRATES

The Clouds again.
of course. A simple process of Convection.

STREPSIADES

I admire you.
but I don't follow you.

SOKRATES

Listen. The Clouds are a saturate water-solution.
Tumescence in motion, of necessity, produces precipitation.
When these distended masses collide—*boom!*
Fulmination

STREPSIADES

But who makes them move before they collide? Isn't that
Zeus?

SOKRATES

Not Zeus, idiot. The Convection-principle!

STREPSIADES

Convection? That's a
new one.
Just think. So Zeus is out and convection-principle's in.
Tch, tch.
But wait: you haven't told me who makes it thunder.

SOKRATES

But I just *finished* telling you! The Clouds are water-packed;
they collide with each other and explode because of the
pressure.

STREPSIADES

Yeah?
And what's your proof for *that?*

SOKRATES

Why, take yourself as example.
You know that meat-stew the vendors sell at the Panathenaia? How it gives you the cramps and your stomach
starts to rumble?

STREPSIADES

Yes,
by Apollo! I remember. What an awful feeling! You feel
sick and your belly churns and the fart rips loose like
thunder. First just a gurgle, *pappapax*; then louder, *pappa-
PAPAXapaX*, and finally like thunder, *PAPAPAPAXA-
PAXAPPAPAXapap!*

SOKRATES

Precisely.
First think of the tiny fart that your intestines make.

Then consider the heavens: their infinite farting is thunder.
For thunder and farting are, in principle, one and the same.

STREPSIADES

Then where does lightning come from? And when it strikes
why is it that some men are killed and others aren't even
touched? Clearly it's *got* to be Zeus. He's behind it, blasting
the liars with bolts of lightning.

SOKRATES

Look, you idiotic Stone-Age relic,
if Zeus strikes the liars with lightning, then why on earth
is a man like Simon still alive? Or Kleonymos? Or Theoros?
They're liars ten times over.
                    But no. Instead of doing that,
he shatters his own shrines, blasts the holiest place names
in Homer and splinters the great oaks. And why, I ask you?
Have you ever heard of an oak tree committing perjury?

STREPSIADES

                                                    Say,
you know, you've got something there. But how do you
explain the lightning?

SOKRATES

                    Attend.

*Illustrating his lecture by means of the potbellied-stove Model
of the Universe.*

                            Let us hypothesize a current of
      arid air
ascending heavenwards. Now then, as this funnelled flatus
slowly invades the limp and dropsical sacks of the Clouds,
they, in turn, begin to belly and swell, distended with gas
like a child's balloon when inflated with air. Then so, pro-
      digious
become the pressures within that the cloud-casings burst
      apart,

exploding with that celestial ratatat called thunder and
   thereby releasing
the winds. These, in turn, whizz out at such incalculable
   velocities
that they catch on fire
                              Result: lightning

STREPSIADES

                                    The very same thing
      that happened to me
at the great feast of Zeus!
                        I was roasting myself a sausage
and forgot to slit the skin Well, suddenly it bloated up
and SPLAT!
                  -singed my eyebrows off and splattered my
      face with guts

CHORUS

   -Ah, how he hungers after learning!

To Strepsiades

                              -Sir, if you can pass our test,
   we guarantee that you shall be
                              -the cynosure of Hellas
   —Our requirements are these:
                              —First, is your memory keen?
   -Do you hanker for researching?
                              -Are you subject to fatigue
from standing up or walking?
                              —Does winter weather daunt you?
   -Can you go without a meal?
                              -Abstain from wine and exercise?
   -And keep away from girls?
                              —Last, do you solemnly swear
adherence to our code?
                  -To wrangle
                              —niggle
                                    —haggle
                                       —battle

*—a loyal soldier of the Tongue, conducting yourself always
like a true philosopher.*

STREPSIADES

Ladies, if all you require
is hard work, insomnia, worry, endurance, and a stomach
that eats anything, why, have no fear. For I'm your man
and as hard as nails.

SOKRATES

And you promise to follow faithfully in
my path,
acknowledging no other gods but mine, to wit, the Trinity—
GREAT CHAOS, THE CLOUDS, and BAMBOOZLE?

STREPSIADES

If I met
another god,
I'd cut him dead, so help me. Here and now I swear off
sacrifice and prayer forever.

KORYPHAIOS

Then, Sir, inform us boldly
what you wish. Providing you honor and revere the Clouds
and faithfully pursue the Philosophical Life, you shall not
fail.

STREPSIADES

Ladies, I'll tell you.
My ambition is modest, a trifling favor.
Just let my muscular tongue outrace the whole of Hellas
by a hundred laps.

KORYPHAIOS

Sir, you may consider your wishes granted.
Never, from this time forth, shall any politician in Athens
introduce more bills than you.

STREPSIADES

　　　　　But I don't want to be a Senator!
Listen, ladies: all I want is to escape the clutches
of my creditors.

KORYPHAIOS

　　　　　Your wishes are modest; we grant them.
And now, Candidate, boldly commit yourself to the hands
of our ministers.

STREPSIADES

　　　　　Ladies, you've convinced me completely
Anyway, thanks to my thoroughbreds. my son. and my wife.
I have no choice

　　　So I hereby bequeath you my body.
　　　　　for better, dear girls. or worse
　　　You can shrink me by slow starvation.
　　　　　or shrivel me dry with thirst

　　　You can freeze me or flay me skinless;
　　　　　thrash me as hard as you please.
　　　Do any damn thing you've a mind to—
　　　　　my only conditions are these:

　　　that when the ordeal is completed.
　　　　　a new Strepsiades rise.
　　　renowned to the world as a WELSHER.
　　　　　famed as a TELLER OF LIES.

a CHEATER,
　　　　　a BASTARD.
　　　　　　　　　a PHONEY.
　　　　　　　　　　　　　a BUM.
SHYSTER,
　　　　　MOUTHPIECE.
　　　　　　　　　TINHORN,
　　　　　　　　　　　　SCUM.
STOOLIE,
　　　　　CON-MAN.

WINDBAG,
                    PUNK,
OILY,
        GREASY,
                HYPOCRITE,
                        SKUNK,
DUNGHILL,
            SQUEALER,
                    SLIPPERY SAM,
FAKER,
        DIDDLER,
                SWINDLER,
                        SHAM,

—or just plain Lickspittle.

And then, dear ladies, for all I care,
    Science can have the body,
to experiment, as it sees fit,
    or serve me up as salami.

Yes, you can serve me up as salami!

KORYPHAIOS

Ah, here's a ready spirit, undaunted, unafraid!
                                —Sir,
complete your course with us and you shall win a glory
that towers to heaven.

STREPSIADES

                    Could you be a little more specific?

KORYPHAIOS

You shall pass your entire existence up in the air, among us,
strolling about with your head in the Clouds. Your life
shall be the envy of all mankind.

STREPSIADES

                    Ah, when shall I see that day?

KORYPHAIOS

Before long thousands of clients will stampede to your doors,
begging, pleading, imploring your service and advice
in all their lawsuits—many involving incredible sums.
I say no more.
              —And now, Sokrates, take this old candidate
and test his worthiness to undergo the solemn rites of initiation. Examine his mental powers; probe his mind and sift
him.

SOKRATES

Now then, tell me something about yourself.
The information is essential if I'm to know
what strategies to employ against you.

STREPSIADES

                                     Strategies?
What do you think I am? A military objective?

SOKRATES

No. I'm merely attempting to ask a few questions.
First, is your memory keen?

STREPSIADES

                          Well, it is and it isn't.
If a man owes me money, I never seem to forget it.
But if I do the owing, I somehow never remember.

SOKRATES

Well, perhaps you have some talents for speaking?

STREPSIADES

No, no talent for talk. But for larceny, lots.

SOKRATES

But how can you possibly learn?

STREPSIADES

Don't you worry.
I'll manage somehow.

SOKRATES

But look: suppose I toss you
some tidbit of higher wisdom? Could you catch it
on the fly?

STREPSIADES

What do you take me for? A puppydog
snapping up wisdom?

SOKRATES

No, a beastly old ignoramus.
In fact, I'm afraid we'll have to whip our wisdom
into your hide.
Hmmm.
Tell me, suppose someone
gave you a thrashing, what would you do?

STREPSIADES

Why,
I'd take my thrashing. Then after a little while
I'd hunt up a witness, and then a little while later
I'd bring suit for Assault and Battery.

SOKRATES

All right, old man.
undress.

STREPSIADES

Undress? But why? Have I said something wrong'

SOKRATES

No, no. But we require all candidates for initiation
to strip naked.

STREPSIADES

But I'm not a burglar,* Sokrates.
Here, search me if you want.

SOKRATES

What do you think I am?
A policeman? This is a solemn philosophical initiation
So stop your idiot blather and get undressed.

STREPSIADES

Starting to undress with extreme reluctance

Oh, all right
No, wait.
First answer me this. If I study very hard
and pay attention in class, which one of your students
will I look like?

SOKRATES

Why, you'll be the spitting image of—
Chairephon.

STREPSIADES

CHAIREPHON! But he's a walking cadaver
I'll graduate a corpse

He feverishly whisks his cloak back on.

SOKRATES

Damnation! Stop this stalling
and GET UNDRESSED!

*He pulls off Strepsiades' cloak and shoves him bodily
toward the black cavelike opening at the rear of
the Thinkery*

Forward Candidate!

STREPSIADES

NO! WAIT!
I'm scared Brr, it's as dark as a snakepit down there.
Give me a honeycake to throw to the snakes, Sokrates,
or they'll eat me alive

SOKRATES

Forward, fool. No hesitation now!

*Sokrates shoves Strepsiades before him into the opening at
the rear of the Thinkery. Then he rushes back, snatches up
Strepsiades' discarded cloak, smiles, tucks it under his tunic,
and vanishes into the Thinkery.*

CHORUS

Farewell, brave soul,
and may your future gleam as bright
as shines your courage now!
May all good fortune come to you
who, sunk in bitter age,
in the somber twilight of your years,
stride forth, undaunted, unafraid,
toward that uttermost frontier of thought
where wisdom lures you on,
O pioneer!

*The Chorus turns sharply and faces the audience. From the
wing appears the poet, the bald Aristophanes; he strides forth
and addresses the audience directly.*

ARISTOPHANES*

Gentlemen, in the name of Dionysos to whom I owe my
    nurture as a poet,
I intend to confront you with my personal complaints,
    frankly and freely,
as a poet should.

My ambitions, of course, are very simply
            stated:

the First Prize and a reputation for talent and wit.
                                                    Accordingly,
firmly convinced that this audience was composed of men
     of taste,
and that this play, *The Clouds*, was the finest of my com-
     edies to date,
I submitted an earlier version, expecting your pleasure and
     approval.
It cost me enormous anguish and labor, and yet I was forced
     to withdraw,
ignobly defeated by cheap and vulgar rivals. My present
     reproaches,
needless to say, are aimed at those self-styled critics and wits
for whom this revision has been made.
                                    However, to the men
of true taste
among you, I say this: I am, as always, your faithful friend,
and never will I willingly or knowingly abandon you or
     reproach you.
After all, I still remember that glorious day when the
     Judges—
men of whose extraordinary taste and discrimination it is a
     joy to speak—
awarded the First Prize to my youthful comedy, *The Ban-
     queters*.
Now at that time, gentlemen, my Muse was the merest slip
     of a girl,
a tender virgin who could not—without outraging all pro-
     priety—
give birth. So I exposed her child, her maiden effort, and a
     stranger
rescued the foundling.* But it was you, gentlemen, whose
     generous patronage
nourished my offspring, and I have never since doubted
     those tokens
of your exquisite taste.
                         And now, gentlemen, like Elektra in
     the play,*
a sister-comedy comes in search of you today, hoping to find

those same tokens of recognition. Let her so much as
  glimpse
a single curl from her brother's head, and she will know
  her own,
as I shall know the tokens of your approval.

                              She's a dainty
  play.
Observe, gentlemen, her natural modesty, the demureness of
  her dress,
with no dangling thong of leather,* red and thick at the tip,
to make the small boys snigger. Note too her delicate refine-
  ment—
her refusal to indulge in cheap cracks at the expense of
  baldness,
and the quiet dignity of her dancing, with nothing salacious
  about it.
Observe the absence of farcical slapstick and sensational
  situations.
Here you see no poor old man drubbing his opponents with
  a stick
in a futile attempt to hide the abysmal poverty of his verses.
Nor does she fling herself on stage with tragic torches
  blazing
and bloodcurdling fustian. No, gentlemen, my comedy
  comes to you
relying upon herself and her poetry.

                              This is what she is,
and I am the poet, her adoring father. Now I may be bald-
  headed
(as some of my competitors so tirelessly point out), but I
  am *not* vapid;
and it has never been *my* practice to serve you up some
  réchauffeé
of stale and tired plots. No, my fictions are always fresh,
no two of them the least alike, and all of them uproariously
  funny.
Observe, moreover, gentlemen, that it was *I* who punched
  Kleon
in the paunch in his hour of pride; yet once I had him on
  the ground,

I refused to kick him.

But consider my competitors, note their conduct

with poor Hyperbolos. Once they had him floored, they never stopped

grinding him down in the dirt—*plus* his mother into the bargain.

It was Eupolis, of course, who led the mass-attack upon Hyperbolos;

he gutted my *Knights*, botched it, and then dragged the resultant abortion

on stage—a stunning new plagiarism entitled (of *course*) *The Pederast*.

Even as larceny, a complete flop: Eupolis wanted a dirty dance,*

so what did he do but introduce a drunken old hag to shake her hips?

Not that *she* was original either; he lifted her from an ancient play

by Phrynichos (who quite sensibly fed the old bitch to a sea monster).

So much for Eupolis.

After him, Hermippos opened up on Hyperbolos,

and before long every imitator in town was after Hyperbolos' hide,

and every last one of them plagiarized my celebrated simile on the eels.*

I devoutly pray that those who like such stuff are bored to death

by mine. But as for you men of taste who enjoy your Aristophanes

and applaud his talent, why, posterity will endorse your judgment.

Exit Aristophanes.

CHORUS

You, our king, we summon first.
Omnipotence, in glory throned,

look down upon our dances.
          O Zeus, be with us now!

And you, steward of the sea,
whose savage trident's power
heaves the shattered world
and pries the waters up,
          O Poseidon, hear our prayer!

And you, O Father, Ether,
pure presence of Air,
nourisher, sustainer,
          O Spirit, quicken us now!

And you whose flaring horses blaze
across the skies! O benison,
splendor whose shining spills
on earth, on heaven,
          O Light, illuminate us all!

KORYPHAIOS

Gentlemen, Critics, and Clever Fellows:
                              YOUR ATTENTION
     PLEASE.
Because our agenda includes a few complaints and home
     truths,
we shall be blunt.
                    WE ARE TIRED OF BEING IGNORED.
Of all the gods
               to whom this city stands in debt for benefits
     conferred,
no god has brought more benefits than we. Yet we alone,
forsaken and forgotten gods, receive no sacrifice at all.
But surely we need not remind you of all our loving care,
the unsleeping devotion lavished, gentlemen, on your be-
     half?
          For example,
whenever you launch some exceptionally crack-brained
     project,
we promptly thunder our objection; we drizzle our dis-
     pleasure.

Or look to recent history. Have you forgotten that black day
when a low tanner, a repulsive atheist nicknamed Paphlagon*
was running for election as General? And how we re-
sponded?
How we furrowed our beetling brows and rumbled with
rage,
and *hard on the heels of the Levin rattled the steeds of
Thunder?*
How the moon, in dudgeon, snuffed her flame amongst the
rack,
and the sun in sullenness withdrew,* curling his blazing wick
back beneath his globe, refusing to shine if this Kleon
were elected?
                So you elected—Kleon!
                              As native Athenians,
gentlemen,
you are all familiar with that local brand of statesmanship
sometimes known as Blundering Through—the curious belief
which holds that, by virtue of some timely divine intervention,
all your most appalling political blunders will sooner or later
redound to the interest of Athens.
                        Whence the question arises:
why not make a good thing of this latest glaring example
of Blundering Through?
                How?
                      By convicting this cormorant
Kleon
of bribery and peculation. Then muzzle his omnivorous
maw
and slap a yoke around his neck. Not only is such action
in perfect accord with your long tradition of Blundering
Through,
but with one shrewd stroke all your bungling is redeemed
as statesmanship, manifestly furthering the noblest interests
of Athens.

CHORUS

> O lord of Delos, you
> who haunt the cliffs and scarp,
> where the ridge of Kynthos rises,
> > *O Phoibos, be with us now!*
>
> And you of Ephesos, lady,
> glory of the shrine of gold
> where the Lydian women worship,
> > *O Artemis, come to the dance!*
>
> And you, goddess on the hill,
> mistress of this lovely land
> beneath your aegis guarded,
> > *O Athene, be with us now!*
>
> And you, dancer of Delphoi,
> runner upon the peaks, at dark
> when the trailing torches flicker
> and the whirling Maenads cry their joy,
> > *O Dionysos, dance with us now!*

KORYPHAIOS

Our cluster of Clouds had gathered for the outing down to
  Athens
when we chanced to run into the Moon, who asked us to
  deliver
the following message on her behalf:
                              GREETINGS SALU-
  TATIONS ETCET
TO ATHENS AND ALLIES STOP MY DEITY MOR-
  TALLY OFFENDED
BY YOUR SCANDALOUS RUDENESS DESPITE
  MANY SUBSTANTIAL CONTRIBUTIONS
TO WELFARE OF ATHENS STOP AM WOMAN OF
  ACTIONS REPEAT ACTIONS
NOT WORDS
              (Signed)
              THE MOON.
                        And the Moon has a
  point, gentlemen.

Thanks to her shining efforts on your behalf, your average savings
on lighting alone run more than a drachma a month. Why,
I can hear you now, instructing your slaves as you leave the house,
"No need to buy torches tonight, lad. The moonlight's lovely."
And moonlight is merely one of her many services.
    Nonetheless,
you brusquely refuse to devise an Accurate Lunar Calendar,
and your month is a consequent chaos,* a masterpiece of temporal confusion.
Worse still, when the gods come hungrily trudging home at night
and find they must do without their dinner because you celebrate
your festivals on the wrong day, it's the poor innocent Moon
who bears the brunt of their heavenly grumbling. What's more,
on the days when you ought to sacrifice to the gods, you're bustling
about holding trials or torturing some poor witness on the rack.
And conversely, no sooner do the gods fast or go into mourning
for Memnon or Sarpedon, than you Athenians start carousing
and boozing.
              So be warned, gentlemen.
                         Very recently the gods
stripped Hyperbolos of his seat* on the Commission for Public Festivals
and Other Red-Letter Days—a measure designed to teach him
and all such Johnnies-Come-Lately a little respect for time.

While the Chorus resumes its customary position, the doors of the Thinkery are thrown open and Sokrates appears.

SOKRATES

Almighty Effluvium! Ozone and Chaos! Never
in all my days have I seen such peerless stupidity,
such a bungling, oblivious, brainless imbecile as this!
I no sooner teach him the merest snippets of science
than he suffers an attack of total amnesia. Still,
the Truth is my mistress and I obey.

He goes to the Thinkery door and peers into the darkness.

                          —Strepsiades,
where are you?
                Fetch your mattress and come outside.

Strepsiades appears at the door, tugging at his mattress.

STREPSIADES

I can't come. The little bugs won't let me leave.

SOKRATES

Down with it, blockhead. Now your attention, please.

STREPSIADES

Ready.

SOKRATES

        To resume then, what particular discipline
in that vast array of choices offered by your ignorance
would you especially like to acquire? For instance,
would you prefer diction or rhythm or measures?

STREPSIADES

                            Measures.
Why, just the other day the flourman swindled me
of half a peck.

SOKRATES

Not dry measures, dunderhead!
I want to know which *meter* you'd prefer to master—
trimeter or tetrameter.

STREPSIADES

Well, I like the yard
as well as anything.

SOKRATES

Rubbish. Palpable rubbish.

STREPSIADES

What would you like to bet that your trimeter isn't
exactly three feet?

SOKRATES

Why, you illiterate numskull!
However, perhaps you'd do better with rhythm.

STREPSIADES

Rhythm?
Will rhythm buy the groceries?

SOKRATES

Sensitivity to rhythm
confers a certain ineluctable social *savoir-faire*
Polite society will accept you if you can discriminate, say.
between the martial anapest and common dactylic—
sometimes vulgarly called finger-rhythm.*

STREPSIADES

Finger-rhythm?
I know *that*.

SOKRATES

Define it then.

STREPSIADES

Extending his middle finger in an obscene gesture.

Why, it's tapping time
with *this* finger. Of course, when I was a boy—

Raising his phallus to the ready.*

I used to make rhythm with *this* one.

SOKRATES

Why, you lout!

STREPSIADES

But look, you goose, I don't want to learn this stuff.

SOKRATES

Then what *do* you want to learn?

STREPSIADES

Logic! Logic!
Teach me your Immoral Logic!

SOKRATES

But, my dear fellow,
one must begin by mastering the rudiments of language.
For instance, can you list me the male quadrupeds?

STREPSIADES

Pooh, I *would* be a damnfool if I didn't know *them*.
Listen: the ram, the buck, the stallion, the bull,
the duck—

SOKRATES

And now the females of the same quadrupeds.

STREPSIADES

Let's see: the ewe, the doe, the mare, the cow,
the duck—

SOKRATES

Stop right there. A gross solecism.
According to you, the word *duck* apparently applies
to both the male and female of the species.

STREPSIADES

Huh?

How do you mean?

SOKRATES

In *your* usage, they're both ducks.

STREPSIADES

Holy Poseidon, you're right! What should I have said?

SOKRATES

The male is a *duck*; the female's a *duchess*.*

STREPSIADES

A *duchess?*

Bravo! Almighty Ozone, that's a good one!
For that little lesson, you can bring out your basket
and I'll fill it with seed.

SOKRATES

Oops. Another solecism.
You've made *basket* masculine, when it's feminine.*

STREPSIADES

What?

Basket is masculine? But why?

SOKRATES

Because the ending *-et*
is what in grammar we call a masculine termination.
Like the *-os* ending of *Kleonymos.*

STREPSIADES

Wait. I don't see.

SOKRATES

I repeat: *basket* and *Kleonymos* are masculine in form
and ending.

STREPSIADES

Kleonymos *masculine?* But *he's* feminine.
Form and ending. Queer as they come.

But look,
what *should* I call a basket?

SOKRATES

Why, a *baskette*, of course.
By analogy with *toilette.*

STREPSIADES

Baskette, eh?

SOKRATES

That's it.
Now you're talking Greek.

STREPSIADES

The *baskette* of *Kleonymette?*

SOKRATES

Precisely. Which brings us to the distinction between
men's names and women's names.

STREPSIADES

Oh, I know the female names

SOKRATES

For example?

STREPSIADES

For example, Lysilla, Philinna, Demetria,
Kleitagora—

SOKRATES

And now recite some masculine names.

STREPSIADES

Easy. There's thousands of them. Like Philoxenos, Melesias,
Amynias—

SOKRATES

Stop, you nincompoop. I asked for men's names,
not women's names.

STREPSIADES

You mean those *aren't* men's names?

SOKRATES

Not men's names at all. A transparent confusion
between singular and plural. Suppose, for instance,
we drop the plural s from Amynias, what would we have?

STREPSIADES

Why, Amynia.*

SOKRATES

> You see, by dropping the plural *s*,
you've made Amynias a singular woman.

STREPSIADES

> Well, the draftdodger,
it serves him right. But why am I learning stuff
any damn fool knows?

SOKRATES

> Fool, you flatter yourself.
However, lie down on your mattress and—

STREPSIADES

> And what, Sokrates?

SOKRATES

And lucubrate upon your dilemma.

STREPSIADES

> Please, no, Sokrates!
Anywhere but there. Couldn't I just go and lubricate
on the ground?

SOKRATES

> Permission refused.

STREPSIADES

> Ohh, what a fate!
Those little bugs are sure to crucify me now.

*Strepsiades burrows under the infested sheepskins on his
mattress while Sokrates chants encouragement.*

SOKRATES

First concentrate
Then cerebrate
  Now concentrate again.

Then lucubrate.
Next, speculate.
  Now ruminate And then,

if your mind gets stuck,
don't curse your luck.
  Get up! Quick as a wink,

cut through the knot,
swift as a thought,
  but THINK. Candidate. THINK!

Now hence, ye Syrops of Sleep! Come hither, O Pain!

STREPSIADES

Yooooooow! Yooooooow!

SOKRATES

Look here, what's biting you now?

STREPSIADES

Biting, you say?
THEY'RE MURDERING ME!
Out of the ticking
the bugs come creeping.
They're biting my ribs.
They're swilling my blood.
My balls are all sores.
My ass is a shambles
THEY'RE MURDERING ME!

SOKRATES

There, there, old fellow. Don't take it so hard.

STREPSIADES

> DON'T TAKE IT SO HARD?
> When my money's gone?
> When my skin's gone?
> When my blood's gone?
> And then what's more,
> when I tried to hum
> and forget these bites,
> I DAMN NEAR DIED!

There is a brief interval of silence during which Strepsiades hums and thrashes under his covers. Then Sokrates picks up a sheepskin and peers under.

SOKRATES

Here, what's this? Have you stopped lucubrating?

STREPSIADES

Who, *me?*

By Poseidon, I *have not!*

SOKRATES

What thoughts have you had?

STREPSIADES

Only this. I've been thinking how much of me would be left when the bugs got through.

SOKRATES

Bah! Consume you for an ass.

STREPSIADES

I *am* consumed.

SOKRATES

Courage, gaffer. We mustn't repine.
Pull back your covers and concentrate. What we need

is some clever quibbling subterfuge with which to frustrate and fleece your creditors.

STREPSIADES

                Who's fleecing *who*, Sokrates?
That's what I'd like to know.

Another brief silence follows.

SOKRATES

                Hmmm. I wonder
what he's up to now? I'll peek under the covers.

He lifts the sheepskin.

What's this? Asleep on the job, are you?

STREPSIADES

                By Apollo,
I'm *not* sleeping!

SOKRATES

        Any thoughts yet?

STREPSIADES

                Not a thing.

SOKRATES

Surely you've found *something*.

STREPSIADES

                Well, only this thing
I've got in my hand.

SOKRATES

        Buffoon! Get back to your pallet
and cogitate.

STREPSIADES

But, Sokrates, what am I cogitating *about?*

SOKRATES

A moot question, friend, whose answer lies with you.
When *you* know what *you* want, kindly illuminate *me.*

STREPSIADES

But I've told you ten thousand times already, Sokrates.
It's my debts. I want to welsh on my debts.

SOKRATES

Splendid.
Then back to your pallet.

Strepsiades dutifully crawls under his sheepskin.

And now distill your mind
to its airiest essence, allowing the subtle elixirs of thought
to permeate and penetrate every pore of the problem.
Then Analyze, Refine, Synthesize, Define—

STREPSIADES

Frantically thrashing to escape the bugs.

OUCH!

SOKRATES

Stop fidgeting!
—However, in the case of a dilemma,
defer your inquiry briefly. When refreshed, return,
sift your conclusions and knead vigorously Then mull
the results.

STREPSIADES

Suddenly illuminated.

Ooooh, Sokrates!

SOKRATES

Yes?

STREPSIADES

EUREKA!

I've got it. A glorious dodge for ditching my debts!

SOKRATES

Aha. Expatiate.

STREPSIADES

Well, just suppose—

SOKRATES

Supposing *what?*

STREPSIADES

Just suppose I rented one of those witchwomen from
Thessaly* and ordered her to charm down the moon from
the sky. And then I snatch up the moon and I pop her into
a box, and polish her face until she shines like a mirror.

SOKRATES

And what would you gain by that?

STREPSIADES

What would I gain?

Why, think what would happen if the moon never rose.
I wouldn't have to pay interest.

SOKRATES

No interest? But why?

STREPSIADES

Because interest falls due on the last day of the month,
before the New Moon, doesn't it?

SOKRATES

A superlative swindle!
Now then, let me propose a somewhat thornier case.
You are threatened, we assume, with a suit for five talents.
Problem: how do you quash the verdict?

STREPSIADES

How? *I* don't know.
I'd have to meditate on *that*.

SOKRATES

By all means meditate;
but beware of immuring your mind with excessive intro-
spection. Allow your intellect instead to sally forth upon
her own, as though you held a cockroach on a leash.

STREPSIADES

Suddenly illuminated.

Ooh, Sokrates, I've found a glorious bamboozle! I've got it!
Admit it, it's wonderful!

SOKRATES

Kindly expound it first.

STREPSIADES

Well, have you ever noticed in the druggists' shops
that beautiful stone, that transparent sort of glass
that makes things burn?

SOKRATES

A magnifying glass, you mean?

STREPSIADES

That's it. Well, suppose I'm holding one of these,
and while the court secretary is recording my case,

I stand way off. keeping the sun behind me.
and scorch out every word of the charges.*

SOKRATES

By the Graces,
a magnificent bamboozle!

STREPSIADES

Whew. and am I glad
to get *that* suit quashed!

SOKRATES

Now then, try your teeth
on this little teaser

STREPSIADES

Shoot.

SOKRATES

This time imagine
that you find yourself a defendant without a witness.
Your case is absolutely hopeless. Problem: to prevent
your opponent's suit from coming to trial

STREPSIADES

Pooh.
nothing to it at all.

SOKRATES

Elaborate.

STREPSIADES

But it's a pushover.
Sokrates While they were trying the case before mine.
I'd go hang myself

SOKRATES

Preposterous!

STREPSIADES

It's *not* preposterous.
You can't sue a corpse.

SOKRATES

Poppycock. Palpable rubbish.
As your tutor, I hereby resign. And now, GET OUT!

STREPSIADES

You resign? But why?

Falling on his knees in supplication.

Oh, please. I implore you, Sokrates . . .

SOKRATES

But you forget everything as fast as you learn it, numskull!
Tell me, what was the first lesson?
Well, speak up.

STREPSIADES

Let me think.
The first lesson?
The *first* lesson?
Ummm. That whoozit you put seeds in!
For god's sake.
what *is* it called?

SOKRATES

Why, you blithering bungler!
You senile incompetent! You . . . you mooncalf! Clear out!

STREPSIADES

Sweet gods in heaven, what's to become of me now?
I'm a goner unless I master those sleights-of-tongue.

Falling on his knees before the Chorus

O most gracious Clouds, please advise me. Tell me
what to do

KORYPHAIOS

Our counsel, reverend sir, is this.
Have you a grown-up son perhaps? Then send him off
to study in your place

STREPSIADES

It's true, ladies, I have a son,
but he's a gentleman, you see, with a true gentleman's
natural distaste for learning. So what can I do?

KORYPHAIOS

Is he the boss?

STREPSIADES

Well, he's a strapping, sturdy boy,
and there's a bit of eagle-blood on his mother's side.
Still, I'll go fetch him anyway. If he refuses
to learn his lessons, by god, he'll never set foot
in my house again!

To Sokrates.

—I won't be gone a moment.

Exit Strepsiades into his house

CHORUS

Now, sir, you see
what blessings we,
the Clouds, have brought to pass.

E.g. this fool-
ish, willing tool,
    this frantic, eager ass.

But seize your prey.
Avoid delay.
    No matter how well hooked,

your fish is not
fried fish till caught—
    and goose is better cooked.

Exit Sokrates. Enter Strepsiades, dragging Pheidippides.

STREPSIADES

Out with you! By Condensation, you won't stay here!
Go cut your teeth on Megakles' money!

PHEIDIPPIDES

                          But Father,
what's the matter with you? Are you out of your head?
Almighty Zeus, you must be mad!

STREPSIADES

                       "Almighty Zeus!"
What musty rubbish! Imagine, a boy your age.
still believing in Zeus!

PHEIDIPPIDES

                What's so damn funny?

STREPSIADES

It tickles me when the heads of toddlers like you
are still stuffed with such outdated notions. Now then,
listen to me and I'll tell you a secret or two
that might make an intelligent man of you yet.
But remember: you mustn't breath a word of this.

PHEIDIPPIDES

A word of what?

STREPSIADES

Didn't you just swear by Zeus?

PHEIDIPPIDES

I did.

STREPSIADES

Now learn what Education can do for *you:*
Pheidippides, there is no Zeus.

PHEIDIPPIDES

There is no Zeus?

STREPSIADES

No Zeus. Convection-Principle's in power now.
Zeus has been banished.

PHEIDIPPIDES

Drivel!

STREPSIADES

Take my word for it,
it's absolutely true.

PHEIDIPPIDES

Who says so?

STREPSIADES

Sokrates.
And Chairephon too. The famous expert on fleafeet.

PHEIDIPPIDES

Are you so far gone on the road to complete insanity
you'd believe the word of those' charlatans?

STREPSIADES

                                                    Hush, boy.
For shame. I won't hear you speaking disrespectfully
of such eminent scientists and geniuses. And, what's more,
men of such fantastic frugality and Spartan thrift,
they regard baths, haircuts, and personal cleanliness
generally as an utter waste of time and money—whereas
you, dear boy, have taken me to the cleaner's so many times,
I'm damn near washed up. Come on, for your father's sake,
go and learn.

PHEIDIPPIDES

                    What do they teach that's worth knowing?

STREPSIADES

Worth knowing? Why, the accumulated wisdom of mankind.
For instance, what a blockhead and numskull you are.
Hmmm.
            Wait here. I'll be right back.

Strepsiades darts into his house.

PHEIDIPPIDES

                                        Gods in heaven,
what should I do? My father's gone completely balmy.
Should I hale him into court on charges of insanity
or notify the undertakers?

*Strepsiades reappears with a pair of ducks. He holds up
first one and then the other.*

STREPSIADES

                                        Now then, what's this called?

PHEIDIPPIDES

That? A duck.

STREPSIADES

Excellent. Now what do you call this?

PHEIDIPPIDES

Why, another duck.

STREPSIADES

Another duck? You stupid boy.
From now on you must learn to call them by their right
names. This one is a duck; that one's a duchess.

PHEIDIPPIDES

A *duchess!*
So this is the glorious wisdom you've picked up
from those walking corpses!

STREPSIADES

Oh, there's lots more too,
but I'm so old everything I learn goes in one ear
and right out the other.

PHEIDIPPIDES

Ah. Doubtless that explains
how you lost your cloak.

STREPSIADES

I didn't lose it. I swapped it.
For thoughts.

PHEIDIPPIDES

And where have your sandals gone, you idiot?

STREPSIADES

In the words of Perikles himself when they asked him
where the money went: *Expended as required.*
No comment.*
                        And now, inside with you, boy.
Humor me in this and you can make an ass of yourself
in any way you like. Ah, how well I remember those days
when you were six, and I had to humor your tantrums.
Why, the very first pay I ever drew as a juror
went to buy you a cart at the fair.

PHEIDIPPIDES

                                        All right, Dad.
But someday you'll be sorry.

STREPSIADES

                                Ah, good dutiful boy.
—Hallo there, Sokrates!
                                Hey, Sokrates, come outside.
I've brought my son along—no damn thanks to him.

Enter Sokrates from the Thinkery.

SOKRATES

Why, he's still a baby. How could a toddler like this
possibly operate our Hanging Baskets?

PHEIDIPPIDES

                                As for you,
why don't you hang yourself and skip the basket?

STREPSIADES

                                                Here,
for shame! You'd insult the Master?

SOKRATES

Imitating Pheidippides.

"Thkip the bathket."
Dear me, what adorable, childish prattle. And look
at those great sulking lower lips. How in the world
could this fumbling foetus ever master the arts
of Verdict-Quashing, False Witness, Innuendo,
and Character Assassination? On the other hand, however,
the case is not without precedent. *Even* Hyperbolos,*
after all, somehow mastered the tricks of the trade.
The fee, of course, was prodigious.

STREPSIADES

Now don't you worry,
Sokrates. The boy's a born philosopher. Yes, sir,
when he was just a mite of a shaver, *so* high,
he used to make the cleverest things you ever saw.
Why, there were dollhouses, sailboats, little pushcarts
from scraps of leather, and the sweetest little frogs
carved from fruit peel. He's a scholar, all right.
So tutor him in your two logics—traditional Philosophical
Logic and that flashy modern sophistic logic they call
Immoral because it's so wonderfully wicked. In any case,
if he can't master both logics, I insist that he learn the
Immoral Kind of argument.

SOKRATES

Philosophy and Sophistry*
will instruct your son in person. And now, gentlemen,
if you'll excuse me, I must leave.

STREPSIADES

But remember, Sokrates:
I want him able to make an utter mockery of the truth.

*Exit Sokrates. After his departure the doors of the Thinkery
are thrown open and Philosophy and Sophistry are rolled
forward in great gilded cages. From the shoulders down,
both are human; from the neck up they are fighting-cocks.*
Philosophy (or the Traditional Logic) is a large, muscular

rooster, powerful but not heavy, expressing in his movements that inward harmony and grace and dignity which the Old Education was meant to produce; his plumage is so simple and dignified as to seem almost dingy. Sophistry, by contrast, in comparatively slight, with sloping shoulders, an emaciated pallor, an enormous tongue and a disproportionately large phallus. His body is graceless but extremely quick-moving; his every motion expresses defiant belligerence, and his plumage is brilliant to the point of flashiness. The debate itself should be conducted at top speed with much scratching and spurring. As the Attendants open the cages, the fighters step out and circle each other warily, jockeying for position.

PHILOSOPHY

Front and center, you Feathered Impertinence.
Take your little bow before the audience.
You like to swagger.

SOPHISTRY

                    Why, you Pompous Lump,
with all my heart. The bigger the crowd,
the better I'll rebut you.

PHILOSOPHY

                    You'll rebut *me?*
Who are *you,* runt?

SOPHISTRY

            A Logic.

PHILOSOPHY

                    You,
A Logic? Why, you cheap, stunted Loquacity!
You pipsqueak Palaver!

SOPHISTRY

            I may be called

Mere Sophistry, but I'll chop you down
to size. I'll *refute* you.

PHILOSOPHY

Refute *me?* How?

SOPHISTRY

With unconventionality. With ultramodernity.
With unorthodox ideas.

PHILOSOPHY

For whose present vogue
we are indebted to this audience of imbeciles
and asses.

SOPHISTRY

Asses? These sophisticated gentlemen?
These wits?

PHILOSOPHY

I'll *invalidate* you.

SOPHISTRY

Invalidate *me?*
How, fossil?

PHILOSOPHY

My arguments are Truth and Justice.

SOPHISTRY

Then I'll disarm you and defeat you, friend.
Your Justice doesn't exist.

PHILOSOPHY

What? No Justice?
Preposterous!

SOPHISTRY

Then show it to me. Where is it?

PHILOSOPHY

Where is Justice? Why. in the Lap of the Gods.

SOPHISTRY

In the Lap of the Gods? Then would you explain
how Zeus escaped punishment after he imprisoned
his father?* The inconsistency is glaring.

PHILOSOPHY

Aaaagh.
What nauseating twaddle. It turns my stomach.

SOPHISTRY

Why, you Decrepitude! You Doddering Dotard!

PHILOSOPHY

Why.
you Precocious Pederast! You Palpable Pervert!

SOPHISTRY

Pelt me with roses!

PHILOSOPHY

You Toadstool! O Cesspool!

SOPHISTRY

Wreath my hair with lilies!

PHILOSOPHY

Why, you Parricide!

SOPHISTRY

Shower me with gold! Look, don't you see
I welcome your abuse?

PHILOSOPHY

Welcome it, monster?
In my day we would have cringed with shame.

SOPHISTRY

Whereas *now* we're flattered. Times change.
The vices of your age are stylish today.

PHILOSOPHY

Repulsive Whippersnapper!

SOPHISTRY

Disgusting Fogy!

PHILOSOPHY

Because of *you* the schools of Athens
stand deserted; one whole generation
chaffers in the streets, gaping and idle.
Mark my words: someday this city
shall learn what you have made her men:
effeminates and fools.

SOPHISTRY

Ugh, you're squalid!

PHILOSOPHY

Whereas you've become a Dandy and a Fop!
But I remember your beggared beginnings,
playing as Telephos,* grubby and shifty,
tricked out in Euripidean rags and tatters
and cramming your wallet with moldy leavings
from Pandaletos' loaf.*

SOPHISTRY

What a prodigy of wisdom
was there!

PHILOSOPHY

And what a prodigy of madness here—
your madness, and madder still than you,
this maddened city which lets you live—
you, corrupter and destroyer of her youth!

SOPHISTRY

Throwing a wing about Pheidippides.

Why, you Hoary Fossil! This is one student
you'll never teach!

PHILOSOPHY

Pulling Pheidippides back.

Teach him I *shall*—
unless he's prepared to devote his career
exclusively to drivel.

SOPHISTRY

Bah, rave to yourself.
—Come here, boy.

PHILOSOPHY

You touch him at your peril.

KORYPHAIOS

Intervening.

Gentlemen, forego your wrangling and abuse,
and each present his arguments in turn.
Describe how *you* taught the men of the past,
and *you*, Sir, your New Education.

PHILOSOPHY

                              I second
your proposal.

SOPHISTRY

        As do I.

KORYPHAIOS

                    Excellent.
Who will speak first?

SOPHISTRY

                Let him begin.
I yield the floor. But when he's done,
I'll smother him beneath so huge
a driving hail of Modern Thought
and Latest Views, he cannot speak—
or if he does, my hornet words
and waspish wit will sting him so,
he'll never speak again.

CHORUS

—At last!
            —The Great Debate begins!
                              —Between these two
contending, clever speakers,
                      —matched so fairly,
                                    —who
will win, is anybody's guess.
                        —Both are subtle,
—both facile, both witty,
                    —both masters of rebuttal
—and abuse.
            —The stake? Wisdom.
                                  —Wisdom is the prize.
—For her they fight.
                    —For her their rival hackles rise.

—So listen well.

—Upon their skill, the destinies of Language, Intellect, and Educated Athens hang.

KORYPHAIOS

To Philosophy.

Come, Sir, I summon you—you who conferred your crown of virtue upon the Older Generation—to take the stand. Be bold; rise and with clarion tongue tell us what you represent.

PHILOSOPHY

Gentlemen,
I propose to speak of the Old Education,* as it flourished once
beneath my tutelage, when Homespun Honesty, Plainspeaking, and Truth
were still honored and practiced, and throughout the schools of Athens
the regime of the three D's—DISCIPLINE, DECORUM, and DUTY—
enjoyed unchallenged supremacy.
Our curriculum was
Music and Gymnastic,
enforced by that rigorous discipline summed up in the old adage:
BOYS SHOULD BE SEEN BUT NOT HEARD. This was our cardinal rule,
and when the students, mastered by groups according to region,
were marched in squads to schools, discipline and absolute silence prevailed.
Ah, they were hardy, manly youngsters. Why,
even on winter mornings when the snow, like powdered chaff,
came sifting down, their only protection against the bitter weather
was a thin and scanty tunic. In the classes, posture was stressed

and the decencies firmly enforced: the students stood in
    rows,
rigidly at attention, while the master rehearsed them by rote,
over and over. The music itself was traditional and
    standard—
such familiar anthems and hymns as those, for instance,
    beginning
A *Voice from Afar* or *Hail, O Pallas, Destroyer!**—and the
    old modes
were strictly preserved in all their austere and simple beauty.
Clowning in class was sternly forbidden, and those who
    improvised
or indulged in those fantastic flourishes and trills so much in
    vogue
with the degenerate, effeminate school of Phrynis, were
    promptly thrashed
for subverting the Muses.
                              In the gymnasium too decorum
    was demanded.
The boys were seated together, stripped to the skin, on the
    bare ground,
keeping their legs thrust forward, shyly screening their
    nakedness
from the gaze of the curious. Why, so modest were students
    then,
that when they rose, they carefully smoothed out the ground
    beneath them,
lest even a pair of naked buttocks leaving its trace in the
    sand
should draw the eyes of desire. Anointing with oil was
    forbidden
below the line of the navel, and consequently their genitals
    kept
their boyish bloom intact and the quincelike freshness of
    youth.
Toward their lovers their conduct was manly*: you didn't
    see *them*.
mincing or strutting, or prostituting themselves with girlish
    voices

or coy, provocative glances.

            At table courtesy and good manners

were compulsory. Not a boy of that generation would have dreamed

of taking so much as a radish or the merest pinch of parsley

before his elders had been served. Rich foods were prohibited,

raucous laughter or crossing their legs forbidden. . . .

SOPHISTRY

                       Ugh,

what musty, antiquated rubbish. It reeks of golden grass-hoppers,

all gewgaws and decaying institutions!

PHILOSOPHY

              Nonetheless, these were the precepts

on which I bred a generation of heroes, the men who fought at Marathon.

To Sophistry.

           And what do *you* teach?

                 Modesty?

                   No, vanity and softness,

and the naked beauty of the body muffled in swirling clothes

gross and unmanly. Why, at Panathenaia now it sickens me

to see the boys dancing, ashamed of their own bodies,

effetely forgetting their duty to the goddess while they screen

their nakedness behind their shields.

                   Bah.

To Pheidippides.

           No, young man, by your courage

I challenge you. Turn your back upon his blandishments of vice,

the rotten law courts and the cheap, corrupting softness of
the baths.
Choose instead the Old, the Philosophical Education. Follow
me
and from my lips acquire the virtues of a man:—
A sense of
shame,
that decency and innocence of mind that shrinks from doing
wrong.
To feel the true man's blaze of anger when his honor is
provoked.
Deference toward one's elders; respect for one's father and
mother.
To preserve intact, unsullied by disgrace or stained with
wrong,
that image of Manliness and Modesty by which alone you
live.
Purity:—to avoid the brothels and the low, salacious leer
of prostituted love—which, being bought, corrupts your
manhood
and destroys your name. Toward your father scrupulous
obedience;
to honor his declining years who spent his prime in rearing
you.
Not to call him Dotard or Fogy—

SOPHISTRY

Boy, if you follow his
advice, you'll finish by looking like one of Hippokrates'
sissified sons. They'll call *you* Mollycoddle Milksop.

PHILOSOPHY

Rubbish. I promise
you,
not contentious disputations and the cheap, courtroom cant
of this flabby, subpoena-serving, shyster-jargoned
de-generation,
but true athletic prowess, the vigor of contending manhood

in prime perfection of physique, muscular and hard, glowing
with health.

         Ah, I can see you now, as through an idyl
  moving—
you with some companion of your age, modest and manly
  like you,
strolling by Akademe perhaps, or there among the olives,
sprinting side by side together, crowned with white reed,
breathing with every breath the ecstasy of Spring returning,
the sudden fragrance of the season's leisure, the smell of
  woodbine
and the catkins flung by the poplar, while touching
  overhead,
the leaves of the linden and plane rustle, in love, together.
So follow me, young man, and win perfection of physique.
  To wit—

Demonstrating each attribute individually.

        BUILD, Stupendous.
        COMPLEXION, Splendid.
        SHOULDERS, Gigantic.
        TONGUE, Petite.
        BUTTOCKS, Brawny.
        PECKER, Discreet.

But follow my opponent here, and your reward shall be, as
  follows:

        BUILD, Effeminate.
        COMPLEXION, Ghastly.
        SHOULDERS, Hunched.
        TONGUE, Enormous.
        BUTTOCKS, Flabby.
        PECKER, Preposterous!
(But thereby insuring you an enormous and devoted political
  following.)
What is worse, you shall learn to make a mockery of all
  morality,
systematically confounding good with evil and evil with
  good,

so plumped and pursy with villainy, sodomy, disgrace, and
  perversion.
you resemble ANTIMACHOS himself

                          Depravity can sink

  no lower.

CHORUS

 —Bravo!
        —What brilliance!
                —What finesse!
                        —*This* is wisdom
at its noble best!
                —Such Modesty,
                    —such Decorum
in every lovely word distilled!
                  —Ah, lucky they
  -whose happy lives were lived
                  —beneath your dispensa-
tion,
     —by all the ancient virtues blessed!

To Sophistry.

                      —So, sir.
 —despite your vaunted subtlety and wit,
                    —take care:
 —Your rival's speech has scored.
                —Some crushing *tour de*
force.
 —some master stroke,
             —is needed now.
                 —The stage is yours.

KORYPHAIOS

Unless your strategy is shrewdly planned and your attack
  ferocious,
then your cause is lost. We'll laugh you out of court.

SOPHISTRY

At last!
A few minutes more and I would have exploded from sheer impatience
to refute him and demolish his case.

Now then, I freely admit
that among men of learning I am—somewhat pejoratively—dubbed
the Sophistic, or Immoral, Logic. And why? Because I first
devised a Method for the Subversion of Established Social Beliefs
and the Undermining of Morality. Moreover, this little invention of mine,
this knack of taking what might appear to be the worse argument
and nonetheless winning my case, has, I might add, proved to be
an *extremely* lucrative source of income.

But observe, gentlemen,
how I refute his vaunted Education.

To Philosophy.

Now then, in your curriculum
hot baths are sternly prohibited. But what grounds can you possibly adduce
for this condemnation of hot baths?

PHILOSOPHY

What grounds can I adduce? Why, they're thoroughly vicious. They make a man flabby and effeminate.

SOPHISTRY

You can stop right there, friend. I have you completely at my mercy.

Answer me this: which of the sons of Zeus was the most
  heroic?
Who suffered most? Performed the greatest labors?

PHILOSOPHY

                                        In my opinion,
the greatest hero who ever lived was Herakles.

SOPHISTRY

                                        Very well then.
But when we speak of the famous Baths of Herakles,* are
we speaking of hot baths or cold baths? Necessarily, sir, of
hot baths. Whence it clearly follows, by your own logic,
that Herakles was both flabby and effeminate.
                                        Q.E.D.

PHILOSOPHY

          Q.E.D.! This is the rubbish I mean!
This is the logical claptrap so much in fashion with the
  young!
This is what fills the baths and empties the gymnasiums!

SOPHISTRY

                                        Very well,
if you like, consider our national passion for politics and
  debating,
pastimes which you condemn and I approve. But surely,
  friend,
if politics were quite so vicious as you pretend, old
  Homer—*
our mentor on moral questions—would never have por-
  trayed Nestor
and those other wise old men as politicians, would he?
  Surely
he would not.
                Or take the question of education in oratory—
in my opinion, desirable, in yours the reverse. As for Moderation and Decorum,

the very notions are absurd. In fact, two more preposterous
or pernicious prejudices, I find it hard to imagine. For
   example.
can you cite me *one* instance of that profit which a man
   enjoys
by exercising moderation? Refute me if you can.

PHILOSOPHY

                            Why, instances abound:
Er   Peleus.* for example. His virtue won him a sword.

SOPHISTRY

                            A *sword*,
you say? What a charming little profit for the poor sucker!
Look at our Hyperbolos: nothing virtuous about *him*, god
knows, and yet, what with peddling lamps—plus a knack for
swindling—he piled up a huge profit. All cold cash. No
swords for him. No sir, Hyperbolos and swords just don't
mix.*

PHILOSOPHY

                            Furthermore.
Peleus' chastity earned him the goddess Thetis for his wife.

SOPHISTRY

                            Precisely,
and what did she do? Promptly ditched him for being cold,
no passion for that all-night scrimmage between the sheets
that lusty women love,
                  Bah, you're obsolete.

To Pheidippides.

                        —Young man,
I advise you to ponder this life of Virtue with scrupulous
   care,
all that it implies, and all the pleasures of which its daily
   practice

must inevitably deprive you. Specifically, I might mention
  these:
Sex. Gambling. Gluttony. Guzzling. Carousing. Etcet.
And what on earth's the point of living, if you leach your
  life
of all its little joys?
                    Very well then, consider your natural needs.
Suppose, as a scholar of Virtue, you commit some minor
  peccadillo,
a little adultery, say, or seduction, and suddenly find yourself
caught in the act. What happens? You're ruined, you can't
  defend yourself
(since, of course, you haven't been taught). But follow me,
  my boy,
and obey your nature to the full; romp, play, and laugh
without a scruple in the world. Then if caught *in flagrante*,
you simply inform the poor cuckold that you're utterly
  innocent
and refer him to Zeus as your moral sanction. After all,
  didn't he,
a great and powerful god, succumb to the love of women?
Then how in the world can you, a man, an ordinary mortal,
be expected to surpass the greatest of gods in moral self-
  control?
Clearly, you can't be.

PHILOSOPHY

                    And suppose your pupil, by taking your advice,
is promptly convicted of adultery and sentenced to be
  publicly reamed
up the rectum with a radish?* How, Sir, would you save him
  from *that?*

SOPHISTRY

Why, what's the disgrace in being reamed with a radish?

PHILOSOPHY

Sir, I can conceive of nothing fouler than being buggered
by a radish.

SOPHISTRY

      And what would you have to say, my friend,
if I defeat you on this point too?

PHILOSOPHY

                What *could* I say?
I could never speak again for shame.

SOPHISTRY

                Very well then.
What sort of men are our lawyers?

PHILOSOPHY

Why, they're all Buggers

SOPHISTRY

          Right!
What are our tragic poets then?

PHILOSOPHY

Why, they're Buggers too.

SOPHISTRY

          Right!
And what of our politicians, Sir?

PHILOSOPHY

Why, Buggers to a man.

SOPHISTRY

          Right!
You see how stupidly you spoke?
And now look at our audience.
What about them?

PHILOSOPHY

I'm looking hard.

SOPHISTRY

And what do you see?

PHILOSOPHY

By heaven,
I see an enormous crowd of people,
and almost all of them Buggers.

Pointing to individuals in the audience.

See there? That man's a Bugger,
and that long-haired fop's a Bugger too.

SOPHISTRY

Then how do we stand, my friend?

PHILOSOPHY

I've been beaten by the Buggers.

Flinging his cloak to the audience.

O Buggers, catch my cloak
and welcome me among the Buggers!

With a wild shriek Philosophy disappears into his cage and is wheeled away into the Thinkery, just as Sokrates comes out.

SOKRATES

Well, what are your wishes? Will you take your son home,
or shall I instruct him in the Pettifogger's Art?

STREPSIADES

Teach him—
and flog him too. But remember: I want his tongue

honed down like a razor. Sharpen him on the left side
for piddling private suits, but grind him on the right
for Grand Occasions and Affairs of State.

SOKRATES

                                        Sir,
you may depend upon me. I promise I'll send him home
a consummate little Sophist.

PHEIDIPPIDES

                    God, what a picture of misery—
a nasty, pasty-faced, consummate little stinker!

Exuent Sokrates and Pheidippides into the Thinkery.

KORYPHAIOS

Very well, go in.

To Strepsiades.

                    —You, Sir, shall live to regret your decision.

*Exit Strepsiades into his own house, as the Chorus turns
sharply and faces the audience.*

CHORUS

And now, Gentlemen of the Jury, a few brief words about
    the Prize
and the solid benefits you stand to gain by voting for *The
    Clouds*—
as you certainly should anyway.
                            First of all, when the season sets
for Spring and plowing time has come, we guarantee each
    judge's fields
the top priority in rain. Let others wait. Furthermore,
for his vineyards and orchards, we promise, perfect growing-
    weather:
no drought shall touch them, no flooding rains destroy.

However,
if some presuming mortal dares dishonor our divinity,
let him savor his punishment:

His acres, hard, dry, and barren,
shall see no harvesting. No wine, no fruit, shall ripen for
  him.
And when the olives sprout, and the season's green festoons
the vines, *his* shall wither, battered by our ratatat of rain.
And when he's busy baking bricks, we'll snuff his kiln with
  water
and smash his tiles with cannonades of hail. If he, his friend,
or relatives should celebrate a wedding, we'll send a
  DELUGE down
and drown the wedding night in rain!

By god, we'll make him say
he'd rather be roasting in Egypt than have voted wrong
  today!

Enter Strepsiades from his house, counting on his fingers.

STREPSIADES

Five days, four days, three days, two days, and then
that one day of the days of the month
I dread the most that makes me fart with fear—
the last day of the month, Duedate for debts,*
when every dun in town has solemnly sworn
to drag me into court and bankrupt me completely.
And when I plead with them to be more reasonable—
"But PLEASE, sir. Don't demand the whole sum now.
Take something on account. I'll pay you later."—
they snort they'll never see the day, curse me
for a filthy swindler and say they'll sue.

Well,
let them. If Pheidippides has learned to talk,
I don't give a damn for them and their suits.

Now then,
a little knock on the door and we'll have the answer.

He knocks on Sokrates' door and calls out.

Porter!
     Hey, porter!

Sokrates opens the door.

SOKRATES

Ah, Strepsiades. Salutations.

STREPSIADES

Same to you, Sokrates.

He hands Sokrates a bag of flour.

               Here. A token of my esteem.
Call it an honorarium.* Professors always get honorariums.

Snatching back the bag.

But wait: has Pheidippides learned his rhetoric yet—
that swindling Rhetoric that performed for us just now?

SOKRATES

Taking the bag.
He has mastered it.

STREPSIADES

             O great goddess Bamboozle!

SOKRATES

Now, sir, you can evade any legal action you wish to.

STREPSIADES

Really? Even if I borrowed the money before witnesses?

SOKRATES

Before ten thousand of them. The more the merrier.

STREPSIADES

In parody.

> *Then let my loud falsetto peal*
> *with gladsome paeans plangent!**
> *Mourn, O ye lenders of money,*
> *weep, O principals! Gnash your teeth,*
> *O ye interests compounded.*
> *For lo, within mine halls*
> *a son hath risen,*
> *a son with burnish'd tongue,*
> *yea, with double edges lambent!*
> *Hail, O hero of my halls,*
> *who delivered my domicile,*
> *who fractur'd mine enemies*
> *and drowned a father's dolor!*
> *Ho, fetch forth mine son*
> *forthwith! O my son,*
> *debouch from mine abode!**
> *O heed thy father, prithee!"*

Pheidippides, the very image of "modern youth," slouches contemptuously out of the Thinkery.

SOKRATES

Behold the man!

STREPSIADES

O joy! My boy!

SOKRATES

Take him and go.

STREPSIADES

O my son! O! O!
O! O! O! O!
Oh, how gladly I behold thy pasty face,
that negative and disputatious look! And see there,

how there blossoms on his lips our national rejoinder,
"Huh? G'wan!" How perfectly he is the rogue,
but looks the victim through and through. And on his face
that utter pallor, ah, that true Athenian look!
—All right, Son, you ruined me so it's up to you
to save me.

PHEIDIPPIDES

What's eating *you*, Dad?

STREPSIADES

Your damn debts.
And the date. That's what. Your debts are due today.
Today's Dueday.*

PHEIDIPPIDES

Today's two days? Or two Duedays?
But how can one day be two days?

STREPSIADES

How should *I* know?
It just *is!*

Resuming more calmly, patiently explaining.

Today's Dueday, son. *This* is the day
when creditors are required by law to post their bond*
in court in order to obtain a summons against their debtors.
No bond, no summons.

PHEIDIPPIDES

Ergo, they will forfeit their bond.
By definition, one day cannot be two days.

STREPSIADES

It *can't* be?
But why not?

PHEIDIPPIDES

Because it's a logical impossibility, numskull.
If one day were two days, then *ipso facto* a woman
could be simultaneously a young girl and an old hag.
Which she can't be.

STREPSIADES

But it's the law!

PHEIDIPPIDES

In that case,
I suspect the law on debt has been profoundly misinterpreted.

STREPSIADES

Misinterpreted? But how?

PHEIDIPPIDES

Enigmatically.

Old Solon loved the people.

STREPSIADES

And what in god's name has that got to do with the Duedate?

PHEIDIPPIDES

Solon's sympathies lay with the debtor, not with the creditor.

STREPSIADES

And so?

PHEIDIPPIDES

And so, when Solon promulgated his law on debt,
he carefully specified *two* distinct Duedates

for debts, not *one*, as the current interpretation has it.
Prima facie, a summons *could* be issued on either day,
though in practice this was impossible, since the creditor's
bond could be paid only on the second Duedate.

STREPSIADES

But why did Solon
set two Duedates?

PHEIDIPPIDES'

Read between the lines, moron.
Solon intended that the debtor should present himself in
court on the first date and declare himself absolved of his
debts on the grounds of the creditor's failure to issue a
summons. He won by default. *If*, however, the debtor failed
to take advantage of the deliberate ambiguity of the law,
he had to account to his creditors in court the next day.
Not an attractive prospect.

STREPSIADES

But wait. If that's the law,
then how do you account for the glaring fact that the magistrates actually demand that the creditor's bond be paid on
the first day and not on the second?

PHEIDIPPIDES

Precisely because they
are magistrates.*
Ipso facto, their greed is magisterial and their gluttony
uncontrollable. And because they can't wait to get their
fingers in the pie, they have quietly connived among
themselves to set the Duedate back a day earlier. Their
procedure, of course, is utterly illegal.

STREPSIADES

Still perplexed.

Huh?

But suddenly illuminated.

Hey!

Haw, that's good!

Turning to the audience.

Well, numskulls, what are *you* gawking at?
Yes, *you* down there!
You dumb sheep with the pigeon faces!
Cat's-paws for cleverer men! Any sophist's
suckers!
O shysterbait!
Generation of dupes!
Poor twerps, poor silly saps!
O Audience of Asses,
you were born to be taken!
—And now, gentlemen, a song.
A little ditty of my own, dedicated to me and my son,
offering us warmest congratulations on our success.
Ready,

everybody?

Singing and dancing.

> *Oh, Strepsiades, Strepsiades,*
> *there's no one like Strepsiades!*
> *He went to school with Sokrates*
> *who taught him all his sophistries!*
> *He's smarter than*
> *Euripides,*
> *for only he's,*
> *yes, only he's*
> *Pheidippides'*
> *Old Man!*
> By god, if ever I heard a hit, that's it!

To Pheidippides.

Once you finish off my creditors' suits, the whole town
will go green with envy of Strepsiades.
And now, son,

I'm throwing a dinner in your honor. So let's go in.

Exeunt Strepsiades and Pheidippides into the house. An instant later Pasias arrives, accompanied by his Witness, with a summons against Strepsiades. A notorious spendthrift, drunkard, and glutton, Pasias is grotesquely fat. Essentially a good-natured man, he has prepared himself for a difficult ordeal, and comes equipped with a wine flask from which he periodically fortifies himself.

PASIAS

> Well,
what am I supposed to do? Throw my hard-earned money
down the drain?

Something in his own words reminds him that he needs a drink, a stiff one.

> Playboy Pasias, is it?
> Nossiree.
Bah! Me and my great big heart! Soft-touch Pasias.
But I should have known. You've got to be a bastard.
Hard as nails.

He hardens himself with a drink.

> If I'd sent him packing when he tried
to put the touch on me, I wouldn't be in this fix now.
What a mess!

To Witness.

> I have to drag you around to stand witness,
and what's more, I'll make an enemy of Strepsiades for life.

He fortifies himself with still another drink.

> Well, I'll sue him anyway.
> Yessiree.
> Athens expects it,

and I won't have it said that Pasias ever besmirched
the National Honor *

> Nossiree.

Shouting into the house

> —Strepsiades! I'm suing you!

STREPSIADES

Apearing at the door

Somebody want me?

PASIAS

> I do Today's the Dueday.

STREPSIADES

To the audience

Gentlemen, you're all witness: he distinctly mentioned
two days

To Pasias

> What are you suing me for?

PASIAS

> What *for?* Why.
the money you borrowed from me to buy that horse

STREPSIADES

> Horse?
What horse? Everybody knows I'm allergic to horses.
Ask the audience

PASIAS

> By god, you swore you'd pay me!
You swore it by the gods

STREPSIADES

              Well, by god, now I swear
I won't. Anyway, that was before Pheidippides learned the
Science of Unanswerable Argument.

PASIAS

          And *that*'s why you won't pay me?

STREPSIADES

Can you think of a better reason? I'm entitled to some return
on his education, aren't I?

PASIAS

          And you're prepared to perjure yourself
on an oath sworn by the gods?

STREPSIADES

         By the gods?
              What gods?

PASIAS

What gods?
      Why, Zeus, Poseidon, and Hermes.

STREPSIADES

             Damn right
I would. And what's more, I'd do it again. Gratis,
by god!
    I *like* perjury.

PASIAS

        Why, you barefaced swindler!
You damnable liar!

STREPSIADES

Prodding Pasias in the belly

> Boy. what blubber'
>
> You know,
> that paunch of yours ought to make someone a mighty
> dandy wineskin

PASIAS

> By god. that's the last straw'

STREPSIADES

> Hmmmm. Yup.
> five gallons. I'd guess offhand

PASIAS

> So help me Zeus!
> So help me every god in heaven, you won't get away
> with this!

STREPSIADES

> You know, you and your silly gods tickle me.
> Zeus is a joke to us Thinking Men

PASIAS

> By god. someday
> you'll regret this.
> Now then, for the last time.
> will you pay me or won't you? Give me a straight answer
> and I'll be off

STREPSIADES

> Don't you budge. I'll be right back
> and bring you my final answer.

Strepsiades rushes into the house.

PASIAS

To his Witness

I wonder what he's doing.
Do you think he'll pay me?

STREPSIADES

*Reappearing from the house. in his hands he holds a large
basket*

Now where's that creditor of mine?

Holding up the basket in front of Pasias

--All right. you. what's this?

PASIAS

That? A basket.

STREPSIADES

A *basket?*
And a stupid ignoramus like you has the nerve to come
around badgering me for money? By god. I wouldn't give a
cent to a man who can't even tell a basket from a baskette

PASIAS

Then you won't pay me back?

STREPSIADES

Not if *I* know it.
Look here,
you Colossus of Lard. why don't you quietly melt away?
Beat it, Fatboy'

He threatens to beat him with his baskette

PASIAS

I'm going. Yessiree. And by god,

if I don't post my bond with the magistrates right now,
my name's not Pasias.

        Nossiree.

STREPSIADES

        Tch tch. Poor Pasias.
You'll just lose your bond on top of all your other losses.
And, personally speaking, I wouldn't want to see you suffer
just because your grammar's bad.

Beating Pasias over the head with his baskette.

        Remember?

        Baskette!

*Exit Pasias at a run pursued by Strepsiades. An instant later,
hideous wails and shrieks are heard off-stage, and these are
followed by the pathetic entrance of the notorious effeminate
and gambler, Amynias. He has just had an accident with his
chariot, and his entrance is a picture of misery: his head is
covered with blood, his clothes torn, and his language, a
delirious compound of tragic rhetoric and a marked lisp, is
almost unintelligible.*

AMYNIAS

Alackaday!

      Woe is me!

        Alas! Alas!

STREPSIADES

        Gods in heaven,
what a caterwauling!

      —Look, who *are* you?

        The way you whine
you sound like some poor blubbering god from a tragedy
by Karkinos.*

AMYNIAS

       Wouldst hear how I am high? Know then:
a wretched wight in woe am I. Adversity
yclept.

STREPSIADES

    Then hit the road, Buster.

AMYNIAS

              O Funest Doom!
O Darkling Destiny!
         How fell the fate by which I fall,
ah, Pallas!
      O all unhors'd! O human haplessness
I am!

STREPSIADES

    I get it. You're an actor, and you want me to guess
what part you're practicing.
        Hmm.
         Must be a female role
But of course!
      You're Alkmene in the play by Xenokles,
and you're mourning your brother

AMYNIAS

        You're *such* a tease,
you naughty man.
      Now then, be a dear, and ask Pheidippides
to pay me my money. You see, I'm in the most frightful
way. You simply can't *imagine!*

STREPSIADES

      Money? What money?

AMYNIAS

                        Why, the money
Pheidippides borrowed.

STREPSIADES

             Hmmm. You *are* in a frightful way.
You simply can't *imagine*.

AMYNIAS

            But I *can*. You see, on my way,
I was thrown from my chariot. Literally *hurled* into the air.
It was *too* awful.

STREPSIADES

          It fits. You must have hurt your head.
That would explain that gibberish about money.

AMYNIAS

                   What's gibberish
about wanting my money?

STREPSIADES

            Obvious case of delirium.
Brain damage too, I suspect.

AMYNIAS

           Brain damage?

STREPSIADES

                       Yup.
You'll probably be queer the rest of your life. That's how
I see it.

AMYNIAS

        Pay me my money, or I'll sue you! That's how
I see it.

STREPSIADES

> Is that so?
>> All right, let me ask you a question.
I'm curious to know which theory on rainfall you prefer.
Now then, in your considered opinion, is the phenomenon
of rain best explained as a precipitation of *totally* fresh
water, or is it merely a case of the same old rainwater in
continuous re-use, slowly condensed by the Clouds and then
precipitated once more as rain?

AMYNIAS

>> My *dear* fellow.
I really couldn't care less.

STREPSIADES

>> Couldn't care less, eh?
And a sophomore like you, completely ignorant of Science,
thinks he's got the right to go around pestering people
to pay him money?
>> Boy, some nerve!

AMYNIAS

>> Look here,
if you're temporarily short of cash, then let me have
the interest.

STREPSIADES

> Interest? What the devil's interest?

AMYNIAS

>> Why, interest
is nothing more than the tendency of a cash principal
to reproduce itself by increments over a period of time.
Very gradually, day after day, month after month,
the interest accrues and the principal grows.

STREPSIADES

Dandy.
Then in your opinion there's more water in the ocean now
than last year? Is that right?

AMYNIAS

But, of course, it isn't.
Oceans *can't* grow, you silly man. It's against the Law
of Nature.

STREPSIADES

Then what about you, you unnatural bastard?
If the ocean, with all those rivers pouring into it,
doesn't grow, then who the hell are you to expect your
money to grow?
And now CLEAR OUT! Go peddle your
subpoenas somewhere else.

Amynias stands firm and Strepsiades calls out to his slave.

—Bring me my horsewhip.

*The slave brings the whip and Strepsiades cracks it threaten-
ingly at Amynias.*

AMYNIAS

Appealing in terror to the audience.

—Gentlemen,
you're my witnesses!

STREPSIADES

Still here, are you?

He flicks Amynias with the whip.

Giddeap!
Gallop, you gelding!
Gee!

He flicks Amynias again with his whip, this time in the rear.

AMYNIAS

A hit! A hit!
A palpable hit!

STREPSIADES

Raising his phallus to the ready.

Git, dammit, or I'll sunder your rump
with my ram!

With a wild whinny of fright, Amynias rushes offstage.

Going, are you?
A damned good thing.
And don't come back here nagging me about your money,
or I'll badger your bum!
You'll get the ride of your life!

*Strepsiades re-enters the house to resume his interrupted
dinner with Pheidippides.*

CHORUS

Individually.

—Such is wickedness,
—such is fatal fascina-
tion:
—this senile amateur of fraud,
—by greed
and guile obsessed,
—frantic to disown his debts
—(and,
—such his luck,
—apparently
—succeed-
ing).

—BUT please take note:

                   —soon,

                             —perhaps today,

—this poor man's Sokrates must learn his lesson,

—*viz.*

     —CRIME DOES NOT PAY.

                           —Dishonesty

comes home to roost.

                    —It's Poetic Retribution!

—But *now*, poor fish!

                 —he thinks he's sitting

                             —pretty.

—Success at last!

             —For hasn't his Pheidippides

become

        —so voluble a speaker,

                  —so specious

a sophist,

        —a shyster so vicious,

                  —that he's

now

     —ABSOLUTELY INVINCIBLE?

                       —So

he gloats.

       —But wait!

           —Take note:

                  —the time will come—

Strepsiades howls in pain offstage.

—in fact, it's coming now—

                  —when poor Strepsiades

will wish to god

        —Pheidippides were

                —DUMB!

With a bellow of pain and terror, Strepsiades plunges out of his house, hotly pursued by Pheidippides with a murderous stick.

STREPSIADES

OOOUUUCH!!!
>HALP!
>>For god's sake, help me!

Appealing to the Audience.

>>>>Friends!
Fellow-countrymen! Aunts! Uncles! Fathers! Brothers!
To the rescue!
>>He's beating me!
>>>Help me!
>>>>*Ouuch!*
O my poor head!
>>Ooh, my jaw!

To Pheidippides.

>>>—You great big bully,
Hit your own father, would you?

PHEIDIPPIDES

>>>Gladly, Daddy.

STREPSIADES

You hear that? The big brute *admits* it.

PHEIDIPPIDES

>>>*Admit* it? Hell,
I *proclaim* it.

STREPSIADES

>>You cheap Cutthroat!
>>>You father-beating Bastard!
You Turd!
>>You . . . you . . . you—

PHEIDIPPIDES

Carry on. Don't you know
you're complimenting me?

STREPSIADES

Why, you . . . you . . . you Palpable Pervert!
You Pederast!

PHEIDIPPIDES

Roll me in roses, Daddy!

STREPSIADES

You Bugger!
Hit your own father, would you?

PHEIDIPPIDES

Damn right I would.
God knows, I had good justification.

STREPSIADES

Justification, you say?
Why, you Dunghill, what justification could there *ever* be
for hitting your own father?

PHEIDIPPIDES

Would a logical demonstration
convince you?

STREPSIADES

A logical demonstration? You mean to tell me
you can *prove* a shocking thing like that?

PHEIDIPPIDES

Elementary, really.

What's more, you can choose the logic. Take your pick.
Either one.

STREPSIADES

> Either *which?*

PHEIDIPPIDES

> > Either *which?* Why,
Socratic logic or pre-Socratic logic. Either logic.
Take your pick.

STREPSIADES

> *Take my pick*, damn you? Look,
who do you think paid for your shyster education anyway?
And now you propose to convince *me* that there's nothing
wrong in whipping your own father?

PHEIDIPPIDES

> > > I not only propose it;
I propose to *prove* it. Irrefutably, in fact. Rebuttal
is utterly inconceivable.

STREPSIADES

> By god, *this* I want to hear!

CHORUS

> Old friend, WATCH OUT.
> Upon this bout
> > may hang your own survival.
>
> What's more, unless
> I miss my guess,
> > the odds are on your rival.
>
> That curling lip,
> that sneer's a tip,
> > and you'd be wise to heed it.

The tip? A trap.
But, *verbum sap.*
I wish you luck. *You*'ll need it.

KORYPHAIOS

To Strepsiades.

And now, Sir, I suggest you brief the Chorus Begin at the beginning and describe your little fracas exactly as it happened.

STREPSIADES

Yes'm.
The whole damn dirty squabble from start to finish.

As you know.
we both went in to celebrate. Well, Ladies, a custom's a
    custom,*
after all, and there's nothing like a little music, I always say,
to get a party off to a good start. So naturally I asked him
to get down his lyre and sing a song. For instance,
Simonides'
*Shearin' o' the Ram.**
Well, you know what the little stinker answered?
That singing at table was—Obsolete,

Old Hat,

Lowbrow,

Bullshit!

Strictly for grandmothers.

PHEIDIPPIDES

You damn well got what you
deserved. Asking me to sing on an empty stomach! What is
this anyway? A banquet or a cricket-concert?

STREPSIADES

You hear that?
A cricket-concert!

His exact words.

And then he started sneering at Simonides!
Called him—get this—Puny Pipsqueak Hack!

Was I *sore?*
Brother!

Well, somehow I counted to ten, and then I asked
him to sing me some Aischylos.

Please.

And you know what he
replied?

That he considered Aischylos "a poet of colossal stature:"—

Yup,
"the most colossal, pretentious, pompous, spouting, bombastic bore in poetic history."*

I was so damn mad I just about went
through the roof. But I gritted my teeth together, mustered
up a sick smile and somehow managed to say, "All right,
son, if that's how you feel, then sing me a passage from
one of those highbrow modern plays you're so crazy
about."

So he recited—you can guess—
Euripides! One of those slimy tragedies* where, so help me,
there's a brother who screws his own sister!

Well, Ladies, *that* did it!

I jumped up,
blind with rage, started cursing at him and calling him
names, and he started screaming and cursing back and
before I knew it, he hauled off and—*wham!*—he biffed me
and bashed me and clipped me and poked me and choked
me and—

PHEIDIPPIDES

And, by god, you
had it coming! Knocking a genius like Euripides!

STREPSIADES

Euripides!
A GENIUS??
That . . .

That . . . that . . . !

Pheidippides raises his stick threateningly.

HALP! He's hitting me!

PHEIDIPPIDES

You've got it

coming, Dad!

STREPSIADES

Got it coming, do I?

Why, you ungrateful brat, I *raised* you!
When you were a baby I pampered you! I waited on you
   hand and foot!
I understood your babytalk. You babbled GOO and I
   obeyed. Why,
when you whimpered WAWA DADA, who brought your
   water?
DADA did.
When you burbled BABA, who brought your Baby Biscuits?
   DADA did.
And when you cried GOTTA GO KAKA DADA, who
   saved his shitty darling?
Who rushed you to the door? Who held you while you did
   it? Damn you,
            DADA did!
         And in return you choked me
         and when I shat in terror,
         would you give your Dad a hand,
         would you help me to the door?
         No, you left me there alone
         to do it on the floor!

   Yes, to do it on the floor!

CHORUS

   YOUR ATTENTION, PLEASE!
   Pheidippides
      now makes his demonstration—

a proof which will,
I'm certain, thrill
    the younger generation.

For if this lad
defeats his Dad,
    there's not an older man

or father in
this town, whose skin
    is worth a Tinker's Damn!

KORYPHAIOS

And now that Doughty Champion of Change, that Golden-
    Tongued Attorney
for Tomorrow, that Harbinger of Progress
                                    —PHEIDIPPIDES!

To Pheidippides.

                                    Remember, Sir,
we want the truth
            —or a reasonable facsimile.

PHEIDIPPIDES

                        Gentlemen, Eloquence
is sweet, sweeter than I ever dreamed! This utter bliss of
speech! This rapture of articulation! But oh, the sheer Attic
honey of subverting the Established Moral Order!
                        And yet when I look back
on those benighted days of pre-Sokratic folly, upon the boy
I used to be, whose only hobby was horses, who could not
speak three words of Greek without a blunder, why . . .
                        words fail me.
But *now*, now that Sokrates has made a fresh Pheidippides
of me, now that my daily diet is Philosophy, Profundity,
Subtlety, and Science, I propose to prove beyond the
shadow of a doubt the philosophical propriety of beating
my Father.

STREPSIADES

For the love of Zeus,
go back to your damn horses! I'd rather be stuck with a
stable than be battered by a stick.

PHEIDIPPIDES

I ignore these childish interruptions
and proceed with my demonstration.
Now then, answer my question:
did you lick me when I was a little boy?

STREPSIADES

Of course I licked you.
For your own damn good. Because I loved you.

PHEIDIPPIDES

Then *ipso facto*,
since you yourself admit that loving and lickings are
synonymous, it's only fair that I—for your own damn good,
you understand?—whip you in return.
In any case by what right do you whip me
but claim exemption for yourself?
What do you think I am? A slave?
Wasn't I born as free a man as you?*
Well?

STREPSIADES

But . . .

PHEIDIPPIDES

But what?
Spare the Rod and Spoil the Child?
Is that your argument?
If so,
then I can be sententious too. *Old Men Are Boys Writ Big,*

as the saying goes.

A *fortiori* then, old men logically deserve to be beaten more, since at their age they have clearly less excuse for the mischief that they do.

STREPSIADES

But it's unnatural! It's . . . *illegal!* *Honor your father and mother.*

That's the law.

Everywhere.

PHEIDIPPIDES

The *law?*

And who made the law?

An ordinary man. A man like you or me. A man who lobbied for his bill until he persuaded the people to make it law.

By the same token, then, what prevents me now from proposing new legislation granting sons the power to inflict corporal punishment upon wayward fathers?

Nothing vindictive, of course.

In fact, I would personally insist on adding a rider, a Retroactive Amnesty for Fathers, waiving our right to compensation for any whippings we received prior to the passage of the new law. However, if you're still unconvinced, look to Nature for a sanction. Observe the roosters, for instance, and what do you see?

A society whose pecking-order envisages a permanent state of open warfare between fathers and sons. And how do roosters differ from men, except for the trifling fact that human society is based upon law and rooster society isn't?

STREPSIADES

Look, if you want to imitate the roosters, why don't you go eat shit and sleep on a perch at night?

PHEIDIPPIDES

Why? Er . . .
because the analogy doesn't hold, that's why. If you don't
believe me, then go ask Sokrates.

STREPSIADES

Well, whatever your roosters happen to do,
you'd better not lick me. It's your neck if you do.

PHEIDIPPIDES

My neck?
How so?

STREPSIADES

Because look: I lick you. All right, someday you'll
have a son and you can even the score with me by licking
the hell out of him. But if you lick me, then your son will
follow your precedent by licking you. If you have a son.

PHEIDIPPIDES

And if I don't have a son?
You've licked me, but where am I? I'm left holding the bag,
and you'll go to your grave laughing at me.

*There is a long tense silence as the full force of this crushing
argument takes its effect upon Strepsiades.*

STREPSIADES

What?
But how . . . ?
Hmm,
by god, you're right!

To the Audience.

—Speaking for the older generation, gentlemen, I'm compelled to admit defeat. The kids have proved their point: naughty fathers should be flogged.

PHEIDIPPIDES

Of course, I nearly forgot. One final matter.

STREPSIADES

The funeral?

PHEIDIPPIDES

Far from it. In fact, it may even soothe your feelings.

STREPSIADES

How to be licked and like it, eh? Go on. I'm listening.

PHEIDIPPIDES

Well, now, Misery Loves Company, they say. So I'll give you some company.

I'll horsewhip Mother.

STREPSIADES

You'll *WHAT???*
HORSEWHIP YOUR OWN MOTHER?

But this is worse! Ten thousand times worse!

PHEIDIPPIDES

Is that so? And suppose I prove by Sokratic logic the utter propriety of horsewhipping Mother?

What would you say to that?

STREPSIADES

> What would I
> *say?*
>> By god, if you prove *that*,
>> then for all I care, you heel,
>> you can take your stinking Logics
>> and your Thinkery as well
>> with Sokrates inside it
>> and damn well go to hell!

To the Chorus.

> —You Clouds got me into this! Why in god's name
> did I ever believe you?

KORYPHAIOS

>> The guilt is yours, Strepsiades,
> yours and yours alone. The dishonesty you did
> was your own choice, not ours.

STREPSIADES

>> But why didn't you warn me
> instead of luring a poor old ignoramus into trouble?
> Why did you encourage me?

KORYPHAIOS

>> Because this is what we are,
> the insubstantial Clouds men build their hopes upon,*
> shining tempters formed of air, symbols of desire;
> and so we act, beckoning, alluring foolish men
> through their dishonest dreams of gain to overwhelming
> ruin. There, schooled by suffering, they learn at last
> to fear the gods.

STREPSIADES

>> Well, I can't say much for your methods,
> though I had it coming. I was wrong to cheat my creditors,
> and I admit it.

To Pheidippides

—All right, boy, what do you say?
Let's go and take revenge on Sokrates and Chairephon
for swindling us. Are you game?

PHEIDIPPIDES

What? Raise a finger
against my old Philosophy professor? Count me out.

STREPSIADES

Show a little respect for Zeus.

PHEIDIPPIDES

Zeus?
You old fogy,
are you so stupid you still believe there's such a thing
as Zeus?

STREPSIADES

Of course there's a Zeus.

PHEIDIPPIDES

Not any more
there isn't. Convection-Principle's in power now.
Zeus has been deported.

STREPSIADES

That's a lie! A lot of cheap
Convection-Principle propaganda circulated by those
windbags in the Thinkery!
I was brainwashed! Why, they told me
that the whole universe was a kind of potbellied stove

Pointing to the model in front of the Thinkery.

like that model there, an enormous cosmical barbecue,
and the gods were nothing but a lot of hot air and gas
swirling around in the flue. And I swallowed it,
hook, line, and sinker!

PHEIDIPPIDES

                              Rave to yourself. Madman.
I'm leaving.

Exit Pheidippides.

STREPSIADES

                    O Horse's Ass, Blithering Imbecile,
Brainless Booby, Bonehead that I was to ditch the gods
for Sokrates!

*He picks up Pheidippides' stick and savagely smashes the
potbellied model of the Universe in front of the Thinkery. He
then rushes to his own house and falls on his knees before the
statue of Hermes.*

                    —Great Hermes, I implore you!
                                        Be gracious,
lord! Forego your anger and give me your compassion.
Pity a poor old codger who was hypnotized with hogwash,
drunk on drivel.
                    O Hermes, give me your advice,
tell me what to do.
                              Should I sue?

*He puts his ear close to the dog's mouth as though listening
to whispered advice.*

                                        What?
Ummm.
        Good.
              Got it.
                    DON'T SUE
                              Go on.

Yes?

BURN DOWN THE THINKERY . . . SMOKE OUT
THE CHARLATANS . . .
INCINERATE THE FAKES!

Aye aye, Sir!

Shouting to his slave.

—Xanthias! come here!
Quick, get me your ladder!

Bring me an axe!

Xanthias runs up with a ladder and an axe.

Now
scramble up there on the Thinkery and rip up the tiles
until the roof caves in.

Shoo. boy!

*Xanthias sets his ladder against the Thinkery, clambers up,
and starts chopping at the tiles and prying them up with his
axe.*

—Quick,
bring me a torch!

Another slave runs up with a blazing torch.

By god, I'll fix those fakes
for what they did to me or my name's not Strepsiades!
Let's see if they can fast-talk their way out of this.

*He bounds up the ladder to the roof, furiously firing the
rafters and beams with his torch, while Xanthias pries at the
tiles with the axe. The smoke billows up in clouds and the
whole roof begins to glare luridly, while inside the Thinkery
are heard the first signs of alarm and confusion.*

FIRST STUDENT

From within.

FIRE!! FIRE!!
                    HELP!

STREPSIADES

                              Scorch 'em, Torch!
Go get 'em!

When Xanthias stops to stare at the holocaust, Strepsiades tosses him the torch, snatches up the axe. and starts slashing furiously at the rafters.

FIRST STUDENT

Rushing out of the Thinkery and peering up to the roof.

                    —Sirrah, what dost?

STREPSIADES

                                        Dust? That's chips,
Buster. I'm chopping logic with the rafters of your roof.

SECOND STUDENT

From within.

Who roasteth our rookery?

STREPSIADES

                    A man without a coat.

SECOND STUDENT

Rushing outside.

But we're burning alive!

STREPSIADES

              Hell, I'm freezing to death!

FIRST STUDENT

But this is Arson! Deliberate Arson! We'll die!

STREPSIADES

Splendid. Exactly what I had in mind—

*He narrowly misses his leg with the axe and then teeters
dangerously on the roof.*

                        Oops!—

so long as I don't split my shins with this axe
or break my neck in the process.

*Wheezing, hacking, and gagging, Sokrates scuttles out of
the Thinkery, closely followed by an incredible procession
of emaciated, ghostlike Students, all gibbering with terror.
Finally, at the very rear, squawking and clucking like two
frightened roosters, come Philosophy and Sophistry.*

SOKRATES

                    You there, sirrah!
What is thy purpose upon my roof?

STREPSIADES

                  Ah, sir,
I walk upon the air and look down upon the sun
from a superior standpoint.

SOKRATES

Choking on the smoke and almost incoherent with rage.

             Why, you—
                agh!
                I'm gagging . . .

argh
   I . . .

grhuahg

CAN'T

TALK!!

Arrggghhh.

As Sokrates collapses into a spasm of choked coughing, Strepsiades and Xanthias come scrambling down the ladder from the roof. Then Chairephon, totally covered with soot and cinders and his cloak smouldering, streaks from the holocaust of the Thinkery

CHAIREPHON

Yiyi!

HALP!
It's like an oven in the Thinkery! I'm burnt to a crisp.
I'm a cinder

STREPSIADES

Belaboring him with a stick as Xanthias lashes Sokrates.

Then why did you blaspheme the gods?
What made you spy upon the Moon in heaven?

KORYPHAIOS

Thrash, them,
beat them, flog them for their crimes, but most of all
because they dared outrage the gods of heaven!

Strepsiades and his slaves thrash Sokrates and his followers until the whole herd of thinkers. followed by Philosophy and Sophistry, stampedes madly toward the exit Here they meet—and flatten—Pasias and Amynias* returning to the Thinkery armed with summonses and accompanied by their witnesses. Exeunt omnes in a general rout. Behind them the Thinkery with an enormous crash collapses into blazing ruin.

CHORUS

> Now ladies, let us leave
> and go our way.
> Our dances here are done,
> and so's our play.

Slowly and majestically, the Chorus files out.

Notes

page 21. *Strepsiades:* A name derived from στρέψις (turning twisting, wriggling). That is, Strepsiades is etymologically The Debtdodger and his name is played upon throughout the play.

22. *desert to the Spartans:* The annual invasions of Attika by the Spartans and their allies during the first few years of the Peloponnesian War meant that maltreated or discontented Athenian slaves could easily desert to the enemy, and the fear of desertion was common in Athens.

23. *ponytails:* Pheidippides wore his hair long and curling in the style affected by the younger knights.

25. *bumbailiff:* B. B. Rogers' solution, perhaps too English for American ears; but the pun is almost untranslatable. The Greek word here translated as bumbailiff is δήμαρχος, inserted as a surprise in place of the expected "bedbug" or "flea."

25. *Blueblood Megakles:* Megakles was a common male name of the Alkmaionid family, one of the oldest and most aristocratic in Athens. It is largely because of the prominence of Alkmaionid names in the play that Pheidippides has frequently—and not

improbably—been regarded as a caricature of Alkibiades, also an Alkmaionid and notorious for his dissolute youth.

Strepsiades' marriage to an Alkmaionid wife is, of course, a *mésalliance* between a prosperous farmer and a daughter of the dissolute and luxurious city nobility. Presumably, such alliances were not uncommon in the late fifth century, and Aristophanes clearly intends to show the progress of corruption in Strepsiades, ruined by his playboy son and his luxurious wife.

page 26. *hippos:* "Horse." A common component in aristocratic names, since in early Athens the ownership of a horse automatically meant membership in the military cavalry or the social chivalry.

Pheidonides: The name means Parsimonious.

Pheidippides: The compromise means Parsimonious Chevalier of The Scrimping Aristocrat.

horse-god oaths: As Poseidon Hippios, Poseidon was the patron god of horsemen. Cf. *Knights* 551 ff.

29. *Cosmical Oven:* The theory advanced in this passage is of uncertain provenience. In *Birds* 1001, Aristophanes attributes it to Meton, though the comedian Kratinos attributed it to Hippo in his *Panoptai*, and both Herakleitos and Parmenides held that the heavens were made of Fire. Here, however, it is probably best taken as a representative— and, for Aristophanes, representatively ridiculous— example of contemporary physical theory. Some of the Sophists may have held something like it; so far as we know, Sokrates did not.

But the metaphore of the Cosmical Oven is central to the play, and for this reason Aristophanes has placed a visible model of it in front of the Thinkery (cf. 11. 1473–74). Moreover, unless I am mistaken, the metaphor is a surprisingly consistent one, whose every detail and principle would have been instantly understood by an Athenian— but not an American—audience. For the principle here is that of an ordinary, humdrum, home-made charcoal-burner's "kiln," used incongruously as a diagram of high-falutin' Socratic physics, and it is in the appreciation of the details that the humor of the finale lies. It is, according to Aristophanes, a kiln designed for very slow heat and very little air (i.e., a πνιγεύς); in shape it is like an inverted bowl (i.e., a δῖνος—cf. 1. 1473), bellied at the bottom and tapered at the top; set inside it are charcoals (i.e., ἄνθρακες—1.97) and *above* the charcoals are the swirling heated gases and flames (i.e., αἰθέριος δῖνος—1.380) under whose steady heat wood becomes charcoal. Translated into the physics of the Aristophanic Sokrates, the humble charcoal-burner's oven becomes the Universal Crucible, in which the gods are the lightning and the slow, downward-burning heat of the heavens, the forces which slowly carbonize the world and the creatures below; in which living is a form of burning and the dead are only ashes. Against this background, with only minor modifications, Sokrates' student can demonstrate to Strepsiades the cosmical principles involved in the gnat's buzz and Sokrates can explain the thunder as elemental farting. And it is, of course, the same metaphor which informs the finale of the play where the Thinkery itself becomes an enormous blazing kiln. Sokrates chokes on the smoke (ἀποπνιγήσομαι—1. 1504), Chairephon is roasted alive (κατακαυθήσομαι—1. 1505), while Strepsiades, like a blazing god, fires the roof *above* them.

Such, I believe, is Aristophanes' meaning. Because, however, charcoal kilns are unfamiliar nowadays, I have been compelled to make the Cosmical Oven an ordinary potbellied stove and to introduce a pseudoscientific equivalent for Δῖνος, i.e., Convection-Principle.

page 29. *for a fee:* The perennial gibe. The Sophists expected to be paid for the instruction they gave, an attitude which seemed mercenary to the wealthy

Plato and which Platonists since have never tired of condemning. Doubtless many of the Sophists were mercenary and several were rich men, but the mere fact of accepting a salary for professional services rendered does not—except in aristocratic societies where cash payments are regarded as vulgarizing those who receive them—convict a man of intellectual dishonesty. But perhaps I am prejudiced. In any case, the sophistic movement made headway in Athens, not because the Sophists were greedy mountebanks in a gullible age, but because there was a rising class with a desperate need for new skills and techniques and for this class the existing education was worse than useless. If the New Education began by being *vocational*—offering precisely those legal and verbal skills which were so urgently required for the conduct of Athenian imperialism—it ended by being genuinely *revolutionary*, that is, by systematically questioning and overturning all the established beliefs of the old order. It could never have become this, however, had not the fact of payment *freed* the Sophists from the old order as much as it *bound* them to the new. Hence the hostility and open contempt of such conservatives as Aristophanes and Plato.

Sokrates, it is true, did *not* accept payment, and this is Sokrates' glory. But Sokrates' glory is not necessarily the Sophists' shame.

page 29. *The Technique of Winning Lawsuits:* Literally, "to overcome the truth by telling lies," i.e., the familiar accusation that the Sophists made "the worse cause appear the better." It was precisely this charge that was brought against Sokrates by his accusers later, and Aristophanes may be responsible for the suspicion. That some Sophists professionally claimed this ability is beyond dispute. Equally, however, the sophistic attack upon traditional beliefs must have seemed both perverse and illogical to staunch conservatives. Passionately held convictions tend, i.e., to defend themselves by their look of being self-evident: those who question them are *ipso facto* guilty of dishonesty or faulty reasoning. And this is especially true of an age when logic was in a state of comparative infancy. Plato, for instance, constantly attacks the Sophists for their devotion to specious logic (i.e., sophistry), and yet his own *Republic* contains dozens of logical fallacies and grotesque equivocations that even a schoolboy could detect. And presumably these are honest mistakes. But the Sophists normally receive no mercy.

page 30. *two kinds of Logic:* i.e., the so-called Just (or Major or Better) Logic and the Unjust (or Minor or Weaker) Logic, here rendered as Philosophy and Sophistry respectively.

The originator of the Doctrine of the Two Logics (or *Antilogoi*) was Protagoras of Abdera. If we are right in assuming that Protagoras' famous dictum ("Man is the measure of all things") means that the truth is subjective, then the same statement also implies that a proposition can be simultaneously both true and false. And it is a fact that Protagoras taught his students to argue *both* sides of a given statement with equal plausibility— presumably as an exercise in forensic virtuosity. The very willingness of Athenian courts to consider matter that would now be regarded as inadmissible supports the view that these exercises were practical in scope and not deliberate attempts to subvert justice. But for Aristophanes the *Antilogoi* are transparent sophistry, humbug on a huge scale, and he accordingly makes the debate between the two *Logoi* the climax of the comedy.

It is customary, of course, to translate Λόγος as "Logic" or "Argument," and this is the literal meaning of the word. But the issue here is larger, and to translate this way tends to obscure the fact that Aristophanes is talking, not about systems of formal logic, but about a whole system of Reason, discursive and nondiscursive alike. Λόγος also means Reason; but Reason includes several modes of discourse ranging from the work of the imagination to moral reason and strictly logical reason in the narrow sense. The so-called Just Argument, for instance, is not really an argument or a logical system at all; it is a personification of the kind of Reason spoken by a certain kind of society before logic, strict logic, existed: a' Reason which expressed itself in education, in morals, in imagination, in the criteria of values and the justifications offered for those values. As opposed to the Unjust Argument, it represents the rational power of poetry—and the peculiar logic of poetic imagination—against the rational power of prose and formal logic (and for this very reason Aristophanes lets the Just Argument speak in splendid anapests while the Unjust Argument uses prosy iambics). In ethics, it represents the power of rational suasion— by means of models and parallels drawn from the great body of lyric and epic poetry—in contrast to a system of ethics, just as rational but rational in a different way, sanctioned by inferences drawn from Nature and animal existence (cf. Pheidippides' inferences from the life of the rooster, 11. 1427–29). In culture, it is the rational guidance of Custom (not Blind Custom), the corrective rightness of traditional experience as against the restless innovations and risky isolation from experience and history of the pure intellect. It is not what the modern world normally means by Reason, and certainly not what Protagoras meant, but it is, I think, what Aristophanes meant and what most Greeks would have understood him to mean. But for this very reason, because his *Logos* is not a logic but a prelogical discourse of the whole human reason, the Just Argument is helpless against his opponent. His case cannot be expressed logically, and yet it remains rational.

All this may seem like compounding old humbug with new, but it is the justification I make for translating Δίκαιος Λόγος as Philosophy and "Αδικος Λόγος as Sophistry. Sophistry, of course, should be taken in the strict sense of the word, Philosophy in the loose and unprofessional sense (as in the catchphrase, "a philosophy of life").

page 31. *miscarriage:* Probably a conscious echo of Sokrates' claim to be midwife of ideas.

35. *Spartan prisoners from Pylos:* Cf. Glossary, under *Pylos.* After their imprisonment, the Spartans must have been considerably emaciated.

35. *geological research:* Literally, "they are exploring the things under the earth." This was, in fact, one of the accusations brought against Sokrates by his accusers in 399 B.C. In substance the charge implies that scientific research is blasphemous, insofar as the very act of investigating Nature suggests that the inquirer has doubts about the received cosmology. In the *Apology,* Sokrates admits to having dabbled in scientific research in his earlier days; the later Sokrates, Plato implies, had quite outgrown such nonsense.

37. *And as patriotic as it is useful:* During the years preceding the Peloponnesian War, Athens sometimes confiscated the territory of rebellious subject cities. The land so confiscated was then divided by lot and portioned out among the poorer citizens of Athens. Such allotments, needless to say, were enormously popular—at least in Athens.

37. *a single lawcourt in session:* The Athenian love of litigation was notorious, and Aristophanes never misses a chance of hitting it. Cf. *Wasps.*

38. *Perikles squeezed it dry:* Cf. Glossary: EUBOIA.

41. *Bars of iron, like the Byzantines?:* Sokrates' statement that the gods are an expression coined by vulgar superstition causes Strepsiades to think of a less vulgar sort of coinage. And so he comes up with the Byzantines who, alone in the Greek world, used coins made of iron.

42. *the mystical couch:* Probably a very battered settee. The reader should perhaps be aware that the whole

scene of Strepsiades' admission to the Thinkery and introduction to the Clouds is an elaborate "philosophical" initiation rite, probably paralleling initiation into one of the many Greek mysteries. Thus Sokrates' researches are *mysteries;* Sokrates powders Strepsiades as a *purification;* Strepsiades wears a *chaplet* and is forced to strip *naked* (like a candidate at the Eleusinian Mysteries) before entering the *cave* at the rear of the Thinkery (which reminds him of the cave of the oracular Trophonios, a Theban seer). After his entrance he must undergo an *ordeal* (whippings, bedbugs, etc.) before being vouchsafed rebirth as a *new man.*

page 42. *poor Athamas:* Cf. Glossary: ATHAMAS. Athamas attempted to kill his son Phrixos; when sentenced to be sacrificed for the attempt, he was saved by Herakles. The point here is that Strepsiades' mythology is inaccurate and his literary education has been neglected. But since no conceivable modern audience can be expected to know—or even to care—whether Athamas was killed or saved, I have deliberately intruded the two succeeding lines in the hope of making them seem Aristophanic and the situation a little clearer.

47. *That's why they write:* Presumably all the effusions which follow this are genuine examples of what happened when the Murky Muse inspired a dithyrambic soul.

60. *But I'm not a burglar:* According to the Scholiast, this line is explained by the customary Athenian procedure for searching a house in which stolen goods might have been hidden. The searcher was required to strip so that he could not, under pretense of carrying out his search, convey into the house of the accused the goods presumed to have been stolen. Sokrates' reply in the following line is an intruded gloss of my own manufacture, designed to give the situation a possible point for a contemporary audience.

61. *ARISTOPHANES:* In the Greek text the speech

which I have here assigned to Aristophanes is given to the Chorus in accordance with the normal convention of the *parabasis*. But if the Chorus in a normal *parabasis* speaks *on behalf of* the poet, the parabasis of *Clouds* is unique in having the Chorus speak, in the first person, *as* the poet himself. Doubtless in the original version of this play, the *parabasis* was spoken by the Chorus on the poet's behalf; but in the revision Aristophanes has laid aside the mask and speaks directly for himself. In the circumstances it seemed unnatural to give the Chorus the poet's lines, and I have therefore brought Aristophanes on stage to speak for himself in person.

page 62. *a stranger rescued the foundling:* Aristophanes had produced his comedy *The Banqueters* under the name of Kallistratos. His reason for so doing, he claims, was natural modesty and observation of Athens' neglect and mistreatment of her comic poets (cf. *Knights* 514–45); more likely, he was too young to enter the contest under his own name.

62. *Elektra in the play:* Cf. Glossary: ELEKTRA

63. *dangling throng of leather:* The comic phallus. Despite the almost unanimous consensus of scholars that Aristophanic characters did *not* wear the phallus, and Aristophanes' explicit denial here, I am nonetheless convinced they did. My only argument is the text and the near impossibility of explaining the dramatic action of numerous scenes in the absence of the phallus. In *Clouds*, Strepsiades' little play on "finger-rhythm" (652 ff.) literally requires the phallus, as does his parting threat to Amynias (1299–1302). The masturbation-jingle in *Knights* (24 ff.) is unactable without it; the Wasps are stingless, etc., etc. Nor am I in the least deterred by Aristophanes' denial—the prize evidence of those who deny the phallus in Aristophanes—simply because it would be the height of ingenousness, I think, to take Aristophanes' word for it, especially here. *The Clouds* may very well be a daintier, wittier play than the comedies of

Aristophanes' rivals, but the disclaimers here are slyly contradicted by the play: several scenes are pure slapstick, Strepsiades beats his opponents with a stick, etc.

page 64. *a dirty dance:* That is, the *kordax.* Cf. Glossary: KORDAX.

64. *my celebrated simile on the eels:* Cf. *Knights* 864–67.

66. *Paphlagon:* Cf. Glossary: PAHLAGON.

66. *hard on the heels of the Levin rattled the steeds of Thunder?:* A quotation from Sophokles' (lost) *Teukros.*

66. *How the moon, in dudgeon, snuffed her flame amongst the rack, and the sun in sullenness withdrew:* An eclipse of the moon took place in October 425, and a solar eclipse in March 424, just before the election of Kleon as general.

68. *your month is a consequent chaos:* An allusion to the confusion created in the Hellenic calendar by the Athenian astronomer Meton. Instituted in 432 B.C. and then gradually adopted throughout Greece, the Metonic calendar changes made for initial difficulties. Because the reform was not uniformly adopted throughout Greece, the same festivals in different places would fall on different dates, etc.

68. *stripped Hyperbolos of his seat:* Hyperbolos (cf. Glossary) had been appointed Athenian delegate to the Amphictyonic Council of Delphoi in 424 B.C. The Council was a religious and juridical federation of Greek city-states whose primary concerns at this time would have been the war and infractions of such "international law" as existed at the time. Presumably, this Council would have been responsible for smoothing the way to general Greek adoption of the Metonic calendar. Exactly what happened to Hyperbolos is not known; the Chorus says that it "stripped him of his crown"—which may mean, as Rogers suggests, that the wind blew off the sacred chaplet which he wore in his official capacity. From the animosity of the Clouds, it can

be reasonably assumed that Hyperbolos had supported the Metonic reform.

page 70. *vulgarly called finger-rhythm:* δάκτυλος in Greek means both "finger" and "dactylic meter."

71. *Raising his phallus to the ready:* Cf. note on pp. 157–58: *dangling thong of leather.*

72. *the female's a duchess:* An anachronistic pun of my own invention; the Greeks had ducks but no dukes. Literally, the Greek says "the male is a rooster (ἀλέκτωρ), the female a roosterette (ἀλεκτρύαινα)."

72. *You've made basket masculine, when it's feminine:* "Basket" is my own contribution. In the Greek, the word is κάρδοπος, "a kneading-trough," whose -ος termination is normally the sign of the masculine gender, though κάρδοπος is in fact feminine. This pun, of course, leads directly to discussion of Kleonymos, another instance of a masculine ending for an actual effeminate.

74. *Why, Amynia:* In the original, this whole passage is based upon a play on the Greek vocative (whereby the nominative *Amynias* becomes *Amynia*—which has the -*a* termination of the feminine nominative). Because English has no vocative, I have recast the play here as a confusion between singular and plural. For Amynias, cf. Glossary: AMYNIAS.

80. *witchwomen from Thessaly:* Throughout antiquity, Thessaly was famous for its red-headed witches. Cf. Apuleius *Metamorphoses* I; Plato *Gorgias* 513 a.

82. *scorch out every word of the charges:* The charges would have been written down on a wax tablet.

89. *Expended as required. No comment:* When asked to account for the expenditure of several talents (actually used to purchase the withdrawal of the Spartans), Perikles answered only: "I spent them as required."

90. *Even Hyperbolos:* Hyperbolos had evidently studied under the Sophists for a fee of one talent—a large sum.

page 90. *Philosophy and Sophistry:* Cf. note on pp. 153–54: *two kinds of Logic*.

90. *from the neck up they are fighting-cocks:* According to a Scholiast, the Logics were garbed as fighting-cocks and brought out in cages. This statement has rarely won the approval of scholars, who are quick to point out that it is contradicted by the references throughout the debate to hands, clothing, and other parts of the *human* anatomy. If I am right, the Logics wore rooster masks and a few feathers with perhaps a great vivid bustle of tail feathers; but from the neck down they were visibly human. After their adoption by the Birds, Pisthetairos and Euelpides appear garbed in this very way (cf. *Birds*). Such a solution allows Aristophanes to present the Logics as fighting-cocks or as wrestlers as his dramatic needs required, and the text seems to me to support this.

93. *how Zeus escaped punishment after he imprisoned his father?:* Zeus dethroned his father Kronos and bound him in chains. The same argument is used by Euthyphro (cf. Plato *Euthyphro*) to justify his prosecution of his own father. But the argument here is interesting because it shows clearly the mythological rationale of the Old Education and the way in which the New Education refuted it. For the Old Education, mythology was a rational corpus of heroic behavior and morality was taught in mythological terms, quite despite the fact that the morality of mythology was incompatible in many instances with the operative moral values of the fifth century. The greatest artists of the older generation—Aischylos and Pindar—had in fact attempted to reconcile myth and moral behavior by rewriting the offensive myths and expelling their crudities or giving them new—and moral—interpretations. The exponents of the New Education quite naturally turned their characteristic invention—formal logic—against the Old Education by pointing out the inconsistencies of its morality and

mythology. The same purpose informs many of Euripides' tragedies, and for this reason he incurred the suspicion and contempt of Athenian conservatives—quite despite the fact that his own artistic intentions were really very much like those of Aischylos, an attempt to harmonize mythology and morality. But because the morality was relatively new—or looked that way—and was supported by a logic which was destructive of the old morality, he was not understood by conservatives. Few artistic feuds seem, in fact, more futile than Aristophanes' with Euripides, since—apart from dramatic differences—the two men basically believed the same things.

page 94. *Telephos:* Cf. Glossary; TELEPHOS.

94. *Pandaletos' loaf:* Cf. Glossary: PANDALETOS.

97. *the Old Education:* Readers interested in knowing more about the conflict between different views of education in fifth-century Athens and the rationale of the Old Education should consult the relevant chapers of Werner Jaeger's *Paideia*. Suffice it to say here that it was basically a curriculum comprising two major fields called respectively Music and Gymnastic. By Music was meant the education of the inward man; the schooling not merely of the mind, but of the emotions, the "soul," the feelings and the thoughts in their rational ensemble. The basic instrument of this inward education was poetry joined to music, a blend in which poetry taught by means of example and emulation and was sustained by music which was believed to inculcate the moral virtues. Gymnastic was, of course, vigorous and disciplined athletics. The intended product of this theory of education was a disciplined reason in a disciplined body, an outward grace which expressed the grace and harmony within, the whole person embodying the classical virtues: self-control, decorum, respect for others, piety toward the gods, moderation in all things, dignity and courage. It was, in short, far

more what we would call moral education, education in "character," than intellectual training. It was also, for obvious reasons, the education of a restricted and exclusive class. It taught no skills, prepared for no career, and was obviously impractical for Athenian society of the late fifth century. For these reasons, it has always appealed to the exponents of "education of character," British public schools and their American imitators. Aristophanes put his whole heart into its exposition here, and I have done my best to overcome my own repugnance, though probably unsuccessfully.

It would, of course, have been a pleasure to modernize the debate and present it in topical terms as a struggle between the views of education represented—less than ideally, of course—by American universities and that preposterous pretence of education perpetrated by the professional "educationists" in the secondary schools of America. But this is a suggestion which might be adopted by a producer in search of a topical Aristophanes; for a translation, it is out of the question.

page 98. *A Voice from Afar* or *Hail, O Pallas, Destroyer!*: According to the Scholiast, the second of these hymns is ascribed to Lamprokles of Athens; the first to Kydeides of Hermione.

98. *their conduct was manly*: The point is precisely the manliness. The fashionable homosexuality of the Athenian upper classes was essentially borrowed from Sparta, where homosexuality was not only tolerated but even encouraged as a military virtue (because "lovers" would fight well for each other). Hence the contempt with which Philosophy regards the effeminate homosexuals of the Athenian New Education. Only among the Athenian lower classes was homosexuality viewed with contempt. The modern image of an Athens populated exclusively by happy philosophical pederasts is largely due to the fact that the surviving literature is a

leisure-class production; poor men were very rarely Platonists.

page 104. *Baths of Herakles:* Greeks normally named hot baths everywhere the Baths of Herakles. Another example of specious logic against which Philosophy is helpless.

104. *old Homer:* This argument must have hurt. Of all the poets, Homer was regarded by the Old Education as the greatest, the Bible of true belief. And now, like the devil, Sophistry quotes scripture.

105. *Peleus:* Cf. Glossary: PELEUS.

105. *Hyperbolos and swords just don't mix:* Because Hyperbolos presumably attempted to avoid military service.

106. *reamed up the rectum with a radish?:* The poetic punishment meted out to adulterers in Athens.

110. *Duedate for debts:* Strepsiades does not actually say this. What he says is that the day he fears is "the-Old-and-The-New." By this he means the effective last day of the lunar month, the day on which both the last of the waning Old Moon and the first of the waxing New Moon could be seen. The-Old-and-The-New, in short, was the normal name given to the last day of the month, the day on which debts were payable. And this nomenclature continued to be used even when the calendar was no longer lunar. The term is, to modern ears, grotesquely unfamiliar, but it is also crucial to an understanding of the action, and for this reason I have had considerable misgivings about altering it. But upon reflection it seemed to me that "Duedate" might possibly do, and I have so rendered it. But see the note on p. 164: *Today's Dueday.*

111. *Call it an honorarium:* Aristophanes, that is, hints that Sokrates was not above receiving "tokens of esteem" from his disciples. This may be pure satirical malice, but then again it may not be Sokrates' students were mostly rich aristocrats; he himself was poor. And in the circles which Plato frequented, a distinction was probably drawn be

tween a payment and a "gratuity"—the common sophistry of "good society." But this is guesswork.

page 112. *with gladsome paeans plangent!:* An echo, according to the Scholiast, from the *Satyrs* of Phrynichos—or Euripides' *Peleus*. Probably the latter.

112. *debouch from mine abode!:* A very slight modification of Euripides' *Hekabe* 173 ff.

113. *Today's Dueday:* Cf. note p. 163: *Duedate for debts.* For a more literal rendering of Pheidippides' sophistic analysis of the-Old-New-Day in the following lines, readers should consult any prose translation of the play. I have preferred to use the "Dueday—two day" pun because it made the equivocation instantly visible as glib hocus pocus, though it also meant a necessary change—a slight one—in the interpretation of Solon's legislation which Pheidippides offers. But I suppose most readers of the *Clouds* to be more interested in a comedy than in the details of Athenian debt legislation.

113. *to post their bond:* Before commencing a legal action against a defaulting debtor, a creditor had to post with the prytanies, as caution money to defray court expenses, the sum of 10 per cent of the amount of the debt.

115. *Precisely because they are magistrates:* A deliberate distortion of the literal meaning of the Greek. The text actually says: "They act like Foretasters; in order to devour the meal as quickly as possible, they have the deposits paid a day in advance." The Foretasters seem to have been officials responsible for sampling the dishes to be served at a public feast the following day.

118. *the National Honor:* The National Honor (and, one might add, the public interest) of Athens required that every citizen be as litigious as possible.

122. *tragedy by Karkinos:* Karkinos was a frigid, fourth-rate tragedian with an apparent penchant for introducing querulous beggar-gods in his plays. Most of the fustian which follows is presumably the

work of Karkinos or his son Xenokles. Talent did not run in the family.

page 132. *a custom's a custom:* The festive custom of *paroinia*, according to Rogers, an old convivial tradition of singing at table.

132. *Shearin' o' the Ram:* Krios (which also means "Ram") was a wrestler, probably the victim of an overwhelming defeat in a wrestling match, and hence the "Shorn Ram." Simonides' poetry was very highly regarded by the older generation.

133. *bombastic bore in poetic history:* The charge was common in antiquity. In an age of discursive prose and colloquial poetry, the gorgeousness of Aischylos and his extravagant metaphorical bravura made him look like a drunken lord of language. For Aristophanes, of course, Aischylos is the Model Poet who "makes men better citizens" as opposed to the Arch-Corrupter, Euripides Cf. *Frogs.*

133. *One of those slimy tragedies:* A reference to Euripides' (lost) *Aiolos.*

136. *Wasn't I born as free a man as you?:* A parody of Euripides' *Alkestis* 691.

140. *the insubstantial Clouds men build their hopes upon:* This line and most of the two which follow it are Arrowsmith, not Aristophanes. I have intruded them in order to give just a little more resonance to the meaning of the Clouds. For although English has idioms in plenty which more or less parallel the Greek—to "have one's head in the Clouds," "to build on the clouds," "castles in the clouds," etc.—a little further rounding out seemed necessary. The Clouds are the patrons of visionaries and woolgatherers the world over; here they are cloudy deceivers, the shining hopes that deceive Strepsiades.

146. *Pasias and Amynias:* The Greek plays, of course, have come down to us without footnotes or stage directions other than what the Scholiasts tell us. And I admit that there is no textual justification for bringing back Pasias and Amynias here, nor is it

suggested by any Scholiast. They are here because Pasias threatened to pay his bond and return with a summons, and because I think Aristophanes would have liked them to be foiled again, even at Strepsiades' moment of truth.

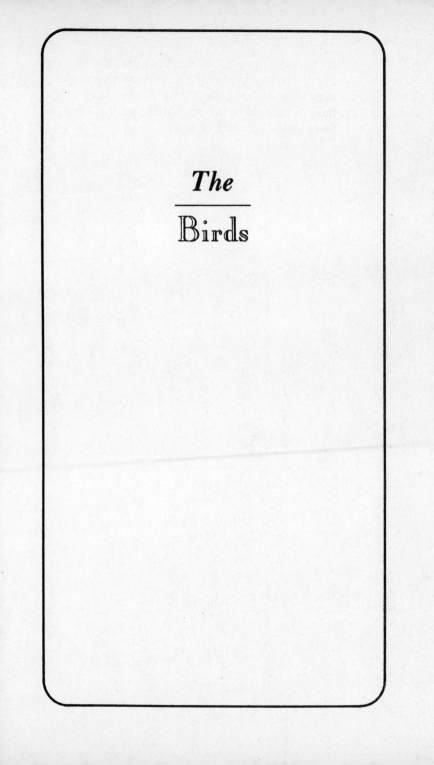

The
Birds

CONTENTS

FOR
Jean

Introduction

The Play and Its Interpretation

Nobody denies that *The Birds* is a masterpiece, one of the greatest comedies ever written and probably Aristophanes' finest. Splendidly lyrical, shot through with gentle Utopian satire and touched by the sadness of the human condition, its ironic gaiety and power of invention never flag; in no other play is Aristophanes' comic vision so comprehensively or lovingly at odds with his world.

But if the play is by common consent a great one, there is little agreement about what it means. Thus it has, with great ingenuity and small cogency, been interpreted as a vast, detailed comic allegory of the Sicilian expedition: Pisthetairos stands for Alkibiades; Hoopoe is the general Lamachos; the Birds are Athenians, the gods Spartans, and so on. Alternatively, the play has been viewed as Aristophanes' passionate appeal for the reform and renewal of Athenian public life under the leadership of the noble Pisthetairos, a true Aristophanic champion cut from the same cloth as Dikaiopolis in *The Acharnians*. Again, probably in revenge for so much unlikely ingenuity, it has been claimed that *The Birds* is best understood as a fantastic escapist extravaganza created as a revealing antidote to the prevalent folly of Athenian political life. And, with the exception of the word "escapist," this last view seems to me essentially correct. But whatever else *The Birds* may be, it is not escapist.

Any translation worth the name necessarily involves an interpretation, and it is my hope that my version will make my interpretation clear and convincing. But because in some respects my view of the play is unorthodox and this is crucial to the interpretation, I offer the following points for the reader's consideration.

1) *The life of The Birds*. Like many Aristophanic comedies, *The Birds* takes its title from its chorus; but unlike, say, *Wasps*, which is based upon a simple simile (jurors are waspish: they buzz, swarm, sting, etc.). *Birds* and *Clouds* are titles around which cluster a great many traditional associations, idioms, and ideas. Thus in *Clouds* the chorus symbolizes the Murky Muse, that inflated, shining, insubstantial, and ephemeral power which inspires sophists, dithyrambic poets, prophets, and other pompous frauds. Similarly, in *Birds* there is the same natural clustering of association and standard idiom, and the associations are crucial to the play's understanding. On the most natural level, of course, the life of the Birds symbolizes precisely what one would expect: the simple, uncomplicated rustic life of peace. But behind this natural symbolism, deepening it and particularizing it, lies the chronic and pervasive escape-symbolism of late fifth-century Athens. In play after play of Euripides, for instance, chorus and characters alike, when confronted by the anguish of tragic existence, cry out their longing to escape, to be a bird, a fact of which Aristophanes makes extensive use, shaping his play around the symptomatic mortal infatuation with the birds. It is for this reason, this pervasive hunger for escape from intolerable existence which haunts tragedy and society alike, that Aristophanes makes his Birds address his audience with words of tragic pathos:

O suffering mankind.
               lives of twilight,
                              race feeble and fleeting

like the leaves scattered!
> *Pale generations,*
>> *creatures of clay,*
the wingless, the fading!
> *Unhappy mortals,*
>> *shadows in time,*
flickering dreams!
> *Hear us now,*
>> *the ever-living Birds,*
the undying,
> *the ageless ones,*
>> *scholars of eternity.*

And these lines in their turn look forward to the ironic apotheosis of the mortal Pisthetairos with which the play closes. Mankind's crazy comic dream is a wish-fulfillment darkened by death. But the dream survives.

My point is this: far from writing an escapist extravaganza, Aristophanes dramatizes the ironic fulfillment in divinity of the Athenian man who wants to escape. What begins as hunger for the simple life ends—such is the character of Athenians and true men—in world-conquest and the defeat of the gods; or it would end there, if only it could. This is the *hybris* of enterprise and daring, the trait from which no Athenian can ever escape. Aristophanes' irony is, I think, loving.

2) *The Theme.* It is commonly said that *The Birds* is unlike other Aristophanic comedies in having no pointed central theme or particular concern (e.g., peace in *Acharnians* and *Peace*; demagoguery in *Knights*, sophistry in *Clouds*, etc.), and at first blush this seems to be true. But unless I am badly mistaken, the central concern of the play is less noticeable only because it is more comprehensive, including in itself most of the targets of the earlier plays. That concern is *polupragmosunē*, a concept which Athenians used as a general description of their most salient national characteristics. At its broadest *polupragmosunē* is that quality of spectacular restless energy that made the Athenians both the glory and the bane of the Hellenic world. On the positive side, it connotes energy, enterprise, daring, ingenuity, originality, and curiosity;

negatively it means restless instability, discontent with one's lot, persistent and pointless busyness, meddling interference, and mischievous love of novelty. The Athenian Empire itself is a visible creation of political *polupragmosunē*, and so too are the peculiar liabilities to which empire made the Athenians subject: the love of litigation, the susceptibility to informers and demagogues, the violent changes in national policy and, most stunning example of all, the Sicilian expedition. In political terms, *polupragmosunē* is the very spirit of Athenian imperialism, its remorseless need to expand, the *hybris* of power and energy in a spirited people; in moral terms, it is a divine discontent and an impatience with necessity, a disease whose symptoms are disorder, corruption, and the hunger for change.

Athens with its *polupragmosunē* is unbearable for Pisthetairos and Euelpides, and so, rational escapists both, they set out to find among the Birds precisely what they miss in Athens: the quiet, leisurely, simple, uncomplicated peace-loving life of the Birds, which is called *apragmosunē*. Confronted by the hostility of the Birds to man, Pisthetairos ingeniously conceives the idea of Cloudcuckooland. And from this point on, totally forgetting his quest for *apragmosunē*, he becomes the open and skillful exponent of *polupragmosunē*: persuasive, ingenious, cunning, meddlesome, and imperialistic. The characterization could hardly be more explicit or the change more deliberate, as the peace-loving escapist, with ruthless policy and doubtful arguments, pushes ahead with his scheme for the New Athens of the Birds. It is both comic and ironic, and Aristophanes' point is that no Athenian can escape his origins. His character is *polupragmosunē*, and character is destiny, as Herakleitos said. Put an Athenian among the Birds, and he will be an imperialist with wings and fight with gods.

3) *Pisthetairos*. It is sometimes said—quite wrongly, I believe—that Aristophanes' characters move on a single plane, without depth or complexity. If I am right, Pisthetairos' character, like Dikaiopolis' and Strepsiades', displays itself in action, not in professions; its basic simplicity, the thrust for power, is not something given but something defined in action. Like Dikaiopolis and Strepsiades, he *realizes* his name;

but whereas Dikaiopolis' purpose is good and his methods roguish, Pisthetairos has no purpose but power and his methods are the appropriate ones. He compels assent and even admiration, as politicians do, by sheer persuasiveness and virtuosity and energy, but the energy is the dither of power for its own sake, without a rational goal in sight, restless and unappeasable: sheer *polupragmosunē*. He is Aristophanes' example of a politician without a policy, or nearly without one, unless we count to his credit his success in protecting Cloudcuckooland from ravenous interlopers, gods, and other pests.

4) *Cloudcuckooland*. Like Pisthetairos, Cloudcuckooland itself is treated ironically. On the one hand it is a pipedream Utopia from which a few of the nuisances and spongers that infest cities are driven out by an enraged Pisthetairos; on the other it is, especially in the methods of its founding, a visible parody of the Athenian Empire. Historical parallels and allusions here can be overdone, but I wonder what Athenian could have failed to notice the way in which, point for point, the policies and strategies of imperial Athens toward the member-states of her empire are adapted to Cloudcuckooland's campaign against the gods. Pisthetairos specifically proposes to exterminate the gods by "Melian starvation," and the general proposals of boycott vividly recall the Megarian Decree. Also pertinent, I think, the close resemblance between Pisthetairos and the Birds and Athens and her subject-cities, once her allies: slowly the Birds, like the allies, yield to the initiative of the stronger, putting their strength at the service of another intellect, thereby losing their freedom. It is Aristophanes' point that the Birds, like the allies, are stupid; Athens and Pisthetairos clever and unscrupulous. And significantly, I think, the play closes with a light irony as Pisthetairos and the gods prepare to celebrate their truce with a dinner of—poultry; jailbirds, true, but birds for all that. It is, for the Birds, an ominous sign of things to come. All their campaign against the gods has brought them is a new tyrant, no less voracious than the old and just as treacherous.

But if Cloudcuckooland serves to parody the growth of Athenian power and imperialistic politics. it also serves as a convenient and satisfying appeal for Athens to renew herself by ridding the city of the informers, sponges, charlatans, sophists, bureaucracy, and abuses that have made it almost unliveable. Irony here crosses with irony, as Pisthetairos, the champion of *polupragmosunē*, beats out the rival champions. So too, in *Knights*, the improbable cause of Demos' resurgence is none other than the tripe-peddling demagogue who has out-Kleoned Kleon.

5) *The Apotheosis*. In Aristophanes' eyes the logical terminus of Athenian restlessness and aggressiveness is that man should become god, wear wings and rule the world. The blasphemy is prevented only by the impossibility of its realization. But the ambition survives and luxuriates in man's discontent with his condition, his mortal *hybris*. For Aristophanes that discontent was tragic and meant man's loss of his only possible happiness: peace lost in war, traditional dignity swallowed up in the restless greed for wealth and power, honor lost in the inhumanity of imperialism and political tyranny. But he also knew that such discontent was born of life and aggressive hunger for larger life.

Date and Circumstances

The Birds was first performed at the Great Dionysia in late March, 414 B.C. and was awarded the Second Prize. The First Prize was taken by Ameipsias with his *Komastai* ("The Revellers") and the Third Prize by Phrynichos with his *Monotropos* ("The Hermit"). The year preceding the play's performance, during its composition, must have been a grim and bitter time in Athens, especially for an exponent of peace and rational politics like Aristophanes. In May, 415, just as the Athenian fleet was about to sail for Sicily on its disastrous expedition, the entire city was thrown into a superstitious panic by the mutilation of the pillars of Hermes, the work either of drunken carousers or of a political faction bent on discrediting Alkibiades, the commander of the Sicilian expedition. As a result, the whole expedition seemed to hang under a heavy cloud; accusations were being made on all sides, and the general atmosphere of the city was one of suspicion, horror, and frenetic political activity. Finally, after the fleet had sailed, evidence was found which seemed to incriminate Alkibiades and a state galley was sent out with orders to bring him back to Athens to stand trial. It is unlikely that Alkibiades' escape and defection to Sparta were known at Athens at the time the play was performed.

The Translation

This translation is meant to provide a faithful, but not a literal, version of *The Birds*. Literalness in any case is out of the question: a literal Aristophanes would be both unreadable and unplayable, and therefore unfaithful: But fidelity is clearly a matter of degree and relation: *how* faithful and faithful to *what?*

It was my purpose to create a lively, contemporary acting version of the play, a translation which might also, I hoped, be read for pleasure or study, and which would be as loyal to Greek and Greek experience as I could make it without involving myself in disloyalty to English. Only by so doing, I thought, could I remain faithful to two languages and two cultures at the same time. For the same reason I have deliberately avoided wholly modernizing or "adapting" the play. If the diction of this version is essentially contemporary American English, its experience, I believe, is basically Athenian. Some modernization, of course, was not only inevitable but also desirable. But generally I have preferred to suggest the similarities between Athens and America without asserting, or forcing, an identity. If the language does its work, the experience should translate itself with only a little occasional help from the translator. Or so I thought.

For fidelity's sake, this is also a poetic version. A prose Aristophanes is to my mind as much a monstrosity as a limerick in prose paraphrase. And for much the same reasons. If Aristophanes is visibly obscene, farcical, and colloquial, he is also lyrical, elegant, fantastic, and witty. And a translation which, by flattening incongruities and tensions, reduces one dimension necessarily reduces the other. Bowdlerize Aristophanes and you sublimate him into something less vital and whole; prose him and you cripple his wit, dilute his obscenity and slapstick, and weaken his classical sense of the wholeness of human life.

Translating comedy is necessarily very different from translating tragedy; not only is it more demanding, but its principles, because they are constantly being improvised or modified, are harder to state. Insofar as I can describe them or deduce them from my own practice, my general principles are these:

1) *Meter*. Aristophanes' basic dialogue line is a loose, colloquial iambic hexameter (*senarii*), and my English equivalent is a loose five-stress line. It was my opinion that the flexibility required by the Greek could best be achieved by a meter capable of modulating, without jarring or unnaturalness, back to the norm of English dramatic verse, the blank. At its most humdrum such a line is indistinguishable from prose, but worked up, patterned with regular stresses, it can readily be traditionalized as tragic parody or cant or realized as speakable poetry in its own right. The longer anapestic and trochaic lines I have rendered by a six-beat movement (except in the first section of the *parabasis*, where I have adapted William Carlos William's triplet-line to my own purposes). Because the convention of *stichomythia* seemed deadening when brought over into English and served no useful dramatic purpose, I have everywhere taken the liberty of breaking it down.

2) *Obscenity*. I have refused on principle to bowdlerize. Equally, I have tried to avoid the quicksands of archness or cuteness on the one hand and sledgehammer shock-tactics on the other. Where Aristophanes is blunt, I have left him blunt, but generally I have tried to realize his rhetorical obscenities with the elegance and neatness that might make them truly obscene.

3) *Stage Directions*. The Greek plays have come down to us almost entirely without stage directions. To some small degree they are supplied by the ancient scholiasts, but because this is an acting version of the play and because comedy constantly suggests and requires stage action, I have freely supplied stage directions. Wherever possible, I have relied on

indications in the text, but when a direction was clearly required and the text offered no help, I have used my imagination.

4) *Improvisation*. There are occasions (e.g., a pun, an obscure reference, or a tangle of politics, pun and idiom) when the Greek is simply untranslatable. On such occasions it has been my practice to improvise (see, for instance, the note on p. 209. *Her lover*), on the grounds that literal translation would have slowed or obscured the dramatic situation, and this is fatal to comedy. Normally I have indicated when I have improvised and why. But I should also confess that there are a few passages in which I have improvised on my own, without warrant. My only excuse is the self-indulgent one that I thought they might be justified as compensation for losses elsewhere.

5) *Tragic and Poetic Parody*. Aristophanes constantly parodies tragedy and poetry, and these parodies were meant to be recognized. Since modern audiences cannot be expected to recognize them—especially since most of the originals are no longer extant—the translator is required to do the impossible and create the illusion of parody. This means in effect that the parodies must be so grotesque as to be instantly recognizable as parody, and to this end I have deliberately heightened fustian, archaism, and bombast. Thus the Poet in this play speaks a parody of Pindar that is sheer doggerel and utterly un-Pindaric. I can only plead that my purpose was not to slander Pindar but to make the Poet an obvious hack.

6) *Dialects and Nonsense*. Aristophanic comedy abounds with dialects—Skythian policemen, Spartan heralds, sham Persians, Boiotians, Megarians, and the pure jabberwocky god of *The Birds*, Triballos. Because these dialects seemed to me both comic and conventional, I have everywhere rendered them by an apposite contemporary comic dialect: mint-julep Southern, broad Brooklynese, Katzenjammerkids German, etc. Nothing, in my opinion, is less comic or more tiresome than dialectal realism; for comedy, a recognizable *comic* convention is required, whatever the cost in anachronism. In the case of Triballos, who speaks pure nonsense, I have preferred to

invent some genuine English nonsense rather than transliterate his Greekish gibberish. Herakles, it should be noted, does *not* in the original speak a dialect at all, but his hungry lowbrow character seemed to me to require conventional treatment, and I accordingly arranged it

7) *Rhetorical Conventions and Jargon.* What is true of dialects is also true of professional rhetoric and jargon: if they are to be comic, they have to be translated into an apposite convention of English rhetoric or jargon. Invariably, this means that their language must be heightened and made even more ponderous than it is in the Greek. The astronomer Meton, for instance, is used by Aristophanes to parody the jargon and abstruse pomposity of sophistic science. But because Greek scientific jargon was a relatively immature growth (at least when compared with the jargons of modern science), his words, literally translated, sound to modern ears merely somewhat silly. In the circumstances I deliberately heightened his language, adding technical terms and jargonizing it further, in the belief that only by so doing could I create the effect of gobbledegook that Meton's demonstration was intended to have for Athenian ears.

8) *Personal and Topical Allusions.* Aristophanes' frequent allusions to persons and events present the translator with a ticklish problem. Some of them are so obscure as to be meaningless to anybody but a prosopographer; others exist because they offer happy opportunities for puns or gibes at topical personalities; still others are crucial to the play's meaning. In general, it has been my practice to simplify, suppressing totally obscure allusions (see, for instance, the note on p. 187. *this stinking, jabbering Magpie here*) altogether, and avoiding such cumbersome and evasive phrases as "you know who I mean" and the like. In the first case, it seemed important not to slow the action on a minor obscurity; in the second, no allusion at all seemed preferable to an unsatisfactory echo of one. But where names and events seemed essential to the meaning, I have retained them, wherever possible intruding a gloss which might minimize the difficulty even though it expanded the text. So far as I know, every suppressed allusion is mentioned and explained in the notes.

Text and Acknowledgments

The texts on which I have chiefly relied for this translation are those of R. Cantarella and Victor Coulon (Budé) supplemented by the Oxford text of Hall and Geldart. Like every modern English or American translator of Aristophanes, I have derived invaluable aid and comfort from the splendid text and commentary of Benjamin Bickley Rogers.

For suggestions, corrections, and *trouvailles* I owe thanks to colleagues and friends too many to mention. But my chief mentor has been my wife. It was she who endured with unflinching patience and even good humor the successive versions, and it is to her, as orniphile and critic, that this translation is dedicated.

Finally, I should like to thank both the Yaddo Corporation and the American Academy in Rome for grants of money and leisure which made this translation possible, and the Research Institute of the University of Texas for secretarial assistance.

Austin, Texas   WILLIAM ARROWSMITH

Characters of the Play

EUELPIDES
(i.e., Hopeful), an Athenian
PISTHETAIROS
(i.e., Plausible), an Athenian
SANDPIPER,
servant of Epops the Hoopoe
EPOPS, OR HOOPOE,
otherwise known as Tereus
CHORUS OF BIRDS
KORYPHAIOS
PRIEST
POET
PROPHET
METON
INSPECTOR
LEGISLATOR
FIRST MESSENGER
SENTRY
IRIS
HERALD
DELINQUENT

KINESIAS,
  a dithyrambic poet
INFORMER
PROMETHEUS
POSEIDON
TRIBALLOS
HERAKLES
SECOND MESSENGER

SCENE: *A desolate wilderness.* In the background is a single tree and the sheer rock-face of a cliff. Enter, in the last stages of exhaustion, Euelpides and Pisthetairos. On his arm Euelpides carries a Magpie; Pisthetairos holds a Crow. They are followed by slaves with their luggage, consisting mostly of kitchen equipment, cauldrons, pots, spits, etc.*

EUELPIDES

To his Magpie.

Straight ahead, croaker? Over by that tree?

PISTHETAIROS

Damn this cracked Crow! He keeps cawing me backwards.

EUELPIDES

Look, halfwit, what's the point of hiking these hills?
If we don't stop this zigzagging pretty soon,
I'm through.

PISTHETAIROS

        I must have been mad—trusting a Crow
to go trudging off on this hundred-mile hike.

EUELPIDES

                        You're mad?

Look at me, man—hitched to a Magpie
and my toenails worn away right down to the nub.

PISTHETAIROS

I'll be damned if I know where we are.

EUELPIDES

                                                    Say,
do you suppose we could find our way back home from
here?

PISTHETAIROS

Friend, even Exekestides couldn't do *that.**

EUELPIDES

Stumbling.

                                                    Hell.

PISTHETAIROS

That's just where we're headed now, old man.

EUELPIDES

                                          You know,
that birdseller Philokrates who sold us these damn Birds
was a filthy fraud, that's what. Swearing up and down
that these two Birds here would lead us to the Hoopoe,
old Tereus the Bird who used to be a man,*
and swindling us with this stinking, jabbering Magpie here*
for two bits and that cluckhead Crow of yours for six!
And what do they do but nip our fingers off?

To the Magpie.

Well, what are you gaping at, imbecile? Where?
Straight into the cliff? But there's no road there, idiot.

PISTHETAIROS

A road? Sweet gods, there isn't even a track!

EUELPIDES

Say, isn't your Crow croaking something about a road?

PISTHETAIROS

You know, now that you mention it, I think he *is* croaking
in a different key.

EUELPIDES

Something about a road, isn't it?

PISTHETAIROS

Naw, he's cawing he'll gnaw my fingers off.

EUELPIDES

It's a filthy shame, that's what. Think of it, man:
here we are dying to go tell it to the Birds,*
and then, by god, we can't even find the way.

To the Audience.

Yes, dear people, we confess we're completely mad.
But it's not like Sakas'* madness. Not a bit.
For he, poor dumb foreigner, wants in, while we,
born and bred Athenians both, true blue,
true citizens, not afraid of any man,
want out.
                    Yes, we've spread our little feet
and taken off. Not that we hate Athens—
heavens, no. And not that dear old Athens
isn't grand, that blessed land where men are free—
to pay their taxes.*
                    No, look to the locust
who, one month or two, drones and shrills
among the little thickets, while the men of Athens,

perched upon the thorny thickets of the law, sit
shrilling out their three score years and ten.
Because of legal locusts,* gentlemen, we have left,
lugging these baskets and pots and boughs of myrtle,
looking for some land of soft and lovely leisure*
where a man may loaf and play and settle down
for good. Tereus the Hoopoe is our journey's end.
From him we hope to learn if he has seen
in all his many travels such a place
on earth.

PISTHETAIROS

   Pssst! Hey!

EUELPIDES

    What's up?

PISTHETAIROS

        Look at my Crow
staring up in the air.

EUELPIDES

      And my Magpie's gaping too.
It looks as though he's pointing his beak at the sky.
I'll bet that means there's Birds somewhere hereabouts.
We'll find out soon enough if we make a ruckus.

PISTHETAIROS

I know. Try kicking the side of the cliff with your foot.*

EUELPIDES

Go bash it with your head. You'll make more noise.

PISTHETAIROS

Pick up a rock and pound.

EUELPIDES

Good idea. I'll try.

He picks up a rock and pounds on the cliff, shouting.

Boy! Hey, boy!

PISTHETAIROS

Don't call old Hoopoe "boy."
You'd better say, "Ho, Hoopoe!" or "Hey, Epops!"

EUELPIDES

Hey, Hoopoe!

No answer.

Hmmm. Shall I try him again?
Yoohoo, Hoopoe!

*A concealed door in the cliff suddenly swings open and a
Sandpiper with an enormous curved beak peers out, almost
spitting Pisthetairos.*

SANDPIPER

What are you whooping about?

EUELPIDES

Apollo help us! What a beak on the Bird!

*In his fright he lets go of his Magpie who flaps off. Pisthetairos
falls backward, losing his Crow, while the Sandpiper retreats
in horror.*

SANDPIPER

Halp!
Nest-robbers! Egg-stealers! Bird-catchers!
Halp!

EUELPIDES

You hear that? His bark is worse than his beak.

SANDPIPER

Mortals, you die!

EUELPIDES

But we're not men.

SANDPIPER

What are you?

EUELPIDES

Me? I'm *turdus turdus*. An African migrant.*

SANDPIPER

What nonsense.

EUELPIDES

Not nonsense, crap. Look at my feet.

SANDPIPER

Indicating Pisthetairos.

And that bird over there? What's his species?

PISTHETAIROS

Me?

Brown-tailed Smellyrump. Quail family.

EUELPIDES

To Sandpiper.

Say,
what about you, Birdie? What the hell are you?

SANDPIPER

I'm a Slavebird.*

EUELPIDES

I see. Some bantam thrash you
in a scrap?

SANDPIPER

No, but when the boss got himself changed
into a Hoopoe, I put in my application for feathers too
so I could stay in his service, doing odd jobs and buttling.

EUELPIDES

And since when have our Birds been having butlers?

SANDPIPER

He gets the habit, I think, from having once been human.
But suppose he wants some sardines. Up I jump,
dash down with a dish and catch him some fish.
If it's soup he wants, I grab a little ladle
and skitter to the kettle.

EUELPIDES

Quite the runner, eh?
Tell you what, runner-bird: just skitter inside
and fetch your master out.

SANDPIPER

But he's napping now.
He gorged himself silly on a mess of midges and myrtle.

EUELPIDES

His nap be damned. Go wake him.

SANDPIPER

I warn you:
He'll be grumpy. But just for a favor I'll do it.

Exit Sandpiper.

PISTHETAIROS

And then drop dead.

To Euelpides.

—Whoosh, I'm still shaking.

EUELPIDES

Me too. And guess what. My Magpie's gone,
got clear away.

PISTHETAIROS

Got away? Why you big baby,
were you so scared you dropped your load?

EUELPIDES

Well,
what about you? Where's your bird?

PISTHETAIROS

Where's my bird?
Right here in my hand.*

EUELPIDES

Right where?

PISTHETAIROS

Well, he was here.

EUELPIDES

And where were you? Holding on for dear life?

HOOPOE

From within.

CLEAR THE COPSE, I SAY, AND WHEEL ME OUT!

The eccyclema wheels out the Hoopoe, sitting on a pile of brush and peering out from a thicket. Except for his huge crest and beak and a few bedraggled feathers here and there, the Hoopoe is human.

EUELPIDES

Holy Herakles! That's no Bird, it's a freak.
Get a load of that plumage! What a tiara!

HOOPOE

Who *are* you?

EUELPIDES

      Birdie, you looked bedraggled.
I'll bet the gods* gave you some nasty knocks.

HOOPOE

You dare sneer at my plumage? I, strangers,
was once a man.

EUELPIDES

      Oh, we're not laughing at you.

HOOPOE

Then, what's so funny?

EUELPIDES

      Your beak. It tickles me.

HOOPOE

I am dressed as the poet Sophokles disfigures me*
in that atrocious tragedy of his entitled *Tereus.*

EUELPIDES

                                                    Gee,

you're Tereus in person?

                        Are you Bird or Peacock?

HOOPOE

With ferocious dignity.

I am a Bird.

EUELPIDES

            Then what happened to your feathers, Bird?

HOOPOE

They've fallen out.   −

EUELPIDES

                    Caught the mange, I suppose?

HOOPOE

I'll ignore that remark.

                All Birds moult in winter,*
and then in spring we grow fresh feathers back.
Now then, suppose you tell me who *you* are.

EUELPIDES

                                            Mortals.

HOOPOE

Country?

EUELPIDES

        Athens, land of lovely—warships.

HOOPOE

Then you must be jurymen.*

EUELPIDES

                    No, just the reverse:
we're non-jurymen.

HOOPOE

            I thought that species had become extinct
in Athens.

EUELPIDES

        You can still find a few growing wild—*
if you look hard enough.

HOOPOE

                But what brings you here, gentlemen?

EUELPIDES

Your assistance and advice.

HOOPOE

                    My advice? About what?

EUELPIDES

You were mortal once as we are mortal now.
You once were plagued with creditors, and we're plagued
    now.
You welshed on your debts; we welsh on our debts now.
But though you were mortal once, you became a Bird
and flew the circuit of the spreading earth and sea;
yet both as Bird and Man you understand.
And so we come to you, to ask your help,
bearing our hope that you may know some land,
some country like a blanket, soft and snug,*
between whose folds two tired men might flop.

HOOPOE

And Athens won't do? You want something more . . .
splendid?

EUELPIDES

It wasn't exactly splendor we had in mind. No,
we wanted a country that was made for just *us*.

HOOPOE

Ah, something more exclusive? An Aristocracy perhaps?

EUELPIDES

Ugh. Can't abide that Aristokrates.

HOOPOE

                              But my dear fellow,
what *do* you want?

EUELPIDES

                    Oh, the sort of country
where the worst trouble I could have would be
friends trooping to my door bright and early
in the morning to pester me with invitations to dinner:
"C'mon, old boy, I'm throwing a big celebration.
So fresh up, give your kiddies a bath,
and come on over. And don't go standing me up,
or I won't turn to you when I'm in trouble."

HOOPOE

Zeus, you like your troubles pleasant, don't you?

To Pisthetairos.

And you?

PISTHETAIROS

      I like pleasant troubles too.

HOOPOE

                              For instance?

PISTHETAIROS

For instance, this. Some pretty little boy's old man
comes up, really peeved, giving me hell:
 'Fine way you treat my son, you old stinker!
You met the boy coming home from the baths
and never fondled him, never even kissed him
or tickled his balls And *you*, his daddy's pal!''

HOOPOE

Poor old bastard, you *are* in love with trouble.
Well, I've got just the place to please you both.
Now, down on the Red Sea—

EUELPIDES

                              Sweet gods, not the sea!
No, sir. I don't want any court-officials with summons*
and subpoenas showing up on ships at the crack of dawn.
Look here, don't you know of some city in Hellas?

HOOPOE

Well now, there's always Lepreus? How would that suit you?

EUELPIDES

Lepreus? Never heard of it. Offhand, I'd say no.
Smacks of old Melanthios. He's leprous.

HOOPOE

                              Hmmm.
Well, how about Opous then?

EUELPIDES

                              Count me out
If Opountios comes from Opous,* then Opous
isn't for me. You couldn't pay me to live there.
But look here, what kind of life do you Birds lead?
You should know. You've lived here long enough.

HOOPOE

Life among the Birds? Not bad. And you don't need cash.

EUELPIDES

Well, that's the worst of life's big swindles disposed of.

HOOPOE

We scour the gardens for food, pecking mint,
scrabbling for poppyseed, sesame and myrtle-berries . . .

EUELPIDES

Gods alive, that's not life! That's a honeymoon!*

PISTHETAIROS

Suddenly illuminated.

WAIT!
    WONDERFUL!
        I'VE GOT IT!
            WHAT A SCHEME!
If you Birds will just do what I say, we'll make it succeed.

HOOPOE

Do what?

PISTHETAIROS

      First, take my advice. For instance,
stop flapping around with your beaks hanging open.
It looks undignified and people jeer at the Birds.
In Athens whenever we see some silly ass,
we ask, "Hey, who's that Bird? and people say,*
"Oh, *him?* He's a real bat, dumb as a dodo,
booby, that's what, hasn't got the brains of a Bird."

HOOPOE

A palpable hit. And we deserve it too.
But what remedy do you suggest?

PISTHETAIROS

Found your own city.

HOOPOE

Found *our own city?* But who ever heard
of a City of Birds?

PISTHETAIROS

O Hebetude, thy name is Hoopoe!
Look down there.

HOOPOE

I'm looking.

PISTHETAIROS

Now look up there.

HOOPOE

I'm looking.

PISTHETAIROS

Way up. Crane your neck.

HOOPOE

By Zeus,
I'll be a helluva sight if I sprain my neck looking.

PISTHETAIROS

See anything?

HOOPOE

Nothing but clouds and a mess of sky.

PISTHETAIROS

Precisely. That mess of sky is the sphere of the Birds.

HOOPOE

Sphere? How do you mean?

PISTHETAIROS

Habitat, as it were.
The heavens, you see, revolve upon a kind of pole*
or axis, whence we call the sky a sphere.
Well then, you settle in your sphere, you build your walls,
and from this sphere of yours a city will appear.
And then, my friend, you'll be lords of all mankind
as once you were merely lords of locusts and bugs.
As for the gods, if they object or get in your way,
you can wipe them all out by starvation.*

HOOPOE

Wipe them out?
But *how?*

PISTHETAIROS

Your air is the boundary between earth and heaven.
Now just as we, when we make a trip to Delphi,
are required to secure a visa from the Theban government,
so you, when men propose a sacrifice to heaven,
impose a boycott, refusing your passport to these offerings
and forbidding any transit through your land,
until the gods agree to pay you tribute.

HOOPOE

By Earth!
Holy Snares! Sweep Springes and Nets!
A trickier gimmick I never heard of yet!
We'll put it to a vote. A referendum. We'll enlist your help
and build our city, provided the Birds agree.

PISTHETAIROS

But who will make the motion?

HOOPOE

You, of course.
Don't worry. They don't twitter nonsense any more.
They used to chirp, but now I've taught them Greek.

PISTHETAIROS

But can we muster a quorum?

HOOPOE

Nothing simpler.
I'll just step behind this little thicket here
and wake my sleeping wife, my lovely Nightingale.
We'll do a small duet and whistle them here.
They'll all come flocking in when they hear our song.

PISTHETAIROS

Hoopoe, old Bird, you're wonderful!
But hurry. Quick.
Go wake your sleeping Nightingale and sing your song.

The Hoopoe retires and begins to sing.

HOOPOE

Awake from sleep, my love!
Sing, O tawnythroat,
bird with honeyed tongue!
Awake and sing
your song and mine,
Itys, Itys!

*From the thicket the flute beings its obbligato in imitation
of the song of the Nightingale at her most melancholy.*

Pure sound of sorrow!
Hear it rise,
a grief that goes,
Itys, Itys!
from the ivy's dark,

the tangled leaves,
and climbs and soars,
　　　Itys, Itys!
till lord Apollo hears,
god with golden hair,
and sweeps his lovely lyre
in echo of your song,
　　　Itys, Itys!
and throats that cannot die
sing the sorrow back,
　　　Itys! Itys! Itys!

*There is a short coda by the flute, accompanied now by the
distant sweeping of the lyre.*

EUELPIDES

Holy Zeus, just hear the little Birdie's song!
A sound like honey streaming through the woods . . .

PISTHETAIROS

　　　　　　　　　　　　　　　　　Pssst.
Hush.

EUELPIDES

　Hush? But why?

PISTHETAIROS

　　　　　Shush.

EUELPIDES

　　　　　　　　But why?

PISTHETAIROS

The Hoopoe is preening to sing another song.

HOOPOE

Singing, with flute obbligato.

Epopopopopopopopoi!

Popopopopopopoi!

Io! Io! Io!

Hear ye ye ye ye ye ye ye!

Calling first to the landbirds.

O Birds of fellow feather come!
Come, you Birds who graze, who feed
over the farmers' fresh-sown fields!
Barley-eating tribes, in thousands come!
O peckers after seeds, hungry nations,
swift of wing! Come, O chirrupers!
All you who flitter in the furrows,
who throng, who flock the new-turned sod,
who sing your chirrup, chirrup-song,
    tio tio tio tio tio tio tio!

All you who in the gardens nest,
who perch beneath the ivy's leaves!
O rangers on the mountain, come,
arbutus-stealers, olive-thieves!
Flock, fly to my call! Come, O come!
    trio trio trio totobrix!

To the Birds of marsh and meadow.

O Birds of swamp and river, come!
You whose beaks snap up the whining gnats,
who splash in water where the earth is wet
or skim the meadows over Marathon!
O Birds of blazoned feather, come!

To the Seabirds.

Come, Birds who soar upon the sea
where the kingfisher swoops!
O Birds with delicate necks,
O taper-throated, come!
Come and see the world remade!
Come and see the Birds reborn!

Lo, a MAN has come, of skill and craft,
  whose wit cuts like a knife,
and to the Birds he brings the Word
  of more abundant life.

Hear ye, hear ye, hear ye!
Come to council, come!
Hither, hither, hither!

> *Toro ,toro toro tix*
> *kikka bau, kikka bau*
> *toro toro toro li*
>   *li lix!*

PISTHETAIROS

Hey, seen any Birds yet?

EUELPIDES

                    Not a sign of one.
And my neck's damn near broken from looking too.

PISTHETAIROS

The way it looks to me, the Hoopoe hopped in
and whooped himself hoarse, and all for nothing.

HOOPOE

            Toro tix! Toro tix!

*As the Hoopoe's call ends, the first member of the Chorus
enters. He is dressed as a Flamingo and is shortly followed
by other members, each costumed in broad representation of
some bird.*

PISTHETAIROS

Pssst. Euelpides! Look over there! There's a Bird coming in!

EUELPIDES

By Zeus, it *is* a Bird! What do you suppose he is? A
Peacock?

Enter Hoopoe.

PISTHETAIROS

The Hoopoe will tell us.
                    —Say, what sort of Bird is that?

HOOPOE

That, my friend, is a rare marshbird. Not the sort of Bird
you run into every day.

EUELPIDES

                    Golly, what a flaming red!

HOOPOE

Exactly. That Bird's a Flamingo.

EUELPIDES

                              Oooh. Look.

PISTHETAIROS

                                        What is it?

EUELPIDES

That Bird.

*Enter a second bird, dressed in gorgeous Persian costume,
with a magnificent strut.*

PISTHETAIROS

          Say, he's exotic. Like something out of Aischylos.*
Prithee, sir,
how is yon strange and mountain-ranging mantic Bird
yclept?

HOOPOE

We call him the Bedouin Bird.

PISTHETAIROS

You don't say? The Bedouin Bird! But how could a Bedouin Bird get to Greece without a Camel Bird?

EUELPIDES

And look there! There comes another Bird with a whopping crest.

Enter a Hoopoe.

PISTHETAIROS

Say, that's odd. You mean you aren't the only Hoopoe going? Is he a Hoopoe too?

HOOPOE

Yes indeed, he's a Hoopoe too. But he's the son of the Hoopoe in Philokles' tragedy of *Tereus.** I'm his grandpa, and he's my namesake, Hoopoe Jr.—You know the pattern, the way Kallias calls his son Hipponikos, and then these Hipponikoses call all their sons Kalliases.

EUELPIDES

So this is the Kallias Hoopoe. Well, he sure looks plucked.

HOOPOE

He's quite the bird about town, so parasites strip him bare and the chorus girls keep yanking his pretty feathers out.

Enter a dazzlingly brilliant bird with an enormous crest and a great protruding belly.

EUELPIDES

Sweet Poseidon! Look at that gorgeous Birdie strutting in! What's he called?

HOOPOE

That one? He's the Crested Guzzleguzzle.

EUELPIDES

The Guzzleguzzle, eh? I thought that was our boy
Kleonymos.*

PISTHETAIROS

No, this Bird has a crest. Our man is crestfallen now.
Don't you remember how he ditched his helmet and ran
away?

EUELPIDES

Look, Hoopoe, what's the point of all this crestwork on the
Birds?* Dress parade?

HOOPOE

No. Partly self-defense, partly
sanitation.
Some towns are built on crests of hills, others in the passes.
So some Birds sport their plumes on top, but others on
    their asses.

PISTHETAIROS

What an ungodly crowd of Birds! It gives me the jitters.

*The rest of the Chorus, birds of every size and description,
now stream into the orchestra.*

Look, Birds everywhere!

EUELPIDES

Apollo, what a bevy of Birds:
Why, when they lift up their wings, they block out the
entrance.

PISTHETAIROS

Look, there's the Partridge!

EUELPIDES

And here's the Hooded Ptarmigan!

PISTHETAIROS

And there's a Widgeon. I think.

EUELPIDES

Here comes a female Plover.
But who's that Bird on her tail?

PISTHETAIROS

Her lover. The Horny Pecker.*

EUELPIDES

What does her husband say?

PISTHETAIROS

He's a queer Bird and doesn't care.

HOOPOE

Here's the Owl.

PISTHETAIROS

Now there's a thought! Bringing Owls to Athens.*

HOOPOE

And Jay and Pigeon. Lark, Wren, Wheatear, and
Turtledove. Ringdove, Stockdove, Cuckoo, and Hawk.
Firecrest and Wren, Rail and Kestrel and Gull. Waxwing.
Woodpecker, and Vulture . . .

In one last surge the remaining members of the Chorus

*stream into the orchestra, ruffling their feathers and chirping
and hissing.*

PISTHETAIROS

Birds, Birds, billions of Birds!

EUELPIDES

Indicating the Audience

But most of them Cuckoos and Geese

PISTHETAIROS

What a skittering and cackling!

EUELPIDES

Unless I'm much mistaken.
I detect a note of menace.*

PISTHETAIROS

They *do* seem somewhat peeved.
You know, I think they're glaring at *us*

EUELPIDES

Damn right they are.

KORYPHAIOS

Who-oo-chee-who-chee-who-oo-oo-oo
who-oo-chee-oo-oo has summoned me?

HOOPOE

Me, that's who. Your old friend Hoopoe.

KORYPHAIOS

Spea-pea-pea-pea-speak, Hoopopopopopoi.

HOOPOE

Listen. Great news! Glorious news!
News of Profit, gravy for all!
Two brilliant men have come to call
on me.

KORYPHAIOS

On YOU?
But HOW?
And WHO?

HOOPOE

But I'm trying to tell you.
Two old men have come to call.
two old refugees who have renounced the human race for
good
and who bring us a glorious scheme, a Plan of fantastic
proportions,
gigantic, sublime, colossal—

KORYPHAIOS

Colossal's the word for your blunder.
Have you lost your mind?

HOOPOE

Wait. listen . . .

KORYPHAIOS

Explain. And fast.

HOOPOE

Listen. I welcomed two old men. Harmless ornithologists.
infatuated with the Birds. They want to live with their
Feathered Friends.

KORYPHAIOS

What? You welcomed TWO MEN?

HOOPOE

What's more, I'd do it again.

KORYPHAIOS

You mean they're *here?* In our midst?

HOOPOE

As much as I. Look.

He raises his wings, revealing the two men cowering behind him.

CHORUS

—O Treachery!
O Treason!
—O!
BAD Hoopoe, to betray us so!
To think that you, the Birdies' friend,
could come to such a wicked end!
To think that I should one day see
the Bird who pecked the corn with me
dishonor and disgrace
The MAGNA CARTA of our race,
and sell us to our foe!
—O Treachery!
O Treason!
—O!

KORYPHAIOS

All right, we'll settle accounts with this treacherous Hoopoe
later
As for these venerable old fools, we'll settle with them right
now.
We'll shred them into tatters.

PISTHETAIROS

> Gods, they're shredding us to tatters!

EUELPIDES

Well, it's all your fault. This whole damn trip was your idea.
Why in god's name did you lead me here?

PISTHETAIROS

> To bring up my rear.

EUELPIDES

It's so hopeless I could cry.

PISTHETAIROS

> Fat chance you'll have of crying.

Once those Birds are through with you, you won't have any
eyes.

CHORUS

> Advance the wings and charge the flanks!
> > The Rooster shrills ATTACK!
> Aerial squadrons, take to the air!
> > Beat your enemy back.
>
> These men are spies, their lives are lies,
> > so kill without regrets!
> The skill to kill lies in your bills.
> > Your beaks are bayonets.
>
> No cloud exists, no breaker is,
> > no fog on mountain peaks,
> quite big or thick or black enough
> > to save them from our beaks!

KORYPHAIOS

Mount the attack!

> Charge them, Birds! Bite them, tear them!

On the double!
   Captain on the right! Advance your wing and charge!

*The Chorus wheels in massed formation toward the stage.
Euelpides in terror starts to run.*

EUELPIDES

They're charging! Where can we run?

PISTHETAIROS

         Run, man? Stand and fight!

EUELPIDES

And get torn to tatters?

PISTHETAIROS

       What good's running? *They*'re flying.

EUELPIDES

But what should I do?

PISTHETAIROS

      Listen to me and follow my orders.
First pick up that platter and use it as a shield. Now HOLD
 THAT LINE!

EUELPIDES

But what good's a platter?

PISTHETAIROS

        Birds are skittish of platters.*
        They'll scatter.

EUELPIDES

Yeah? Well, what about that vulture there?

PISTHETAIROS

Snatch up a skewer.
Now stick it out front like a spéar.

EUELPIDES

But what about my eyes?

PISTHETAIROS

Jam a jug on your head. Now cover your eyes with saucers.

EUELPIDES

What a kitchen tactician! What crockery-strategy! Gee,
old Nikias is tricky, but he can't compare with you.

KORYPHAIOS

FORWARD!
Spit them with your beaks! At 'em, Birds!
CHARGE!
Rip 'em, scratch 'em, flay 'em, bite! BUT BREAK THAT
POT!

HOOPOE

Intervening.

Truce, truce.
No more of this bitterness. You Birds should be
ashamed.
Why should you kill these men? What harm have they done
to you?
Somewhat more to the point, they're both closely related to
my wife.*

KORYPHAIOS

Why spare these men any more than wolves? What worse
enemy than men do we Birds have?

HOOPOE

Enemies by nature, I admit.
But these men are exceptions to the rule. They come to you
    as friends.
Moreover, they bring a scheme from which we Birds stand
    to profit.

KORYPHAIOS

Are you suggesting that Birds should take advice from men?
What can *we* learn from men?

HOOPOE

If wise men learn from their enemies,
then why not you?
Remember the advantage of keeping
an open mind.
Preparedness, after all, is not a lesson taught us by our
    friends
but by our enemies. It is our enemies, not our friends, who
    teach us to survive.
I might cite the case of cities: was it from their friends or
    their foes
that mankind first learned to build walls and ships in self-
    defense?
But that one lesson still preserves us all and all we have.

KORYPHAIOS

There's something in what you say.
Perhaps we'd better hear them

PISTHETAIROS

To Euelpides.

They're beginning to show signs of reason. Don't say a word.

HOOPOE

To the Chorus.

That's better, friends. You're doing right, and you'll thank
me for it later.

KORYPHAIOS

We've never disobeyed your advice before.

PISTHETAIROS

                                                                    They seem more
                                                                    peaceful now.
                        So you can ground the pan
                        and put the platter down.
                        But stand your ground
                        and keep that spit on hand,
                        while I look round
                        our little camp of crocks
                        and see how matters stand
                        by peeking over pots.

EUELPIDES

                        Chief, suppose we die
                        in combat?

PISTHETAIROS

                                Then we'll lie
                        in Athens at public cost.*
                        They'll give us hero's honors
                        and bury us like gods
                        when we say our lives were lost
                        fighting foreign soldiers
                        at very heavy odds.
                        In fact, I'll use those very words
                        (omitting, for effect, of course
                        any reference to Birds.)*

KORYPHAIOS

                        All right, you Birds, FALL IN!
                        The war's over.

AT EASE!
You there, quiet!
QUIET, PLEASE!

*The Chorus returns to its normal position in the orchestra.
Much whispering, nodding, and shuffling. Then silence.*

Now we have to inquire
who these strangers are
and why they've come.
Look here, Hoopoe.

HOOPOE

Um?

KORYPHAIOS

Who are these fellows?

HOOPOE

Two humans from Hellas
where genius grows greener than grass.

KORYPHAIOS

But why have they come?
What do they hope to get from the Birds?

HOOPOE

Their motive is Love.
Love is the burden of all their words.
Love of your life
and Love of you,
to live with you
in Love always.

KORYPHAIOS

Is *that* what they say?
But what is the gist of their scheme?

HOOPOE

> They envisage a vision of glory,
> > a dream so fantastic
> it staggers the sensible mind.

KORYPHAIOS

> Well, it doesn't stagger mine.
> > What's in it for them?
> Who are they trying to stick?

HOOPOE

> No one.
> > This is no trick.
> > What this means is bliss.
> Believe me, utter bliss. Sheer
> and absolute.
> > *Viz.*
> all shall be yours,
> whatever is,
> here or there,
> far or near,
> all, everywhere.
> And this they swear.

KORYPHAIOS

> Crackpots, eh?

HOOPOE

> Right as rain.
> Foxes, not men.
> Boxes of slyness,
> brimming with brain.

KORYPHAIOS

Then let them talk! We're all in a twitter to hear.

HOOPOE

So be it, then.
                    —Men, take these weapons inside
the house and hang them up beside the blazing hearth
where the god of fire presides. They'll bring us luck.

*Servants pick up the pots and plates and skewers and carry
them inside. The Hoopoe turns to Pisthetairos.*

Pisthetairos, you have the floor. Proceed with your case.
Explain your proposal.

PISTHETAIROS

                    By Apollo, only on condition
that you Birds agree to swear a solemn truce with me
like the truce which that armor-making baboon—you know
   who I mean—*
signed with his wife: no biting, scratching, or cutting,
no hauling around by the balls, no shoving things—

EUELPIDES

Bending over.

—Up there?

PISTHETAIROS

              In my eyes, I was going to say.

KORYPHAIOS

We accept your terms.

PISTHETAIROS

                    First you have to swear to them.

KORYPHAIOS

We swear it then, but on this one condition only:
that you guarantee that this comedy of ours will win First
Prize by completely unanimous vote of the Judges.

PISTHETAIROS

                               Agreed.

KORYPHAIOS

Splendid. If. however. we Birds should break the truce,
we agree to forfeit. say. forty-nine per cent
of the votes.

HOOPOF

To the Chorus

                Fall out!
                        Pick up your weapons, men
and return at once to your quarters On the double!
Company Assignments will be posted on the bulletin boards.

CHORUS

        —Man by nature is a liar made.
         He plays a double game:
        —Dishonesty's his stock-in-trade.
         Deception is his name.
        —We say no more.
                       —But it may be
         your canny mortal brain may see
         what our poor feeble wits cannot—
        —some gift of noble intellect
         we once possessed and then forgot
         as our race declined;
        —some genius of the will
         or wisdom of the mind,
        —grown rusty with neglect,
         but fusting in us still.
        —It seems to us fantastic.
        —But still, it *could* be true.
        —And, of course, we'd split the profits—
        —if any such accrue.

222   **ARISTOPHANES**

KORYPHAIOS

Pisthetairos, proceed. You may say whatever you wish. With
   impunity.
We pledge you our words as Birds: we won't renege on the
   truce.

PISTHETAIROS

By god, I'm wild to begin!
                          The dough of my vision has risen,
and there's nothing now but the kneading.
                          —Boy, bring me a wreath.
Someone fetch water for my hands.*

EUELPIDES

                                        Hey, we going to a feast?

PISTHETAIROS

A dinner of words, a fat and succulent haunch of speech,
a meal to shiver the soul.
                          —Unhappy Birds, I grieve for you,
you who once were kings—

KORYPHAIOS

                          —Kings? Of what?

PISTHETAIROS

                                        Kings of everything.
Kings of creation. My kings. This man's kings. Kings of
   king Zeus.
More ancient than Kronos. Older than Titans. Older than
   Earth.

KORYPHAIOS

Older than Earth?

PISTHETAIROS

                     Older than Earth.

KORYPHAIOS

> And to think I never suspected!

PISTHETAIROS

Because you're a lazy Bird* and you haven't reread your
  Aesop.
For Aesop states that the Lark is the oldest thing in the
  world,
older than Earth. So ancient, in fact, that when her father
  died,
she couldn't find him a grave, for the Earth hadn't yet been
  made,
and therefore couldn't be dug. So what on earth could she
  do?
Well, the little Lark was stumped. Then suddenly she had it!
She laid her daddy out and buried him under her tail.

EUELPIDES

She did for a fact.
> And that's how Asbury* got its name.

PISTHETAIROS

Hence my argument stands thus: if the Birds are older than
  Earth,
and therefore older than gods, then the Birds are the heirs
  of the world.
For the oldest always inherits.

EUELPIDES

> It stands to reason, friends.
So pack some bone in your bills and hone them down to
  a point.
Old Zeus won't rush to resign and let the Woodpeckers
  reign.*

PISTHETAIROS

Think of it, the springtime of the world!

The Age of the Birds!
Primal lords of Creation! Absolute masters of man!
But the gods are mere upstarts and usurpers of very recent
  date.
And proof abounds.
                    Let me adduce, for instance, the case of
                        the Rooster.
Aeons and aeons ago, ages before the age of Darius,
the kingdom of Persia lay prostrate beneath the sway of the
  Rooster
And the Rooster, ever since, has been called the Persian Red.

EUELPIDES

And that's why, even now, he swaggers and struts like a
  king
and keeps a harem of hens. And, unique among the Birds,
he wears the royal red tiara of the ancient Persian kings.

PISTHETAIROS

And talk of power!
                    Why, even now its memory remains,
enshrined in habit. For when the Cock his matins crows,
mankind goes meekly off to work—bakers, smiths, and
  potters,
tanners and merchants and musical-instrument makers.
And when he crows at dusk, the night-shift goes.

EUELPIDES

                                        I'll vouch for that.
It was thanks to his night-shift crowing that I lost my
  warmest coat.
I'd gone downtown to dinner, see, in honor of a birth.
Well, after a while I'd had five or six and passed out cold,
when that blasted Rooster started to crow. Needless to say,
I thought it was dawn, jumped into my clothes and tore off
  to work.
But just outside the gate, somebody conked me with a club
and I passed out cold again. And when I came to, no coat!

PISTHETAIROS

What's more, once upon a time the Kites were the kings of
Hellas.

KORYPHAIOS

The *kings* of Hellas?

PISTHETAIROS

                Right. The Kites were the kings of Hellas.
And it was during their reign that the custom began in
    Greece
of falling flat on your face whenever you saw a Kite.*

EUELPIDES

You know, I once spotted a Kite and went down on the
    ground—
so damn hard I swallowed my money* and two of my teeth.
I damn near starved.

PISTHETAIROS

                And once the Cuckoo was king of Egypt.
And when the call of the Cuckoo was heard in the land,
    every Egyptian
grabbed his scythe and ran to the fields to reap.

EUELPIDES

                            That's a fact.
And that's why, even today, we still call the Egyptians
cuckoo.*

PISTHETAIROS

Why, so great was the power of the Birds that even the
    greatest kings—
Agamemnon and Menelaos, to name only two of the
    greatest—
had their sceptres tipped with Birds, and the Birds got a cut
    in the take.

EUELPIDES

So *that's* it. That explains all that funny business in the plays
I never understood before—where Priam, for instance,
      walks in,
and there on his sceptre, large as life, some Bird is perching.
I used to think he was there to keep an eye peeled down
      below
on the rows where the politicians sit,* to see where our
      money goes.

PISTHETAIROS

But the crowning proof is this: the present incumbent, Zeus,
wears an Eagle upon his helmet as the symbol of royal
      power.
Athena uses the Owl, and Apollo, as aide to Zeus, a Hawk.

EUELPIDES

By Demeter, they do! But why do the gods use these Birds
as emblems?

PISTHETAIROS

An unconscious admission of the Birds' ancient power and
      supremacy.
That's why when men sacrifice to the gods, the Birds swoop
      down and snatch the food,
thereby beating out the gods, and so asserting their old
      priority.
Again, no one ever swore by the gods, but always by the
      Birds.

EUELPIDES

Doctors still swear by the Duck.* That's why we call them
      quacks.

PISTHETAIROS

But these were the honors you held in the days of your
greatness.

Whereas now you've been downgraded.
You're the slaves, not lords, of men.
They call you brainless or crazy.
They kill you whenever they can.

The temples are no protection:
the hunters are lying in wait
with traps and nooses and nets
and little limed twigs and bait.

And when you're taken, they sell you
as tiny *hors d'oeuvres* for a lunch.
And you're not even sold alone,
but lumped and bought by the bunch.

And buyers come crowding around
and pinch your breast and your rump,
to see if your fleshes are firm
and your little bodies are plump.

Then, as if this weren't enough,
they refuse to roast you whole,
but dump you down in a dish
and call you a *casserôle*.

They grind up cheese and spices
with some oil and other goo,
and they take this slimy gravy
and they pour it over you!

Yes, they pour it over you!

It's like a disinfectant,
and they pour it piping hot,
as though your meat were putrid,
to sterilize the rot!

Yes, to sterilize the rot!

As Pisthetairos finishes, a long low susurrus of grief runs
through the Chorus and the Birds sigh, weep, and beat their
breasts with their wings.

CHORUS

Stranger, forgive us if we cry,
    reliving in your words
those years of cowardice that brought
    disaster to the Birds:—
    that tragic blunder
    and our fathers' crime,
    complacency whose cost
    was greatness and our name,
    as dignity went under
    in a chicken-hearted time,
    and all was lost.

But now, by luck,
or heaven-sent,
a Man has come
to pluck us from disgrace.

Hail, Pisthetairos!
Hail, Savior of the Birds,
Redeemer of our Race!
To you we now commit:
        ourselves,
        our nests,
        our chicks,
            et cet.

KORYPHAIOS

Sir, you have the floor once more. Proceed with your
explanation. Until our power is restored, life means less
than nothing to the Birds.

PISTHETAIROS

        My Plan, in gist, is this—a city of the Birds,
whose walls and ramparts shall include the atmosphere of
    the world
within their circuit. But make the walls of brick, like
    Babylon.

EUELPIDES

A Babylon of the Birds!* What a whopping, jumbo-size city!

PISTHETAIROS

The instant your walls are built, reclaim your sceptre from
   Zeus.
If he shilly-shallies or fobs you off with a lot of excuses,
proclaim a Holy War, a Great Crusade against the gods.
Then slap embargoes on their lust, forbidding any gods
in manifest state of erection to travel through your sky
on amatory errands down to Earth to lay their women—
their Semeles, Alkmenes, and so forth. Then, if they attempt
   to ignore
your warning, place their offending peckers under bond
as contraband and seal them shut. That will stop their fun,
I think.
          Second, appoint some Bird as your official ambassador
to men, and serve them formal notice that the Birds demand
   priority
in all their sacrifices. The leftovers, of course, will go to the
   gods.
But for the future, even when they offer sacrifices to the
   gods,
each Bird must be paired with a god*—whichever one seems
   most apt.
Thus, if Aphrodite is offered a cake, the Wagtail will get one
   too.
When Poseidon gets his sheep, the Seagull must have his
   wheat.
Greedy Herakles shall eat—when the glutton Jay is fed.
And as for Zeus, why, Zeus must wait his turn until the
   Kinglet,
lord of all the Birds, receives his sacrificial gnat.

EUELPIDES

I *like* that gnat. Old has-been Zeus can rumble with rage!

KORYPHAIOS

But why should men believe we're gods and not just shabby
Birds? These wings are a giveaway.

PISTHETAIROS

                Rubbish. Hermes is a god, isn't he?
But he goes flapping around on wings. And so do loads of
   gods.
There's Victory on ''gildered wings,'' and don't forget the
   god of Love.
And Homer says that Iris looks like a dove with the jitters.

EUELPIDES

And lightning too, that's got wings. Hey, what if lightning
fell on us?

KORYPHAIOS

And what if men are blind and go on truckling to Olympos
and refuse to worship the Birds?

PISTHETAIROS

               Then swarms of starving Sparrows
shall descend on their fields in millions and gobble up their
   seeds.
They'll damn well go hungry. We'll see then if Demeter will
   feed them.

EUELPIDES

If I know that Demeter, she'll have plenty of excuses ready.

PISTHETAIROS

Then we'll muster the Crows and Ravens and send them
   down in droves
to peck out the eyes of the oxen and make the sheep go
   blind.
Dr. Apollo can cure them—but I'd hate to pay the fee.

EUELPIDES

Give me the nod when you're ready. I want to unload my
ox.

PISTHETAIROS

If, on the other hand, mankind accepts you as their gods,
their manifest Poseidon, their Earth, their Principle of Life,
all their wishes shall come true.

KORYPHAIOS

                            All their wishes? For instance?

PISTHETAIROS

Why, enormous plagues of locusts will not infest their vines:
a single regiment of our Owls will wipe the locusts out.
And the gallfly and the mite will no longer blight their figs
since we'll send down troops of Thrushes to annihilate the
   bugs.

KORYPHAIOS

But what about money? Money's Man's dominant passion.

PISTHETAIROS

Duck soup for you. Your oracles will tell them what they
want—the whereabouts of the richest mines, when the
market is right to make a killing, and so forth. And no
more shipwrecks either.

KORYPHAIOS

No more shipwrecks?

PISTHETAIROS

            No shipwrecks. You take your omens, you see,
and some Bird pipes up, "Bad weather brewing" or "Fore-
cast: fair."

EUELPIDES

To hell with the Birds! A ship for me! I'm off to sea!

PISTHETAIROS

You'll show them buried treasure; you'll tell them where to
    find gold.
For Birds know all the answers, or so the saying goes—
"A little Bird told me." People are always saying that.

EUELPIDES

The hell with the sea! A shovel for me! I'm off to dig for
gold!

KORYPHAIOS

But how will we give them health? That lies in the hands of
the gods.

PISTHETAIROS

Give them wealth, you give them health. They're really
much the same.

EUELPIDES

And that's a fact. The man who's sick is always doing badly.

KORYPHAIOS

But longevity and old age also lie in the hands of the gods.
How will a man grow old if the gods refuse him Old Age?
Will he die in childhood?

PISTHETAIROS

                        Die? The Birds will add to his life
three centuries at least.

KORYPHAIOS

                    But how?

PISTHETAIROS

From their own lives, of course.
What doth the poet say?
"Five lives of men the cawing Crow
outliveth."*

EUELPIDES

Long live the Birds! Down with Zeus!

PISTHETAIROS

I'm with you there,
and think of the money we'll save!

For Birds won't want any shrines;
    marble just leaves them cold.
They don't give a hoot for temples
    with doors of beaten gold.

They'll live in woodses and copses—
    that's plenty of shrine for them.
And the social-register swells
    can strut on an olive limb.*

And we'll go no more to Delphi!
    To hell with Ammon's seat!
We'll amble out under the olives
    and toss them bits of wheat,

and hold up our paws to heaven
    and make the Birds a prayer,
and the Birds will grant all our wishes
    for cutting them a share.

And we won't be out of pocket.
    No, the only dough we'll need
is a little loaf of barley
    and a tiny pinch of seed.

KORYPHAIOS

The Birds' best friend! And to think how we misjudged you

once, most generous of men!
                    Ask us what you will. It shall be done.

CHORUS

Amen, we say.
              And now, presuming you concur,
                  we Birds propose an oath
              of mutual assistance, sir,
                  and binding on us both.

              Arm to wing, we'll soar to war!
                  Our cause needs no excuse.
              We'll storm up Mt. Olympos, friend,
                  and make a pulp of Zeus!

KORYPHAIOS

We await your orders, sir. Tasks that need mere brawn and
    muscle
we Birds can do. The complicated mental stuff we leave to
    you.

HOOPOE

Action, dammit, action! That's what we need.
Strike while the iron's hot. Not dawdling around
like slowpoke Nikias.
                    —Dear me, I nearly forgot.
You two gentlemen must see my little nest,
my trash of sticks and straw and kickshaw stuff.
And good heavens! We haven't been formally introduced.

PISTHETAIROS

Pisthetairos here.

HOOPOE

                    Ah. And this gentleman?

EUELPIDES

                                        Euelpides.

From Athens.

HOOPOE

        Enchanted, I'm sure.

PISTHETAIROS

                The pleasure's ours.

HOOPOE

Please come in

PISTHETAIROS

        No, after you.

HOOPOE

              This way, gentlemen.

The Hoopoe begins to flap his wings to flutter into his nest

PISTHETAIROS

Hey, you!
        Damn it, stop! Back water, blast you!
Look here, what sort of partnership is this supposed to be
if you start taking off when we can't even fly?

HOOPOE

Does it matter?

PISTHETAIROS

        Remember what old Aesop tells us*
in his fable of the Eagle and the Fox in business
who couldn't get along? The Fox got swindled by the Eagle.

HOOPOE

Don't be nervous. I know of a wonderful magic root.
Merely nibble on it and you'll sprout a set of wings.

PISTHETAIROS

Splendid. Then let's go in.
                              —You there, Xanthias.
Hey, Manodorus! Bring our luggage inside the house.

KORYPHAIOS

One moment, please, Hoopoe, when you go inside . . .

HOOPOE

                                                      Yes?

KORYPHAIOS

By all means take your hùman guests and feast them well.
But first do one little favor for the Chorus, please.
Bring out your wife, your lovely Nightingale,
the bird with honeyed tongue, the Muses' love,
and let the Chorus play with her a little while.

PISTHETAIROS

I add my entreaty to theirs. In the name of heaven,
bring her out from the bed of rushes where she hides.

EUELPIDES

Please, please do. Bring the pretty Birdie out.
I've never met a Nightingale before.

HOOPOE

                                        With all my heart.
I'd be delighted, gentlemen.

Calling inside.

                              Oh Prokne! Prokne.
Please come out, my dear, and meet our visitors.

*A lovely well-rounded young flutegirl shyly appears. She is
dressed in the rich gold-encrusted robes of a young Athenian*

matron of high birth. On her head she wears the mask of the Nightingale.

PISTHETAIROS

Almighty Zeus! Gosh, what a baby of a Birdie!
What curves! What grace! What a looker!

EUELPIDES

                              Gee! By god,
I'd like to bounce between her thighs right now!

PISTHETAIROS

And what a shimmer of gold! Just like a bride.

EUELPIDES

By god, I've got half a mind to kiss her!

PISTHETAIROS

                              Look out,
you old lecher, her beak's a pair of skewers.

EUELPIDES

                              Very well.
Then I'll treat her like an egg and peel her shell.
I'll lift her little mask and kiss her—so.

HOOPOE

Harrumph. This way.

PISTHETAIROS

                    And may good fortune go with us.

Exeunt Pisthetairos, Euelpides, and Hoopoe, followed by the slaves with the luggage.

CHORUS

O love,
          tawnythroat!
Sweet nightingale,
musician of the Birds
Come and sing,
          honey-throated one!
Come, O love,
          flutist of the Spring,
accompany our song.

The Chorus turns sharply and faces the audience, while the
flutegirl begins the song of the nightingale at its most
mournful. The flute obbligato accompanies the Chorus
throughout.*

O suffering mankind,
                    lives of twilight,
                              race feeble and fleeting,
like the leaves scattered!
                    Pale generations,
                              creatures of clay,
the wingless, the fading!
                    Unhappy mortals,
                              shadows in time,
flickering dreams!
                    Hear us now,
                              the ever-living Birds,
the undying,
          the ageless ones,
                    scholars of eternity.
Hear and learn from us
                    the truth
                              of all there is to know—
what we are,
          and how the gods began,
                              of Chaos and Dark.
(And when you know
                    tell Prodikos to go
                              hang:* he's had it!)

There was Chaos at first
           and Night and Space
                and Tartaros.
There was no Earth.
        No Heaven was.
              But sable-wingèd Night
laid her wind-egg there*
        in the boundless lap
             of infinite Dark.
And from that egg,
        in the seasons' revolving,
             Love was born,
the graceful, the golden,
        the whirlwind Love
           on gleaming wings.
And there in the waste
        of Tartaros,
           Love with Chaos lay
and hatched the Birds.
        We come from Love.
              Love brought us
              to the light.
There were no gods
        till Love had married
           all the world in love.
Then the world was made.
        Blue Heaven stirred,
           and Ocean,
the Earth and ageless gods,
        the blessèd ones
           who do not die.
But we came first.
        We Birds were born
           the first-born sons of
           Love,
in proof whereof
        we wear Love's wings,
           we help his lovers.
How many pretty boys,
        their prime not past,
           abjuring Love,

have opened up their thighs
                 and yielded,
                              overborne by us,
bribed by a Bird,
              a Coot, a Goose,
                              a little Persian Cock!
Think of the services
                 we Birds perform
                              for all mankind.
We mark your seasons off,
                       summer, spring,
                                   winter, fall.
When for Africa
            the screaming Crane departs,
                              you sow your fields.
And then the sailor
                 takes his ease
                              and hangs his rudder up,
and thief Orestes
              weaves himself a cloak
                              and robs no man.
And then the Kite appears,
                    whose coming says
                                 the Spring is here,
the time has come
              to shear the sheep.
                              And so the Swallow
brings his summer,
               when mankind lays
                             its winter weeds away.
And we are Ammon
              and Dodona.
                        We are your Apollo,
that prophetic voice
              to whom you turn
                          in everything you do—
practical affairs,
              commerce and trade,
                           and marriage too.

Birds are your signs,
            and all your omens
                        are governed by Birds:
words are omens
            sent by the Birds.
                        And the same for sneezes,
meetings, asses, voices:
            all are omens,
                        and omens are Birds.
Who are we then
            if we are not
                        your prophetic Apollo?

*The obbligato of the flute ceases as the Chorus now shifts to a
lighter vein and a quicker tempo.*

            So elect us as your gods
            and we, in turn, shall be
            your weathervane and Muse,
            your priests of prophecy,
                foretelling all,
            winter, summer, spring, and fall.

            Furthermore, we promise we'll
            give mankind an honest deal.
            Unlike our smug opponent, Zeus,
            we'll stop corruption and abuse.
            NO ABSENTEE ADMINISTRATION!
            NO PERMANENT VACATION
            IN THE CLOUDS!
                        And we promise
            to be scrupulously honest.

            Last of all, we guarantee
            to every single soul on earth,
            his sons and their posterity:
                        HEALTH
                        WEALTH
                        HAPPINESS
                        YOUTH
                        LONG LIFE

LAUGHTER
PEACE
DANCING
and
LOTS TO EAT!
We'll mince no words.
Your lives shall be
the milk of the Birds!
We guarantee
you'll all be
revoltingly
RICH!

O woodland Muse
with lovely throat,
tio tio tio tinx!
who with me sing
whenas in glade or mountain, I,
perched upon the ashtree cry,
tio tio tio tinx!
my tawny-throated song of praise,
to call the Mother to the dance,
a song of joy for blessed Pan,
totototototinx!
whence, like a bee,
the poet stole his honeyed song,*
my ravished cry,
tio tio tio tinx!

Do *you* suffer pangs of conscience?
Nervous?
Jumpy?
Scared?
Need a hideout from the law? Some cozy place to pass the
time? Well, step right up, friend!
We'll get you a berth with the Birds.
We do things differently up here.
What your laws condemn,
the things that you think shady or immoral are compulsory
with us.

Consider the case, for instance, of a boy who beats up his
    dad.
Admit it: you're shocked. The idea! But *we* call it courage
when some bantam twirps, "C'mon, old Bird, put up your
                         spurs and fight!"
Or suppose you've deserted. You're a runaway, branded
    with shame.
Hell, come and live with us! We'll call you a Yellow
    Chicken.
Or perhaps you happen to come from some foppish hole in
    Asia?
Come on up, you fairy fop, and be an Asiatic Finch.
Or suppose you're a slave from Krete, like our friend
    Exekestides—
We'll call you little Cuckoo and pawn you off as our own.
Was Peisias your father?
                          Are you a future traitor too?
Hell, make like a Partridge then. That's what your Daddy
    did.
And who are we Birds to fuss at shamming hurt and
    partridge tricks?

          And so the swans
          their clamor cry,
          tio tio tio tinx!
          and beating wings
          and bursting throats
          lord Apollo sing,
          tio tio tio tinx!
  by Hebros' waters, swarming, crying,
          tio tio tio tinx!
And every living thing is still.
On bird, on beast, the hush of awe.
The windless sea lies stunned when—
          totototototinx!
          All Olympos rings,
  and wonder breaks upon the gods,
  and echoing, the Graces sing,
  and lovely Muses raise the cry,
          tio tio tio tinx!

Friends, you haven't really lived till you've tried a set of
    FEATHERS!
Think, spectators.

              Imagine yourselves with a pair of wings!
The sheer joy of it! Not having to sit those tragedies out!
No getting bored. You merely flap your little wings and fly
    off home.
You have a snack, then make it back to catch the COMIC
    play.
Or again, suppose you're overtaken by a sudden need to crap.
Do you do it in your pants?

              Not a bit.

                      You just zoom off,
fart and shit to your heart's content and whizz right back.
Or perhaps you're having an affair—I won't name any names.
You spot the lady's husband attending some meeting or
    other.
Up you soar, flap your wings, through the window and into
    bed!
You make it a quickie, of course, then flutter back to your
    seat.
So what do you say?

              Aren't wings just the most *wonderful* things?
Look at Dieitrephes, our vulgar Ikaros of trade,*
who started life on wicker wings but rose to captain's rank,
and now, still riding high, is colonel of a wing of horse.
From horse's ass to Pegasos! But *that's* what wings can do!

*The Chorus now turns and faces the stage Pisthetairos and
Euelpides return. Both of them now sport tiny wings, a few
feathers, and outsize beaks.*

PISTHETAIROS

Well, here we are.

EUELPIDES

              Sweet gods, in all my days,
I've never seen a sillier sight than you!

PISTHETAIROS

                      Yeah,
what's so damn funny?

EUELPIDES

               You and those baby wings.
They tickle me. You know what you look like, don't you?

PISTHETAIROS

You look like an abstraction of a Goose.

EUELPIDES

                    Yeah?
Well, if you're supposed to be a Blackbird, boy,
somebody botched the job. You're more bare than Bird.

PISTHETAIROS

We made the choice that gave these barbs their bite.
Remember the poor Birds in that Aischylos play*—
"Shot down by shafts of their own feathers made?"

EUELPIDES

What's the next move?

PISTHETAIROS

             First, we'll give our city
some highfalutin' name. Then a special sacrifice
to our new gods.

EUELPIDES

          A special sacrifice? Yummy.

KORYPHAIOS

To work, men. How do you propose to name our city?

PISTHETAIROS

How about Sparta? That's a grand old name
with a fine pretentious ring.

EUELPIDES

                        Great Herakles.
call my city Sparta? I wouldn't even insult
my mattress by giving it a name like Sparta.*

PISTHETAIROS

                                        Well.
what do you suggest instead?

EUELPIDES

                        Something big, smacking
of the clouds. A pinch of fluff and rare air
A swollen sound.

PISTHETAIROS

                I've got it! Listen—
                        CLOUDCUCKOOLAND!

KORYPHAIOS

That's it! The perfect name. And it's a *big* word too.

EUELPIDES

CLOUDCUCKOOLAND!
                        Imagination's happy home,
where Theogenes builds castles in the air, and Aischines
becomes a millionaire.

PISTHETAIROS

                Better yet, here we have
the plain of Phlegra, that windy battlefield of blah and bluff.
where the gabbling gods outbragged the wordy giants

KORYPHAIOS

A suave and splendid city.
                    —But which of the gods
should we designate as patron and protector?

EUELPIDES

                                        Why not Athena?

PISTHETAIROS

But it's bound to seem a bit, odd, isn't it? I mean,
a female goddess protecting our walls with a spear
while men like Kleisthenes sit home with their knitting?

KORYPHAIOS

And, come to think of it, who will guard our Storkade?*

PISTHETAIROS

A Bird.

KORYPHAIOS

        One of us, you mean?

PISTHETAIROS

                        Why not the Rooster?
They're terrible scrappers and famous fighting Birds.
Little chicks of Ares.

EUELPIDES

                Little Corporal Cock!
He's the perfect Bird for protecting our rock.

PISTHETAIROS

To Euelpides.

    Hop it, man!*
                Quick, up the rigging of the air!

Hurry! Done? Now supervise the workers on the wall.
Run the rubble up!
                         Quick, mix the mortar, man!
Up the ladder with your hod—and then fall down!
Don't stop!
                    Post the sentries!
                                        Bank the furnace!
Now the watchman's round.
                                        All right, catch two winks.
Rise and shine!
                    Now send your heralds off,
one to the gods above, one to the mortals below
Then scurry back.

EUELPIDES

                        As for you, just stay right here—
and I hope you choke.

PISTHETAIROS

                        Obey your orders, friend.
Unless you do your share, we shan't get done.

Exit Euelpides.

Now, let me see.
                    First, a priest to supervise
our sacrifice.
                    —Boy!

An Acolyte appears.

                        Boy, go fetch me a priest.
And when you're finished, bring me a basket and a laver.

Exit Acolyte.

CHORUS

                        The Birds agree
                        most heartily.
                            You're absolutely right.

Hymns and laud
are dear to god,
    but dinner's their delight

Yes, gratitude
is shown with food,
    so rise and offer up,

in witness of
our shrunken love,
    one miserable lamp chop!

'KORYPHAIOS

    Flutist, come in.*
    Now let our sacrifice begin

*Enter the Flutist, a Raven whose beak is an enormous flute
which is strapped to his mouth by means of a leather harness
After strenuous huffing, he manages to produce what are
unmistakably caws.*

PISTHETAIROS

Stop that raucous Rook!
               In the name of god,
what are you anyway?
                 I've seen some weird sights,
but this is the first time in my life I ever saw
a Blackbird propping his beak with a leather belt.*

*Exit Flutist. Enter Priest, followed by the Acolyte with the
paraphernalia of the sacrifice.*

At last.
    —Eminence, you may begin the inaugural sacrifice

PRIEST

Your humble servant, sir.
            —But where's my acolyte?

*The Acolyte steps forward. The Priest raises his hands and
begins the Bidding Prayer of the Birds.**

Now let us pray—
   PRAY TO THE HESTIA OF NESTS,
   TO THE HOUSEHOLDING HARRIER HAWK,
   TO ALL THE OLYMPIAN COCKS AND
      COQUETTES.
   TO THE SWOOPING STORK OF THE SEA—

PISTHETAIROS

ALL HAIL, THE STORK! HAIL, POSEIDON OF
   PINIONS!

PRIEST

   TO THE SWEETSINGER OF DELOS,
   THE APOLLONIAN SWAN,
   TO LETO THE QUEEN OF THE QUAIL,
   TO ARTEMIS THE PHOEBE—

PISTHETAIROS

HAIL TO THE PHOEBE, VIRGIN SISTER OF
   PHOIBOS!

PRIEST

   PRAY TO WOODPECKER PAN,.
   TO DOWITCHER KYBELE,
   MOTHER OF MORTALS AND GODS—

PISTHETAIROS

HAIL, DOWAGER QUEEN, GREAT MOTHER OF
   BUSTARDS!

PRIEST

   PRAY THAT THEY GRANT US
   HEALTH AND LENGTH OF LIFE,
   PRAY THAT THEY PROTECT US,
   pray for the Chians too*—

PISTHETAIROS

You know, I like the way he tacks those Chians on.

PRIEST

> COME, ALL HERO BIRDS,
> ALL HEROINE HENS AND PULLETS!
> COME, O GALLINULE!
> BRING DICKYBIRD AND DUNNOCK,
> COME, CROSSBILL AND BUNTING!
> ON DIPPER, ON DIVER,
> ON WHIMBREL AND FINCH!
> COME CURLEW AND CREEPER,
> ON PIPIT, ON PARROT,
> COME VULTURE, COME TIT—

PISTHETAIROS

Stop it, you fool! Stop that rollcall of the Birds!
Are you utterly daft, man, inviting Vultures and Eagles
and suchlike to our feast? Or weren't you aware
one single beak could tuck it all away?
Clear out, and take your blasted ribands with you.
So help me, I'll finish this sacrifice myself.

Exit Priest.

CHORUS

> Again we raise
> the hymn of praise
>   and pour the sacred wine.
>
> With solemn rite
> we now invite
>   the blessed gods to dine.
>
> But don't *all* come—
> perhaps just one,
>   and maybe then again,
>
> there's not enough
> (besides, it's tough),
>   so stay away. Amen.

PISTHETAIROS

Let us pray to the pinion'd gods—

Enter a hungry, ragged Poet, chanting.

POET

In all thy songs, O Muse,
let one city
praisèd be—
CLOUDCUCKOOLAND THE LOVELY!

PISTHETAIROS

Who spawned this spook?
        —Look here, who are you?

POET

One of the tribe of dulcet tongue and tripping speech—
        "the slave of Poesy,
        whose ardent soul
        the Muses hold in thrall,"
        as Homer hath it.*

PISTHETAIROS

Judging from your clothes, friend, your Muses must be
bankrupt. Tell me, bard, what ill wind plopped you here?

POET

I've been composing poems in honor of your new city—
oodles of little odes, some dedication-anthems,
songs for soprano voice, a lyric or two
à la Simonides—

PISTHETAIROS

        How long has your little poetic mill
been grinding out this chaff?

POET

> Why, simply ages.
> Long, long since my Muse commenced to sing
> Cloudcuckooland in all her orisons.

PISTHETAIROS

> Long ago?
> But that's impossible. This city's still a baby.
> I just now gave birth. I just baptised her.

POET

> *Ah, but swift are the mouths of the Muses,*
> *more swift than steeds the galloping news*
> *of the Muses!*

He turns to the altar and with outstretched hands invokes it in Pindaric parody.

> O Father,
>   Founder of Etna,*
>   of thy bounty give,
>   O Hiero, O Homonym,
>   Great Hero of the Fire,
>   just one slender sliv-
>   er to my desire,
>   some tidbit to savor,
>   some token of favor—

PISTHETAIROS

> You know, I think we'd better bribe this beggar bard
> to leave before we die of doggerel.

To the Acolyte.

> —You there,
> strip and let the beggar poet have your overcoat.

He hands the coat to the Poet.

Dress.

Why, you poor poet, you're shivering with cold.

POET

>My Muse accepts with thanks
>　　this modest donation.

>But first, before I leave,
>　　one brief quotation,
>　　a snatch of Pindar
>　　you might ponder—

PISTHETAIROS

Gods above, will this poor man's Pindar never leave?

POET

Undressed amidst the nomad Skyths,*
*　　the Frozen Poet fareth,*
as Beastly Cold as Bard may be,
*　　who Next-to-Nothing weareth.*

Genius, ah, hath deck'd his Song,
*　　but oh, th' Ingratitude!*
Whilst other Blokes be warm as Toast,
*　　the Poet's damn near Nude.*

You catch my drift?

PISTHETAIROS

Yes, I catch your drift.
You want some underwear.

To the Acolyte.

All right. off with it, lad.
We can't allow our delicate poets to freeze to death.
And now clear out, will you?

POET

I go, I go,
but first my final valediction to this little village—

Singing.

> *O Muse on golden throne,*
> *Muse with chattering teeth*
> *sing this capitol of cold,*
> *this frigorifical city!*

I have been where the glebe is frozen with frore.
I have traipsed where the furrows are sown with snow.

Alalai!

Alalai!

G'bye.

Exit Poet.

PISTHETAIROS

Well, how do you like that? Griping about the cold
after making off with an entire new winter outfit!
And how in the name of heaven did that poetic plague
discover us so fast?

To the naked and shivering Acolyte.

—You there, to work again.
Take up your laver and circle the altar, boy,
and we'll resume our inaugural sacrifice once again.
Quiet now, everyone.

As Pisthetairos approaches the altar with the sacrificial knife,
an itinerant Prophet with a great open tome of oracles makes
his appearance.

PROPHET

HALT! Forbear, I say!
Let no one touch the victim.

PISTHETAIROS

Who the hell are you,
may I ask?

PROPHET

I am a Prophet, sir, in person.

PISTHETAIROS

Then beat it.

PROPHET

Ah, the naughty wee scamp.
                        But we mustn't scoff.
Friend, I have brought you an oracle of the prophet Bakis,
transparently alluding to the city of Cloudcuckooland.

PISTHETAIROS

Why did you wait till after I founded my city
before disgorging this revelation of yours?

PROPHET

                                    Alas,
I could not come. The Inner Voice said No.

PISTHETAIROS

I suppose we'll have to hear you expound your oracle.

PROPHET

                                    Listen—

LO, IN THAT DAY WHEN THE WOLF AND THE
    CROW DO FOREGATHER AND COMPANION,
AND DOMICILE IN THE AIR, AT THAT POINT
    WHERE KORINTH KISSETH SIKYON*—

PISTHETAIROS

Look here, what has Korinth got to do with me?

PROPHET

                                    Why,
it's ambiguous, of course. Korinth signifies "air."

Resuming.

> PRESENT, I SAY, A WHITE SHEEP TO PANDORA,
> BUT TO THE SEER WHO BRINGS MY BEHEST:
> *IN PRIMIS*, A WARM WINTER COAT
> PLUS A PAIR OF SANDALS (THE BEST)—

PISTHETAIROS

The *best* sandals, eh?

PROPHET

Yup. Look in the book.

Resuming.

> ITEM, A GOBLET OF WINE,
> ITEM, A GIBLET OF GOAT—

PISTHETAIROS

Giblet? It says giblet?

PROPHET

Yup. Look in the book.

Resuming.

> IF, O BLESSÉD YOUTH, THOU DOST AS I ENJOIN,
> REGAL EAGLE WINGS THIS VERY DAY ARE
>   THINE.*
> NOT SO MUCH AS PIGEON FLUFF, IF THOU
>   DECLINE.

PISTHETAIROS

It really says that?

PROPHET

Yup. Look in the book.

PISTHETAIROS

Drawing out a huge tome from under his cloak.

You know, your oracles somehow don't mesh with mine,
and I got these from Apollo's mouth.

Listen—

LO, IF IT CHANCE THAT SOME FAKER INTRUDE,
TROUBLING THY WORSHIP AND SCROUNGING
    FOR FOOD,
            LET HIS RIBS BE BASHED
            AND HIS TESTICLES MASHED—

PROPHET

I suspect you're bluffing.

PISTHETAIROS

Nope. Look in the book.

Resuming.

SMITE ON, I SAY, IF ANY PROPHET SHOULD
    COME,
YEA, THOUGH HE SOARETH LIKE THE SWALLOW.
FOR THE GREATER THE FAKER,* THE HARDER
    HIS BUM
SHOULD BE BATTERED.
                    GOOD LUCK.
                            Signed,
                                APOLLO.

PROPHET

Honest? It says that?

PISTHETAIROS

Yup. Look in the book.

Suddenly throwing his tome at him and beating him.

Take that!
    And that!
        And that!

PROPHET

Ouch. Help!

PISTHETAIROS

Scat. Go hawk your prophecies somewhere else.

Exit Prophet. From the other side enters the geometrician and surveyor Meton,* his arms loaded with surveying instruments.

METON

The occasion that hath hied me hither—

PISTHETAIROS

                                    Not another!
State your business, stranger. What's your racket?
What tragic error brings you here?

METON

                                My purpose here
is a geodetic survey of the atmosphere of Cloudcuckooland
and the immediate allocation of all this aerial area
into cubic acres.

PISTHETAIROS

        Who are *you?*

METON

                    Who am *I?*
Why, Meton, of course. Who else could *I* be?
Geometer to Hellas by special appointment.
Also Kolonos.

PISTHETAIROS

And those tools?

METON

Celestial rules,
of course.
                Now attend, sir.
                        Taken *in extenso*,
our welkin resembles a cosmical charcoal-oven*
or potbellied stove worked by the convection principle,
though vaster. Now then, with the flue as my base,
and twirling the calipers thus, I obtain the azimuth,
whence, by calibrating the arc or radial sine—
you follow me, friend?

PISTHETAIROS

No, I don't follow you.

METON

No matter. Now then, by training the theodolite here
on the vectored zenith tangent to the Apex A,
I deftly square the circle, whose conflux, or C,
I designate as the center or axial hub of Cloudcuckooland,
whence, like global spokes or astral radii,
broad boulevards diverge centrifugally, forming,
as it were—

PISTHETAIROS

Why, this man's a regular Thales!

Whispering confidentially.

Pssst. Meton.

METON

Sir?

PISTHETAIROS

I've taken quite a shine to you.
Take my advice, friend, and decamp while there's still time.

METON

You anticipate danger, you mean?

PISTHETAIROS

The kind of danger
one meets in Sparta. You know, nasty little riots,
a few foreigners beaten up or murdered, knifings,
fighting in the streets and so on.

METON

Dear me, you mean
there might actually be revolution?

PISTHETAIROS

I certainly hope not.

METON

Then what *is* the trouble?

PISTHETAIROS

The new law. You see,
attempted fraud is now punishable by thrashing.

METON

Er, perhaps I'd best be going.

PISTHETAIROS

I'm half afraid
you're just a bit too late.
Yes!
Look out!
Here comes your thrashing!

He batters Meton with a surveying rod.

METON

HALP! MURDER!

PISTHETAIROS

I warned you. Go survey some other place, will you?

Exit Meton. From the other side enters an Inspector,* dressed in a magnificent military uniform and swaggering imperiously.

INSPECTOR

Fetch me the Mayor, yokel.

PISTHETAIROS

Who's this popinjay?

INSPECTOR

Inspector-general of Cloudcuckooland County, sir.
invested, I might add, with plenary powers—

PISTHETAIROS

Invested?
On whose authority?

INSPECTOR

Why, the powers vested in me
by virtue of this piddling piece of paper here
signed by one Teleas of Athens.

PISTHETAIROS

Look. Let me propose
a little deal, friend. I'll pay you off right now,
provided you leave the city.

INSPECTOR

                    A capital suggestion.
As it so happens, my presence is urgently required
at home. They're having one of their Great Debates.
The Persian crisis, you know.*

PISTHETAIROS

                         Really? Splendid.
I'll pay you off right now.

Violently beating the Inspector
                    Take that!
                         And that!

INSPECTOR

What does this outrage mean?

PISTHETAIROS

                    The payoff. Round One
of the Great Debate.

INSPECTOR

                    But this is mutiny! Insubordination!

To the Chorus.

Gentlemen, I call on you Birds to bear me witness
that this man wilfully assaulted an Inspector.

PISTHETAIROS

                         Shoo, fellow,
and take your ballot boxes with you* when you go.

Exit Inspector.

What confouded gall! Sending us one of their Inspectors
before we've even finished the Inaugural Service.

Enter an itinerant Legislator reading from a huge volume of laws

LEGISLATOR

BE IT HEREBY PROVIDED THAT IF ANY CLOUD-
CUCKOOLANDER SHALL WILFULLY INJURE OR
WRONG ANY CITIZEN OF ATHENS—

PISTHETAIROS

Gods, what now? Not *another* bore with a book?

LEGISLATOR

A seller of laws and statutes, sir, at your service.
Fresh shipment of by-laws on special sale
for only—

PISTHETAIROS

Perhaps you'd better demonstrate your wares.

LEGISLATOR

Reading.

BE IT HEREBY PROVIDED BY LAW THAT FROM
    THE DATE SPECIFIED BELOW
THE WEIGHTS AND MEASURES OF THE CLOUD-
    CUCKOOLANDERS ARE TO BE ADUSTED
TO THOSE IN EFFECT AMONG THE OLOPHYX-
    IANS—

PISTHETAIROS

Pummelling him

By god, I'll Olo-phyx you!

LEGISLATOR

Hey, mister, stop!

PISTHETAIROS

Get lost, you and your laws, or I'll carve mine
on the skin of your tail.

Exit Legislator. Enter Inspector

INSPECTOR

                    I summon the defendant Pisthetairos
to stand trial in court on charges of assault and battery
not later than April.

PISTHETAIROS

                    Good gods, are *you* back too?

He thrashes Inspector who runs off. Re-enter Legislator.

LEGISLATOR

IF ANY MAN, EITHER BY WORD OR ACTION, DO
  IMPEDE OR RESIST
A MAGISTRATE IN THE PROSECUTION OF HIS
  OFFICIAL DUTIES, OR REFUSE
TO WELCOME HIM WITH THE COURTESY PRE-
  SCRIBED BY LAW—

PISTHETAIROS

Great thundery Zeus are *you* back here too?

He drives the Legislator away. Re-enter Inspector.

INSPECTOR

I'll have you sacked. What's more, I'm suing you
for a fat two thousand.

PISTHETAIROS

                    By Zeus, I'll fix you
and your blasted ballot boxes once and for all!

Exit Inspector under a barrage of blows. Re-enter Legislator

LEGISLATOR

Remember that evening when you crapped in court?

PISTHETAIROS

                                                      Dammit

Someone arrest that pest!

Exit Legislator.

                              And this time stay away!
But enough's enough.
                              We'll take our goat inside
and finish this sacrifice in peace and privacy.

*Exit Pisthetairos into house, followed by Acolyte with basket
and slaves with the sacrifice.*

CHORUS*

Wheeling sharply and facing the audience.

> Praise Ye the Birds, O Mankind!
>   Our sway is over all.
> The eyes of the Birds observe you:
>   we see if any fail.
>
> We watch and guard all growing green,
>   protecting underwing
> this lavish lovely life of earth,
>   its birth and harvesting.
>
> We smite the mite, we slay the pest,
>   all ravagers that seize
> the good that burgeons in your buds
>   or ripens on your trees.
>
> Whatever makes contagion come,
>   whatever blights or seeks
> to raven in this green shall die,
>   devoured by our beaks.

KORYPHAIOS

You know, gentlemen, that proclamation that's posted
   everywhere in town–
WANTED, DEAD OR ALIVE! DIAGORAS OF MELOS.
ONE TALENT'S REWARD FOR ANY MAN WHO
   KILLS THE TYRANT!
Well, we Birds have published our own public procla-
   mation:–
"HEAR YE!
            WANTED DEAD OR ALIVE!
                         PHILOKRATES
   THE BIRDSELLER!
DEAD, 1 TALENTS REWARD. 4 TALENTS IF
TAKEN ALIVE,
       BUT PROCEED WITH CAUTION. THIS MAN
   IS DANGEROUS.
WANTED FOR MURDER AND CRUELTY TO BIRDS
   ON THE FOLLOWING COUNTS:–
For the Spitting of Finches, seven to a skewer;
item, for Disfiguring Thrushes by means of inflation;
item, for Insertion of Feathers in Blackbirds' nostrils:
item, for Unlawful Detention of Pigeons in Cages;
item, for Felonious Snaring of Innocent Pigeons;
item, for Flagrant Misuse of Traps and Decoy-devices."
So much for Philokrates.
               But as for you, dear spectators.
we give you solemn warning.
               If any boy in this audience
has as his hobby the keeping of Birds in captivity or cages.
we urgently suggest that you let your pets go free. Disobey.
and we'll catch *you* and lock you up in a wicker cage
or stake you out to a snare as a little decoy boy!

CHORUS

      How blessèd is our breed of Bird.
         dressed in fluff and feather,
      that, when hard winter holds the world,
         wears no clothes whatever.

And blazoned summer hurts no Bird,
  for when the sun leaps high,
and, priestly in that hellish light,
  the chaunting crickets cry,

the Birds keep cool among the leaves
  or fan themselves with flight;
while winter days we're snug in caves
  and nest with nymphs at night.

But Spring is joy, when myrtle blooms
  and Graces dance in trio,
and quiring Birds cantatas sing
  vivace e con brio.

KORYPHAIOS

Finally, gentlemen, a few brief words about the First Prize
and the striking advantages of casting your vote for *THE
  BIRDS* of Aristophanes—
advantages compared to which that noble prince,
poor Paris of Troy, was very shabbily bribed
indeed.
          First on our list of gifts comes a little item
that every judge's greedy heart must be panting to possess.
I refer, of course, to those lovely little owls of Laurium,
sometimes called the coin of the realm.
                              Yes, gentlemen,
these lovely owls, we promise, will flock to you by the
thousand, settle down in your wallets for good and hatch
you a brood of nice little nest eggs.
                        Secondly, gentlemen, we promise
to redesign your houses.
                        See, the sordid tenements vanish,
while in their place rise splendid shrines whose dizzy
heights, like Eagle-eyries,* hang in heaven.
                              Are you perhaps
a politician faced with the vexing problem of insufficient
plunder? Friend, your problems are over. Accept as our gift
to you a pair of Buzzard claws designed with special hooks

for more efficient grafting.

As for heavy eaters,
those suffering from biliousness, heartburn, acid indigestion
or other stomach ailments and upsets, we proudly present
them
with special lifetime Bird-crops, guaranteed to be virtually
indestructible.

If, however, gentlemen, you withhold your vote,
you'd better do as the statues do and wear a metal lid
against our falling guano.

I repeat.

Vote against *THE BIRDS*,
and every Bird in town will cover you with—vituperation!

The Chorus turns and faces the stage. Enter Pisthetairos.

PISTHETAIROS

Birds, the omens are favorable. Our sacrifice has been
auspicious. But I wonder where in the world our messenger
is with news about our wall.

A sound of furious panting offstage.

Aha. There he is now.
I'd recognize that awful huffing and puffing anywhere.
Those are the true Olympic pants and puffs I hear.

Enter Messenger, panting.

MESSENGER

Where anh where hoo where uh where can he be?
Where is Pisthetairos hanh?

PISTHETAIROS

Here hunh here.

MESSENGER

Whew, the wall's all up! The wall's done!

PISTHETAIROS

Splendid!

MESSENGER

What a wonderful, whopping, well-built wall! Whew!
Why, that wall's so wide that if you hitched up
four Trojan Horses to two huge chariots
with those braggarts Proxenides in one and Theogenes in the
 other,
they could pass head-on. *That's* the width of your wall!

PISTHETAIROS

Wow, what a width!

MESSENGER

And what a height! Measured it myself.
Six hundred feet high!

PISTHETAIROS

Poseidon, what a height!
Who in the world could have built a wall like that?

MESSENGER

The Birds.
Nobody but Birds.
Not one Egyptian.
No bricklayers. No carpenters. Or masons.
Only the Birds. I couldn't credit my eyes.
What a sight it was:
Thirty thousand Cranes
whose crops were all loaded with boulders and stones,*
while the Rails with their beaks blocked out the rocks
and thousands of Storks came bringing up bricks
and Plovers and Terns and seabirds by billions
transported the water right up to the sky!

PISTHETAIROS

                                      Heavens!
But which Birds hauled the mortar up?

MESSENGER

                                      Herons,
in hods.

PISTHETAIROS

    But how was the mortar heaped in the hods?

MESSENGER

Gods, now *that* was a triumph of engineering skill!
Geese burrowed their feet like shovels beneath
and heaved it over their heads to the hods.

PISTHETAIROS

                                      They did?
Ah Feet! Ah, Feet! O incredible feat!*
What can compete with a pair of feet?

MESSENGER

                                      And, sir,
you should have seen the Ducks with their aprons on
go hauling the bricks! And how the Swallows came
swooping, dangling their trowels behind them like boys,
and darting and dipping with mouthfuls of mortar!

PISTHETAIROS

                                      Why,
if this is true, then human labor is obsolete.
But what happened next? Who finished off the job?
Who did the woodwork on the wall?

MESSENGER

                              Mastercraftsmen birds.

It was Pelicans, like carpenters, with handy hatchet-beaks
who hewed the gates, and what with the racket and hubbub
of all that hacking and chopping and hewing and banging,
sir, you'd have sworn it was a shipyard down at the docks.
Or so it sounded to me.

But the gates are done,
the bolts shot home, watchbirds make their rounds
with clanging bells, the guards patrol their beats
and every tower along the circuit of the wall
blazes with its watchfire. And in three words, sir,
all is well.

But I must go and wash my face.
My job is done. The rest is up to you.

Exit Messenger.

KORYPHAIOS

Well,
wasn't it a wonder the way that wall of ours shot up?

PISTHETAIROS

A damn sight too wonderful. If you're asking me,
I think it's all a lie.
—But look what's coming:
another messenger, and a sentry judging by his looks.

Enter Sentry, whirling on stage in the wild steps of a military dance.

—What are you, fellow? A soldier or a ballerina?

SENTRY

ALAS! ALACKADAY!
OCHONE!
WOE IS ME!

PISTHETAIROS

Well, what's troubling *you?*

SENTRY

                            Sir, we are diddled
and undone.
                   Some god has given us the slip,
I wot not which. Carommed through the gates
out into territorial air. The Daws on guard
never spotted him.

PISTHETAIROS

                   Gad. A national scandal.
Which god?

SENTRY

               We couldn't tell. But he was wearing wings,
that much we know.

PISTHETAIROS

                 Were Pursuitbirds sent up
to intercept him?

SENTRY

              Everything we had took off, sir.
The Sparrowhawk Reserve, thirty thousand Falcons,
every claw-carrying Harrier we could throw
in the sky:—Kestrels, Buzzards, Owls, Eagles,
Vultures, you name it.
                 Why, the whole atmosphere
is throbbing and buzzing with the whirr of beating wings
as they comb the clouds for that sneaky little god.
If you're asking me, he's not so far away either.
He's hereabouts. I'm sure.

Exit Sentry.

PISTHETAIROS

                 Where's my bow?
Bring me my sling!

Archerbirds, fall in!
Now shoot to kill.
Dammit, where's my sling?

CHORUS

Now words are weak
and ACTIONS speak
ineffably of War.

Let every Bird
for battle gird:
the gods are at our door:

Rise up, defend
your native land!
Go mobilize the Air!

Immortal spies
now prowl our skies.
And saboteurs. Take care.

KORYPHAIOS

Quiet.
I hear the whirr of beating wings.
Listen. Some god comes whizzing through our air.

*With a loud whoosh and a burst of baroque movement and
color, Iris descends in the machine. She is a young girl with
golden wings and billowing rainbow-colored robes. From her
dress and hair, in gracious and extravagant loops of color,
pennants and ribbons and streamers trail out behind.*

PISTHETAIROS

Ship ahoy!
Belay!
Where are you cruising?
Down anchors!
And stop luffing those wings.
Now who are you? Home Port? Purpose of voyage?

IRIS

I am Iris the fleet.

PISTHETAIROS

> Clippership or sloop?

IRIS

What does this mean?

PISTHETAIROS

> Some Buzzard flap up

and arrest that bitch.

IRIS

> You dare arrest *me?*

What sort of joke is this?

PISTHETAIROS

> You'll see, sister.

IRIS

But I must be dreaming. This can't be real.

PISTHETAIROS

What gate did you enter by? Answer, you slut.

IRIS

Gates? What would a goddess know about gates?

PISTHETAIROS

A glib little piece. Just listen to those lies.
—Well, did you report to the Daw on duty at the gate?
Mum, eh?
> Where's your Storkpass?

IRIS

I must be mad.

PISTHETAIROS

What? You never even applied?

IRIS

You must be mad.

PISTHETAIROS

Was your form filled out by Colonel Cock
and properly punched?

IRIS

Just let him try!
Why, the very idea!

PISTHETAIROS

So that's your game, is it?
To sneak in here, infiltrate our territorial air,
spy on our city—

IRIS

But where can a poor god go?

PISTHETAIROS

How should I know? But not here, by god!
You're trespassing. What's more, it would serve you right
if I ordered you put to death this very instant.
If ever a god deserved to die, that god is you.

IRIS

But I *can't* die.

PISTHETAIROS

Well, you damn well should.

A pretty pickle it would be if the whole world
obeyed the Birds while you gods got uppity
and defied your betters.

           Now then, you aerial yacht,
state your business here.

IRIS

           My business? Why,
I am bearing the following message from my father Zeus
to mankind:
           "LET HOLOCAUSTS MAKE GLAD THY
GODS AND MUTTON BARBECUES ON BEEFY
ALTARS TOAST, YEA, TILL EVERY STREET DOTH
REEK WITH ROAST AMBROSIALLY."

PISTHETAIROS

           Hmm. I think he wants a sacrifice.
But to which gods?

IRIS

           To *which* gods? To *us*, of course.
Who else could he mean?

PISTHETAIROS

           But that's quite absurd.
You, gods? I mean, really!

IRIS

           Name me any other gods.

PISTHETAIROS

Why, the Birds, madam. Birds are now the gods.
Men worship Birds, not gods. Good gods, no!

IRIS

*In the high tragic manner.**

Then beware, O Mole, lest thou court the choler
of the gallèd gods, and Justice with the angry pick
of peevèd Zeus prise up thy pedestals
and topple all thy people, leaving not a smitch;
yea, and forkèd levin sear thee to a crisp,
lambasted low amongst thy mortal porticoes
by lightnings blunderbuss'd, yea—

PISTHETAIROS

                                        Listen, lady,
stow the tragic guff. You're starting to slobber.
And kindly stop twitching.
                                        What do you think I am?
Some poor Lydian or Phrygian slave* you can browbeat
with the bogey-talk?
                                        Go back and tell your Zeus
if he messes around with me, I'll fry him to a cinder!
What doth the poet say?*
        Aye, with eagles belching levin,
        I shall scorch the halls of heav'n,
        till Zeus doth frizzle in his juice
        and Amphion, e'en Amphion—
                                        —But what am I saying?
How does Amphion fit in here?
                                        Well, no matter.
But you tell your Zeus that if he crosses me, by god,
I'll send six hundred Porphyrions up against him,
and every Bird-Jack of the lot tricked out as a panther.
I'd like to see his face. I remember the time
when one poor piddling little Porphyrion
was one too many for Zeus.
                                        But as for *you*,
Miss Messenger Iris, sail my way once more
and I'll lay my course right up your lovely legs,
and board you at the top.
                                        Mark my words:
you'll be one flabbergasted little goddess
when you feel the triple ram on this old hulk.

IRIS

What a disgusting way to talk.

PISTHETAIROS

Skedaddle, slut.

IRIS

Just you wait till my Father hears about this.

PISTHETAIROS

Heaven defend me from this flying flirt. Beat it!
Go singe some youngster with your lechery, will you?

Exit Iris in the machine.

CHORUS

The gods' attack
has been rolled back,
    rebuffed by our Blockade.

Let god and man
now heed our ban:
    NO TRANSETHEREAL TRADE!

No more, no more
do victuals soar;
    no savory ascends;

and chops and stew
are now taboo:
    the party's over, friends!

PISTHETAIROS

You know, its rather odd about that other messenger
we despatched to earth. He should be back by now.

*Enter Herald in great haste. He throws himself to the ground
at Pisthetairos' feet and salaams profoundly.*

HERALD

O Pisthetairos! O Paragon! O Pink!
Thou Apogee of Genius! Sweet Flower of Finesse!
O Phoenix of Fame! Flimflam's Non-Pareil!
O of every noble attribute the Plus!
O Happy Happy Chap! O Blest! O Most!
O Best!—
             oh, balls.

PISTHETAIROS

                        You were about to say, my friend,
when you so rudely interrupted yourself?

HERALD

Rising and crowning Pisthetairos.

Deign, my lord, to accept this crown of solid gold,
proffered in honor of your glorious wisdom and chicane
by an adoring world.

PISTHETAIROS

                        I am deeply honored sir.
But why should man's election fall on me?

HERALD

O fabulous founder of great Cloudcuckooland,
how can you ask such a question? Have you not heard
that Pisthetairos has become the darling of the mortal
      world,
a name to conjure with? That all mankind
has gone Cloudcuckoolandophile,
madly, utterly?
                        And yet, only yesterday,
before your dispensation in the skies became a fact,
the Spartan craze had swept the faddish world.
Why, men went mad with mimicry of Sokrates,*
affected long hair, indifferent food,
rustic walking sticks, total bathlessness,

and led, in short, what I can only call
a Spartan existence.
             But then suddenly, overnight,
the Birds became the vogue, the *dernier cri*
of human fashion.* And men immediately began
to feather their own nests; to cluck and brood;
play ducks and drakes; grub for chickenfeed;
hatch deals, and being rooked or gulled,
to have their little gooses cooked. But if they grouse,
they still are game.
             In sum, the same old life,
‚but feathered over with the faddish thrills of being
chic.
        But the latest word in Birds is names.
The gimpy peddler is tagged Old Partridge now;
Menippos is called Cuckoo; Opountios, Stool Pigeon;
Philokles is the Lark; Theogenes, the Pseudo-Goose;
Lykourgos, Lame Duck; Chairephon is Bats;
Syrakosios, of course, is called the Jaybird,
and as for Meidias, why, he's the Sitting Duck—
and judging from that ugly clobbered beak of his,
no man ever missed.
            And that's not all.
Mankind has gone so utterly batty over Birds
that all the latest songs are filled with them—
Swallows, Pigeons, Ducks, Geese, you name it.
Any tune with feathers in it or a pinch or fluff
becomes a hit.
           And that's how matters stand
below.
        But one last point before I leave.
Vast swarms and coveys of men are on the move,
all migrating here to Cloudcuckooland in quest of wings
and the Feathered Way of Life. Somehow, sir,
you'll have to wing these mortal immigrants.

Exit Herald.

PISTHETAIROS

                                       Gad!

We'd best get busy.

To a Slave.

> —You there.
>   Run inside.
> Stuff every hamper you can find with sets of wings
> and tell Manes to bring them out. I'll stay here
> to give my greeting to these wingless refugees in person.

Exit Slave.

CHORUS

> Upon thy head, Cloudcuckooland,
>   the crown of praise we set:
> O Beautiful for Swarming Skies—

PISTHETAIROS

> —Don't count your chickens yet.

CHORUS

> This feather'd isle, this pinion'd place,
>   where martyr-Birds have bled,
> where men aspire on wings of fluff—

Enter Manes, slowly and empty-handed.

PISTHETAIROS

> —Their legs are made of lead.

Exit Manes.

CHORUS

> What greater bliss can men require?
>   Here the lovely Graces go,
> and Wisdom strolls with sweet Desire,
>   and Peace comes tripping slow.

Enter Manes carrying two wings.

PISTHETAIROS

She's miles ahead of Manes.

                    —Dammit, blockhead, move!

CHORUS

            To work, dull clod! Heave-ho the wings!

Exit Manes.
To Pisthetairos.

                Now show him you're the master.
                Flog him, thrash him—

Enter Manes with two more wings.

PISTHETAIROS

                                —What's the use?
                A mule could manage faster.

Exit Manes.

CHORUS

                Now sort the wings in pinion-piles
                    by order of professions:
                Seabirds' wings for nautical types,
                Warblers' for musicians—

Enter Manes with three wings.

PISTHETAIROS

    —So help me, Kestrels, if I don't bash your head
        to a pulp, you lazy, stupid, bungling ass!

*Beats him. Manes scurries off, instantly reappearing with
crates and hampers of wings which he quickly dumps and
sorts into the appropriate piles. Suddenly from offstage is
heard the tenor voice of Delinquent, singing:*

If I had the wings of an Eagle,*
o'er this barren blue brine I would fly . . .

PISTHETAIROS

That messenger of ours was telling the truth, by god.
Here comes someone crooning Eagle-ballads.

Enter Delinquent,* a strapping boy in his teens.

DELINQUENT

Some kicks!
There's nothin' on earth like flyin'! Whee!
                                        Chee,
Cloudcuckooland's the roost for me! Hey, man,
I'm bats about the Birds! I'm with it chum!
I wanna be a Bird! I want your way of life!

PISTHETAIROS

Which way? We Birds have bushels of ways.

DELINQUENT

If it's strictly for the Birds, then it's for me, man.
But best of all I like that splendid custom you've got
that permits a little Bird to choke his daddy dead.

PISTHETAIROS

True. We think it very manly of a young Bird
if he walks up and takes a poke at his old man.

DELINQUENT

                                   That's it, Dad.
Exactly why I'm here. I want to throttle
the old man and inherit his jack.

PISTHETAIROS

                          One moment.

We Birds observe another custom older still.
You'll find it preserved in the Scrolls of the Storks. I quote:
"ONCE THE AGED STORK HATH REARED HIS
    BROOD
AND HIS CHICKS HAVE MADE THEIR MAIDEN
    FLIGHT ALONE,
THEY MUST IN TURN SUPPORT THEIR FATHER IN
    HIS AGE."

DELINQUENT

A fat lot of good I've got from coming here, chum,
if I have to go back home and support the old man.

PISTHETAIROS

I tell you what. You seem a decent lad,
and I'll adopt you as our city's official Mascot-Bird.
But first some good advice I received as a toddler
at my mother's knee:
                        Don't drub your dad.
Take this wing instead.
                        With your other hand,
accept this spur. Here, your helmet is this crest.
Now march off, rookie. Drill, stand your guard,
live on your pay and let your father be.
You look aggressive: flutter off to Thrace.
There's fighting there.

DELINQUENT

                        By god, I think you're right.
What's more, I'm game.

PISTHETAIROS

                        You damn well better be.

*Exit Delinquent. From the other side enters the dithryambic
poet Kinesias. His splay-footed galumphing entrance is in
sharp contrast to his aerial pretensions.*

KINESIAS

> On gossamer I go,
> delicately wending,*
> up, up, up the airy stairs
> of Poesy ascending—

PISTHETAIROS

By god, we'll need a boatload of wings at least
to get this limping poet off the ground!

KINESIAS

> —forth through the Vast Unknown,
> original, alone—

PISTHETAIROS

Welcome, Kinesias, bard of balsa-wood!
What made you whirl you splay-foot hither, bard?

KINESIAS

> I yearn, I burn, thou know'st it well,
> to be a lilting Philomel.

PISTHETAIROS

A little less lilt, please. Could you stoop to prose?

KINESIAS

Wings, dull wight, wings!
                    Vouchsafe me wings
to percolate amidst the churning scud and rack
of yon conceited clouds from which I'll pluck and cull
tornado similes of blizzard speech.

PISTHETAIROS

You mean you plagiarize the clouds?

KINESIAS

> Ah, my dear sir,
> but our poet's craft depends completely on the clouds.*
> Why, the most resplendent poem is but the insubstantial
> shimmer refracted from that blue and bubbled murk of
> froth, that featherfillip'd air.
>> Judge for yourself.

PISTHETAIROS

I won't.

KINESIAS

> Ah, but you shall, dear boy, you shall.
> I'll do my Aerial Aria, and just for you.
>> Ready?

Singing.

> *Now wingèd wraiths*
> *of the hovering Plover*
> *over yon Ether rove—*

PISTHETAIROS

GALE WARNINGS POSTED! STAND BY, ALL SHIPS
AT SEA!

KINESIAS

> *—over the billows pillow'd aloft,*
> *in the buffeting gust of the gathered gale—*

PISTHETAIROS

By god, I'll give you some buffets you won't like!

*He snatches a pair of large wings from a pile and beats
Kinesias who runs about, still spouting.*

KINESIAS

> *—now north, now south,*
> *and where they fare, fare I,*
> *cutting my wake*
> *on the harborless lake*
> *of the featherfillip'd sky.*

Get that, old boy? A catchy figure, what?

PISTHETAIROS

Lashing him again.

Get that? What? No taste for featherfillips, poet?

KINESIAS

What a beastly way to welcome a poetic genius
for whose services the entire civilized world competes!

PISTHETAIROS

Then stay with us. You can train an All-Bird
Chorus. Leotrophides will conduct his own compositions.
He likes the delicate stuff.

KINESIAS

> Durst despise me, sir?

Know then, I ne'er shall cease from Poesy
until with wings I waltz upon Cloudcuckooland.

> Farewell.

Exit Kinesias. Enter an Informer in a tattered coat, singing.

INFORMER

> *What suspicious Birds are these**
> *that own no clothes and house in trees?*
> *O Cuckoo, Cuckoo, tell me true!*

PISTHETAIROS

We've passed the nuisance stage. This is crisis.
Here comes a warbler humming treason-trills.

INFORMER

                               Ho!
Again I cry:
        O Cuckoo, Cuckoo, tell me true!

PISTHETAIROS

I think it must be an epigram on his tattered coat.
He's so cold he's calling the Cuckoo to bring the Spring.*
Poets are always talking out loud to Cuckoos in April.

INFORMER

You there. Where's the guy who's handing out the wings?

PISTHETAIROS

You're looking at him now. What do *you* want, friend?

INFORMER

Wings, fellow, wings! Got it?

PISTHETAIROS

                            I get it:
to hide the holes in your coat.*

INFORMER

                       Listen, Buster:
my business is the indictment of islands for subversive
activities.* You see in me a professional informer.

PISTHETAIROS

                          A splendid calling

INFORMER

Also an *agent provocateur* of lawsuits and investigations.
That's why I want the wings. They'd come in handy

for whizzing around the islands delivering my indictments
and handing out subpoenas in person.

PISTHETAIROS

I see. And these wings
would increase your efficiency?

INFORMER

Increase my efficiency?
Impossible. But they'd help me dodge the pirates I meet
en route. Then, coming home, I'd load the crops of the
Cranes with writs and suits for ballast.

PISTHETAIROS

And *that's* your trade?
A husky lad like yourself earning his livelihood
by indicting foreigners?

INFORMER

But what am I supposed to do?
I don't know how to dig.

PISTHETAIROS

Great Zeus Almighty,
Aren't there enough honest means of earning a living
without this dirty little dodge of hatching suits?

INFORMER

Listen, mister: it's wings I want, not words.

PISTHETAIROS

But my words *are* wings.

INFORMER

Your words are *wings?*

PISTHETAIROS

But of course. How else do you think mankind won its
wings if not from words?

INFORMER

From words?

PISTHETAIROS

Wings from words.
You know the old men, how they loll around at the
   barbershop*
grousing and bitching about the younger generation?—
"Thanks to that damned Dieitrephes* and his damned
advice," growls one, "my boy has flown the family nest
to take a flier on the horses."
                     "Hell,"
pipes another, "you should see that kid of mine:
he's gone so damn batty over those tragic plays,
he flies into fits of ecstacy and gets goosebumps
all over."

INFORMER

And *that's* how words give wings?

PISTHETAIROS

Right.
Through dialectic the mind of man takes wing and soars;
he is morally and spiritually uplifted. And so I hoped
with words of good advice to wing you on your way
toward some honest trade.

INFORMER

It just won't work.

PISTHETAIROS

But why won't it?

INFORMER

     I can't disgrace the family name
We've been informers now for several generations,
you see.
    So give me wings—Hawk's or Kestrel's
will suit me fine, but anything's all right by me
provided they're fast and light. I'll slip them on,
dart out to the islands with stacks of subpoenas and
summons, whizz back home to defend the case in court
then zip right back to the islands again.

PISTHETAIROS

           I get it.
When they arrive, they find their case is lost by default
they've been condemned *in absentia*.

INFORMER

           You've got it

PISTHETAIROS

And while they're coming here, you're going there
to confiscate their property? Right?

INFORMER

           You've got it.
I'll whirr around like a top.

PISTHETAIROS

        Right. I've got it:
you're a top. And guess what I've got here for you,
a lovely little set of Korkyrean wings.

He pulls out a whip.

INFORMER

Hey, that's a whip!

PISTHETAIROS

>   Not a whip, it's wings
> to make your little top go round

He lashes Informer with the whip

>   Got it?

INFORMER

Ouch! Owwooooo!

PISTHETAIROS

>   Flap your wings, Birdie!
> That's it, old top, wobble on your way!
>   By god,
> I'll make this legal whirligig go round!

*Exit Informer under the lash. Pisthetairos signals to his slaves
to pick up the piles of wings.*

>   —Hey,
> you there. Gather up the wings and bring them inside

Exeunt Pisthetairos and Attendants with the hampers of wings.

CHORUS*

> Many the marvels I have seen,
>   the wonders on land and sea;
> but the strangest sight I ever saw
>   was the weird KLEONYMOS-tree.
>
> It grows in faraway places;
>   its lumber looks quite stout,
> but the wood is good for nothing,
>   for the heart is rotten out.
>
> In Spring it grows gigantic
>   with sycophantic green,
> and bitter buds of slander
>   on every bough are seen.

But when. like war, cold winter comes
  this strange KLEONYMOS yields.
instead of leaves like other trees.
  a crop of coward's shields

And far away (but not so far).
  we saw a second wonder.
a place of awful, dismal dark–
  when the sun goes under

And there by day dead heroes come
  and talk with living men.
and while it's light no ghost will hurt.
  but when it's dark again.

then thieves and ghosts take common shape.
  and who knows which is which?
So wise men dodge that dive at night–
  but most of all the rich

For any man who ventures in
  may meet ORESTES there.
the ghost who paralyzes men.
  the thief who strips them bare.

Enter Prometheus. so muffled in blankets as to be com
pletely unrecognizable. His every motion is furtive. but his
furtiveness is hampered by an immense umbrella which he
carries underneath his blankets. He speaks in a whisper*

PROMETHEUS

Easy does it. I hope old Zeus can't see me.

To a Bird.

Psst. Where's Pisthetairos?

PISTHETAIROS

                    What in the world is *this?*
–Who are you. blanket?

PROMETHEUS

        Shh. Are there any gods
on my trail?

PISTHETAIROS

        Gods? No. not a god in sight.
Who *are* you?

PROMETHEUS

        What's the time? Is it dark yet?

PISTHETAIROS

You want the time? It's still early afternoon.
Look, who the hell *are* you?

PROMETHEUS

        Is it milking-time. or later?

PISTHETAIROS

Look. you stinking bore—

PROMETHEUS

        What's the weather doing?
How's the visibility? Clear skies? Low ceiling?

PISTHETAIROS

Raising his stick

        By god.
if you won't talk—

PROMETHEUS

        Dark. eh? Good. I'm coming out.

Uncovers

PISTHETAIROS

Hullo: it's Prometheus!

PROMETHEUS

Shh. Don't make a sound.

PISTHETAIROS

What's the matter?

PROMETHEUS

Shh. Don't even whisper my name.
If Zeus spots me here, he'll cook my goose but good.
Now then, if you want to learn the lay of the land
in heaven, kindly open up this umbrella here
and hold it over my head while I'm talking.
Then the gods won't see me.

*Pisthetairos takes the umbrella, opens it up, and holds it over
Prometheus.*

PISTHETAIROS

Say, that's clever.
Prometheus all over.*
—All right. Pop underneath
and give us your news.

PROMETHEUS

Brace yourself.

PISTHETAIROS

Shoot.

PROMETHEUS

Zeus has had it.

PISTHETAIROS

Since when?

PROMETHEUS

Since the moment
you founded the city of Cloudcuckooland. Since that day
not a single sacrifice, not even a whiff of smoke,
no savories, no roast, nothing at all
has floated up to heaven. In consequence, my friend,
Olympos is starving to death. And that's not the worst of it.
All the Stone Age gods* from the hill country
have gone wild with hunger, screaming and gibbering away
like a lot of savages. And what's more, they've threatened
war unless Zeus succeeds in getting your Bird-embargo lifted
and the tidbit shipments back on the move once more.

PISTHETAIROS

You mean to say there are *other* gods in Heaven?
Stone Age gods?

PROMETHEUS

Stone Age gods for Stone Age people.
Exekestides must have something to worship.

PISTHETAIROS

Heavens,
they *must* be savages. But what do you call them?

PROMETHEUS

We call them Triballoi.

PISTHETAIROS

Triballoi? From the same root
as our word "trouble," I suppose.

PROMETHEUS

Very probably, I think
But give me your attention. At present these Triballoi gods
have joined with Zeus to send an official embassy

to sue for peace. Now here's the policy you must follow:
flatly reject any offers of peace they make you
until Zeus agrees to restore his sceptre to the Birds
and consents to give you Miss Universe* as your wife.

PISTHETAIROS

But who's Miss Universe?

PROMETHEUS

A sort of Beauty Queen,
the sign of Empire and the symbol of divine supremacy.
It's she who keeps the keys to Zeus' thunderbolts
and all his other treasures—Divine Wisdom,
Good Government, Common Sense, Naval Bases,
Slander, Libel, Political Graft, Sops to the Voters—

PISTHETAIROS

And *she* keeps the keys?

PROMETHEUS

Take it from me, friend.
Marry Miss Universe and the world is yours.
—You understand
why I had to tell you this? As Prometheus, after all,
my philanthropy is proverbial.

PISTHETAIROS

Yes, we worship you
as the inventor of the barbecue.*

PROMETHEUS

Besides, I loathe the gods.

PISTHETAIROS

The loathing's mutual, I know.

PROMETHEUS

                     Just call me Timon:
I'm a misanthrope of gods.

                    —But I must be running along.
Give me my parasol. If Zeus spots me now,
he'll think I'm an ordinary one-god procession. I'll pretend
to be the girl behind the boy behind the basket.

PISTHETAIROS

Here—take this stool and watch yourself march by.

*Exit Prometheus in solemn procession, draped in his blanket,
the umbrella in one hand, the stool in the other. Pisthetairos
and the Attendants retire.*

CHORUS*

        There lies a marsh in Webfoot Land,
           the Swamp of Dismal Dread,
      and there we saw foul SOKRATES
           come calling up the dead.

      And there that cur PEISANDROS came
           to see if he could see
      the soul he'd lost while still alive
           by dying cowardly.

      He brought a special sacrifice,
           a little camel lamb;
      then, like Odysseus, slit its throat—
           he slits its throat and ran!

      And then a phantom shape flew down,
           a specter cold and wan,
      and on the camel's blood he pounced—
           the vampire CHAIREPHON!

*Enter the Peace Delegation from Olympos: first, Poseidon, a
god of immense and avuncular dignity, carrying a trident,
then Herakles with lion skin and club, a god with the
character and build of a wrestler and an appetite to match.*

and finally Triballos, hopelessly tangled up in the unfamiliar robes of Olympian civilization.

POSEIDON

Here we are. And there before us, ambassadors,
lies Cloudcuckooland.

Triballos, by now hopelessly snarled up in his robes, trips and falls flat on his face.

         —Damn you! Back on your feet,
you hulking oaf. Look, you've got your robes
all twisted up.
        No. Screw them around to the right.
This way. Where's your dignity, you heavenly hick?
O Democracy, I fear your days are numbered
if Heaven's diplomatic corps is recruited like this!
Dammit, stop twitching! Gods, I've never seen
a gawkier god than you!
        —Look here, Herakles,
how should we proceed in your opinion?

HERAKLES

            You hoid me,
Poseidon. If I had my way, I'd throttle the guy,
any guy, what dared blockade the gods.

POSEIDON

          My dear nephew,
have you forgotten that the purpose of our mission here
is to treat for peace?

HERAKLES

        I'd throttle him all the more.

Enter Pisthetairos, followed by Attendants with cooking utensils. He pointedly ignores the presence of the Divine Delegation.

PISTHETAIROS

To Attendants

Hand me the cheese grater. Vinegar, please. All right.
now the cheese. Poke up that fire, somebody.

POSEIDON

Mortal, three immortal gods give you greeting.

Dead Silence.

Mortal, three immortal—

PISTHETAIROS

Shush: I'm slicing pickles.

HERAKLES

Hey, what kind of meat is dat?

PISTHETAIROS

Those are jailbirds
sentenced to death on the charge of High Treason
against the Sovereign Birds.

HERAKLES

And dat luscious gravy
gets poured on foist?

PISTHETAIROS

Looking up for the first time.

Why hullo there: it's Herakles!
What do you want?

POSEIDON

Mortal, as the official spokesman
for the Divine Delegation, I venture to suggest that—

PISTHETAIROS

Holding up an empty bottle.

Drat it. We're out of oil.

HERAKLES

Out of oil?
Say, dat's a shame. Boids should be basted good.

POSEIDON

—As I was on the point of saying, official Olympos
regards the present hostilities as utterly pointless.
Further, I venture to observe that you Birds
have a great deal to gain from a kindlier Olympos.
I might mention, for instance, a supply of clean rainwater
for your Birdbaths and a perpetual run, say,
of halcyon days. On some such terms as these
we are formally empowered by Zeus to sign the articles
of peace.

PISTHETAIROS

Poseidon, you forget: it was not the Birds
who began this war. Moreover, peace is our desire
as much as yours. And if you gods stand prepared
to treat in good faith, I see no obstacle to peace.
None whatsoever. Our sole demand is this:
Zeus must restore his royal sceptre to the Birds.
If this one trifling concession seems agreeable to you,
I invite you all to dinner.

HERAKLES

Youse has said enough.
I vote Yes.

POSEIDON

You contemptible, idiotic glutton!
Would you dethrone your own Father?

PISTHETAIROS

I object, Poseidon.
Look at it in this light.
Can you gods be unaware
that you actually stand to increase, not diminish your power,
by yielding your present supremacy to the Birds? Why,
as things stand now, men go skulking around
under cover of the clouds, with impunity committing perjury
and in your name too. But conclude alliance with the Birds,
gentlemen, and your problems are over forever. How?
Suppose, for instance, some man swears a solemn oath
be Zeus and the Raven and then breaks his word. Suddenly
down swoops a Raven when he's least suspecting it
and pecks out his eyes!

POSEIDON

Holy Poseidon! You know,
I think you've got something there.

HERAKLES

Youse is so right.

POSEIDON

To Triballos.

What do you say?

TRIBALLOS

Fapple gleep.

HERAKLES

Dat's Stone Age for Yeah.*

PISTHETAIROS

And that's not all.
Suppose some fellow vows to make a sacrifice to the gods
and then later changes his mind or tries to procrastinate.

thinking, *The mills of the gods grind slow;*
well, so do mine.
We Birds, I can promise you,
will put a stop to sophistry like that.

POSEIDON

Stop it? But how?

PISTHETAIROS

Someday our man will be busily counting up his cash
or lolling around in the tub, singing away.
and a Kite will dive down like a bolt from the blue.
snatch up two of his sheep or a wad of cash
and whizz back up to the gods with the loot.

HERAKLES

Friend.
youse is right. Zeus should give dat sceptre
back to the Birds.

POSEIDON

What do *you* think, Triballos''

HERAKLES

Threatening him with his club.

Vote Yes, bub, or I'll drub youse.

TRIBALLOS

Schporckl nu?
Momp gapa birdschmoz kluk.

HERAKLES

See? He votes wid me

POSEIDON

If you both see eye to eye, I'll have to go along.

HERAKLES

Dat does it. Hey, youse. The sceptre's yours.

PISTHETAIROS

Dear me, I nearly forgot one trifling condition.
We Birds willingly waive any claim we might have to Hera:
Zeus can have her. We don't object in the slightest.
But I must have Miss Universe as my wife. On that demand
I stand absolutely firm.

POSEIDON

Then you won't have peace.
Good afternoon.

The Delegation prepares to leave, Herakles with great reluctance.

PISTHETAIROS

It's all the same to me.
—Oh chef:
make the gravy thick.

HERAKLES

God alive, Poseidon, where in the
world is youse going? Are we going to war for the sake of a
dame?

POSEIDON

What alternative would you suggest?

HERAKLES

Peace, peace!

POSEIDON

You poor fool, don't you realize that you're being tricked?
What's more, you're only hurting yourself.

Listen here.
if Zeus should abdicate his throne in favor of the Birds
and then die. you'd be left a pauper Whereas now
you're the legal heir of Zeus. Heir. in fact.
to everything he owns.

PISTHETAIROS

Watch your step. Herakles.
You're being hoodwinked.

Taking Herakles by the arm and withdrawing a little

—Now. just step aside with me
I have something to tell you.
Look. you poor chump.
your uncle's pulling a fast one. Not one cent
of Zeus' enormous estate will ever come to you
You see. my friend. you're a bastard.

HERAKLES

What's dat. fella?
I'm a bastard?

PISTHETAIROS

Of course you're a bastard—by Zeus.
Your mother. you see. was an ordinary mortal woman.
not a goddess. In other words. she comes
of foreign stock. Which makes you legally a bastard.*
pure and simple.
Moreover, Pallas Athene
is normally referred to as The Heiress.* That's her title
But how in the name of Zeus could Athene be an heiress
if Zeus had any legitimate sons?

HERAKLES

Maybe.
Youse could be right. But what if the Old Man
swears I'm his son?

PISTHETAIROS

The law still says No.
In any case. Poseidon here. who's been egging you on.
would be the first person to challenge the will in court
As your father's brother. he's the next-of-kin. and hence
the legal heir
Let me read you the provisions of the law

He draws a lawbook from his robes

In the words of Solon himself:
SO LONG AS LEGITIMATE ISSUE SHALL SURVIVE
THE DECEASED. NO BASTARD SHALL INHERIT
IN THE CASE THAT NO LEGITIMATE ISSUE SUR-
VIVES. THE ESTATE SHALL PASS TO THE NEXT
OF KIN

HERAKLES

Youse mean to say I won't inherit a damn thing
from the Old Man?

PISTHETAIROS

Not a smitch. By the way.
has your Father ever had your birth legally recorded
or had you registered in court as his official heir?

HERAKLES

No. never. I always thought there was something fishy

PISTHETAIROS

Come, my boy. chin up. Don't pout at heaven
with that sullen glare. Join us. Come in with the Birds.
We'll set you on a throne and you can guzzle pigeon's milk
the rest of your endless days.

HERAKLES

You know. fella.

I been thinking about that dame you want so bad.
Well, I vote youse can have her.

PISTHETAIROS

                                        Splendid.
What do you say, Poseidon?

POSEIDON

                          No. A resounding No

PISTHETAIROS

Then it rests with Triballos.
                          —What's your verdict, my friend?

TRIBALLOS

Gleep? Schnoozer, skirt wotta twatch snock!
Birdniks pockle. Ugh.

HERAKLES

                    He said she's for the Boids.
I hoid him.

POSEIDON

          And I distinctly heard him say the opposite:
A firm No—with a few choice obscenities added.

HERAKLES

The poor dumb sap never said a doity word.
All he said was: *Give 'er to the Boids.*

POSEIDON

                              I yield
You two can come to terms together as you please.
Since you seem to be agreed on everything, I'll just abstain.

HERAKLES

To Pisthetairos.

Man. youse is getting everything youse wants.
Fly up to Heaven wid us, and get your missus
and anything else your little heart desires.

PISTHETAIROS

And we're in luck. This feast of poultry I've prepared
will grace our wedding supper

HERAKLES

                              Youse guys push along
I'll stay here and watch the barbecue.

POSEIDON

                              Not on your life
You'd guzzle grill and all. You'd better come along
with us, my boy

HERAKLES

                  Aw, Unc, but it woulda tasted so good.

PISTHETAIROS

To Attendants

   ·You there, servants.
                        Bring my wedding clothes along.

Exeunt Pisthetairos. the gods and Attendants.

CHORUS*

                  Beneath the clock in a courtroom.
                     down in the Land of Gab,
                  We saw a weird race of people.
                     earning their bread by blab

Their name is the Claptraptummies.
　Their only tool is talk.
They sow and reap and shake the figs
　by dexterous yakkity-yak.

Their tongues and twaddle mark them off,
　barbarians every one;
but the worst of all are in the firm
　of GORGIAS & SON.*

But from this bellyblabbing tribe,
　one custom's come to stay:
in Athens, when men sacrifice,
　they cut the tongue away.

Enter a Messenger.

MESSENGER

O blessèd, blessèd, blessèd breed of Bird,
more happy than human tongue can tell:
welcome your lord and King as he ascends to heaven!
Attend him now!
　　　　　　Praise him, whose glory glisters
more brightly than the rising stars at dusk
flare their loveliness upon the golden evening air,
purer than the blazoned sun!
　　　　　　He comes, he comes,
and with him comes the splendid glory of a bride
whose beauty has no peer. In his hand he shakes
the wingèd thunderbolt at Zeus, the flash of lightning.
Unspeakably sweet, a fragrance ascends to heaven
and curls of incense trace their love spirals
on the drinking air.
　　　　　　He comes!
　　　　　　　　　　Greet your King with song!
Raise the wedding song the lovely Muses sing!

Re-enter Pisthetairos, gorgeously attired, his long golden
train carried by the three gods. Beside him, dressed in the*

*magnificent golden robes of a bride, walks the veiled figure
of Miss Universe.*

KORYPHAIOS

Make way! Make way!
                              Fall back for the dancers!
Welcome your King with beating wings!
Dance, dance!
                    Praise this happy Prince!
sing the loveliness of brides!
Weave with circling feet, weave and dance
in honor of the King, in honor of his bride!
Now let the Golden Age of Birds begin
    by lovely marriage ushered in.
                              Hymen Hymenaios O!

CHORUS

                    To such a song as this,
                    the weaving Fates once led
                    the universal King,
                    Zeus, the lord of all,
                    to lovely Hera's bed.
                        O Hymen! Hymenois O!

                    And blooming Love was there,
                    Love with shimmering wings,
                    Love the charioteer!
                    Love once held the reins,
                    Love drove the happy pair!
                        O Hymen! Hymenaios O!

PISTHETAIROS

I thank you for your songs and dance. Thank you, thank
    you,
one and all.

KORYPHAIOS

                    Now praise the lightnings of your King!

Sing his thunders crashing on the world!
Sing the blazing bolts of Zeus, praise the man
who hurls them!
                    Sing the flare of lightning;
praise, praise the crashing of its awful fire!

CHORUS

               O Lightning, flash of livid fire,
               O javelin of Zeus,
                                   everliving light!

A great low roll of thunder is heard.

O thunders breaking on this lovely world,
rumble majestic that runs before the rain!
O Lightning and Thunders,
                         bow low, bow down,
bow before this man, bow to the lord of all!

Another great crack of thunder.

He wields the thunder as his very own.
Lightnings flare at the touch of his hand,
               winning, achieving
the Bride of Heaven and the Crown of God!
               O Hymen! Hymenaios O!

PISTHETAIROS

Now follow our bridal party, one and all.
Soar on high, you happy breed of Birds,
to the halls of Zeus, to the bed of love!

*He extends his hand to his bride and together they dance
toward the waiting machine.*

               Reach me your hand, dear bride.
               Now take me by my wings,
               oh my lovely,
                         my sweet,

and let me lift you up,
and soar beside you
through the buoyant air!

*Pisthetairos and his bride dance toward the waiting machine.
With slowly beating wings they rise gradually heavenward.
The gods and Attendants bow down in homage, the Chorus
divides and flocks triumphantly toward the exits, chanting as
they go.*

CHORUS

> *Alalalai!*
> > *Io!*
> > > *Paion!*
> O greatest of the gods!
> *Tenella Kallinikos O!*

Notes

page 186. *A desolate wilderness:* The locale of the Hoopoe's
nest belongs, of course, to the same fabulous geog-
raphy as Cloudcuckooland itself. Since in mythology Tereus was the king of the Daulians, a Thracian
people, the scene may be laid "somewhere in
Thrace"—an extremely imprecise designation.

187. *even Exekestides couldn't do* that: Cf. Glossary,
EXEKESTIDES. From the frequent allusions in the
play to men who, technically ineligible, had somehow managed to get themselves enrolled as Athenian
citizens, it is tempting to believe that proposals to
revise the citizenship lists were in the air or had
recently been carried out. The climax of these
allusions comes in the final scene of the play, in
which Pisthetairos attempts to prove that Herakles
is technically a bastard (and hence cannot inherit
Zeus' estate) because his mother was an ordinary
mortal, i.e., of foreign stock.

187. *Old Tereus the bird who used to be a man:* Cf.
Glossary, TEREUS.

Despite the violent story which tells how Tereus
became the Hoopoe, Prokne the Nightingale, and

315

Philomela the Swallow, Aristophanes' Tereus and
Prokne live happily together in marital bliss.

page 187. *this stinking, jabbering Magpie here:* In the Greek,
the Magpie is actually called "son of Tharraleides."
According to the Scholiast, Tharraleides' son was
Asopodoros, a diminutive man commonly ridiculed
as a runt. There may also be a pun on the word
θαρραλέος, loquacious or impudent.

188. *dying to go tell it to the Birds:* Literally, the Greek
says "dying to go to the crows," a common
Athenian imprecation, and roughly equivalent to
"go to perdition" or "go to hell" in English.
Pisthetairos and Euelpïdes propose merely to follow the imprecation in its literal meaning—only to
get lost en route.

188. Cf. Glossary, SAKAS and the note on *even Exekestides*, above.

188. *to pay their taxes:* A slight modernization of the
Greek which says "to pay fines."

189. *Because of legal locusts:* Aristophanes' favorite
complaint against Athens, and one to which the
entire *Wasps* is devoted. But although Aristophanes
here develops Athens' love of litigation as the
major source of dissatisfaction, elsewhere throughout the play the other grievances emerge: the
restless and mischievous Athenian character (called
πολυπραγμοσύνη); the plague of informers; the
victimization of the Allies; the ambition for power,
an ambition which knows no limits and whose
only goal is World Mastery (βασιλεία).

189. *soft and lovely leisure:* Pisthetairos and Euelpides
are looking, that is, for a place that offers them what
Athens does not: release from the tortured, nervous,
frenetic restlessness of Athenian life.

In Greek this quality of Athenian national restlessness was called πολυπραγμοσύνη, and its lexi-
cal meanings include "officiousness," "meddling,"
and "the activities of the busybody." Translated
to social and political life, the word connotes those
national characteristics which made the Athenians

at once the wonder and the bane of the Greek world: national enterprise and energy vs. a spirit of unsatisfied restlessness; adventurous daring of action and intellect as against a spirit that seemed destructive of tradition and the life of rural peace; hunger for innovation and change undercut by the inability to temporize or be still. The word, in short, expresses precisely those qualities—daring, energy, ingenuity, strain, dynamic action, restlessness, ambition for acquisition and conquest, glory in change—that typify the Athens of the fifth century. It was these qualities that had made Athens great; they also made Athens imperial and thereby propagated themselves; they were responsible for the senseless protraction of the Peloponnesian War and they would, Aristophanes believed, eventually destroy Athens as they had already destroyed the countryside of Attika and the virtue it fostered: ἀπραγμοσύνη, the contented leisure of traditional order and the rural conservatism of peaceful life.

The word is, of course, crucial to the play. For if Aristophanes shows us in Pisthetairos here an Athenian exhausted by years of national restlessness and in search of ἀπραγμοσύνη among the Birds, it is precisely his point that no Athenian can escape his origin. And once arrived among the Birds, Pisthetairos promptly exhibits the national quality from which he is trying to escape. He is daring, acquisitive, ruthlessly energetic, inventive, and a thorough-paced imperialist. And finally, in the apotheosis that closes the play, he arrives at his logical destination—divinity. For πολυπραγμοσύνη, as Aristophanes ironically observed, is moved by nothing less than man's divine discontent with his condition, and the hunger of the Athenians to be supreme, and therefore god.

page 189. *Try kicking the side of the cliff with your foot:* As the Scholiast explains it, this line is an echo of a children's jingle: "Kick the rock with your foot. and the birds will fall down."

page 191. *I'm turdus turdus. An African migrant:* I have taken a liberty here in an attempt to make English of the Greek which literally says: "I'm a Scared-stifflet. A Libyan species." *Turdus turdus* (the scientific name of the thrush) seemed to introduce the right scientific note, as well as to accommodate the obscenity which follows.

192. *I'm a Slavebird:* Cock-fighting cant. Greeks called the loser in a cock-fight the "slave" of the winner

193. *Right here in my hand:* If, as I suspect—contrary to the belief of most scholars—the phallus was worn in Aristophanic comedy, these words have a point that is otherwise lacking. Pisthetairos, having let his bird escape, finds himself holding his own phallus in terror. It is good fun based on good observation.

194. *I'll bet the gods:* The Greek introduces the official *Twelve* Gods here, probably for emphasis. I have omitted them for clarity's sake.

194. *as the poet Sophokles disfigures me:* Sophokles had produced a tragedy called *Tereus* (lost) in which he may have described Tereus' metamorphosis into a Hoopoe. In the Aristophanic play, Tereus is obviously only slightly—and rather shabbily—metamorphosed, and he ascribes his shabbiness to his Sophoklean origins.

In appearance the European Hoopoe is a stunning and unusual bird, with brilliant black and white wing pattern and pink plumage and splendid black-tipped erectile crest.

195. *All Birds moult in winter:* With this statement the Hoopoe realistically accounts for his bedraggled plumage in March, when the play was performed.

195. *Then you must be jurymen.* The familiar taunt: everybody in Athens is on a jury

196. *You can still find a few growing wild:* Aristophanes means that the only Athenians still untouched by the national disease of litigation were countrymen

The countryside breeds ἀπραγμοσύνη; the city.
πολυπραγμοσύνη which finds expression in the
suits brought by informers, etc

page 196 *some country like a blanket, soft and snug*
ἀπραγμοσύνη again.

198. *court-officials with summons:* Euelpides is terrified
by the thought of officials with summonses who
may show up *anywhere* near the sea, even the Red
Sea. The Greek mentions the ''Salaminia,'' the
galley used in Athens for official business, and the
very vessel which had, a few months earlier, been
despatched to Sicily with orders for the recall of
Alkibiades to Athens to stand trial.

198. *If Opountios comes from Opous:* The pun here is
untranslatable. Opountios was a one-eyed Athenian
informer; Opous was a town in Lokris, and the
word Oupountios designates an inhabitant of Opous
as well as the Athenian informer.

199. *That's a honeymoon!:* Poppyseed was used in making wedding cakes, and myrtle berries were used
for wedding wreaths.

199. *and people say:* In the manuscript it is Teleas—
and not people—who sneers at the Birds. Teleas was
evidently an extremely flighty and silly Athenian
official and Aristophanes' point is the obvious one
it takes a Bird to recognize a Bird.

201 *The heavens, you see, revolve upon a kind of pole*
This line and the three that follow it involve a
series of untranslatable puns and some difficult
scientific jargon. The Greek for ''the vault of the
heavens'' is πόλος, which leads naturally to πολεῖται
(revolves), which resembles πολῖται (citizens),
which in turn yields πόλις (city). The argument is
a fine specimen of sophistic doubletalk.

201 *wipe them all out by starvation:* The manuscript says
literally, ''wipe them out with a Melian famine ''
The year before the performance of *The Birds*, the
small neutral island of Melos had been blockaded
by an Athenian fleet and reduced by slow starvation
When finally captured, the entire male population

was put to the sword and the women and children enslaved.

It is, of course, a deliberate part of Aristophanes' general ironic design that the tactics used by Pisthetairos against the gods are, in fact, the brutal military tactics of Athenian imperialism. However fantastic the play may seem, its purpose is the relentless satirical equation of Athens and Cloudcuckooland.

page 206. *Like something out of Aischylos:* The line which follows is a quotation from the (lost) *Edonoi* of Aischylos.

207. *the son of the Hoopoe in Philokles' tragedy of* Tereus: The passage is a complicated one. But its basis seems to be an elaborate comparison between three generations of Hoopoes and three generations of the family of Kallias, and its point is surely (1) a charge of plagiarism against the tragedian Philokles and (2) the charge of profligacy against the younger Kallias.

There are three *Hoopoes*: (1) Hoopoe *grandpère* (the Hoopoe who married Prokne and the hero of Sophokles' *Tereus*); (2) Hoopoe *père* (the Hoopoe of Philokles' *Tereus*, a plagiarism of—and therefore descended from—Sophokles' play); and (3) Hoopoe *fils*, the dissolute and bedraggled Hoopoe of the Chorus. To these correspond: (1) Kallias *grandpère*, a distinguished Athenian; (2) Hipponikos son of Kallias (1), and also distinguished; and (3) Kallias *fils*, the unworthy and profligate scion of a distinguished line. (The family was evidently addicted to alternating names with each generation: Kallias, Hipponikos, Kallias, Hipponikos, etc.)

208. *our boy Kleonymos:* Kleonymos was a notorious glutton and an equally notorious coward. Since cowards have lost their crests (by throwing away their helmets on the battlefield), the Crested Guzzleguzzle should not be confused with Kleonymos.

208. *this crestwork on the Birds:* This joke depends

upon a pun on the word λόφος, which means: (1) the crest of a bird, (2) the summit—or crest—of a hill.

page 209. *Her lover. The Horny Pecker:* This is Arrowsmith. not Aristophanes, and so too is the following line. But the lines seemed to me utterly untranslatable since they involved an impossible pun on the word κειρύλος (which means both "kingfisher" and "barber") and an obscure barber by the name of Sporgilos. In the circumstances it seemed better to betray the letter than the spirit.

209. *Bringing Owls to Athens:* The Athenian equivalent of "bringing coals to Newcastle."

210. *I detect a note of menace:* The effect of the entire following scene depends upon our understanding of the *natural* hostility between Birds and Man (cf. l. 369 ff.). In a country policed by the bird-loving vigilantes of the Audubon Society, Aristophanes' Birds might seem unreasonably hostile and suspicious of human motives. But anyone who has ever seen a Mediterannean bird-market or been offered pickled thrushes or *uccellini con polenta* will understand. Those who do not are advised to read closely the second Parabasis (1058 ff.) and to ponder Pisthetairos' little poem at 523 ff. Seen in the light of this total hostility, Pisthetairos' persuasion of the Birds is an extraordinary feat, designed, I believe. in order to exhibit his characteristic Athenian resourcefulness and eloquence and cunning.

214 *Birds are skittish of platters:* In the Greek it is owls who are said to be skittish of platters. The reason for this skittishness is not known; it may be because owls are sacred to Athena and Athena was supposed to have invented the art of pottery I preferred in the circumstances to emphasize the Birds' terror of becoming a meal.

215 *closely related to my wife:* Tereus' wife Prokne was Athenian and all Athenians regarded themselves as related by virtue of the very kinship-structure of the city.

217 *in Athens at public cost:* Soldiers who fell on the

battlefield for Athens were buried at public expense
in the Kerameikos outside the city.

page 217. *any reference to Birds:* Literally, the Greek says,
"we will say that we died fighting the enemy at
Orneai." "At Orneai" in the Greek is a pun on ορνις
(bird), i.e., "at Birdland," and the town of Orneai
which lay between Korinth and Sikyon and which,
in 416, underwent a bloodless one-day siege.

220. *you know who I mean:* "The armor-making baboon"
seems to have been a certain knife-maker called
Panaitios who was married to an extremely promis-
cuous shrew. They managed to arrive at a marital
modus vivendi only by making a formal compact
of truce.

222. *Someone fetch water for my hands:* An orator put
on a crown of myrtle before beginning his speech,
but the wreath and the washing of hands are the
customary preparations for a feast; hence Euelpides'
question.

223. *Because you're a lazy Bird:* In the Greek κού
πολυπράγμων, uninquisitve, notonone'stoes, sluggish,
without curiosity. The Birds' fallen estate and
decadence is directly traceable to their lack of
πολυπραγμοσύνη, Pisthetairos' most outstanding
trait. Cf. note on p. 316 *soft and lovely leisure.*

223. *And that's how Asbury got its name:* A complicated bit of foolery crowned by Euelpides' elaborate pun, which I have freely altered for the
effect. Pisthetairos actually says that, according to
"Aesop," the Lark buried her father in her own
head. The word for "head" in Greek is κεφαλή,
which is also the name of an Athenian deme.
Hense Euelpides' crack: the father of the Lark is
buried at κεφαλή.

223. *and let the woodpeckers reign:* Since the oak tree
was sacred to Zeus and the woodpeckers attacked
the oaks, Zeus would be particularly unwilling to
yield his sceptre to the Woodpecker.

225. *falling flat on your face whenever you saw a Kite:*
The Kite was a harbinger of Spring, according to

the Scholiast, and one which was evidently welcomed with almost religious joy.

page 225. *I swallowed my money:* It was common in antiquity for people to carry their coins in their mouth, probably as a precaution against theft.

225. *we still call the Egyptians cuckoo:* The cuckoo's call was in Egypt a call to reap, as Pisthetairos explains. To this Euelpides replies with a proverbial expression whose meaning is obscure— though, almost certainly obscene. Since I could not translate what I could not understand, I have tried to make Euelpides' reply consistent with his zaniness elsewhere.

226. *on the rows where the politicians sit:* Literally, the Greek says that the birds on sceptres were keeping an eye on Lysikrates, to see whether he was bribed. Lysikrates was an Athenian general of a dishonest and corrupt character.

226. *Doctors still swear by the Duck:* A deliberate improvisation of my own to circumvent the complexity of the Greek. Literally, the line reads: "Lampon swears by the Goose when he's trying to cheat you." Lampon was a notorious soothsayer, but evidently superstitious enough that he tried to mitigate his perjury when fleecing a victim: instead of swearing an oath by Zeus (Ζῆνα), he swore by the Goose (Χῆνα).

229. *A Babylon of the Birds!:* Cf. Glossary, BABYLON.

229. *each Bird must be paired with a god:* These pairs, depend upon similarity in character or upon puns, and I have altered several of them accordingly Thus in the manuscript Aphrodite is paired with the phalarope (which is suggested by *phallos*); Poseidon, god of the sea, is matched by a seabird; the glutton Herakles by the cormorant; and Zeus, king of the gods, by the wren, king of the birds.

233. *"Five lives of men the cawing Crow outliveth":* A garbled echo of Hesiod, frag. 50.

233. *can strut on an olive limb:* The olive was sacred to

ARISTOPHANES

Athena and hence should be acceptable even to aristocratic birds.

page 235. *Remember what old Aesop tells us:* According to the Scholiast, the fable should be ascribed to Archilochos rather than Aesop. But the gist of the fable seems to be as follows. The Fox and the Eagle swore lasting friendship and built their homes close together: the Eagle up in the tree, the Fox at the foot. During the Fox's absence one day, the Eagle swooped down, carried off the Fox's cubs, and proceeded to make a meal of them. The Fox, unable to climb the tree, could not take vengeance.

238. *The Chorus turns sharply and faces the audience:* The Parabasis, (or Digression), that part of an Aristophanic comedy in which the Chorus steps forth and addresses the audience directly, usually on behalf of the poet. In this play the Parabasis is linked with unusual coherence to the action, whereas in most comedies the Chorus employs the Parabasis to expound the topical social and political views of the comedian.

The opening anapestic section of the Parabasis is devoted to what might be called an Avine Cosmogony, a splendid and eloquent exposition of the origins of the world and the creation of the Birds and the gods. This defense of the antiquity of the Birds then passes into an overtly humorous bid for support, as though the Birds were campaigning for the votes which will make them gods. This is followed by a lovely lyric strophe. ("O woodland Muse") which is succeeded by the *epirrhema* in a more topical and satirical vein; then the lyric antistrophe ("And so the swans") and the farcical *antepirrhema* ("You haven't really lived till you've tried a set of FEATHERS!").

The relevance of the opening cosmogony to the theme of the play has been questioned, but unreasonably I think. If Cloudcuckooland is an Athenian Utopia, the meaning of Utopia is scored when Pisthetairos achieves his apotheosis in the finale.

He has built Utopia by becoming god, and escaping his human condition. It is to the reality and sadness of man's condition that the cosmogony of the blessed Birds is addressed, and these lovely opening lines ("O suffering mankind, lives of twilight, race feeble and fleeting") are intended as a tragic counterweight to the crazy comic dream of mankind with which the play closes.

page 238. *tell Prodikos to go hang:* Prodikos was a sophist whom Aristophanes seems to have respected. The point here is that, wise as Prodikos may be, as a teacher of truth he is not to be compared with the Birds.

239. *laid her wind-egg there:* A wind-egg is an unfertilized pullet's egg.

242. *the poet stole his honied song:* i.e., the tragic poet, Phrynichos, famous for his lyric sweetness.

244. *Dieitrephes, our vulgar Ikaros of trade:* For Dieitrephes, see Glossary. Aristophanes, like most conservatives, is a convinced snob, and he almost never forgives a man his business background, especially if the man has succeeded, as Dieitrephes had, in making his way into the *élite* ranks of the chivalry.

245. *the poor Birds in that Aischylos play:* A reference to, followed by a quotation from, the lost *Myrmidones* of Aischylos.

246. *insult my mattress by giving it a name like Sparta:* A pun on Σπάρτη (Sparta and σπάρτη, a kind of broom from which rope and bed-cording were made). Euelpides detests Sparta so much that he wouldn't attach σπάρτη to his bed.

247. *who will guard our Storkade?:* The wall which surrounded the Akropolis of Athens was usually called the Pelasgic Wall but sometimes the Pelargic Wall, both related forms. Aristophanes here uses Pelargic Wall, fancifully deriving it from πελαργός ("stork"). "Storkade" is B. B. Rogers' *trouvaille* and one which I gratefully adopt here.

page 247. *Hop it, man.:!* Pisthetairos' officiousness with Euelpides here is a stunning example of πολυπραγμοσύνη.

249. *Flutist, come in!* At these words the flutist Chairis, dressed as a Blackbird or a Crow, steps forward. Chairis' music seems to have grated intolerably on Aristophanes' ears; he is a *bête noire* in *The Acharnians* (425 B.C.) and still obnoxious by the time of *The Birds* eleven years later.

249. *propping his beak with a leather belt:* Evidently a mouth band or flutist's lip protector.

249. *the Bidding Prayer of the Birds:* This entire prayer is a parody of the customary invocation of the gods, in each case, by pun or burlesqued attributes or cult titles, linking a god with a bird. Because of the elaborateness of the puns and the obscurities of cult titles, literal translation is out of the question, and I have tried to make my own puns where I could not re-create the Greek—as I rarely could. Thus my Artemis is not a Finch but an American Phoebe, an appropriate name, I thought, for the sister of Phoibos; Kybele, Mother of Gods and Men, is not an Ostrich, as she is in the Greek, but a Dowitcher, a bird which suggested "dowager," and the Great Mother of Bustards. Those who are interested in discussion of the literal Greek should consult Rogers' commentary on the passage.

250. *pray for the Chians too:* Cf. Glossary, CHIANS

252. *as Homer hath it:* Everything about this poet is begged, borrowed, or stolen. Here he attributes lines to Homer which either are not Homeric or Homer so muddled as to be unrecognizable.

253. *O Father, Founder of Etna:* This whole passage is evidently a hideously garbled and atrociously adapted burlesque of Pindar's ode dedicated to the Syracusan tyrant Hiero on the founding of the town of Etna.

254. *Undressed amidst the nomad Skyths:* More Pindar, perhaps quoted almost verbatim, but doggerlized deliberately by me since no contemporary reader could be expected to recognize the Pindaric man-

ner or its incongruous humor in this particular context.

page 256. *WHERE KORINTH KISSETH SIKYON:* That is, at Orneai. Cf. Note on p. 322, *any reference to Birds*. Itinerant prophets in Athens could live well by supplying ambiguous predictions of conquest and victory to the ambitious Athenians. This particular prophet may very well be quoting from an actual oracle which predicted the sack of Orneai and thereby prompted the expedition; he then attempts to resell the same article, differently interpreted, to Cloudcuckooland.

257. *REGAL EAGLE WINGS THIS VERY DAY ARE THINE:* This is said to have been the favorite prediction of the Athenian Demos (cf. *Knights*, 1013). The Eagle, of course, symbolized supremacy and conquest.

258. *FOR THE GREATER THE FAKER:* The manuscript specifies by name two of these fakers. The first is Lampon, Athens' most renowned soothsayer; the second, Diopeithes, the accuser of the philosopher Anaxagoras.

259. *METON:* Cf. Glossary.

260. *our welkin resembles a cosmical charcoal-oven:* Meton's whole lecture is an elaborate spoof of technical "scientific" jargon of the age. But because Greek scientific jargon is almost chaste compared to our splendid modern proliferations, I have worked it up in order to create an effect analogous to that intended for Greek ears.

262. *enters an Inspector:* The Inspector, or Commissioner, was a regular Athenian official sent out from Athens to supervise subject states or to organize newly founded colonies. Their salaries seem to have been paid by the colonies they supervised, and some of them, like the Inspector here, had become rich men in the course of their careers.

263. *The Persian crisis, you know:* A free rendering. In the original the Inspector alludes loftily to his negotiations with the Persian satrap Pharnakes; he is

needed at home for consultation about these weighty negotiations. Persia at this time, however, was more and more becoming a crucial factor in Greek political life.

page 263. *and take your ballot boxes with you:* Wherever Athenian inspectors are found, there will also be ballot boxes, the typical device of Athenian democracy, and arbitrarily instituted throughout the empire.

264. *Enter an itinerant Legislator:* During the war the Athenian Assembly had passed so many decrees, regulations, etc., that it became virtually impossible for the subject-cities and colonies to keep abreast of them. In the circumstances the practice of peddling the latest crop of statutes became a flourishing trade.

266. *CHORUS:* The second Parabasis: The Birds eulogize themselves and the blessings they bring, issue their own proclamation, and explain to the Judges the advantages of awarding *The Birds* the first prize.

268. *shrines whose dizzy heights, like Eagle-eyries:* In Greek the word ἀετός meant (1) an Eagle, and (2) the triangular pediment which crowned the pillars.

270. *Thirty thousand Cranes whose crops were all loaded with boulders and stones:* Cranes were believed to use stones to ballast themselves; the ballast was held in the crop.

271. *Ah Feet! Ah, Feet! O incredible Feat!:* This is a common proverb with the word "feet" substituted for "hands."

272. *the wild steps of a military dance:* The *pyrrhichē* danced in full armor. Actually, the sentry is not dancing; the dancing is in his eyes, i.e., ablaze with martial ardor.

277. *In the high tragic manner:* Iris' tragic fulmination is probably a pastiche of all the tragedians, patched out with some Aristophanic inventions.

278. *Some poor Lydian or Phrygian slave:* A direct quotation from Euripides' *Alkestis*, 675.

278. *What doth the poet say?:* A quotation from the lost *Niobe* of Aischylos, incongruously incorporated into

the passage without alteration. In order to clarify the deliberate incongruity (the mention of Amphion), I have intruded the line which follows the quotation.

page 280. *mimicry of Sokrates:* A gibe at the Spartan affectations of the Socratic circle and especially Sokrates' personal uncleanliness. To some extent this may be merely an exploitation of the common man's stereotype of the intellectual and philosopher. I remember a Princeton landlady telling me that Einstein never took a bath; this was her revenge on his genius. As for Sokrates, who knows?

281. *the dernier cri of human fashion:* The examples of the avine vogue which follow are all of my own invention. The Greek cannot be literally translated into English because it is based upon an untranslatable pun ($\nu o\mu ó\varsigma$, meaning both "law" and "pasture" or "feeding-place"), designed to parody, in avine terms, the Athenian love of litigation.

284. *If I had the wings of an Eagle:* A quotation, according to the Scholiast, from the lost *Oinomaos* of Sophokles.

284. *Delinquent:* The Greek is $\pi a\tau\rho o\lambda o ía\varsigma$, a word which it is usual to translate as "parricide," although it means merely "father-beater." Since our young man merely *wants* to murder his father, I have made him an adolescent punk and called him Delinquent.

286. *On gossamer I go, delicately wending:* According to the Scholiast, a parody of Anakreon.

287. *our poet's craft depends completely on the clouds:* For the Clouds as patron goddesses of dithyrambic poets, cf. *Clouds*, 355 ff. Poets whose compositions are a characteristic blend of obscurity, turbid emptiness and inflated language naturally depend upon the Murky Muse for inspiration.

288. *What suspicious Birds are these:* Adapted from a poem by Alkaios.

289. *he's calling the Cuckoo to bring the Spring:* In the Greek it is the Swallow who brings the Informer's Spring.

page 289. *to hide the holes in your coat:* Literally the manuscript has Pisthetairos say: "Are you planning to fly to Pellene?" Pellene was famous for its heavy woolen clothing, offered as prizes in the contests celebrated there.

289. *the indictment of islands for subversive activities*
By "islands" is meant the subject-states of the Athenian Empire, very largely comprised of the Aegean islands. Since the islanders were compelled to refer their more important lawsuits to the verdict of Athenian juries, they were therefore in a disadvantageous position and easily victimized by professional informers.

291. *they loll around at the barbershop:* The barbershop was *par excellence* the nerve center of Athenian gossip, rumor, and political speculation.

291 *that damned Dieitrephes:* Cf. Glossary, DIEITRE PHES. Dieitrephes was a notorious horse-racing enthusiast and hence in high favor with the wastrels among the Athenian *jeunesse dorée.*

293. *CHORUS:* With this strophe Aristophanes commences a series of brief Travelogues by the Birds: strange sights and marvels which their word-traveling has enabled them to visit. Actually, of course, all of the wonders are merely fabulized versions of familiar Athenian institutions and personages: the coward-sycophant Kleonymos, the thief Orestes, the psychagogue Sokrates and his accomplice Chairephon, the incredible tongue-worship of the wondrous men of Athens.

In this strophe Kleonymos is compared to a tree which grows enormous in the Spring and in winter sheds, not leaves, but shields The Spring was the banner season for informers and sycophants, when men like Kleonymos (physically fat to begin with) were bloated with the profits of their trade In winter the Kleonymos-tree sheds its shields, an allusion to Kleonymos' cowardice in battle (i.e throwing down his shield and running away)

The second part of the strophe deals with the

notorious footpad Orestes and concludes with a play on the name: (1) the Athenian thief, (2) his famous legendary predecessor, the son of Agamemnon The point seems to be that those who venture out in Athens at night may meet Orestes the thief (who stripped his victims) or Orestes the heroic ghost (who paralyzed his victims—a power possessed by heroes, according to the Scholiast).

page 294. *Enter Prometheus:* Mankind's greatest champion and arch foe of Zeus makes his ridiculously furtive entrance on still another philanthropic mission: to warn Pisthetairos of Zeus' plans and secrets. Needless to say, he is extremely anxious to avoid observation by the gods.

296. *Say, that's clever. Prometheus all over:* Pisthetairos is impressed by the ingenuity of Prometheus' umbrella, and compliments him as deserving of his name (Prometheus meant "Foresight").

297 *All the Stone Age gods:* A free—but I thought plausible—rendering of the "barbarian gods" of the text. If Triballos is a representative of the barbarian gods, then the divinities meant are not merely uncivilized but Neolithic.

298. *Miss Universe:* The Greek gives βασιλεία, which means "sovereignty," "empire," "supreme power " Because she is an unfamiliar abstraction and not a genuine Olympian at all, I have felt free to turn her into a "sort of Beauty Queen" and to gloss her in the text as "the symbol of divine supremacy " In this play she symbolizes the logical conclusion of the Athenian (or the Birds') struggle for domination and universal supremacy She is what Thoukydides called ἀρχή ("empire," "domination") and what I believe Euripides everywhere in his tragedies meant by the figure of Helen: the prize for which the (Peloponnesian) War was fought

298. *the inventor of the barbecue:* Because Prometheus gave fire to man

299 *CHORUS* The second installment of the Birds Travelogue The subject is Sokrates as psychagogue

or psychopomp, the guide of the soul, engaged in calling up spirits from the dead in a little sacrifice which resembles that of Odysseus in Book XI of the *Odyssey*. Sokrates' Stygian assistant is his cadaverous colleague of Athenian life, Chairephon.

The scene takes place in the land of Shadowfeet (according to Ktesias, a curious web-footed tribe which lived in Libya; when they lay down for a nap, they held up their huge webfeet as awnings against the sun. To this the Scholiast adds that they had four legs, three of which were used for walking, and the fourth as a tentpole for their tentlike feet). Here, beside a Stygian swamp, haunted by terror, Sokrates summons the soul of Peisandros, an Athenian coward in search of his *psyche* (i.e., courage), by means of sacrifice; but so faint-hearted is Sokrates that he runs away in terror, leaving the bloody victim to the spectral vampire Chairephon.

page 303. *Dat's Stone Age for Yeah:* Cf. note on p. 331, *All the Stone Age gods.*

306. *Which makes you legally a bastard:* According to Athenian laws on citizenship, citizens must be born of Athenian fathers and mothers. Herakles, as the son of Zeus (a *bona fide* Olympian) and Alkmene (an ordinary woman, i.e., a foreigner) would be both illegitimate and ineligible for citizenship—according to Athenian law.

306. *Pallas Athene is normally referred to as The Heiress:* Because Athens was Athena's "portion," she was officially called The Heiress.

309. *CHORUS:* The concluding section of the Birds' Travelogue, a pointed satire on the Athenian worship of the Clacking Money-Making Tongue in thin anthropological disguise.

310. *of GORGIAS & SON:* To Gorgias the manuscript adds the name of Philippos, son or disciple of Gorgias the sophist. It was believed that the persuasive tongue of Gorgias served to stimulate the disastrous interest in Sicily among Athenians which culminated in the Sicilian Expedition.

page 310. *Re-enter Pisthetairos. gorgeously attired:* The
culmination of the play in the apostheosis of
Pisthetairos and the marriage with Miss Universe
Man's comic dream is completed; by building
Cloudcuckooland and winning Miss Universe. Man
becomes supreme, escapes his mortal condition,
and achieves divinity. It would be blasphemous if it
were not so terribly ironic a wish-fulfillment of the
god-intoxicated Athenian Dream.

Lysistrata

CONTENTS

Introduction

The Play

Lysistrata was first performed at Athens in the year 411 B.C., probably during the Lenaia. Of the achievement of that first production, we know nothing at all; of more recent developments, we are better informed.

Regular translation, frequent adaptation, persistent production, and occasional confiscation—these are the signs of success, making *Lysistrata* today's popular favorite among Aristophanes' surviving comedies. A not altogether joyous eminence. Even the most rabid advocate of the wide circulation of the classics-in-any-form must blanch slightly at the broadcast misconception that this play is a hoard of applied lubricity. Witness its latest American publication, bowdlerized-in-reverse, nestled near some choice gobbets from Frank Harris' autobiography in a slick and curious quarterly called *Eros*, now under indictment. If this be success, there is scant comfort in it.*

---

*Some, however: It is refreshing to conjecture what treatment Harris might have received from Aristophanes, who is by most standards quite orthodox in matters sexual. Compare his remarks on Ariphrades, especially at *Knights* 1280 ff.

What profit in outwearing time's ravages, only to win through
to a general snigger? Both Aristophanes and his audience
deserve better

Happily. they do receive it. *Lysistrata* is Aristophanes'
most popular play. not because it is his most obscene (it is
not) nor his most prurient (he is never prurient), but because.
to a present-day reader or viewer, it is his most comprehensible.
capable of assimilation with the least violence to preconceptions.
Indeed. when we examine its preoccupation with sex. the
source of its notoriety. we find the treatment rather more
soothing than shocking. Those facets of the subject at which
we. uneasy in our daintiness. are wont to boggle, have nearly
disappeared. Gone, almost, is the homosexuality (now a
clinical matter. hardly the object of fun); gone the scatology
(so uncomfortable in Monuments of the Western Tradition).
Lysistrata centers on what has become for us the last refuge
of genteel ribaldry—heterosexual intercourse. If the presentation is more explicit than we usually expect on a stage. we can
still understand it and conclude with the comforting generality
that the Greeks were. after all, just like us.

They were not. of course. They invested sex with little
transcendental significance. and nothing could have been more
foreign to them than the two most current misconstructions of
Lysistrata—the mid-Victorian ("Brute Man Saved from Himself by the Love of a Good Woman") and the Reichian
("Happy Ganglia Make the Whole World Kin"). *Lysistrata*
concurs with Aristophanes' other briefs for peace. *The
Acharnians* and *The Peace*, in its basically hedonistic approach:
To the discomforts of war are opposed the joys of fulfilled
desire. Admittedly. there have been changes. The earlier plays
interweave a triad of desires—Wine. Food, and Sex; here. the
first two members of the triad are muted (though not dis-
pensed with entirely). and the third is explored to the full.

Predictably. this exploration of single theme rather than
cluster is preferred by certain critics to Aristophanes' normal
practice in that it generates something curiously close to the
modern notion of a plot. Abetting this is the split Chorus.
which not only performs its normal function of a control
which limits and defines the main action. but parallels that
action with one of its own: gaffer loses crone. gaffer gets

crone. Put the parts together, let individual action be succeeded by the appropriate choral action, and the result seems positively Well-Made. Though objection is occasionally raised to a presumed lack of connection between the sex-strike and the seizure of the Akropolis, anyone who considers the terms in which that seizure is first defined—the old men's attack on the locked gates with logs they cannot lift, with fires they cannot light—will hardly be persuaded. And just as well. The connection is not just a structural ploy, but central to the play's meaning. The Akropolis, the heart of the city, is fused with the objects of desire, and its restoration is Love Achieved.

Love, not merely Sex—a vital distinction. If *Lysistrata* is not an exaltation of rut, neither is it a nihilistic satire which undercuts all human progress, all collective action, cynically opposing to it the basic animality of the individual. Upsetting as it may seem to us, the heirs of a Puritan ethic, Aristophanes' hedonism is rarely anarchic. Certainly not here. The fundamental relationship is not blind sexual gratification, the force that drives the water through the rocks, any rocks, but love in its civic manifestation—the bond between husband and wife. Once this is established and identified with the City itself, Aristophanes can and does develop it into other areas. He can turn it around to show the wife and mother's proper share in the State, broaden it into a plea for Panhellenism, push it beyond sex entirely (in the split Choruses) to its irreducible residue. The neural itch is only the beginning; the goal is a united City, and a unified Hellas at peace, the gift of Aphrodite. Significantly, the play ends with, not an orgy, but an invocation by Spartans and Athenians of the whole pantheon. *Eros* and *sophia*, sex and wisdom, join as the civilizing force of love.

Nobility of conception, of course, does not confer dignity of execution, and the basic ridiculousness of sex is rarely lost sight of. It is precisely this tension between intent and accomplishment, a tension all too visible in this most phallic of all comedies, that makes the play work. No character is exempt. Not even the heroine, whose somewhat prissy idealism cracks wide open for a moment at line 715 (all line numbers refer to original Greek text) in the inclusive cry *binêtiômen*—"we want to get laid." *Lysistrata* is a great play, not a so-so tract.

Still, there does exist a minority view. The play's technical excellences are unquestionable: tight formal unity, economy of movement, realism in characterizations, range of feeling. They are also rather un-Aristophanic excellences, and thé specialist who prefers earlier, comparatively messy pieces may perhaps be forgiven Certainly one point must be conceded him: At spots in *Lysistrata*, particularly during debates, Aristophanes' linguistic exuberance deserts him. I do not mean eloquence, but wit, the constant subterranean interplay of sound and sense which elsewhere makes poetry of argumentation. Whether this comes from haste, or from despair, or from the lack of balance which accompanies an overpowering desire to convince—the same lack that, to my mind, deforms the end of *The Clouds*—I cannot say. For whatever reason, it constitutes a blemish.

But a minor blemish on a major work, one tough-minded about sex, tough-minded about war. *Lysistrata*'s greatness ultimately resides in its sheer nerve, its thoroughgoing audacity in confronting, after twenty years of conflict, an Athens poised between external and internal disasters, between the annihilation of her Sicilian expeditionary force in 413 and the overthrow of her constitution in 411. With an astigmatism born of centuries, we are only too liable to misconstrue it, by refusing to see the heroine whole, by regarding the women's revolt as more possibility than fantasy, giving way to sentimentality. But somehow we cannot do it much harm. Even when he writes like someone else, Aristophanes, servant of the Muses and Aphrodite, is Aristophanes still.

Translation

In general, the principles of this translation remain those guiding my versions of *The Acharnians* and *The Wasps*. It is interpretive rather than literal. It cannot be used as a by-the-line crib, but aims at recreating in American English verse what I conceive to have been Aristophanes' essential strategies in Greek. To do this, fields of metaphor have often been changed, jokes added in compensation for jokes lost, useless proper names (primarily those of chorus members and supernumeraries) neglected. Not all of these changes have been indicated in the notes. Some particular points:

Obescenity: Though its workings may seem rococo at times, this version tries to be unblushing, and thus avoid the second greatest sin against Aristophanes, coyness. However, there is one area of compromise that must be justified: The language of the women has been slightly muted, not in the interest of propriety, but to make their characters viable to a modern audience. Lysistrata, for example, has more than a little of the *grande dame* about her, also an intriguing reluctance to refer directly to the relations between the sexes. When she must so refer, it is incongruous and funny—but a literal Englishing of *peous*, the last word in line 124 (here rendered, "Then here's the program: Total Abstinence from SEX!"), either by "penis" or by some curt Saxonism, would stretch the only available stereotype till it shattered, and reduced her assimilated social rank disastrously for the play.

Proper Names: Such is the power of tradition that the name of the heroine, and hence of the play, is here presented in its Latin form rather than in the straight transliteration from the Greek—"Lysistrate"—which would follow the normal practice for this series. But, in any case, the Latin rules for accent should hold, and the name be pronounced LySIStrata. Pronunciations of other principals: KleoNIky. MYRrhiny, LAMpito. KiNEEsias.

Staging: Those who hold that the Theater of Dionysos possessed, in the fifth century B.C., a stage raised above the level of the orchestra (i.e., of the Chorus' dancing area) will find ample proof of their contention in *Lysistrata*; those who maintain that such a raised stage was a fourth-century innovation will find it easy to discount such proof; I prefer to avoid the hassle altogether, though I lean to the fourth-century theory. But all the setting that is really needed is a building, center, with double doors, representing the entrance to the Akropolis, or Propylaia, on whose roof Lysistrata and her women can appear after the coup d'état. The prologue might profit slightly in the direction of literality by the presence of Lysistrata's house, right, and Kleonike's house, left. The first entrance of the Chorus of Men might gain (in the absence of parodoi) by a climbable hill; squeamish audiences might be helped over the Kinesias-Myrrhine encounter if it took place inside a Cave of Pan, Myrrhine appearing (rather than disappearing) briefly to obtain her props. All these are matters of individual taste, and affect the translation not at all. But one principle is at work throughout and must be observed: *Characters and Chorus do not normally mingle.* It is important to note certain applications of this general rule for this play: The Chorus of Women *at no time* enters the Akropolis, nor does it attack the Commissioner and his Skythians; these are the actions of different women, the younger women (most of them supers) who have joined in the oath toward the end of the Prologue. In my reading of the play, I see only one exception to the rule, and it is more apparent than actual: The abortive storming of the Akropolis by the united Chorus in the last scene, an attempt repulsed by the torch-bearing Commissioner.

Text

I have worked most closely with Coulon's Budé text of 1928, and its immediate source, Wilamowitz' edition of 1927, supplementing them with little profit by the text of Cantarella (1956) and with great profit by those of Rogers (second edition, 1911) and Van Leeuwen (1903). But these worthies, singly or collectively, are not to be held responsible for certain features of the Greek underlying my translation. The characteristic weakness of the manuscripts of Aristophanes—their inability to answer with any certainty the recurrent question, "Who's talking?"—breaks out in its most virulent form in this most susceptible play; the translator, trying desperately to make dramatic sense of everything, must formulate his own replies. I have indicated in the notes my major departures from Coulon. Certain of these, particularly the continued presence of the Commissioner and Kinesias after their respective frustrations, may seem violent in the extreme. I can only state here that they are not arbitrary, but proceed from a reasoned examination of the problems involved.

Some minor solutions *are* arbitrary, of course, and scarcely susceptible of proof, as in line 122, where I have distributed between Kleonike and Myrrhine two words assigned by the manuscripts to Kleonike alone, for a purely pragmatic reason: it plays better that way. Again, my answer to the hackneyed query. "What woman delivers lines 447-448?"—to make Ismenia the the Theban, heretofore mute, the speaker of two lines in Attic Greek—is an impossible solution to an impossible problem. Its only virtue is to bring in a previously introduced character without breaking the pattern—which, at that. is better than assigning the lines to the leader of the Women's Chorus.

This seeming disrespect for received writ has had its disturbing consequences, primarily an itch to fiddle further The oath, for example: In the manuscripts, Lysistrata administers it (212 ff.) to the bibulous Kleonike as representative of the assembled women. In view of subsequent developments, might the responsions not better be made by Myrrhine. who will illustrate the practical applications of the oath? Or, to take the Commissioner, whose part I have already fattened considerably: Certain tricks of speech, coupled with his determination at 1011-1012 to make the necessary arrangements, suggest that he, rather than the Chorus (or Koryphaios), might be the official greeter of both the Spartan and the Athenian delegations, beginning the iambs at 1074 (p. 441, "Men of Sparta, I bid you welcome!"). But, though the will to refrain comes hard. I have, for the moment. stopped.

Acknowledgments

My thanks go the University of California, for typing grants: to Eleanore Stone. who fearlessly and impeccably typed and proofread the present version; to colleagues at Riverside, especially William Sharp, who enlightened me on drama; to colleagues in Washington. especially Kenneth Reckford, who enlightened me on Aristophanes. More than thanks to William Arrowsmith, who has taught me more about translation than I shall ever know; and to my wife, the dedicatee of this volume. who taught me about women without being a traitor to her sex.

DOUGLASS PARKER

Characters of the Play

LYSISTRATA
KLEONIKE } *Athenian women*
MYRRHINE
LAMPITO, *a Spartan woman*
ISMENIA, *a Boiotian girl*
KORINTHIAN GIRL
POLICEWOMAN
KORYPHAIOS OF THE MEN
CHORUS OF OLD MEN *of Athens*
KORYPHAIOS OF THE WOMEN
CHORUS OF OLD WOMEN *of Athens*
COMMISSIONER *of Public Safety*
FOUR POLICEMEN
KINESIAS, *Myrrhine's husband*
CHILD *of Kinesias and Myrrhine*
SLAVE
SPARTAN HERALD
SPARTAN AMBASSADOR
FLUTE-PLAYER
ATHENIAN WOMEN
PELOPONNESIAN WOMEN
PELOPONNESIAN MEN
ATHENIAN MEN

SCENE: *A street in Athens. In the background, the Akropolis; center, its gateway, the Propylaia. The time is early morning.* Lysistrata is discovered alone, pacing back and forth in furious impatience.*

LYSISTRATA

Women!

Announce a debauch in honor of Bacchos,
a spree for Pan, some footling fertility fieldday,
and traffic stops—the streets are absolutely clogged
with frantic females banging on tambourines. No urging
for an orgy!
                    But *today*—there's not one woman here.

Enter Kleonike.

Correction: one. Here comes my next door neighbor.
—Hello, Kleonike.*

KLEONIKE

                    Hello to *you*, Lysistrata.
—But what's the fuss? Don't look so barbarous, baby;
knitted brows just aren't your style.

LYSISTRATA

                              It doesn't
matter, Kleonike—I'm on fire right down to the bone.
I'm positively ashamed to be a woman—a member
of a sex which can't even live up to male slanders!
To hear our husbands talk, we're *sly*: deceitful,
always plotting, monsters of intrigue. . . .

KLEONIKE

Proudly.

                              That's us!

LYSISTRATA

And so we agreed to meet today and plot

an intrigue that really deserves the name of monstrous . . .
and WHERE are the women?

       Slyly asleep at home—
they won't get up for anything!

KLEONIKE

       Relax, honey.
They'll be here. You know a woman's way is hard—
mainly the way out of the house: fuss over hubby,
wake the maid up, put the baby down, bathe him,
feed him . . .

LYSISTRATA

    Trivia. They have more fundamental busi-
ness to engage in.

KLEONIKE

    Incidentally, Lysistrata, just why are
you calling this meeting? Nothing teeny, I trust?

LYSISTRATA

Immense.

KLEONIKE

    Hmmm. And pressing?

LYSISTRATA

       Unthinkably tense.

KLEONIKE

Then where IS everybody?

LYSISTRATA

      Nothing like that. If it were,
we'd already be in session. Seconding motions.

—No, *this* came to hand some time ago. I've spent
my nights kneading it, mulling it, filing it down. . . .

KLEONIKE

Too bad. There can't be very much left.

LYSISTRATA

Only this:
the hope and salvation of Hellas lies with the WOMEN!

KLEONIKE

Lies with the women? Now *there's* a last resort.

LYSISTRATA

It lies with us to decide affairs of state
and foreign policy.
The Spartan Question: Peace
or Extirpation?

KLEONIKE

How *fun!*
I cast an Aye for Extirpation!

LYSISTRATA

The utter Annihilation of every last Boiotian?

KLEONIKE

AYE!—I mean Nay. Clemency, please, for those
scrumptious eels.*

LYSISTRATA

And as for Athens . . . I'd rather not put
the thought into words. Just fill in the blanks, if you will.
—To the point: If we can meet and reach agreement
here and now with the girls from Thebes and the
Peloponnese,
we'll form an alliance and save the States of Greece!

KLEONIKE

Us? Be practical. Wisdom for women? There's nothing
cosmic about cosmetics—and Glamor is our only talent.
All we can do is *sit*, primped and painted,
made up and dressed up.

Getting carried away in spite of her argument.

                              ravishing in saffron wrappers,
peekaboo peignoirs, exquisite negligees, those chic,
expensive little slippers that come from the East . . .

LYSISTRATA

Exactly. You've hit it. I see our way to salvation
in just such ornamentation—in slippers and slips, rouge
and perfumes, negligees and décolletage. . . .

KLEONIKE

                                                How so?

LYSISTRATA

So effectively that not one husband will take up his spear
against another . . .

KLEONIKE

                    Peachy!
                              I'll have that kimono
dyed . . .

LYSISTRATA

          . . . or shoulder his shield . . .

KLEONIKE

                                        . . . squeeze into that
daring negligee . . .

LYSISTRATA

. . . or unsheathe his sword!

KLEONIKE

. . . and buy those slippers!

LYSISTRATA

Well, now. Don't you think the girls should be here?

KLEONIKE

Be here? Ages ago—they should have flown!

She stops.

But no. You'll find out. These are authentic Athenians: no matter what they do, they do it late.

LYSISTRATA

But what about the out-of-town delegations? There isn't a woman here from the Shore; none from Salamis . . .

KLEONIKE

That's quite a trip. They usually get on board at sunup. Probably riding at anchor now.

LYSISTRATA

I thought the girls from Acharnai would be here first. I'm especially counting on them. And they're not here.

KLEONIKE

I think Theogenes' wife is under way. When I went by, she was hoisting her sandals . . .*

Looking off right.

But look!

Some of the girls are coming!

Women enter from the right. Lysistrata looks off to the left where more—a ragged lot—are straggling in.

LYSISTRATA

And more over here!

KLEONIKE

Where did you find *that* group?

LYSISTRATA

They're from the outskirts.*

KLEONIKE

Well, that's something. If you haven't done anything else, you've really ruffled up the outskirts.

Myrrhine enters guiltily from the right.

MYRRHINE

Oh, Lysistrata,
we aren't late, are we?
Well, *are* we?
Speak to me!

LYSISTRATA

What is it, Myrrhine? Do you want a medal for tardiness? Honestly, such behavior, with so much at stake . . .

MYRRHINE

I'm sorry. I couldn't find my girdle in the dark.
And anyway, we're here now. So tell us all about it, whatever it is.

KLEONIKE

No, wait a minute. Don't
begin just yet. Let's wait for those girls from Thebes
and the Peloponnese.

LYSISTRATA

Now *there* speaks the proper attitude.

*Lampito, a strapping Spartan woman, enters left, leading a
pretty Boiotian girl (Ismenia) and a huge, steatopygous
Korinthian.*

And here's our lovely Spartan.
Hel*lo*, Lampito
dear.
Why darling, you're simply ravishing! Such
a blemishless complexion—so clean, so out-of-doors!
And will you look at that figure—the pink of perfection!

KLEONIKE

I'll bet you could strangle a bull.

LAMPITO

I calklate so.*
Hit's fitness whut done it, fitness and dancin'. You know
the step?

Demonstrating.

Foot it out back'ards an' toe yore twitchet.

The women crowd around Lampito.

KLEONIKE

What unbelievably beautiful bosoms!

LAMPITO

Shuckins,

whut fer you tweedlin' me up so? I feel like a heifer
come fair-time.

LYSISTRATA

Turning to Ismenia.

And who is this young lady here?

LAMPITO

Her kin's purt-near the bluebloodiest folk in Thebes—
the First Fam'lies of Boiotia.

LYSISTRATA

As they inspect Ismenia.

Ah, picturesque Boiotia:
her verdant meadows, her fruited plain . . .

KLEONIKE

Peering more closely.

Her sunken
garden where no grass grows. A cultivated country.

LYSISTRATA

Gaping at the gawking Korinthian.

And who is *this*—er—little thing?

LAMPITO

She hails
from over by Korinth, but her kinfolk's quality—mighty
big back there.

KLEONIKE

On her tour of inspection.

She's mighty big back *here.*

LAMPITO

The womenfolk's all assemblied. Who-all's notion
was this-hyer confabulation?

LYSISTRATA

                          Mine.

LAMPITO

                                    Git on with the give-out.
I'm hankerin' to hear.

MYRRHINE

                    Me, too! I can't imagine
what could be so important. Tell us about it!

LYSISTRATA

Right away
              —But first, a question. It's not
an involved one. Answer yes or no.

A pause.

MYRRHINE

                              Well, ASK it!

LYSISTRATA

It concerns the fathers of your children—your husbands,
absent on active service. I know you all have men
abroad.
          —Wouldn't you like to have them home?

KLEONIKE

My husband's been gone for the last five months! Way up
to Thrace, watchdogging military waste.* It's horrible!

MYRRHINE

Mine's been posted to Pylos for seven whole months!

LAMPITO

My man's no sooner rotated out of the line
than he's plugged back in. Hain't no discharge in this
war!

KLEONIKE

And lovers can't be had for love or money,
not even synthetics. Why, since those beastly Milesians
revolted and cut off the leather trade, that handy
do-it-yourself kit's *vanished* from the open market!

LYSISTRATA

If I can devise a scheme for ending the war,
I gather I have your support?

KLEONIKE

                    You can count on me!
If you need money, I'll pawn the shift off my back—

Aside.

and drink up the cash before the sun goes down.

MYRRHINE

Me, too! I'm ready to split myself right up
the middle like a mackerel, and give you half!

LAMPITO

Me, too! I'd climb Taygetos Mountain plumb
to the top to git the leastes' peek at Peace!

LYSISTRATA

Very well, I'll tell you. No reason to keep a secret.

Importantly. as the women cluster around her

We can force our husbands to neogitate Peace.
Ladies, by exercising steadfast Self-Control–
By Total Abstinence

A pause

KLEONIKE

> From WHAT?

MYRRHINE

> Yes, what?

LYSISTRATA

> You'll do it?

KLEONIKE

Of course we'll do it! We'd even *die!*

LYSISTRATA

> Very well.
then here's the program:
> Total Abstinence
> from SEX!

The cluster of women dissolves.

–Why are you turning away? Where are you going?

Moving among the women.

–What's this? Such stricken expressions! Such gloomy
gestures!
–Why so pale?
> –Whence these tears?
> –What IS this?
Will you do it or won't you?
> Cat got your tongue?

KLEONIKE

Afraid I can't make it. Sorry.
                    On with the War!

MYRRHINE

Me neither. Sorry.
                    On with the War!

LYSISTRATA

                              This from
my little mackerel? The girl who was ready. a minute
ago, to split herself right up the middle?

KLEONIKE

Breaking in between Lysistrata and Myrrhine

Try something else. Try anything. If you say so,
I'm willing to walk through fire barefoot
                              But not
to give up SEX—there's nothing like it, Lysistrata!

LYSISTRATA

To Myrrhine.

And you?

MYRRHINE

     Me, too! I'll walk through fire.

LYSISTRATA

                              Women!
Utter sluts, the entire sex! Will-power,
nil. We're perfect raw material for Tragedy,
the stuff of heroic lays. "Go to bed with a god
and then get rid of the baby"—that sums us up!

Turning to Lampito.

—Oh, Spartan, be a dear. If *you* stick by me,
just you, we still may have a chance to win.
Give me your vote.

LAMPITO

>   Hit's right onsettlin' fer gals
to sleep all lonely-like, withouten no humpin'.
But I'm on your side. We shore need Peace, too.

LYSISTRATA

You're a darling—the only woman here
worthy of the name!

KLEONIKE

>   Well, just suppose we *did*,
as much as possible, abstain from . . . what you said,
you know—not that we *would*—could something like
that bring Peace any sooner?

LYSISTRATA

>   Certainly. Here's how it works:
We'll paint, powder, and pluck ourselves to the last
detail, and stay inside, wearing those filmy
tunics that set off everything we *have*—
>   and then
slink up to the men. They'll snap to attention, go
absolutely *mad* to love us—
>   but we won't let them. We'll Abstain.
—I imagine they'll conclude a treaty rather quickly.

LAMPITO

Nodding.

Menelaos he tuck one squint at Helen's bubbies
all nekkid, and plumb throwed up.

Pause for thought.

                                        Throwed up his sword

KLEONIKE

Suppose the men just leave us flat?

LYSISTRATA

                                        In that case.
we'll have to take things into our own hands.

KLEONIKE

There simply isn't any reasonable facsimile!
—Suppose they take us by force and drag us off
to the bedroom against our wills?

LYSISTRATA

                                        Hang on to the door

KLEONIKE

Suppose they beat us!

LYSISTRATA

                            Give in—but be bad sports
Be nasty about it—they don't enjoy these forced
affairs. So make them suffer.
                            Don't worry; they'll stop
soon enough. A married man wants harmony—
cooperation, not rape.

KLEONIKE

                            Well. I suppose so.

Looking from Lysistrata to Lampito.

If *both* of you approve this. then so do we

LAMPITO

Hain't worried over our menfolk none. We'll bring 'em
round to makin' a fair, straightfor'ard Peace
withouten no nonsense about it. But take this rackety
passel in Athens: I misdoubt no one could make 'em
give over thet blabber of theirn.

LYSISTRATA

They're our concern.
Don't worry. We'll bring them around.

LAMPITO

Not likely.
Not long as they got ships kin still sail straight,
an' thet fountain of money up thar in Athene's temple.*

LYSISTRATA

That point is quite well covered:
We're taking over
the Akropolis, including Athene's temple, today.
It's set: Our oldest women have their orders.
They're up there now, pretending to sacrifice, waiting
for us to reach an agreement. As soon as we do,
they seize the Akropolis.

LAMPITO

The way you put them thengs,
I swear I can't see how we kin possibly lose!

LYSISTRATA

Well, now that it's settled, Lampito, let's not lose
any time. Let's take the Oath to make this binding.

LAMPITO

Just trot out thet-thar Oath. We'll swear it.

LYSISTRATA

>>> Excellent.

—Where's a policewoman?

A huge girl, dressed as a Skythian archer (the Athenian police) with bow and circular shield, lumbers up and gawks.

>>> —What are *you* looking for?

Pointing to a spot in front of the women.

Put your shield down here.

The girl obeys.

>>> No, hollow *up!*

The girl reverses the shield. Lysistrata looks about brightly.

—Someone give me the entrails.

A dubious silence.

KLEONIKE

>>> Lysistrata, what kind
of an Oath are we supposed to swear?

LYSISTRATA

>>> The Standard.
Aischylos used it in a play, they say—the one where
you slaughter a sheep and swear on a shield.

KLEONIKE

>>> Lysistrata,
you *do not* swear on Oath for *Peace* on a *shield!*

LYSISTRATA

What Oath do you want?

Exasperated.

Something bizarre and expensive?
A fancier victim—"Take one white horse and
disembowel"?

KLEONIKE

White horse? The symbolism's too obscure.*

LYSISTRATA

*Then how
do we swear this oath?*

KLEONIKE

Oh, *I* can tell you
that, if you'll let me.
First, we put an enormous
black cup right here—hollow up, of course.
Next, into the cup we slaughter a jar of Thasian
wine, and swear a mighty Oath that we won't . . .
dilute it with water.

LAMPITO

To Kleonike.

Let me corngratulate you—
that were the beatenes' Oath I ever heerd on!

LYSISTRATA

Calling inside.

Bring out a cup and jug of wine!

*Two women emerge, the first staggering under the weight of
a huge black cup, the second even more burdened with a
tremendous wine jar. Kleonike addresses them.*

KLEONIKE

You darlings!
What a tremendous display of pottery!

Fingering the cup.

A girl
could get a glow just *holding* a cup like this!

She grabs it away from the first woman, who exits.

LYSISTRATA

Taking the wine jar from the second serving woman (who exits), she barks at Kleonike.

Put that down and help me butcher this boar!

Kleonike puts down the cup, over which she and Lysistrata together hold the jar of wine (the "boar"). Lysistrata prays.

> O Mistress Persuasion,
> O Cup of Devotion,
> Attend our invocation:
> Accept this oblation,
> Grant our petition,
> Favor our mission.

Lysistrata and Kleonike tip up the jar and pour the gurgling wine into the cup. Myrrhine, Lampito, and the others watch closely.

MYRRHINE

Such an attractive shade of blood. And the spurt—
pure Art!

LAMPITO

Hit shore do smell mighty purty!

Lysistrata and Kleonike put down the empty wine jar.

KLEONIKE

Girls, let me be the first

Launching herself at the cup.

to take the Oath!

LYSISTRATA

Hauling Kleonike back.

You'll have to wait your turn like everyone else.
—Lampito, how do we manage with this mob?

Cumbersome.

—Everyone place her right hand on the cup.

The women surround the cup and obey.

I need a spokeswoman. One of you to take
the Oath in behalf of the rest.

*The women edge away from Kleonike, who reluctantly finds
herself elected.*

The rite will conclude
with a General Pledge of Assent by all of you, thus
confirming the Oath. Understood?

Nods from the women. Lysistrata address Kleonike.

Repeat after me:

LYSISTRATA

I will withhold all rights of access or entrance

KLEONIKE

I will withhold all rights of access or entrance

LYSISTRATA

From every husband, lover, or casual acquaintance

KLEONIKE

from every husband, lover, or casual acquaintance

LYSISTRATA

Who moves in my direction in erection.
                                    —Go on

KLEONIKE

who m-moves in my direction in erection.
                                    Ohhhhh!
—Lysistrata, my knees are shaky. Maybe I'd better . . .

LYSISTRATA

I will create, imperforate in cloistered chastity,

KLEONIKE

I will create, imperforate in cloistered chastity,

LYSISTRATA

A newer, more glamorous, supremely seductive me

KLEONIKE

a newer, more glamorous, supremely seductive me

LYSISTRATA

And fire my husband's desire with my molten allure—

KLEONIKE

and fire my husband's desire with my molten allure—

LYSISTRATA

But remain, to his panting advances, icily pure.

KLEONIKE

but remain, to his panting advances, icily pure.

LYSISTRATA

If he should force me to share the connubial couch,

KLEONIKE

If he should force me to share the connubial couch,

LYSISTRATA

I refuse to return his stroke with the teeniest twitch.

KLEONIKE

I refuse to return his stroke with the teeniest twitch.

LYSISTRATA

I will not lift my slippers to touch the thatch

KLEONIKE

I will not lift my slippers to touch the thatch

LYSISTRATA

Or submit sloping prone in a hangdog crouch.

KLEONIKE

or submit sloping prone in a hangdog crouch.

LYSISTRATA

**If I this oath maintain,
may I drink this glorious wine.**

KLEONIKE

*If I this oath maintain,
may I drink this glorious wine.*

LYSISTRATA

**But if I slip or falter,
let me drink water.**

KLEONIKE

*But if I slip or falter,
let me drink water.*

LYSISTRATA

—And now the General Pledge of Assent:

WOMEN

A-MEN!

LYSISTRATA

Good. I'll dedicate the oblation.

She drinks deeply.

KLEONIKE

                      Not too much,
darling. You know how anxious we are to become
allies and friends.
              Not to mention *staying* friends.

*She pushes Lysistrata away and drinks. As the women take
their turns at the cup, loud cries and alarums are heard
offstage.*

LAMPITO

What-all's that bodacious ruckus?

LYSISTRATA

                  Just what I told you:
It means the women have taken the Akropolis. Athene's
Citadel is ours!
            It's time for you to go,
Lampito, and set your affairs in order in Sparta.

Indicating the other women in Lampito's group.

Leave these girls here as hostages.

Lampito exits left. Lysistrata turns to the others.

                 Let's hurry inside
the Akropolis and help the others shoot the bolts.

KLEONIKE

Don't you think the men will send reinforcements
against us as soon as they can?

LYSISTRATA

So where's the worry?
The men can't burn their way in or frighten us out.
The Gates are ours—they're proof against fire and fear—
and they open only on our conditions.

KLEONIKE

Yes!
That's the spirit—let's deserve our reputations:

As the women hurry off into the Akropolis.

UP THE SLUTS!
WAY FOR THE OLD IMPREGNABLES!

The door shuts behind the women, and the stage is empty. A pause, and the Chorus of Men shuffles on from the left in two groups, led by their Koryphaios. They are incredibly aged Athenians; though they may acquire spryness later in the play, at this point they are sheer decrepitude. Their normally shaky progress is impeded by their burdens: each man not only staggers under a load of wood across his shoulders, but has his hands full as well—in one, an earthen pot containing fire (which is in constant danger of going out); in the other, a dried vinewood torch, not yet lit. Their progress toward the Akropolis is very slow.

KORYPHAIOS OF MEN

To the right guide of the First Semichorus, who is stumbling along in mild agony.

Forward, Swifty, keep 'em in step! Forget your shoulder.
I know these logs are green and heavy—but duty, boy,
    duty!

SWIFTY

*Somewhat inspired, he quavers into slow song to set a pace
for his group.*

> I'm never surprised. At my age, life
> is just one damned thing after another.
> And yet, I never thought my wife
> was anything more than a home-grown bother.
>> But now, dadblast her,
>> she's a National Disaster!

FIRST SEMICHORUS OF MEN

> What a catastrophe—
>> *MATRIARCHY!*
> They've brought Athene's statue* to heel,
> they've put the Akropolis under a seal,
> they've copped the whole damned commonweal . . .
> What is there left for them to steal?

KORYPHAIOS OF MEN

*To the right guide of the Second Semichorus—a slower soul,
if possible, than Swifty.*

> Now, Chipper, speed's the word. The Akropolis, on the
>> double!
> Once we're there, we'll pile these logs around them, and
>> convene
> a circuit court for a truncated trial. Strictly impartial:
> With a show of hands, we'll light a spark of justice under
> every woman who brewed this scheme. We'll burn them
>> all
> on the first ballot—and the first to go is Ly . . .

Pause for thought.

is Ly . . .

Remembering and pointing at a spot in the audience.

> Is *Lykon's* wife—and there she is, right over there!*

CHIPPER

Taking up the song again.

> I won't be twitted, I won't be guyed,
> I'll teach these women not to trouble us!
> Kleomenes the Spartan tried
> expropriating our Akropolis*
> some time ago—
> ninety-five years or so—

SECOND SEMICHORUS OF MEN

> but he suffered damaging losses
> - when he ran across US!
> He breathed defiance—and more as well:
> No bath for six years—you could tell.
> We fished him out of the Citadel
> and quelled his spirit—but not his smell.

KORYPHAIOS OF MEN

That's how I took him. A savage siege:
> Seventeen ranks
of shields were massed at that gate, with blanket infantry
   cover.
I slept like a baby.
> So when mere women (who gall the gods
and make Euripides sick) try the same trick, should I
sit idly by?
> Then demolish the monument I won at Marathon!

FIRST SEMICHORUS OF MEN

Singly

> —The last lap of our journey!
> —I greet it with some dismay.
> —The danger doesn't deter me.
> > —but
it's uphill
> —all the way.
> —Please, somebody.

—find a jackass
to drag these logs
                —to the top.
—I ache to join the fracas,
                        —but
my shoulder's aching
                —to stop.

SWIFTY

Backward there's no turning.
Upward and onward, men!
And keep those firepots burning, or
we make this trip again.

CHORUS OF MEN

*Blowing into their firepots, which promptly send forth clouds
of smoke.*

                With a puff (pfffff). . . .
                and a cough (hhhhh). . . .
                The smoke! I'll choke! Turn it off!

SECOND SEMICHORUS OF MEN

Singly.

—Damned embers.
                —Should be muzzled.
—There oughta be a law.
—They jumped me
                —when I whistled
                        —and then
they gnawed my eyeballs
                —raw.
—There's lava in my lashes.
—My lids are oxidized.
—My brows are braised.
                —These ashes are
volcanoes
        —in disguise.

CHIPPER

> This way, men. And remember,
> The Goddess needs our aid.
> So don't be stopped by cinders. Let's
> press on to the stockade!

CHORUS OF MEN

Blowing again into their firepots, which erupt as before

> With a huff (hfffff),
> and a chuff (chffff).
> Drat that smoke. Enough is enough!

KORYPHAIOS OF MEN

Signalling the Chorus, which has now tottered into position before the Akropolis gate, to stop, and peering into his firepot

Praise be to the gods, it's awake. There's fire in the old
  fire yet.
  —Now the directions. See how they strike you:
                                        First, we deposit
these logs at the entrance and light our torches. Next, we
  crash
the gate. When that doesn't work, we request admission
  Politely.
When *that* doesn't work, we burn the damned door
  down, and smoke
these women into submission,
                        That seem acceptable? Good
Down with the load   ouch, that smoke! Sonofabitch!

A horrible tangle results as the Chorus attempts to deposit the logs. The Koryphaios turns to the audience.

Is there a general in the house? We have a logistical
problem.

No answer. He shrugs.

Same old story. Still at loggerheads over in Samos.*

With great confusion. the logs are placed somehow

That's better. The pressure's off. I've got my backbone
back.

To his firepot

What. pot? You forgot your part in the plot?
                                        Urge that smudge
to be hot on the dot and scorch my torch.
                                        Got it. pot?

Praying.

> Queen Athene. let these strumpets
> crumple before our attack
> Grant us victory, male supremacy
> and a testimonial plaque

*The men plunge their torches into firepots and arrange them-
selves purposefully before the gate Engaged in their preparations. they do not see the sudden entrance. from the right. of
the Chorus of Women. led by their Koryphaios These wear
long cloaks and carry pitchers of water They are very old—
though not so old as the men—but quite spry In their turn.
they do not perceive the Chorus of Men*

KORYPHAIOS OF WOMEN

Stopping suddenly

What's this—soot? And smoke as well? I may be all wet.
but this might mean fire. Things look dark. girls; we'll
have to dash

*They move ahead. at a considerably faster pace than the
men.*

FIRST SEMICHORUS OF WOMEN

Singly

Speed! Celerity!   Save our sorority
from arson Combustion   And heat exhaustion

Don't let our sisterhood   shrivel to blisterhood.
Fanned into slag by hoary typhoons.
By flatulent, nasty, gusty baboons.
    We're late! Run!
    The girls might be done!

Tutte.

Filling my pitcher   was absolute torture:
The fountains in town.   are so *crowded* at dawn,
glutted with masses   of the lower classes
blatting and battering,   shoving, and shattering
jugs. But I juggled   my burden, and wriggled
away to extinguish   the igneous anguish

    of neighbor, and sister, and daughter—
      Here's Water!

SECOND SEMICHORUS OF WOMEN

Singly.

Get wind of the news?   The gaffers are loose.
The blowhards are off   with fuel enough
to furnish a bathhouse.   But the finish is pathos:
    They're scaling the heights with a horrid proposal.
    They're threatening women with rubbish disposal!
      How ghastly—how gauche!
      burned up with the trash!

Tutte.

Preserve me, Athene,   from gazing on any
matron or maid   auto-da fé'd.
Cover with grace   these redeemers of Greece
from battles, insanity,.   Man's inhumanity.
Gold-browed goddess,   hither to aid us!
Fight as our ally,   join in our sally
    against pyromaniac slaughter—
      Haul Water!

KORYPHAIOS OF WOMEN

Noticing for the first time the Chorus of Men, still busy at their firepots, she cuts off a member of her Chorus who seems about to continue the song

Hold it What have we here? You don't catch true-blue patriots red-handed These are authentic degenerates. male. taken *in flagrante*

KORYPHAIOS OF MEN

Oops. Female troops. This could be upsetting
I didn't expect such a flood of reserves.

KORYPHAIOS OF WOMEN

Merely a spearhead
If our numbers stun you. watch that yellow streak
spread. We represent just one percent of one percent of
This Woman's Army

KORYPHAIOS OF MEN

Never been confronted with such backtalk. Can't allow
it Somebody pick up a log and pulverize that brass.
Any volunteers?

There are none among the male chorus

KORYPHAIOS OF WOMEN

Put down the pitchers. girls. If they start waving that
  lumber.
we don't want to be encumbered

KORYPHAIOS OF MEN

Look. men. a few sharp jabs
will stop that jawing It never fails.
The poet Hipponax
swears by it.*

Still no volunteers. The Koryphaios of Women advances

KORYPHAIOS OF WOMEN

              Then step right up. Have a jab at me.
Free shot.

KORYPHAIOS OF MEN

Advancing reluctantly to meet her.

           Shut up! I'll peel your pelt. I'll pit your pod.

KORYPHAIOS OF WOMEN

The name is Stratyllis. I dare you to lay one finger on me.

KORYPHAIOS OF MEN

I'll lay on you with a fistful. Er—any specific threats?

KORYPHAIOS OF WOMEN

Earnestly.

I'll crop your lungs and reap your bowels, bite by bite,
and leave no balls on the body for other bitches to
gnaw.*

KORYPHAIOS OF MEN

Retreating hurriedly.

Can't beat Euripides for insight. And I quote:
                    No creature's found
*so lost to shame as Woman.**
              Talk about realist playwrights!

KORYPHAIOS OF WOMEN

Up with the water, ladies. Pitchers at the ready, place!

KORYPHAIOS OF MEN

Why the water, you sink of iniquity? More sedition?

KORYPHAIOS OF WOMEN

Why the fire, you walking boneyard? Self-cremation?

KORHYPHAIOS OF MEN

I brought this fire to ignite a pyre and fricassee your friends.

KORYPHAIOS OF WOMEN

I brought this water to douse your pyre. Tit for tat.

KORYPHAIOS OF MEN

You'll douse my fire? Nonsense!

KORYPHAIOS OF WOMEN

                    You'll see, when the facts soak in.

KORYPHAIOS OF MEN

I have the torch right here. Perhaps I should barbecue *you*.

KORYPHAIOS OF WOMEN

If you have any soap, I could give you a bath.

KORYPHAIOS OF MEN '

                              A bath from those
polluted hands?

KORYPHAIOS OF WOMEN

          Pure enough for a blushing young bridegroom.

KORYPHAIOS OF MEN

Enough of that insolent lip.

KORYPHAIOS OF WOMEN

                    It's merely freedom of speech.

KORYPHAIOS OF MEN

I'll stop that screeching!

KORYPHAIOS OF WOMEN

You're helpless outside the jury-box.

KORYPHAIOS OF MEN

Urging his men, torches at the ready, into a charge.

Burn, fire, burn!

KORYPHAIOS OF WOMEN

As the women empty their pitchers over the men.

And cauldron bubble.

KORYPHAIOS OF MEN

Like his troops, soaked and routed.

Arrrgh!

KORYPHAIOS OF WOMEN

Goodness.

What seems to be the trouble? Too hot?

KORYPHAIOS OF MEN

Hot, hell! Stop it!

What do you think you're doing?

KORYPHAIOS OF WOMEN

If you must know, I'm gardening.

Perhaps you'll bloom.

KORYPHAIOS OF MEN

Perhaps I'll fall right off the vine!

I'm withered, frozen, shaking . . .

KORYPHAIOS OF WOMEN

Of course. But, providentially,
you brought along your smudgepot.
The sap should rise eventually.

Shivering, the Chorus of Men retreats in utter defeat.

A Commissioner of Public Safety* enters from the left, followed quite reluctantly by a squad of police—four Skythian archers. He surveys the situation with disapproval.

COMMISSIONER

Fire, eh? Females again—spontaneous combustion
of lust. Suspected as much.
Rubadubdubbing, incessant
incontinent keening for wine, damnable funeral
foofaraw for Adonis resounding from roof to roof—
heard it all before . . .

Savagely, as the Koryphaios of Men tries to interpose a remark.

and WHERE?
The ASSEMBLY!
Recall, if you can, the debate on the Sicilian Question:
That bullbrained demagogue Demostratos (who will rot,
   I trust)
rose to propose a naval task force.
His wife,
writhing with religion on a handy roof, bleated
a dirge:
"BEREFT! OH WOE OH WOE FOR ADONIS!"
And so of course Demostratos, taking his cue,
outblatted her:
"A DRAFT! ENROLL THE WHOLE OF
ZAKYNTHOS!"
His wife, a smidgin stewed, renewed her yowling:
"OH GNASH YOUR TEETH AND BEAT YOUR
BREASTS FOR ADONIS!"
And so of course Demostratos (that god-detested blot,
that foul-lunged son of an ulcer) gnashed tooth and nail

and voice, and bashed and rammed his program through.
And THERE is the Gift of Women:
MORAL CHAOS!

KORYPHAIOS OF MEN

Save your breath for actual felonies, Commissioner;
see what's happened to us! Insolence, insults.
these we pass over, but not lese-majesty:
We're flooded
with indignity from those bitches' pitchers—like a bunch
of weak-bladdered brats. Our cloaks are sopped. We'll
sue!

COMMISSIONER

Useless. Your suit won't hold water. Right's on their side
For female depravity, gentlemen, WE stand guilty—
we, their teachers, preceptors of prurience, accomplices
before the fact of fornication. We sowed them in sexual
license, and now we reap rebellion.
The proof?
Consider. Off we trip to the goldsmith's to leave
an order:
　　　"That bangle you fashioned last spring for my wife
is sprung. She was thrashing around last night, and the
　prong
popped out of the bracket. I'll be tied up all day—I'm
boarding the ferry right now—but my wife'll be home.
If you get the time, please stop by the house in a bit
and see if you can't do something—anything—to fit
a new prong into the bracket of her bangle."
And bang.
Another one ups to a cobbler—young, but no apprentice.
full kit of tools, ready to give his awl—
and delivers this gem:
　　　　"My wife's new sandals are tight
The cinch pinches her pinkie right where she's
　sensitive.
Drop in at noon with something to stretch her cinch
and give it a little play."

And a cinch it is.
Such hanky-panky we have to thank for today's
Utter Anarchy: I, a Commissioner of Public
Safety, duly invested with extraordinary powers
to protect the State in the Present Emergency, have
   secured
a source of timber to outfit our fleet and solve
the shortage of oarage. I need the money immediately . . .
the WOMEN, no less, have locked me out of the
   Treasury!

Pulling himself together.

—Well, no profit in standing around.

To one of the archers.

                                        Bring
the crowbars. I'll jack these women back on their
pedestals!
   —WELL, you slack-jawed jackass? What's the
attraction? Wipe that thirst off your face. I said *crow*bar,
not saloon!—All right, men, all together. Shove those
bars underneath the gate and HEAVE!

Grabbing up a crowbar.

                              I'll take this side.
And now let's root them out, men, ROOT them out.
One, Two . . .

*The gates to the Akropolis burst open suddenly, disclosing
Lysistrata. She is perfectly composed and bears a large spindle.
The Commissioner and the Police fall back in consternation.*

LYSISTRATA

                  Why the moving equipment?
I'm quite well motivated, thank you, and here I am.
Frankly, you don't need crowbars nearly so much as
brains.

COMMISSIONER

Brains? O name of infamy! Where's a policeman?

He grabs wildly for the First Archer and shoves him toward Lysistrata.

Arrest that woman!
                                Better tie her hands behind her.

LYSISTRATA

By Artemis, goddess of the hunt, if he lays a finger
on me, he'll rue the day he joined the force!

She jabs the spindle viciously at the First Archer, who leaps, terrified, back to his comrades.

COMMISSIONER

What's this—retreat? Never! Take her on the flank.

The First Archer hangs back. The Commissioner grabs the Second Archer.

—Help him.
                                —Will the two of you kindly TIE HER UP?

He shoves them toward Lysistrata. Kleonike, carrying a large chamber pot, springs out of the entrance and advances on the Second Archer.

KLEONIKE

By Artemis, goddess of the dew,* if you so much
as touch her, I'll stomp the shit right out of you!

The two Archers run back to their group.

COMMISSIONER

Shit? Shameless! Where's another policeman?

He grabs the Third Archer and propels him toward Kleonike.

Handcuff *her* first. Can't stand a foul-mouthed female.

Myrrhine, carrying a large, blazing lamp, appears at the entrance and advances on the Third Archer.

MYRRHINE

By Artemis, bringer of light, if you lay a finger
on her, you won't be able to stop the swelling!

The Third Archer dodges her swing and runs back to the group.

COMMISSIONER

Now what? Where's an officer?

Pushing the Fourth Archer toward Myrrhine.

Apprehend that woman!
I'll see that *somebody* stays to take the blame!

Ismenia the Boiotian, carrying a huge pair of pincers, appears at the entrance and advances on the Fourth Archer.

ISMENIA*

By Artemis, goddess of Tauris, if you go near
that girl, I'll rip the hair right out of your head!

The Fourth Archer retreats hurriedly.

COMMISSIONER

What a colossal mess: Athens' Finest—
finished!

Arranging the Archers.

—Now, men, a little *esprit de corps*. Worsted
by women? Drubbed by drabs?
Never!
Regroup,

reform that thin red line.
                              Ready?
                                    CHARGE!

He pushes them ahead of him.

LYSISTRATA

I warn you. We have four battalions behind us—
full-armed combat infantrywomen, trained
from the cradle . . .

COMMISSIONER

                    Disarm them, Officers! Go for the hands!

LYSISTRATA

Calling inside the Akropolis.

MOBILIZE THE RESERVES!

*A horde of women, armed with household articles, begins to
pour from the Akropolis.*

                              Onward, you ladies from hell!
Forward, you market militia, you battle-hardened
bargain hunters, old sales campaigners, grocery
grenadiers, veterans never bested by an overcharge!
You troops of the breadline, doughgirls—
                                    INTO THE FRAY!
Show them no mercy!
                    Push!
                         Jostle!
                                Shove!
Call them nasty names!
                    Don't be ladylike.

The women charge and rout the Archers in short order.

Fall back—don't strip the enemy! The day is ours!

*The women obey, and the Archers run off left. The Commis-
sioner, dazed, is left muttering to himself.*

COMMISSIONER

Gross ineptitude. A sorry day for the Force.

LYSISTRATA

Of course. What did you expect? We're not slaves;
we're freeborn Women, and when we're scorned, we're
full of fury. Never underestimate the Power of a Woman.

COMMISSIONER

Power? You mean Capacity. I should have remembered
the proverb: *The lower the tavern, the higher the
dudgeon.*

KORYPHAIOS OF MEN

Why cast your pearls before swine, Commissioner? I
    know you're a civil
servant, but don't overdo it. Have you forgotten the bath
they gave us—in public,
                        fully dressed,
                                    totally soapless?
Keep rational discourse for *people!*

*He aims a blow at the Koryphaios of Women, who dodges
and raises her pitcher.*

KORYPHAIOS OF WOMEN

                        I might point out that lifting
one's hand against a neighbor is scarcely civilized
behavior—and entails, for the lifter, a black eye.
                        I'm really peaceful by nature,
compulsively inoffensive—a perfect doll. My ideal is a
well-bred repose that doesn't even stir up dust . . .

Swinging at the Koryphaios of Men with the pitcher.

                        unless some no-good lowlife
tries to rifle my hive and gets my dander up!

The Koryphaios of Men backs hurriedly away, and the Chorus of Men goes into a worried dance

CHORUS OF MEN

Singly.

> O Zeus, what's the use of this constant abuse?
> How do we deal with this female zoo?
> Is there no solution to Total Immersion?
> What can a poor man DO?

Tutti.

> Query the Adversary!
> Ferret out their story!
> What end did they have in view,
> to seize the city's sanctuary,
> snatch its legendary eyrie,
> snare an area so very
> terribly taboo?

KORYPHAIOS OF MEN

To the Commissioner.

Scrutinize those women! Scour their depositions—assess
 their rebuttals!
Masculine honor demands this affair be probed to the
 bottom!

COMMISSIONER

Turning to the women from the Akropolis

All right, you. Kindly inform me, dammit, in your own
 words:
What possible object could you have had in blockading
 the Treasury?

LYSISTRATA

We thought we'd deposit the money in escrow and
 withdraw your men
from the war.

COMMISSIONER

The money's the cause of the war?

LYSISTRATA

And all our internal
disorders—the Body Politic's chronic bellyaches: What
causes Peisandros' frantic rantings, or the raucous cau-
cuses of the Friends of Oligarchy?* The chance for graft.
But now, with the money up there,
they can't upset the City's equilibrium—or lower its
balance.

COMMISSIONER

And what's your next step?

LYSISTRATA

Stupid question. We'll budget the money.

COMMISSIONER

You'll budget the money?

LYSISTRATA

Why should you find that so shocking?
We budget the household accounts, and you don't object
at all.

COMMISSIONER

That's different.

LYSISTRATA

Different? How?

COMMISSIONER

The War Effort needs this money!

LYSISTRATA

Who needs the War Effort?

COMMISSIONER

    Every patriot who pulses to save
all that Athens holds near and dear

LYSISTRATA

        Oh. *that*. Don't worry
We'll save you

COMMISSIONER

    You will save us?

LYSISTRATA

       Who else?

COMMISSIONER

      But this is unscrupulous!

LYSISTRATA

We'll save you. You can't deter us.

COMMISSIONER

      Scurrilous!

LYSISTRATA

      You seem disturbed.
This makes it difficult. But, still—we'll save you.

COMMISSIONER

      Doubtless illegal!

LYSISTRATA

We deem it a duty. For friendship's sake.

COMMISSIONER

                          Well, forsake this friend
I DO NOT WANT TO BE SAVED. DAMMIT!

LYSISTRATA

                         All the more reason
It's not only Sparta; now we'll have to save you from
you.

COMMISSIONER

Might I ask where you women conceived this concern
about War and Peace?

LYSISTRATA

Loftily.

                  We shall explain.

COMMISSIONER

Making a fist

                     Hurry up, and you won't
get hurt.

LYSISTRATA

         Then *listen.* And do try to keep your hands to
yourself.

COMMISSIONER

Moving threateningly toward her.

I can't. Righteous anger forbids restraint, and decrees

KLEONIKE

Brandishing her chamber pot.

Multiple fractures?

COMMISSIONER

Retreating.

> Keep those croaks for yourself, you old crow!

To Lysistrata

All right, lady, I'm ready. Speak.

LYSISTRATA

> I shall proceed:
When the War began, like the prudent, dutiful wives that
we are, we tolerated you men, and endured your actions
   in silence. (Small wonder—
you wouldn't let us say boo.)
> You were not precisely the answer
to a matron's prayer—we knew you too well, and found
   out more.
Too many times, as we sat in the house, we'd hear that
you'd done it again—manhandled another affair of
state with your usual staggering incompetence. Then,
masking our worry with a nervous laugh,
we'd ask you, brightly, "How was the Assembly today,
   dear? Anything
in the minutes about Peace?" And my husband would
give his stock reply.
"What's that to you? Shut up!" And I did.

KLEONIKE

Proudly.

> *I* never shut up!

COMMISSIONER

I trust you were shut up. Soundly.

LYSISTRATA

> Regardless, *I* shut up.
And then we'd learn that you'd passed another decree,

fouler than the first, and we'd ask again: "Darling, how
did you manage anything so idiotic?" And my
husband, with his customary glare, would tell me to spin
my thread, or else get a clout on the head
And of course he'd quote from Homer:

> Y^e *menne must husband* y^e *warre.**

COMMISSIONER

Apt and irrefutably right

LYSISTRATA

Right, you miserable misfit?
To keep us from giving advice while you fumbled the
City away in the Senate? Right, indeed!
But this time was really too much
Wherever we went, we'd hear you engaged in the same
 conversation:
"What Athens needs is a Man."*
"But there isn't a Man in the country."
"You can say that again."
There was obviously no time to lose
We women met in immediate convention and passed a
unanimous resolution: To work in concert for safety and
Peace in Greece. We have valuable advice to impart,
and if you can possibly deign to emulate our silence,
and take your turn as audience, we'll rectify you—
we'll straighten you out and set you right

COMMISSIONER

You'll set *us* right? You go too far. I cannot permit
such a statement to

LYSISTRATA

Shush.

COMMISSIONER

I categorically decline to shush
for some confounded woman, who wears—as a constant

reminder of congenital inferiority, an injunction to
public silence—a veil!
Death before such dishonor!

LYSISTRATA

Removing her veil.

>   If that's the only obstacle . . .
>   I feel you need a new panache,
>   so take the veil, my dear Commis-
>   sioner, and drape it thus—
>   and SHUSH!

*As she winds the veil around the startled Commissioner's
head, Kleonike and Myrrhine, with carding-comb and wool-
basket, rush forward and assist in transforming him into a
woman.*

KLEONIKE

>   Accept, I pray, this humble comb.

MYRRHINE

>   Receive this basket of fleece as well.

LYSISTRATA

>   Hike up your skirts, and card your wool,
>   and gnaw your beans—and stay at home!
>   While we rewrite Homer:
> Y^e WOMEN must WIVE ye warre!

*To the Chorus of Women, the Commissioner struggles to
remove his new outfit.*

Women, weaker vessels, arise!
>   Put down your pitchers.
It's our turn, now. Let's supply our friends with some
moral support.

The Chorus of Women dances to the same tune as the Men but with much more confidence.

CHORUS OF WOMEN

Singly.

> Oh, yes! I'll dance to bless their success.
> Fatigue won't weaken my will. Or my knees.
> I'm ready to join in any jeopardy.
>   with girls as good as *these*!

Tutte.

> A tally of their talents
> convinces me they're giants
> of excellence. To commence:
> there's Beauty, Duty, Prudence, Science.
> Self-Reliance, Compliance, Defiance,
> and Love of Athens in balanced alliance
>   with Common Sense!

KORYPHAIOS OF WOMEN

To the women from the Akropolis.

Autochthonous daughters of Attika, sprung from the
soil that bore your mothers, the spiniest, spikiest
nettles known to man, prove your mettle and attack!
Now is no time to dilute your anger. You're
running ahead of the wind!

LYSISTRATA

>   We'll wait for the wind
> from heaven. The gentle breath of Love and his Kyprian
> mother will imbue our bodies with desire, and raise a
> storm to tense and tauten these blasted men until they
> crack. And soon we'll be on every tongue in
> Greece—the *Pacifiers*.*

COMMISSIONER

That's quite
a mouthful. How will you win it?

LYSISTRATA

First, we intend to withdraw
that crazy Army of Occupation from the downtown
shopping section.

KLEONIKE

Aphrodite be praised!

LYSISTRATA

The pottery shop and the grocery stall
are overstocked with soldiers, clanking around like
    those maniac Korybants,
armed to the teeth for a battle.

COMMISSIONER

A Hero is Always Prepared!

LYSISTRATA

I suppose he is. But it does look silly to shop for sardines
from behind a shield.

KLEONIKE

I'll second that. I saw
a cavalry captain buy vegetable soup on horseback. He
carried the whole mess home in his helmet.
                    And then that fellow from Thrace,
shaking his buckler and spear—a menace straight from
    the stage.
The saleslady was stiff with fright. He was hogging her
    ripe figs—free.

COMMISSIONER

I admit, for the moment, that Hellas' affairs are in one hell of a snarl. But how can you set them straight?

LYSISTRATA

                                        Simplicity itself.

COMMISSIONER

Pray demonstrate.

LYSISTRATA

            It's rather like yarn. When a hank's in a tangle, we lift it—*so*—and work out the snarls by winding it up on spindles, now this way, now that way.
                        That's how we'll wind up the War, if allowed: We'll work out the snarls by sending Special
    Commissions—
back and forth, now this way, now that way—to ravel these tense international kinks.

COMMISSIONER

            I lost your thread, but I know there's a hitch. Spruce up the world's disasters with spindles—typically woolly female logic.

LYSISTRATA

            If *you* had a scrap of logic, you'd adopt our wool as a master plan for Athens.

COMMISSIONER

                        What course of action does the wool advise?

LYSISTRATA

            Consider the City as fleece, recently shorn. The first step is Cleansing: Scrub it in a public bath, and remove all corruption, offal, and sheepdip.

Next, to the couch
for Scutching and Plucking: Cudgel the leeches and
similar vermin loose with a club, then pick the prickles
and cockleburs out. As for the clots—those lumps
that clump and cluster in knots and snarls to snag
important posts*—you comb these out,
twist off their heads, and discard.

Next, to raise the City's
nap, you card the citizens together in a single basket
of common weal and general welfare. Fold in our loyal
Resident Aliens, all Foreigners of proven and tested
friendship, and any Disenfranchised Debtors. Combine
   these closely with the rest.
Lastly, cull the colonies settled by our own people:
these are nothing but flocks of wool from the City's
fleece, scattered throughout the world. So gather home
these far-flung flocks, amalgamate them with the
   others.

Then, drawing this blend
of stable fibers into one fine staple, you spin a mighty
bobbin of yarn—and weave, without bias or seam, a
cloak to clothe the City of Athens!

COMMISSIONER

This is too much! The City's
died in the wool, worsted by the distaff side—by women
who bore no share in the War. . . .

LYSISTRATA

None, you hopeless hypocrite?
The quota we bear is double. First, we delivered our
sons to fill out the front lines in Sicily . . .

COMMISSIONER

Don't tax me with that memory.

LYSISTRATA

Next, the best years of our lives were levied. Top-level
strategy attached our joy, and we sleep alone.

> But it's not the matrons
like us who matter. I mourn for the virgins, bedded in
single blessedness, with nothing to do but grow old.

COMMISSIONER

> Men *have* been known
to age, as well as women.

LYSISTRATA

> No, not as well as—better.
A man, an absolute antique, comes back from the war,
    and he's barely
doddered into town before he's married the veriest
    nymphet.
But a woman's season is brief; it slips, and she'll have
no husband, but sit out her life groping at omens—
    and finding no men.

COMMISSIONER

Lamentable state of affairs. Perhaps we can rectify
    matters:

*To the audience.**

TO EVERY MAN JACK, A CHALLENGE:

> ARISE!
Provided you can . . .

LYSISTRATA

Instead, Commissioner, why not simply curl up and *die?*
> Just buy a coffin; here's the place.

*Banging him on the head with her spindle.**

> I'll knead you a cake for the wake—and *these*

Winding the threads from the spindle around him.

        make excellent wreaths. So Rest In Peace.

KLEONIKE

Emptying the chamber pot over him.

        Accept these tokens of deepest grief.

MYRRHINE

Breaking her lamp over his head.

        A final garland for the dear deceased.

LYSISTRATA

        May I supply any last request?
        Then run along. You're due at the wharf:
           Charon's anxious to sail—
           you're holding up the boat for Hell!

COMMISSIONER

This is monstrous—maltreatment of a public official—
maltreatment of ME!
           I must repair directly
to the Board of Commissioners, and present my
colleagues concrete evidence of the sorry specifics of
this shocking attack!

He staggers off left. Lysistrata calls after him.

LYSISTRATA

You won't haul us into court on a charge of neglecting
the dead, will you? (How like a man to insist
on his rights—even his last ones.) Two days between
death and funeral, that's the rule.
           Come back here early
day after tomorrow, Commissioner:
              We'll lay you out.

Lysistrata and her women re-enter the Akropolis. The Koryphaios of Men advances to address the audience.

KORYPHAIS OF MEN

Wake up, Athenians! Preserve your freedom—the time is Now!

To the Chorus of Men.

Strip for action, men. Let's cope with the current mess.

The men put off their long mantles, disclosing short tunics underneath, and advance toward the audience.

CHORUS OF MEN

This trouble may be terminal; it has a loaded odor,
    an ominous aroma of constitutional rot.
My nose gives a prognosis of radical disorder—
    it's just the first installment of an absolutist plot!
        The Spartans are behind it:
        they must have masterminded
some morbid local contacts (engineered by Kleisthenes).
        Predictably infected,
        these women straightway acted
to commandeer the City's cash. They're feverish to freeze
        my be-all,
        my end-all . . .
        my *payroll!**

KORYPHAIOS OF MEN

The symptoms are clear. Our birthright's already
    nibbled. And oh, so
daintily: WOMEN ticking off troops* for improper
    etiquette.
WOMEN propounding their featherweight views on the
    fashionable use
and abuse of the shield. And (if any more proof were
    needed) WOMEN
nagging us to trust the Nice Spartan, and put our heads

in his toothy maw—to make a dessert and call it Peace.
They've woven the City a seamless shroud, bedecked
  with the legend
DICTATORSHIP.
                   But I won't be hemmed in. I'll use
their weapon against them, and uphold the right
  by sneakiness.
               With knyf under cloke,
gauntlet in glove, sword in olive branch.

Slipping slowly toward the Koryphaios of Women.

                     I'll take up my post
in Statuary Row, beside our honored National Heroes,
the natural foes of tyranny: Harmodios,
                  Aristogeiton,
                    and Me.*

Next to her.

Striking an epic pose, so, with the full approval
of the immortal gods,
              I'll bash this loathsome hag in the jaw!

He does, and runs cackling back to the Men. She shakes a fist after him.

KORYPHAIOS OF WOMEN

Mama won't know her little boy when he gets home!

To the Women, who are eager to launch a full-scale attack.

Let's not be hasty, fellow . . . hags. Cloaks off first.

The Women remove their mantles, disclosing tunics very like those of the Men, and advance toward the audience.

CHORUS OF WOMEN

We'll address you, citizens, in beneficial, candid,
  patriotic accents, as our breeding says we must.

since, from the age of seven, Athens graced me with a
    splendid string of civic triumphs to signalize her
        trust:
            I was Relic-Girl quite early,
            then advanced to Maid of Barley;
    in Artemis' "Pageant of the Bear" I played the lead.
        To cap this proud progression,*
        I led the whole procession
    at Athene's Celebration, certified and pedigreed
            —that cachet
            so distingué—
            a *Lady!*

KORYPHAIOS OF WOMEN

To the audience.

I trust this establishes my qualifications. I may, I take it,
address the City to its profit? Thank you.
                    I admit to being a woman—
but don't sell my contribution short on that account.
It's better than the present panic. And my word is as
good as my bond, because I hold stock in Athens—
stock I paid for in sons.

To the Chorus of Men.

—But you, you doddering bankrupts, where are your
shares in the State?

Slipping slowly toward the Koryphaios of Men.

Your grandfathers willed you the Mutual Funds from
    the Persian War*—
and where are they?

Nearer.

                    You dipped into capital, then lost interest . . .
and now a pool of your assets won't fill a hole in the
    ground.
All that remains is one last potential killing—Athens.
Is there any rebuttal?

*The Koryphaios of Men gestures menacingly. She ducks down.
as if to ward off a blow. and removes a slipper*

> Force is a footing resort. I'll take
my very sensible shoe. and paste you in the jaw!

She does so. and runs back to the women.

CHORUS OF MEN

> Their native respect for our manhood is small.
> and keeps getting smaller. Let's bottle their gall.
> The man who won't battle has no balls at all!

KORYPHAIOS OF MEN

All right, men. skin out the skivvies. Let's give them
a whiff of Man, full strength. No point in muffling
the essential Us.

The men remove their tunics.

CHORUS OF MEN

> A century back, we soared to the Heights*
>   and beat down Tyranny there.
> Now's the time to shed our moults
>   and fledge our wings once more.
> to rise to the skies in our reborn force.
>   and beat back Tyranny here!

KORYPHAIOS OF MEN

No fancy grappling with these grannies; straightforward
    strength. The tiniest
toehold. and those nimble. fiddling fingers will have their
foot in the door. and we're done for.
> *No amount of know-how can lick*
a woman's knack.
> They'll want to build ships   next thing we
    know.
we're all at sea. fending off female boarding parties

(Artemisia fought us at Salamis. Tell me, has anyone
caught her yet?)
　　　　But we're *really* sunk if they take up horses. Scratch
the Cavalry:
　　　　　　　A woman is an easy rider with a natural seat.
Take her over the jumps bareback, and she'll never slip
her mount. (That's how the Amazons nearly took
　Athens. On horseback.
Check on Mikon's mural down in the Stoa.)
　　　　　　　　　　　　Anyway,
the solution is obvious. Put every woman in her place—
stick her in the stocks.
　　　　To do this, first snare your woman around the neck.

*He attempts to demonstrate on the Koryphaios of Women.
After a brief tussle, she works loose and chases him back to
the Men.*

CHORUS OF WOMEN

　The beast in me's eager and fit for a brawl.
　Just rile me a bit and she'll kick down the wall.
　You'll bawl to your friends that you've no balls at all.

KORYPHAIOS OF WOMEN

All right, laides, strip for action. Let's give them a whiff
of *Femme Enragée*—piercing and pungent, but not at
all tart.

The women remove their tunics.

CHORUS OF WOMEN

　　We're angry. The brainless bird who tangles
　　　with *us* has gummed his last mush.
　　In fact, the coot who even heckles
　　　is being daringly rash.
　　So look to your nests, you reclaimed eagles—
　　　whatever you lay, we'll squash!

KORYPHAIOS OF WOMEN

Frankly, you don't faze me. *With* me, I have my
    friends—
Lampito from Sparta; that genteel girl from Thebes,
    Ismenia—
committed to me forever. *Against* me, *you*—permanently
out of commission. So do your damnedest.
                                    Pass a law.
Pass seven. Continue the winning ways that have made
your name a short and ugly household word.
                                    Like yesterday:
I was giving a little party, nothing fussy, to honor
the goddess Hekate. Simply to please my daughters,
I'd invited a sweet little thing from the neighborhood—
    flawless pedigree, perfect
taste, a credit to any gathering—a Boiotian eel.
But she had to decline. Couldn't pass the border. You'd
    passed a law.
Not that you care for my party. You'll overwork your
    right of passage
    till your august body is overturned,
                        and you break your silly neck!

*She deftly grabs the Koryphaios of Men by the ankle and
upsets him. He scuttles back to the Men, who retire in
confusion.*

Lysistrata emerges from the citadel, obviously distraught

KORYPHAIOS OF WOMEN

Mock-tragic.

*Mistress, queen of this our subtle scheme,
why burst you from the hall with brangled brow?*

LYSISTRATA

*Oh, wickedness of woman! The female mind
does sap my soul and set my wits a-totter.*

KORYPHAÏOS OF WOMEN

What drear accents are these?

LYSISTRATA

The merest truth

KORYPHAÏOS OF WOMEN

Be nothing loath to tell the tale to friends

LYSISTRATA

'Twere shame to utter, pain to hold unsaid.

KORYPHAÏOS OF WOMEN

Hide not from me affliction which we share.

LYSISTRATA

In briefest compass,

Dropping the paratragedy.

we want to get laid.

KORYPHAÏOS OF WOMEN

By Zeus!

LYSISTRATA

No, no, not HIM!
Well, that's the way things are.
I've lost my grip on the girls—they're mad for men!
But sly—they slip out in droves.
A minute ago,
I caught one scooping out the little hole
that breaks through just below Pan's grotto.*
One
had jerry-rigged some block-and-tackle business
and was wriggling away on a rope.

> Another just flat
deserted.
> Last night I spied one mounting a sparrow,
all set to take off for the nearest bawdyhouse. I hauled
her back by the hair.
> And excuses, pretexts for overnight
passes? I've heard them all.
> Here comes one. Watch.

To the First Woman, as she runs out of the Akropolis.

—You there! What's your hurry?

FIRST WOMAN

> I have to get home.
I've got all this lovely Milesian wool in the house,
and the moths will simply batter it to bits!

LYSISTRATA

> I'll bet.

Get back inside.

FIRST WOMAN

> I swear I'll hurry right back!
—Just time enough to spread it out on the couch?

LYSISTRATA

Your wool sill stay unspread. And you'll stay here.

FIRST WOMAN

Do I have to let my piecework *rot?*

LYSISTRATA

> Possibly.

The Second Woman runs on.

SECOND WOMAN

Oh dear, oh goodness, what shall I do—my flax!
I left and forgot to peel it!

LYSISTRATA

Another one.
She suffers from unpeeled flax.
—Get back inside!

SECOND WOMAN

I'll be right back. I just have to pluck the fibers

LYSISTRATA

No. No plucking. You start it, and everyone else
will want to go and do their plucking, too.

*The Third Woman, swelling conspicuously, hurries on,
praying loudly.*

THIRD WOMAN

*O Goddess of Childbirth, grant that I not deliver
until I get me from out this sacred precinct!*

LYSISTRATA

What sort of nonsense is *this?*

THIRD WOMAN

I'm due—any second!

LYSISTRATA

You weren't pregnant yesterday.

THIRD WOMAN

Today I am—
a miracle!
Let me go home for a midwife, *please!*
I may not make it!

LYSISTRATA

Restraining her.

You can do better than that.

Tapping the woman's stomach and receiving a metallic clang.

What's this? It's hard.

THIRD WOMAN

I'm going to have a boy.

LYSISTRATA

Not unless he's made of bronze. Let's see.

She throws open the Third Women's cloak, exposing a huge bronze helmet.

Of all the brazen . . . You've stolen the helmet from Athene's statue! Pregnant, indeed!

THIRD WOMAN

I am *so* pregnant!

LYSISTRATA

Then why the helmet?

THIRD WOMAN

I thought my time might come while I was still on forbidden ground. If it did, I could climb inside Athene's helmet and have my baby there.
The pigeons do it all the time.

LYSISTRATA

Nothing but excuses!

Taking the helmet.

>   *This* is your baby. I'm afraid
> you'll have to stay until we give it a name.

THRID WOMAN

But the Akropolis is *awful*. I can't even sleep! I saw
the snake that guards the temple

LYSISTRATA

>   That snake's a fabrication.*

THIRD WOMAN

I don't care *what* kind it is—I'm *scared!*

*The other women, who have emerged from the citadel.
crowd around.*

KLEONIKE

And those goddamned holy owls. All night long,
tu-wit. tu-wu—they're hooting me into my grave!

LYSISTRATA

Darlings. let's call a halt to this hocus-pocus.
You miss your men—now isn't that the trouble?

Shamefaced nods from the group

Don't you think they miss you just as much?
I can assure you. their nights are every bit
as hard as yours. So be good girls: endure!
Persist a few days more. and Victory is ours.
It's fated: a current prophecy declares that the men
will go down to defeat before us. provided that *we*
maintain a United Front.

Producing a scroll.

I happen to have
a copy of the prophecy.

KLEONIKE

Read it!

LYSISTRATA

Silence, *please*:

Reading from the scroll.

But when the swallows, in flight from the
    hoopoes, have flocked to a hole
on high, and stoutly eschew their
    accustomed perch on the pole,
yea, then shall Thunderer Zeus to
    their suff'ring establish a stop,
by making the lower the upper . . .

KLEONIKE

Then *we'll* be lying on top?

LYSISTRATA

But should these swallows, indulging their
    lust for the perch, lose heart,
dissolve their flocks in winged dissension,
    and singly depart
the sacred stronghold, breaking the
    bands that bind them together—
then know them as lewd, the pervertedest
    birds that ever wore feather.

KLEONIKE

There's nothing obscure about *that* oracle. Ye gods!

LYSISTRATA

Sorely beset as we are, we must not flag
or faltter. So back to the citadel!

As the women troop inside.

> And if we fail
> that oracle. darlings. our image is absolutely *mud!*

She follows them in. A pause. and the Choruses assemble

CHORUS OF MEN

> I have a simple
> tale to relate you.
> a sterling example
> of masculine virtue:

> The huntsman bold Melanion
>   was once a harried quarry
> The women in town tracked him down
>   and badgered him to marry

> Melanion knew the cornered male
>   eventually cohabits.
> Assessing the odds. he took to the woods
>   and lived trapping rabbits

> He stuck to the virgin stand. sustained
>   by rabbit meat and hate.
> and never returned. but ever remained
>   and alfresco celibate

> Melanion is our ideal:
>   his loathing makes us free.
> Our dearest aim is the gemlike flame
>   of his misogyny

OLD MAN

> Let me kiss that wizened cheek.

OLD WOMAN

Threatening with a fist.

> A wish too rash for that withered flesh.

OLD MAN

> and lay you low with a highflying kick.

He tries one and misses.

OLD WOMAN

> Exposing an overgrown underbrush.

OLD MAN

> A hairy behind, historically, means
> masculine force: Myronides
> harassed the foe with his mighty mane,
> and furry Phormion swept the seas
> of enemy ships, never meeting his match—
> such was the nature of his thatch.

CHORUS OF WOMEN

> I offer an anecdote
> for your opinion,
> an adequate antidote
> for your Melanion:

> Timon, the noted local grouch,
> put rusticating hermits
> out of style by building his wilds
> inside the city limits.

> He shooed away society
> with natural battlements:
> his tongue was edgèd; his shoulder, frigid;
> his beard, a picket fence.

> When random contacts overtaxed him,
> he didn't stop to pack,
> but loaded curses on the male of the species,
> left town, and never came back.

> Timon, you see, was a misanthrope
> in a properly narrow sense:

his spleen was vented only on men . . .
we were his dearest friends.

OLD WOMAN

Making a fist.

Enjoy a chop to that juiceless chin?

OLD MAN

Backing away.

I'm jolted already. Thank you, no.

OLD WOMAN

Perhaps a trip from a well-turned shin?

She tries a kick and misses.

OLD MAN

Brazenly baring the mantrap below.

OLD WOMAN

At least it's *neat.* I'm not too sorry
to have you see my daintiness.
My habits are still depilatory;
age hasn't made me a bristly mess.
Secure in my smoothness, I'm never in doubt—
though even down is out.

*Lysistrata mounts the platform and scans the horizon. When
her gaze reaches the left, she stops suddenly.*

LYSISTRATA

Ladies, attention! Battle stations, please!
And quickly!

A general rush of women to the battlements.

KLEONIKE

What is it?

MYRRHINE

What's all the shouting for?

LYSISTRATA

A MAN!

Consternation.

Yes, it's a man. And he's coming this way!
Hmm. Seems to have suffered a seizure. Broken out
with a nasty attack of love.

Prayer, aside.

O Aphrodite,
Mistress all-victorious,
mysterious, voluptuous,
you who make the crooked straight . . .
don't let this happen to US!

KLEONIKE

I don't care who he is—*where is he?*

LYSISTRATA

Pointing.

Down there—
just flanking that temple—Demeter the Fruitful.

KLEONIKE

My.

Definitely a man.

MYRRHINE

Craning for a look.

I wonder who it can be?

LYSISTRATA

See for yourselves.—Can anyone identify him?

MYRRHINE

Oh lord, I can.
                That is my husband—Kinesias.*

LYSISTRATA

To Myrrhine.

Your duty is clear.
                Pop him on the griddle, twist
the spit, braize him, baste him, stew him in his own
juice, do him to a turn. Sear him with kisses,
coyness, caresses, *everything*—
                but stop where Our Oath
begins.

MYRRHINE

Relax. I can take care of this.

LYSISTRATA

                                Of course
you can, dear. Still, a little help can't hurt, now
can it? I'll just stay around for a bit
and—er—poke up the fire.
                —Everyone else inside!

*Exit all the women but Lysistrata, on the platform, and
Myrrhine, who stands near the Akropolis entrance, hidden
from her husband's view. Kinesias staggers on, in erection
and considerable pain, followed by a male slave who carries
a baby boy.*

KINESIAS

OUCH!!

Omigod.
Hypertension, twinges. . . . I can't hold out much more.
I'd rather be dismembered.

How long, ye gods. how long?

LYSISTRATA

Officially.

WHO GOES THERE?

WHO PENETRATES OUR POSITIONS?

KINESIAS

Me.

LYSISTRATA

A Man?

KINESIAS

Every inch.

LYSISTRATA

Then inch yourself out
of here. Off Limits to Men.

KINESIAS

This *is* the limit.
Just who are *you* to throw me out?

LYSISTRATA

The Lookout.

KINESIAS

Well, look here, Lookout. I'd like to see Myrrhine.
How's the outlook?

LYSISTRATA

>   Unlikely. Bring Myrrhine
> to you? The idea!
>   Just by the by, who are you?

KINESIAS

A private citizen. Her husband, Kinesias.

LYSISTRATA

>   No!
> Meeting you—I'm overcome!
>   Your name, you know,
> is not without its fame among us girls.

Aside.

> —Matter of fact, we have a name for *it*.—
> I swear, you're never out of Myrrhine's mouth.
> She won't even nibble a quince, or swallow an egg,
> without reciting, "Here's to Kinesias!"

KINESIAS

>   For god's sake.
> will you . . .

LYSISTRATA

Sweeping on over his agony.

>   Word of honor, it's true. Why, when
> we discuss our husbands (you know how women are),
> Myrrhine refuses to argue. She simply insists:
> "Compared with Kinesias, the rest have *nothing!*"
> Imagine!

KINESIAS

Bring her out here!

LYSISTRATA

                    Really? And what would I
get out of this?

KINESIAS

                    You see my situation. I'll raise
whatever I can. This can all be yours.

LYSISTRATA

                                        Goodness.
It's really her place. I'll go and get her

*She descends from the platform and moves to Myrrhine.
out of Kinesias's sight.*

KINESIAS

                                        Speed!
·–Life is a husk. She left our home. and happiness
went with her. Now pain is the tenant. Oh, to enter
that wifeless house, to sense that awful emptiness.
to eat that tasteless. joyless food—it makes
it hard, I tell you.
                    Harder all the time.

MYRRHINE

Still out of his sight, in a voice to be overheard

Oh, I *do* love him! I'm mad about him! But he
doesn't want my love. Please don't make me see him.

KINESIAS

Myrrhine darling, why do you *act* this way?
Come down here!

MYRRHINE

Appearing at the wall.

Down there? Certainly not!

KINESIAS

It's me, Myrrhine. I'm begging you. Please come down.

MYRRHINE

I don't see why you're begging me. You don't need me.

KINESIAS

I don't need you? I'm at the end of my rope!

MYRRHINE

I'm leaving.

She turns. Kinesias grabs the boy from the slave.

KINESIAS

No! Wait! At least you'll have to listen
to the voice of your child.

To the boy, in a fierce undertone:

—(Call your mother!)

Silence.

. . . to the voice
of your very own child . . .

—(Call your mother, brat!)

CHILD

MOMMYMOMMYMOMMY!

KINESIAS

Where's your maternal instinct? He hasn't been washed
or fed for a week. How can you be so pitiless?

MYRRHINE

Him I pity. Of all the pitiful excuses
for a father. . . .

KINESIAS

Come down here, dear. For the baby's sake

MYRRHINE

Motherhood! I'll have to come. I've got no choice.

KINESIAS

Soliloquizing as she descends.

It may be me, but I'll swear she looks years younger—
and gentler—her eyes caress me. And then they flash:
that anger, that verve, the high-and-mighty air!
She's fire, she's ice—and I'm stuck right in the middle.

MYRRHINE

Taking the baby.

Sweet babykins with such a nasty daddy!
Here, let Mummy kissums. Mummy's little darling.

KINESIAS

The injured husband.

You should be ashamed of yourself, letting those women
lead you around. Why do you DO these things?
You only make me suffer and hurt your poor,
sweet self.

MYRRHINE

Keep your hands away from me!

KINESIAS

But the house, the furniture, everything we own—you're
letting it go to hell!

MYRRHINE

> Frankly. I couldn't care less

KINESIAS

But your weaving's unraveled—the loom is full of
chickens! You couldn't care less about *that?*

MYRRHINE

> I certainly couldn't

KINESIAS

And the holy rites of Aphrodite? Think how long
that's been.
> Come on, darling, let's go home.

MYRRHINE

I absolutely reufse!
> Unless you agree to a truce
to stop the war.

KINESIAS

> Well, then, if that's your decision.
we'll STOP the war!

MYRRHINE

> Well, then, if that's your decision.
I'll come back—*after* it's done.
> But, for the present.
I've sworn off.

KINESIAS

> At least lie down for a minute.
We'll talk.

MYRRHINE

       I know what you're up to—NO!
—And yet. . . . I really can't say I don't love you . . .

KINESIAS

                      You love me?
So what's the trouble? *Lie down.*

MYRRHINE

               Don't be disgusting.
In front of the baby?

KINESIAS

       Er . . . no. Heaven Forfend.

Taking the baby and pushing it at the slave.

—Take this home.

The slave obeys.

       —Well, darling, we're rid of the kid . . .
let's go to bed!

MYRRHINE

       Poor dear.
               But where does one do
this sort of thing?

KINESIAS

       Where? All we need is a little
nook. . . . We'll try Pan's grotto. Excellent spot.

MYRRHINE

With a nod at the Akropolis.

I'll have to be pure to get back in *there*. How can I
expunge my pollution?

KINESIAS

Sponge off in the pool next door

MYRRHINE

I did swear an Oath. I'm supposed to perjure myself?

KINESIAS

Bother the Oath. Forget it—I'll take the blame

A pause.

MYRRHINE

Now I'll go get us a cot.

KINESIAS

No! Not a cot!
The ground's enough for us

MYRRHINE

I'll get the cot.
For all your faults. I refuse to put you to bed
in the dirt

She exits into the Akropolis

KINESIAS

She certainly loves me That's nice to know

MYRRHINE

Returning with a rope-tied cot

Here. You hurry to bed while I undress

Kinesias lies down

Gracious me—I forgot. We need a mattress

KINESIAS

Who wants a mattress? Not me!

MYRRHINE

Oh, yes, you do.
It's perfectly squalid on the ropes.

KINESIAS

Well, give me a kiss
to tide me over.

MYRRHINE

Voilà.
She pecks at him and leaves.

KINESIAS

OoolaLAlala!
—Make it a quick trip, dear.

MYRRHINE

*Entering with the mattress, she waves Kinesias off the cot
and lays the mattress on it.*

Here we are.
Our mattress. Now hurry to bed while I undress.

Kinesias lies down again.

Gracious me—I forgot. You don't have a pillow.

KINESIAS

I do *not* need a pillow.

MYRRHINE

I know, but *I* do.

She leaves.

KINESIAS

What a lovefeast! Only the table gets laid.*

MYRRHINE

Returning with a pillow.

Rise and shine!

Kinesias jumps up. She places the pillow.

And now I have everything I need.

KINESIAS

Lying down again.

You certainly do.
Come here, my little jewelbox!

MYRRHINE

Just taking off my bra.
Don't break your promise:
no cheating about the Peace.

KINESIAS

I swear to god,
I'll die first!

MYRRHINE

Coming to him.

Just look. You don't have a blanket.

KINESIAS

I didn't plan to go camping—I want to make love!

MYRRHINE

Relax. You'll get your love. I'll be right back.

She leaves.

KINESIAS

Relax? I'm dying a slow death by dry goods!

MYRRHINE

Returning with the blanket.

Get up!

KINESIAS

Getting out of bed.

I've been up for hours. I was up before I was up.

Myrrhine spreads the blanket on the mattress, and he lies down again.

MYRRHINE

I presume you want perfume?

KINESIAS

Positively NO!

MYRRHINE

Absolutely *yes*—whether you want it or not.

She leaves.

KINESIAS

Dear Zeus, I don't ask for much—but please let her spill it.

MYRRHINE

Returning with a bottle.

Hold out your hand like a good boy.

Now rub it in.

KINESIAS

Obeying and sniffing.

This is to quicken desire? Too strong. It grabs
your nose and bawls out: *Try again tomorrow.*

MYRRHINE

I'm *awful!* I brought you that rancid Rhodian brand.

She starts off with the bottle.

KINESIAS

This is just *lovely*. Leave it. woman!

MYRRHINE

                                                    Silly!

She leaves.

KINESIAS

God damn the clod who first concocted perfume!

MYRRHINE

Returning with another bottle.

Here. try this flask.

KINESIAS

                              Thanks—but you try mine.
Come to bed. you witch—
                              and please stop bringing
things!

MYRRHINE

          That is exactly what I'll do.
There go my shoes.

Incidentally, darling, you *will*
remember to vote for the truce?

KINESIAS

I'LL THINK IT OVER!

Myrrhine runs off for good.

That woman's laid me waste—destroyed me, root
and branch!
I'm scuttled,
gutted,
up the spout!
And Myrrhine's gone!

In a parody of a tragic kommos.

Out upon't! But how? But where?
Now I have lost the fairest fair,
how screw my courage to yet another
sticking-place? Aye, there's the rub—
And yet, this wagging, wanton babe
must soon be laid to rest, or else . . .
Ho, Pandar!
Pandar!
I'd hire a nurse.

KORYPHAIOS OF MEN

Grievous your bereavement, cruel
the slow tabescence of your soul.
I bid my liquid pity mingle.

Oh, where the soul, and where, alack!
the cod to stand the taut attack
of swollen prides, the scorching tensions
that ravine up the lumbar regions?
His morning lay
has gone astray.

KINESIAS

In agonay.

> O Zeus, reduce the throbs, the throes!

KORYPHAIOS OF MEN

> I turn my tongue to curse the cause
> of your affliction—that jade, that slut,
> that hag, that ogress . . .

KINESIAS

> No! Slight not
> my light-o'-love, my dove, my sweet!

KORYPHAIOS OF MEN

> Sweet!
> O Zeus who rul'st the sky,
> snatch that slattern up on high,
> crack thy winds, unleash thy thunder,
> tumble her over, trundle her under,
> juggle her from hand to hand;
> twirl her ever near the ground—
> drop her in a well-aimed fall
> on our comrade's tool! That's all.

Kinesias exits left.

A Spartan Herald enters from the right, holding his cloak together in a futile attempt to conceal his condition.

HERALD

This Athens? Where-all kin I find the Council of Elders or else the Executive Board? I brung some news.

The Commissioner, swathed in his cloak, enters from the left.*

COMMISSIONER

And what are you—a man? a signpost? a joint-stock company?

HERALD

A herald, sonny, an honest-to-Kastor herald. I come to chat 'bout thet-there truce.

COMMISSIONER

. . . carrying a concealed weapon? Pretty underhanded.

HERALD

Twisting to avoid the Commissioner's direct gaze.

Hain't done no sech a thang!

COMMISSIONER

Very well, stand still. Your cloak's out of crease—hernia? Are the roads that bad?

HERALD

I swear this feller's plumb tetched in the haid!

COMMISSIONER

Throwing open the Spartan's cloak, exposing the phallus.

You clown, you've got an erection!

HERALD

Wildly embarrassed.

Hain't got no sech a thang! You stop this-hyer foolishment!

COMMISSIONER

What *have* you got there, then?

HERALD

Thet-thur's a Spartan *e*pistle.* In code.

COMMISSIONER

I have the key.

Throwing open his cloak.

Behold another Spartan *e*pistle. In code.

Tiring of teasing.

Let's get down to cases. I know the score,
so tell me the truth.

How are things with you in Sparta?

HERALD

Thangs is up in the air. The whole Alliance
is purt-near 'bout to explode. We-uns'll need barrels,
'stead of women.

COMMISSIONER

What was the cause of this outburst?
The great god Pan?

HERALD

Nope. I'll lay 'twere Lampito,
most likely. She begun, and then they was off
and runnin' at the post in a bunch, every last little gal
in Sparta, drivin' their menfolk away from the winner's
circle.

COMMISSIONER

How are you taking this?

HERALD

Painful-like.
Everyone's doubled up worse as a midget nursin'
a wick in a midnight wind come moon-dark time.
Cain't even tetch them little old gals on the moosey
without we all agree to a Greece-wide Peace.

COMMISSIONER

Of course!
A universal female plot—all Hellas
risen in rebellion—I should have known!
Return
to Sparta with this request:
Have them despatch us
a Plenipotentiary Commission, fully empowered
to conclude an armistice. I have full confidence
that I can persuade our Senate to do the same,
without extending myself. The evidence is at hand.

HERALD

I'm a-flyin', Sir! I hev never heered your equal!

*Exeunt hurriedly, the Commissioner to the left, the Herald
to the right.*

KORYPHAIOS OF MEN

The most unnerving work of nature,*
the pride of applied immorality,
is the common female human.
No fire can match, no beast can best her.
O Unsurmountability,
thy name—worse luck—is Woman.

KORYPHAIOS OF WOMEN

After such knowledge, why persist
in wearing out this feckless
war between the sexes?

When can I apply for the post
of ally, partner, and general friend?

KORYPHAIOS OF MEN

I won't be ployed to revise, re-do,
amend, extend, or bring to an end
my irreversible credo:
Misogyny Forever!
—The answer's never.

KORYPHAIOS OF WOMEN

All right. Whenever you choose.
But, for the present, I refuse
to let you look your absolute worst,
parading around like an unfrocked freak:
I'm coming over and get you dressed.

She dresses him in his tunic, an action (like others in this scene) imitated by the members of the Chorus of Women toward their opposite numbers in the Chorus of Men.

KORYPHAIOS OF MEN

This seems sincere. It's not a trick.
Recalling the rancor with which I stripped,
I'm overlaid with chagrin.

KORYPHAIOS OF WOMEN

Now you resemble a man,
not some ghastly practical joke.
And if you show me a little respect
(and promise not to kick), I'll extract
the beast in you.

KORYPHAIOS OF MEN

Searching himself.

What beast in me?

KORYPHAIOS OF WOMEN

> That insect. There. The bug that's stuck
> in your eye.

KORYPHAIOS OF MEN

Playing along dubiously.

> This gnat?

KORYPHAIOS OF WOMEN

> Yes, nitwit!

KORYPHAIOS OF MEN

> Of course.
> That steady, festering agony. . . .
> You've put your finger on the source
> of all my lousy troubles. Please
> roll back the lid and scoop it out.
> I'd like to see it.

KORYPHAIOS OF WOMEN

> All right, I'll do it.

Removing the imaginary insect.

> Although, of all the impossible cranks. . . .
> Do you sleep in a swamp? Just look at this.
> I've never seen a bigger chigger.

KORYPHAIOS OF MEN

> Thanks.
> Your kindness touches me deeply. For years,
> that thing's been sinking wells in my eye.
> Now you've unplugged me. Here come the tears.

KORYPHAIOS OF WOMEN

> I'll dry your tears, though I can't say why.

Wiping away the tears.

Of all the irresponsible boys. . . .
And I'll kiss you.

KORYPHAIOS OF MEN

Don't you kiss me!

KORYPHAIOS OF WOMEN

What made you think you had a choice?

She kisses him.

KORYPHAIOS OF MEN

All right, damn you, that's enough of that ingrained
   palaver.
I can't dispute the truth or logic of the pithy old proverb:
         Life with women is hell.
         Life without women is hell, too.
And so we conclude a truce with you, on the following
   terms:
in future, a mutual moratorium on mischief in all its
   forms.
Agreed?—Let's make a single chorus and start our song.

The two Choruses unite and face the audience.

CHORUS OF MEN*

We're not about to introduce
the standard personal abuse—
      the Choral Smear
Of Present Persons (usually,
in every well-made comedy,
      inserted here).
Instead, in deed and utterance, we
shall now indulge in philanthropy
      because we feel
that members of the audience
endure, in the course of current events,
      sufficient hell.

Therefore, friends, be rich! Be flush!
Apply to us, and borrow cash
    in large amounts.
The Treasury stands behind us—there—
and we can personally take care
    of small accounts.
Drop up today. Your credit's good.
Your loan won't have to be repaid
    in full until
the war is over. And then, your debt
is only the money you actually get—
    nothing at all.

CHORUS OF WOMEN

Just when we meant to entertain
some madcap gourmets from out of town
    —such flawless taste!—
the present unpleasantness intervened,
and now we fear the feast we planned
    will go to waste.
The soup is waiting, rich and thick;
I've sacrificed a suckling pig
    —the pièce de résistance—
whose toothsome cracklings should amaze
the most fastidious gourmets—
    you, for instance.
To everybody here, I say
take potluck at my house today
    with me and mine.
Bathe and change as fast as you can,
bring the children, hurry down,
    and walk right in.
Don't bother to knock. No need at all.
My house is yours. Liberty Hall.
    What are friends for?
Act self-possessed when you come over;
it may help out when you discover
    I've locked the door.

A delegation of Spartans enters from the right. with difficulty
They have removed their cloaks. but hold them before them
selves in an effort to conceal their condition

KORYPHAIOS OF MEN

What's this? Behold the Spartan ambassadors.
   dragging their beards.
pussy-footing along. It appears they've developed
   a hitch in the crotch

Advancing to greet them

Men of Sparta. I bid you welcome!
                        And now
to the point: What predicament brings you among us?

SPARTAN

We-uns is up a stump. Hain't fit fer chatter

Flipping aside his cloak.

Here's our predicament Take a look for yourselfs

KORYPHAIOS OF MEN

Well. I'll be damned—a regular disaster area.
Inflamed. I imagine the temperature's rather intense?

SPARTAN

Hit ain't the heat. hit's the tumidity.
                       But words
won't help what ails us. We-uns come after Peace
Peace from any person. at any price

Enter the Athenian delegation from the left. led by Kinesias. *
They are wearing cloaks. but are obviously in as much tra-
vail as the Spartans

KORYPHAIOS OF MEN

Behold our local Sons of the Soil. stretching

their garments away from their groins, like wrestlers
Grappling with their plight. Some sort of athlete's disease,
no doubt.
An outbreak of epic proportions.

Athlete's foot?

No. Could it be athlete's . . . ?

KINESIAS

Who can tell us
how to get hold of Lysistrata? We've come as delegates
to the Sexual Congress.

Opening his cloak.

Here are our credentials.

KORYPHAIOS OF MEN

*Ever the scientist, looking from the Athenians to the Spartans
and back again.*

The words are different, but the malady seems the same.

To Kinesias.

Dreadful disease. When the crisis reaches its height,
what do you take for it?

KINESIAS

Whatever comes to hand.
But now we've reached the bitter end. It's Peace
or we fall back on Kleisthenes.

And he's got a waiting list.

KORPHAIOS OF MEN

To the Spartans.

Take my advice and put your clothes on. If someone
from that self-appointed Purity League* comes by, you
may be docked. They do it to the statues of Hermes,
they'll do it to you.

KINESIAS

Since he has not yet noticed the Spartans, he interprets the warning as meant for him, and hurriedly pulls his cloak together, as do the other Athenians

Excellent advice

SPARTAN

Hit shorely is.
Hain't nothing to argue after. Let's git dressed.

As they put on their cloaks, the Spartans are finally noticed by Kinesias

KINESIAS

Welcome, men of Sparta! This is a shameful
disgrace to masculine honor

SPARTAN

Hit could be worser
Ef them Herm-choppers seed us all fired up.
they'd *really* take us down a peg or two

KINESIAS

Gentlemen, let's descend to details Specifically,
why are you here?

SPARTAN

Ambassadors We come to dicker
'bout thet-thur Peace

KINESIAS

Perfect! Precisely our purpose
Let's send for Lysistrata Only she can reconcile
our differences There'll be no Peace for us without her

SPARTAN

We-uns ain't fussy. Call Lysistratos, too, if you want.

The gates to the Akropolis open, and Lysistrata emerges, accompanied her handmaid, Peace—a beautiful girl without a stitch on. Peace remains out of sight by the gates until summoned.

KORYPHAIOS OF MEN

Hail, most virile of women! Summon up all your
    experience:
Be terrible and tender,
                lofty and lowbrow,
                          severe and demure.
Here stand the Leaders of Greece, enthralled by your
    charm.
They yield the floor to you and submit their claims for
    your arbitration.

LYSISTRATA

Really, it shouldn't be difficult, if I can catch them
all bothered, before they start to solicit each other.
I'll find out soon enough. Where's Peace?
                          —Come here.

Peace moves from her place by the gates to Lysistrata. The delegations goggle at her.

Now, dear, first get those Spartans and bring them to me.
Take them by the hand, but don't be pushy about it,
not like our husbands (no savoir-faire at all!).
Be a lady, be proper, do just what you'd do at home:
if hands are refused, conduct them by the handle.

Peace leades the Spartans to a position near Lysistrata.

And now a hand to the Athenians—it doesn't matter
where; accept any offer—and bring *them* over.

*Peace conducts the Athenians to a position near Lysistrata,
opposite the Spartans.*

You Spartans move up closer—right *here*—

To the Athenians.

                              and *you*
stand over *here*.
            —And now attend my speech.

*This the delegations do with some difficulty, because of the
conflicting attractions of Peace, who is standing beside her
mistress.*

I am a woman—but not without some wisdom:
my native wit is not completely negligible,
and I've listened long and hard to the discourse of my
elders—my education is not entirely despicable.
                                 Well,
now that I've got you, I intend to give you hell,
and I'm perfectly right. Consider your actions:
                              At festivals,
in Pan-Hellenic harmony, like true blood-brothers, you
   share
the selfsame basin of holy water, and sprinkle
altars all over Greece—Olympia, Delphoi,
Thermopylai . . . (I could go on and on, if length
were my only object.)
                    But now, when the Persians sit by
and wait, in the very presence of your enemies, you fight
each other, destroy *Greek* men, destroy *Greek* cities!
—Point One of my address is now concluded.

KINESIAS

Gazing at Peace.

I'm destroyed, if this is drawn out much longer!

LYSISTRATA

Serenely unconscious of the interruption.

—Men of Sparta, I direct these remarks to you.
Have you forgotten that a Spartan suppliant once came
to beg assistance from Athens? Recall Perikleidas:
Fifty years ago, he clung to our altar,
his face dead-white above his crimson robe, and pleaded
for an army. Messene was pressing you hard in revolt,
and to this upheaval, Poseidon, the Earthshaker, added
another.
            But Kimon took four thousand troops
from Athens—an army which saved the state of Sparta.
Such treatment have you received at the hands of Athens,
you who devastate the country that came to your aid!

KINESIAS

*Stoutly; the condemnation of his enemy has made him forget
the girl momentarily.*

You're right, Lysistrata. The Spartans are clearly in the
wrong!

SPARTAN

*Guiltily backing away from Peace, whom he has attempted
to pat.*

Hit's wrong, I reckon, but that's the purtiest behind . . .

LYSISTRATA

Turning to the Athenians.

—Men of Athens, do you think I'll let you off?
Have you forgotten the Tyrant's days,* when you wore
the smock of slavery, when the Spartans turned to the
spear, cut down the pride of Thessaly, despatched the
friends of tyranny, and dispossessed your oppressors?
                                                Recall:
On that great day, your only allies were Spartans;
your liberty came at their hands, which stripped away
your servile garb and clothed you again in Freedom!

SPARTAN

Indicating Lysistrata.

Hain't never seed no higher type of woman.

KINESIAS

Indicating Peace.

Never saw one I wanted so much to top.

LYSISTRATA

Oblivious to the byplay, addressing both groups.

With such a history of mutual benefits conferred
and received, why are you fighting? Stop this wickedness!
Come to terms with each other! What prevents you?

SPARTAN

We'd a heap sight druther make Peace, if we was
indemnified with a plumb strategic location.

Pointing at Peace's rear.

We'll take thet butte.

LYSISTRATA

Butte?

SPARTAN

The Promontory of Pylos—Sparta's Back Door.
We've missed it fer a turrible spell.

Reaching.

Hev to keep our
hand in.

KINESIAS

Pushing him away.

The price is too high—you'll never take that!

LYSISTRATA

Oh, let them have it.

KINESIAS

What room will we have left
for maneuvers?

LYSISTRATA

Demand another spot in exchange.

KINESIAS

Surveying Peace like a map as he addresses the Spartan.

Then you hand over to us—uh, let me see—
let's try Thessaly*—

Indicating the relevant portions of Peace.

First of all, Easy Mountain . . .
then the Maniac Gulf behind it . . .
                              and down to Megara
for the legs . . .

SPARTAN

You cain't take all of thet! Yore plumb
out of yore mind!

LYSISTRATA

To Kinesias.

Don't argue. Let the legs go.

Kinesias nods. A pause. General smiles of agreement.

KINESIAS

Doffing his cloak.

I feel an urgent desire to plow a few furrows.

SPARTAN

Doffing his cloak.

Hit's time to work a few loads of fertilizer in.

LYSISTRATA

Conclude the treaty and the simple life is yours.
If such is your decision convene your councils,
and then deliberate the matter with your allies.

KINESIAS

Deliberate? Allies?

　　　　　　　We're over-extended already!
Wouldn't every ally approve our position—
Union Now?

SPARTAN

　　　　　　I know I kin speak for ourn.

KINESIAS

And I for ours.

　　　　　They're just a bunch of gigolos.

LYSISTRATA

I heartily approve.

　　　　　　Now first attend to your purification,
then we, the women, will welcome you to the Citadel
and treat you to all the delights of a home-cooked
banquet. Then you'll exchange your oaths and pledge
your faith, and every man of you will take his wife and
depart for home.

Lysistrata and Peace enter the Akropolis.

KINESIAS

Let's hurry!

SPARTAN

Lead on, everwhich
way's yore pleasure.

KINESIAS

This way, then—and HURRY!

The delegations exeunt at a run.

CHORUS OF WOMEN

I'd never stint on anybody.
And now I include, in my boundless bounty,
    the younger set.
Attention, you parents of teenage girls
about to debut in the social whirl.
    Here's what you get:
Embroidered linens, lush brocades.
a huge assortment of ready-mades.
    from mantles to shifts;
plus bracelets and bangles of solid gold—
every item my wardrobe holds—
    absolute gifts!
Don't miss this offer. Come to my place,
barge right in, and make your choice.
    You can't refuse
Everything there must go today.
Finders keepers—cart it away!
    How can you lose?
Don't spare me. Open all the locks.
Break every seal. Empty every box.
    Keep ferreting—
And your sight's considerably better than mine
if you should possibly chance to find
    a single thing.

CHORUS OF MEN

Troubles, friend? Too many mouths
to feed, and not a scrap in the house
    to see you through?
Faced with starvation? Don't give it a thought.
Pay attention; I'll tell you what
    I'm gonna do.
I overbought. I'm overstocked.
Every room in my house is clogged
    with flour (best ever),
glutted with luscious loaves whose size
you wouldn't believe. I need the space;
    do me a favor:
Bring gripsacks, knapsacks, duffle bags,
pitchers, cisterns, buckets, and kegs
    around to me.
A courteous servant will see to your needs;
he'll fill them up with A-1 wheat—
    and all for free!
—Oh. Just one final word before
you turn your steps to my front door:
    I happen to own
a dog. Tremendous animal.
Can't stand a leash. And bites like hell—
    better stay home.

The united Chorus flocks to the door of the Akropolis. *

KORYPHAIOS OF MEN

Banging at the door.

Hey, open up in there!

*The door opens, and the Commissioner appears. He wears
a wreath, carries a torch, and is slightly drunk. He addresses
the Koryphaios.*

COMMISSIONER

You know the Regulations.
Move along!

He sees the entire Chorus.

—And why are YOU lounging around?
I'll wield my trusty torch and scorch the lot!

The Chorus backs away in mock horror. He stops and looks at his torch.

—*This* is the bottom of the barrel. A cheap burlesque bit.
I refuse to do it. I have my pride.

With a start, he looks at the audience, as though hearing a protest. He shrugs and addresses the audience.

—No choice, eh?
Well, if that's the way it is, we'll take the trouble.
Anything to keep you happy.

The Chorus advances eagerly.

KORYPHAIOS OF MEN

Don't forget us!
We're in this, too. Your trouble is ours!

COMMISSIONER

Resuming his character and jabbing with his torch at the Chorus.

Keep moving!
Last man out of the way goes home without hair!
Don't block the exit. Give the Spartans some room.
They've dined in comfort; let them go home in peace.

The Chorus shrinks back from the door. Kinesias, wreathed and quite drunk, appears at the door. He speaks his first speech in Spartan.*

KINESIAS

Hain't never seed sech a spread! Hit were splendiferous!

COMMISSIONER

I gather the Spartans won friends and influenced people?

KINESIAS

And *we've* never been so brilliant. It was the wine.

COMMISSIONER

Precisely.
        The reason? A sober Athenian is just
non compos. If I can carry a little proposal
I have in mind, our Foreign Service will flourish,
guided by this rational rule:
                No Ambassador
Without a Skinful.
                Reflect on our past performance:
Down to a Spartan parley we troop, in a state
of disgusting sobriety, looking for trouble. It muddles
our senses: we read between the lines; we hear,
not what the Spartans say, but what we suspect
they might have been about to be going to say.
We bring back paranoid reports—cheap fiction, the fruit
of temperance. Cold-water diplomacy, pah!
                    Contrast
this evening's total pleasure, the free-and-easy
give-and-take of friendship: If we were singing,
        Just Kleitagora and me,
        Alone in Thessaly,
and someone missed his cue and cut in loudly,
        Ajax, son of Telamon,
        He was one hell of a man—
no one took it amiss, or started a war;
we clapped him on the back and gave three cheers.

During this recital, the Chorus has sidled up to the door.

—Dammit, are you back here again?

Waving his torch.

Scatter!

Get out of the road! Gangway, you gallowsbait!

KINESIAS

Yes, everyone out of the way. They're coming out.

Through the door emerge the Spartan delegation, a flutist the Athenian delegation, Lysistrata, Kleonike, Myrrhine, and the rest of the women from the citadel, both Athenian and Peloponnesian. The Chorus splits into its male and female components and draws to the sides to give the procession room.

SPARTAN

To the flutist.

Friend and kinsman, take up them pipes a yourn.
I'd like fer to shuffle a bit and sing a right sweet
song in honor of Athens and us'uns, too.

COMMISSIONER

To the flutist.

Marvelous, marvelous—come, take up your pipes!

To the Spartan.

I certainly love to see you Spartans dance.

The flutist plays, and the Spartan begins a slow dance

SPARTAN

> Memory,
> send me
> your Muse,
> who knows

our glory,
knows Athens'—
Tell the story:
At Artemision
like gods, they stampeded
the hulks of the Medes, and
beat them.

And Leonidas
leading us—
the wild boars
whetting their tusks.
And the foam flowered,
flowered and flowed,
down our cheeks
to our knees below.
The Persians there
like the sands of the sea—

Hither, huntress,
virgin, goddess,
tracker, slayer,
to our truce!
Hold us ever
fast together;
bring our pledges
love and increase;
wean us from the
fox's wiles—

Hither, huntress!
Virgin, hither!

LYSISTRATA*

Surveying the assemblage with a proprietary air.

Well, the preliminaries are over—very nicely, too.
So, Spartans,

Indicating the Peloponnesian women who have been hostages.

Take these girls back home. And *you*

To the Athenian delegation, indicating the women from the Akropolis.

take *these* girls. Each man stand by his wife, each wife
by her husband. Dance to the gods' glory, and thank
them for the happy ending. And, from now on, please be
careful. Let's not make the same mistakes again.

*The delegations obey: the men and women of the chorus join
again for a rapid ode.*

CHORUS

> Start the chorus dancing,
> Summon all the Graces,
Send a shout to Artemis in invocation.
> Call upon her brother,
> healer, chorus master,
Call the blazing Bacchus, with his maddened muster.

Call the flashing, fiery Zeus, and
call his mighty, blessed spouse, and
call the gods, call all the gods,
to witness now and not forget
our gentle, blissful Peace—the gift,
> the deed of Aphrodite.
>> Ai!
> Alalai! Paion!
> Leap you! Paion!
> Victory! Alalai!
Hail!   Hail!   Hail!

LYSISTRATA

Spartan, let's have another song from you, a new one.

SPARTAN

> Leave darlin' Taygetos,
> Spartan Muse! Come to us
> once more, flyin'
> and glorifyin'

Spartan themes:
the god at Amyklai,
bronze-house Athene.
Tyndaros' twins.
the valiant ones,
playin' still by Eurotas' streams.

Up! Advance!
Leap to the dance!

Help us hymn Sparta,
lover of dancin',
lover of foot-pats,
where girls go prancin'
like fillies along Eurotas' banks,
whirlin' the dust, twinklin' their shanks.
shakin' their hair
like Maenads playin'
and jugglin' the thyrsis,
in frenzy obeyin'
Leda's daughter, the fair, the pure
Helen, the mistress of the choir.

Here, Muse, here!
Bind up your hair!

Stamp like a deer! Pound your feet!
Clap your hands! Give us a beat!

Sing the greatest,
sing the mightiest,
sing the conqueror,
sing to honor her—

Athene of the Bronze House!
Sing Athene!

Exeunt omnes, dancing and singing.

Notes

page 350. *early morning:* The play's two time scales should be noted. By one, its action encompasses a day, beginning at dawn and lasting until after sundown; by the other, its events logically occupy a period of weeks, if not months—not that this sort of logic has much to do with the case. At no point is the play stopped to indicate the passage of time.

350. *Kleonike:* This is to adopt Wilamowitz' conjecture for the *Kalonike* of the manuscripts, without accepting his views on the character's age. Kleonike's actions approach those of the stock bibulous old woman too closely to indicate a sweet young thing. She is older than Lysistrata, who fits comfortably on the vague borderline between "young matron" and "matron." Quite a bit younger are Myrrhine and Lampito.

352. *those scrumptious eels:* The constant Athenian gustatory passion, rendered sharper by the War's embargo: eels from Lake Kopaïs in Boiotia.

354. *hoisting her sandals:* This rendering follows, with Coulon, Van Leeuwen's emendation at 64—τἀκάτειον "sail"—while suggesting that the

pun plays on the unmetrical reading of the Ravennas, τἀκάτιον "skiff," as a name applied to a woman's shoe. It is tempting to return to an old proposal of Biset and read τἀκάτιον ἀνήρετο.

page 355. *from the outskirts:* Literally, "from Anagyrous," a rural deme of Attika which took its name from the plant *anagyros* "the stinking bean-trefoil." Kleonike's riposte puns on this by reference to an old proverb: "Well, the *anagyros* certainly seems to have been disturbed" = "you've really stirred up a stink" = "the fat's in the fire." Here, as often when geographical names are involved, it is more important to render the fact of a pun than the specifics of the original.

356. *I calklate so:* In employing a somewhat debased American mountain dialect to render the Laconic Greek of Lampito and her countrymen, I have tried to evoke something like the Athenian attitude toward their perennial enemies. They regarded the Spartans as formidably old-fashioned bumpkins, imperfectly civilized, possessed of a determined indifference to more modern value systems.

358. *military waste:* Or perhaps treason. The Greek refers to a General Eukrates, who may be the brother of the illustrious and ill-starred Nikias. If so, he was put to death by the Thirty Tyrants in 404.

364. *in Athene's temple:* In the Opisthodomos, at the back of the Parthenon, was kept the reserve fund of one thousand silver talents established at the beginning of the War twenty years before. Since the fund had been dipped into during the previous year, Lampito's expression constitutes more than a normal exaggeration.

366. *The symbolism's too obscure:* This sentence may seem a startling expansion of the word *poi* (literally, "Whither?"; here, "What is the point of . . . ?"), but is in a good cause—an attempt to explain and motivate the darkest white horse in literature. The sequence is this: Lysistrata, annoyed at the inter-

ruption, sarcastically proposes a gaudy sacrifice;
Kleonike, whose mind is proof against sarcasm,
points out that it has nothing to do with the matter
at hand. For the rationale, I am indebted to
Wilamowitz, though he assigned the lines (191-93)
differently. Other explanations, in terms of Amazons, genitalia, or lovemaking blueprints, are, al-
beit venerable, obscure in themselves. One sympa-
thizes with Rogers, who translated, "grey mare."

page 373. *Athene's statue:* Not one of Pheidias' colossal
statues, but the old wooden figure of Athene Polias
("Guardian of the City") in the Erechtheion.

373. *right over there:* I have given the Koryphaios a bad
memory and placed the object of his anger in the
audience to point up what is happening. Rhodia,
wife of the demagogue Lykon, was a real person,
frequently lampooned for her morals. In a not
unusual breaking of the dramatic illusion, her name
occurs here as a surprise for the expected "Lysistrata." Some commentators, disliking surprise, have
decided that Lysistrata is the wife of someone
named Lykon—thus managing to ruin a joke and
import an obscurity without the change of a word.

374. *expropriating our Akropolis:* Kleomenes' occupation of the Akropolis in 508, high point of his unsuc-
cessful bid to help establish the Athenian aristocrats,
lasted rather less than the six years which the Chorus
seems to remember. The actual time was two days.

376. *at loggerheads over in Samos:* Most of the Athenian
fleet was at the moment based in Samos, practically the only Ionian ally left to Athens, in order to
make ready moves against those states who had de-
fected to Sparta in 412 after the Sicilian fiasco.

379. *Hipponax swears by it:* The Greek refers to one
Boupalos, a Chian sculptor mercilessly lampooned
by the testy poet until, as a doubtful tradition has it,
he hanged himself. The only surviving verse of
Hipponax which bears on the subject ("Hold my
clothes; I'll sock Boupalos in the jaw") does little
to establish the tradition—or, indeed, to dispel the

feeling that Hipponax was about as effective a boxer the Koryphaios.

page 380. *for other bitches to gnaw:* I here adopt John Jackson's transposition of line 363 to follow 367 (*Marginalia Scaenica*, p. 108).

380. *so lost to shame as Woman:* The observation is clearly offered as an illustrative quotation, and the sentiment is certainly Euripidean. But the extant tragic line nearest it in expression is Sophokles *Elektra* 622.

383. *A Commissioner of Public Safety:* That is, *a proboulos,* one of the ten extraordinary Athenian officials appointed in 413 after the Sicilian catastrophe as a check on legislative excesses. Chiefly responsible for drafting the agenda of Senate and Assembly, the commissioners were drawn from men over forty years of age. The two whose names we know were well along: Hagnon was over sixty, Sophokles (if the poet is meant, a matter not absolutely settled) eighty-two. But these instances scarcely prove Wilamowitz' contention that decrepitude was a necessary qualification for the office; and Aristophanes' Commissioner, for all his choleric conservatism, is marked by vigor and intellectual curiosity.

386. *goddess of the dew:* That is, Pandrosos, one of the daughters of Athens' legendary King Kekrops. A tutelary divinity in her own right, she had a shrine in the Erechtheion—and was never identified with Artemis. Having said this, I follow in the translation an unprovable theory of Rogers': that *pandrosos* ''all-bedewing'' just might be an epithet of the moon-goddess, classical antiquity's best-attested virgin, who is otherwise invoked here in three out of four instances.

387. ISMENIA: As stated in the Introduction (p. 347), I here assign two lines in Attic Greek (447-48) to a Theban hostage, for no better reason than symmetry.

391. *the Friends of Oligarchy:* This expansion makes more explicit a reference to the political clubs, or

synōmosiai, who caucussed and combined their votes to gain verdicts and offices, thus paving the road for the oligarchic upheaval in May of 411.

page 395. *Y^e menne must see to ye warre: Iliad* 6.492 (Hektor to Andromache).

395. *"What Athens needs is a Man"* : Traditionally interpreted (perhaps with too much enthusiasm) as a reference to the longing of the Athenian commonality for the return of glory-and-shame Alkibiades, who obliged the following summer.

397. *Pacifiers:* In the Greek, *Lysimachas* "Battlesettlers," a pun on the name of the heroine; also, if D. M. Lewis is right, a reference to her real-life model Lysimache—in 411, priestess of Athene.

400. *to snag important posts:* Most of this rather torturous allegory is self-explanatory, but the "clumps" are the political clubs, or "Friends of Oligarchy," mentioned earlier. See above, note to p. 391.

401. *To the audience:* Or, possibly, to the Chorus of Men. I do not accept Van Leeuwen's emendation here (598), but I do follow him in taking the line to be an interrupted exhortation to all available and qualified males.

401. *with her spindle:* Here and earlier, the women are certainly armed, but with what? The pronouns supplied by the Greek are tantalizingly specific in gender, but in nothing else; solutions usually bring out the worst in interpreters. I have tried to assign appropriate weapons early, and continue them to this denouement—but visualizers (or producers, if any there be) are at liberty, as elsewhere, to use their imaginations. One caveat: the Greek will not bear a direct repetition of the bath given earlier to the Old Men by the Old Women.

403. *my payroll:* The *triobolon*, the three-obol per diem wage for jury duty, which often constituted the only income of elderly men. It would naturally be stored inside the Citadel in the Treasury.

403. *WOMEN ticking off troops:* Emending πολίτας at 626 to ὁπλίτας.

page 404. *Harmodios, Aristogeiton, and Me:* The reference, to a famous statuary group by the sculptor Kritios in the Athenian Agora, picks up an earlier quotation from a popular *skolion*, or drinking-song, on the assassination of the tyrant Hipparchos: "I'll carry my sword concealed in a myrtle bough. . . ." The translation expands on the idea, but hides the quotation in the familiar "sword in olive branch."

405. *this proud progression:* Since this passage is frequently cited as primary evidence for the *cursus honorum* of a high-born young girl in fifth-century Athens, here are the steps set forth a bit more explicitly: (1) *arrêphoros* ("relic-bearer") to Athene, one of four little girls who carried the Goddess' sacred objects in Her semi-annual festival of the *Arréphoria*; (2) *aletris* ("mill-girl") to the Founding Mother (doubtless Athene), one of the girls who ground the meal to be made into sacrificial cakes; (3) *arktos* ("she-bear") at the *Brauronia*, a festival of Artemis held every fifth year at Brauron in Attika, centering on a myth which told of the killing of a tame bear sacred to that goddess; and (4) *kanêphoros* ("basket-bearer"), the maiden who bore the sacrificial cake and led the procession at Athens' most important festivals, such as the City Dionysia and the Great Panathenaia.

405. *the Mutual Funds from the Persian War:* This money originally made up the treasury of the Delian League, an alliance of Greek states against Persia formed by the Athenian Aristeides in 477; following its transfer, for safety's sake, from the island of Delos to Athens in 454, it became for all practical purposes Athenian property, supported by tribute from the Allies. Athens' heavy expenses in Sicily, followed by the Allies' nonpayment and defection, made this question all too pointed in early 411.

406. *to the Heights:* To Leipsydrion, in the mountains north of Athens, where the besieged Alkmaionid exiles held out for a time against the forces of the tyrant Hippias. Since this siege, ever after sym-

bolic of the Noble Lost Cause, took place in 513. commentators find it necessary to point out that the Chorus of Men couldn't *really* have fought in a battle 102 years before; that they are pretending, or speaking by extension for the Athenian Fighting Spirit, or whatever. Seemingly, this goes without saying; actually, it is dead wrong. Dramaturgy has little to do with geriatrics; Aristophanes needed a Chorus of Men old enough to be hidebound, decrepit, so old that they would first see the Women's Revolt, not in terms of sex, but of politics—the recrudescence of a personally experienced tyranny. He was cheerfully prepared to have them average 120 years of age, if anyone cared to count. The critical attitude gives one pause: a modern American playwright who composed a fantastic comedy, set in the present, featuring a Chorus of GAR members—would he be greeted with a flourish of actuarial tables?

page 409. *Pan's grotto:* A cave on the Akropolis containing a shrine to the god, outside the Citadel wall, which it adjoined on the northwest.

413. *That snake's a fabrication:* By inserting this speech (and the reply to it) I do not wish to make Lysistrata a religious skeptic, but to point out the joke. No one had ever seen the snake; even its most famous action, that of assisting Themistokles to persuade the Athenians to abandon the city before the battle of Salamis, had been accomplished by its non-appearance.

419. *Kinesias:* A perfectly good Greek name, but in this context it evokes a pun on a common sexual application of the verb *kinein* "move."

428. *Only the table gets laid:* In the Greek, Kinesias compares his phallus to "Herakles at table"—a stock comedy bit wherein the glutton hero, raving with hunger, is systematically diddled of his dinner by his hosts.

433. *The Commissioner:* I maintain the Commissioner as Athens' representative in this scene (980-1013),

not primarily because of the testimony of the manu-scripts (shaky support at best), but from the logic and structure of the speeches themselves. Coulon assigns them to a *Prytanis*, or member of the Execu-tive Board. In this he follows a whim of Wilamowitz, who took a hesitant suggestion by Van Leeuwen and exalted it into a new principal character in the play—one of the unhappiest changes ever made in an Aristophanic text. The caution of Van Leeuwen, who usually knew no fear as an editor, should have given anyone pause.

page 435 *a Spartan epistle:* Correctly, a *skytalê*, a tapered rod which was Sparta's contribution to cryptography. A strip of leather was wound about the rod, in-scribed with the desired message, and unwound for transmission. A messenger then delivered the strip to the qualified recipient, who deciphered it by wind-ing it around a rod uniform in size and shape with the first. Any interceptor found a meaningless string of letters.

436. *The most unnerving work of nature:* The ensuing reconciliation scene, with its surrogate sexuality, is one of the most curious in Aristophanes. It is not lyric; yet both its diction, oddly diffuse and redundant, and its meter, a paeonic variation on a common trochaic dialogue measure which paradoxi-cally makes it much more regular, seem to call for extensive choreography. I have tried to hedge my bet by stilting the English and employing an irregular scheme depending heavily on off-rhymes.

439. CHORUS OF MEN: Coulon, with most other mod-ern editors, assigns the two strophes here (1043-57, 1058-71, pp. 439-440), plus the two which follow the subsequent scene (1189-1202, 1203-15, pp. 450-451), to the entire Chorus, which thereby dem-onstrates its new-found unity. This seems possible, but unarticulated; even in this play, antistrophic responsion does not necessarily indicate opposition. By paying attention to the matter of this Indian-giving, I have tried to indicate the appropriate

diversity within unity: here, first Men (money), then Women (cooking); following Lysistrata's address, first Women (dress and ornament), then Men (grain). In any case, the manuscript indications, giving the first two strophes to the Women and the last two to the Men, appear impossible.

page 441. *Kinesias:* So I assign the leadership of the Athenians in this scene. Coulon follows Wilamowitz in allotting it to the latter's beloved "Prytanis." The manuscripts commit themselves no further than "Athenians," which is at least safe. It is definitely not the Commissioner.

442. *that self-appointed Purity League:* See Glossary, s.v. "Hermes."

446. *the Tyrant's days:* The reign of Hippias, expelled by the Athenians in 510 with the aid of Kleomenes and his Spartans, who defeated the tyrant's Thessalian allies.

448. *let's try Thessaly:* Puns on proper names, particularly geographical ones, rarely transfer well, as the following bits of sexual cartography will show. "Easy Mountain": an impossible pun on Mt. Oita, replacing the Greek's *Echinous,* a town in Thessaly whose name recalls *echinos* "hedgehog"—slang for the female genitalia. "Maniac Gulf": for Maliac Gulf, with less dimension than the Greek's *Mêlia kolpon,* which puns both on bosom and pudendum. The "legs of Megara" are the walls that connected that city with her seaport, Nisaia.

451. *to the door of the Akropolis:* This stage direction, and what follows it, attempt to make sense of a desperate situation in the manuscripts, whose chief accomplishment is to differentiate between Athenian and Spartan. In the passage 1216-46, I assign to the Commissioner those lines given by Coulon to the "Prytanis," and to Kinesias those he assigns to "an Athenian," with the following exceptions: the Koryphaios of Men receives 1216a ("Prytanis," Coulon) and 1221 ("Athenian," Coulon); the Commissioner receives 1226 ("Athenian," Coulon).

page 452. *in Spartan:* This rendering of 1225 in dialect, and the reading of 1226 as an ironical question, is prompted by a notion of Wilamowitz'. to whom an uncommon verb form seemed clear enough evidence of Spartan to warrant a native informant on stage 18 lines early. I am not sure of the validity of his perception, but it allows other solutions. such as the present one: Kinesias is awash with wine and international amity. and the Commissioner is amused.

455. *LYSISTRATA.* Coulon, following Wilamowitz' ungallant suggestion, takes this speech from Lysistrata (1273-78) and gives it, plus the dubious line following the choral song (1295), to the "Prytanis" —thus crowning the play and turning a superfluous man into an unnecessary hero.

The
Frogs

CONTENTS

Introduction

The Play

The Frogs was produced at the Lenaia of 405 B.C. and won first prize.[1] The Athenians had been at war most of the time since 431 B.C., and their position now was almost desperate. Since the failure in Sicily, they had indeed won several naval battles and had twice been offered peace by Sparta; they were nevertheless in a position where one defeat would lose the war (this happened six months after *The Frogs* was presented). One great victory might still save them, but only if they used it wisely, as a bargaining point for permanent peace.

This, at least, seems to have been the view of Aristophanes. The champion of peace who spoke in *The Acharnians, Peace,* and *Lysistrata*, is still the champion of peace. It was Kleophon who had forbidden the Athenians to accept Spartan terms.

---

[1] . . . "It was presented in the archonship of Kallias . . . at the Lenaia. It was placed first; Phrynichus was second with *The Muses;* Plato third, with *Cleophon*. Our play was so much admired because of the parabasis that it was actually given again, according to Dicaearchus." From the ancient *Hypothesis*, or Introduction. The Plato in question is a well-known comic poet, not the philosopher.

and in this play Aristophanes hates Kleophon as much as ever. But peace cannot now be simply offered or accepted; it must be earned. Aristophanes' program can be summed up as "all hands save ship." All talents and resources, even the doubtful and suspect talents of Alkibiades, must be called on to win one more victory which, if won, must be used as a means to an honorable peace, not as a means to conquest and empire. So, at least, I would read the concluding lines of the play.

In the spring of 405, Athenian literature had suffered too. Aeschylus was dead half a century since, though not forgotten. Euripides and Sophocles, greatest of the moderns, had died within the year. Dionysos, masked though he may be as the preposterous hero of comedy, is also Drama, the spirit and essence of Athenian literature and art. He seeks to bring back good writing to Athens, and with it, the public wisdom which, as Aristophanes maintains against Sokrates, will always be found in the highest poetry.

The first part of *The Frogs*, therefore, takes the form of the Comic Journey beyond the limits of the world, reminiscent in some ways of *Peace* and *The Birds*. During its course, as the Dead are encountered, these are used to speak the poet's own views and to plead for political harmony. At the end of the Journey, a conversation between the two slaves, Xanthias and Aiakos, introduces the grand final *agon* between Euripides and Aeschylus.

This *agon* is, after suitable introductory exhortation and preparation, disputed on five issues, or in five rounds, as follows:

1. 907-1098. General style, subject matter, and effect upon the audiences.
   (1099-1118). Choral interlude.
2. 1119-1250. Prologues, including skill at exposition and the use of iambic metre.
   (1251-60). Choral interlude.
3. 1261-1369. Lyrics and lyric prosody.
   (1370-77). Choral interlude.
4. 1378-1410. The weighing of lines.
   (1411-17). Interlude by Dionysos and Pluto.
5. 1417-65. Advice to the Athenians.

In each round, Euripides attacks first, and in the first three he scores some hits. Nor is his final advice (1446-50) contemptible; at least, it is not unlike the spirit of the poet's own views spoken at 718-37. But Aeschylus, the ultimate winner, has the better position for an *agon*, since the last word is always his.

Briefly, the arguments, round by round, are as follows:

1. Euripides says that Aeschylus is slow-moving, undramatic, turgid, obscure, and too militaristic. His own plays are lucid, plausible, and have meaning for all. Aeschylus retorts that he has always maintained a high heroic standard and incited the citizens to virtue, while Euripides, in bringing Tragedy down to earth, has, especially with his morbid interest in sex, dragged her in the dust, and in so doing has unmanned the Athenians.

2. Euripides alleges an obscure and repetitious style. Aeschylus replies with a charge of metrical monotony. In prologue after prologue of Euripides, the main verb is delayed and a subordinate clause completed in such a way that the phrase

        lost his little bottle of oil
    which scans

$$- \; \cup \; - \cup \; - \; \cup\!\cup \; -$$

will now complete both the sentence and the metrical line.

3. Aeschylus having raised the question of metrical monotony, Euripides retorts in kind. The lyrics of Aeschylus are monotonous. For, however he may begin, he constantly ends with the dactylic phrase

$$\cup\!\!\!\!- \; - \cup\cup \; - \cup\cup \; - \cup\cup \; - -$$

exemplified by his line

    o ho what a stroke come you not to the rescue?

In these metrical criticisms, which are penetrating, the general criticisms of style are repeated, i.e., when Euripides makes sense, he is prosy and pedestrian, when Aeschylus sounds grand, he means little. Aeschylus counters. Euripides writes vers libre, the lyric metres lose their form and the sense loses its coherence. The result is a shoddy, sentimental, drifting sequence, marked in particular by one special fault which Aristophanes loves to detect in Euripides: namely, the unassimilating conjunction of magnificence and homeliness.

4. The weighing of the lines involves a bit of byplay, has been often dismissed as mere fooling, and is mostly that, but nevertheless forwards the constant opinion of Aristophanes (Dionysos): the verse of Aeschylus has more mass, heft, and force than that of Euripides.

5. What shall Athens do? The speakers might represent the poet's own agonizing struggle. Euripides expresses Aristophanes' doubts about the good purposes of the heirs of Perikles, the exponents of naval warfare; but Aeschylus voices Aristophanes' unwilling conclusion, that these men alone have a chance of saving the city.

In this *agon*, Aristophanes has achieved an unfair but telling criticism of Euripides. His Aeschylus, even as parody, fits far less closely the concept which we can form of him from seven complete plays and a number of fragments. Aeschylus was not the Colonel Blimp that Aristophanes makes him. *The Persians* and *The Seven Against Thebes* are not simple glorifications of patriotism and courage. *Agamemnon* condemns war-makers and sackers of cities. The woman's point of view is eloquently stated in every surviving play. And Aphrodite did mean a great deal to Aeschylus; one need only look at the dreaming visions of Helen in *Agamemnon*, or at Klytaimnestra's sadistic ecstasies in the same play. Nor was Aeschylus a reactionary aristocrat. *Prometheus* and *The Eumenides* speak eloquently for progress and reform.

Aristophanes has picked out and exaggerated certain aspects of Aeschylus, not because he was ignorant or blind, but perhaps because he was more concerned with the force of his *agon* than with the inward coherence and validity of his historical persons. The attack is on the moderns. Euripides is their spokesman. Whatever Euripides is, Aeschylus must be the opposite. So, if Euripides is pacific and unmilitary, Aeschylus must be martial. If Euripides is fascinated by women and writes of their problems from their point of view, Aeschylus must despise the sex. And since Euripides was so plainly popular (though not in the sense that he won prizes from the judges), Aeschylus must be in a sense *un*popular, that is, haughty and aristocratic

A byproduct of the pattern is the unhappy position in which Sophocles finds himself: a second-best Aeschylus. Only two could play this game at once. Aeschylus and Euripides were plainly more fun for the parodist, their peculiarities being a great deal more obvious

In translating *The Frogs*, I have found myself surprised into breaking away from several principles which I always stuck to when trying to translate serious Greek poetry. Let me, once again, grimly itemize

1 Notes. I have generally avoided footnotes on the text of tragedy. But Aristophanes is, as the immortal Stephen Leacock put it   "sally after sally, each sally explained in a footnote calling it a sally."[2] I have added some notes.

2. Slang. *The Frogs* opens in the manner, though not altogether in the language, of the vaudeville act or minstrel show. My English is much worse than Aristophanes' Greek. But the vernacular seemed to be the only language into which it would translate itself. Frequently, the translation is in very bad taste And so is Aristophanes.

3. Incongruity. Comedy does not cultivate appropriateness for its own sake.

4 Rhymes. Certain metres, such as short iambic lines, and the long ones in iambic and anapaestic, seemed in English to come out rather lame and labored without rhyme, perhaps because English lacks the flexibility and the bold distinction between long and short of polysyllabic Greek. I have left the parabasis (354-71) unrhymed because it seems, in Greek, rather strained and awkward, and is not funny

5. Clichés. In serious verse, these are absolutely obnoxious (in serious *prose*, too!) Awkwardly enthroned out of context, the cliché is of the stuff of comedy So I have

---

[2]Let me point out that, in accordance with modern convention, this quotation from Stephen Leacock must be accompanied by a footnote calling it a quotation from Stephen Leacock. See Stephen Leacock, *Behind the Beyond* (New York: John Lane Company; London: John Lane, The Bodley Head; Toronto: Bell and Cockburn, 1923), pp. 186-87

written accordingly. Perhaps the alert readers will find that
they have crept into the introduction too.

I have used the *Oxford Classical Text* of Hall and Geldart.
I am deeply indebted to Harry Avery for helpful criticism.

Characters of the Play

DIONYSOS
XANTHIAS. *his slave*
HERAKLES
CORPSE
CHARON
CHORUS (*as Frogs; as Initiates; and as the population of Hades*)
AIAKOS. *the janitor of Hades*
MAID
HOSTESS *of the inn*
PLATHANE. *maid of the inn*
EURIPIDES
AESCHYLUS
PLUTO (*or Hades*)
VARIOUS EXTRAS (*stretcher bearers, dead souls rowing in the boat, assistants to Aiakos, etc.*)

SCENE: *A Door. Enter Dionysos, on foot; Xanthias, riding a donkey, and with a bundle on his back. Dionysos wears a long yellow robe, but over it the lion skin affected by Herakles, and he carries a primitive knobby club.*

XANTHIAS

Shall I give them any of the usual jokes, master?
You know, the ones that are always good for a laugh?

DIONYSOS

Go ahead. *Any* of them. Except ``what a day!``
Don't give them that one. It's gone awfully sour.

XANTHIAS

But something witty, like . . .

DIONYSOS

                    *Any*thing. Except ``my poor back.``

XANTHIAS

Well, can I tell the really funny one?

DIONYSOS

                              Yes, do,
go right ahead. Only don't say *this* one.

XANTHIAS

                         Don't say what?

DIONYSOS

Don't shift your load because ``you need to go to the
baffroom.``

XANTHIAS

Can't I even tell the people I'm so over-loaded
that unless somebody unloads me I'll blow my ——
bottom?

DIONYSOS

No, don't, please don't. Wait till I *need* to vomit.

XANTHIAS

So what did I have to carry all this stuff for,
if I can't pull any of the jokes Phrynichos* pulls,
or what Lykis pulls, or what Ameipsias pulls?

DIONYSOS

Well, just don't do it. When I'm in the audience
and have to watch any of these conscious efforts,
I'm a year older when I leave the place.

XANTHIAS

Poor me. Oh, my poor neck. I think it's broken now.
It won't say anything funny.

DIONYSOS

Now isn't this a sassy slave? I've spoiled him.
Here am I, Dionysos, son of Grapejuice,
wearing out my own feet, and I let him ride
so that he won't get tired carrying the bundles.

XANTHIAS

What do you mean, not carrying them?

DIONYSOS

                                        How can you?
You're riding.

XANTHIAS

            But I'm carrying.

DIONYSOS

                        How?

XANTHIAS

                                With an effort.

DIONYSOS

Isn't the donkey carrying what you're carrying?

XANTHIAS

Not carrying what I'm carrying no, by golly.

DIONYSOS

How can you carry it, when somebody's carrying you?

XANTHIAS

Dunno. I only know my shoulder's falling apart.

DIONYSOS

All right, so the donkey isn't doing any good,
why don't you pick him up and carry him?

XANTHIAS

Why wasn't I in that sea battle,* where they freed the
slaves who fought? Then I could tell you to go jump in
the lake.

DIONYSOS

Get down, you bum. Here we are at the door.
This is the place I was trying to find. First stop. Get
down.

Knocks on the door.

Hey there! You inside! Hey. Anybody home? Bang bang

Herakles half opens the door, pokes his head out.

HERAKLES

Who was pounding on my door? Sounded like a Centaur
kicking it or something. What goes on?

DIONYSOS

To Xanthias.

Slave boy!

XANTHIAS

What is it?

DIONYSOS

You noticed, didn't you?

XANTHIAS

Noticed what?

DIONYSOS

How scared he was.

XANTHIAS

Yeah, scared. Scared you were going bats.

HERAKLES

Demeter! I have to laugh.
I'm biting my lip to hold it in, but I can't help it.

DIONYSOS

Come here, dear boy. I have a favor to ask of you.

HERAKLES

Wait till I get rid of the giggles. Only I can't stop them.
That lion skin being worn over that buttercup nightie!
Haw haw haw.

Collapses. Recovers.

What's the idea, this meeting of the warclub and slipper?
Where were you bound?

DIONYSOS

Well. I served aboard a kind of dreamboat named the Kleisthenes.*

HERAKLES

And did you engage?

DIONYSOS

I did. We sank a dozen, a baker's dozen, of the enemy craft.

HERAKLES

You two?

DIONYSOS

So help me Appolo.

XANTHIAS

And then I woke up.

DIONYSOS

So then I'm sitting on deck, see, reading this new book: *Andromeda*, by Euripides: all of a sudden it hits me over the heart, a craving, you can't think how hard.

HERAKLES

A craving, huh. A big one?

DIONYSOS

Little one Molon*-size

HERAKLES

A craving. For a woman?

DIONYSOS

No.

HERAKLES

For a boy?

DIONYSOS

No no.

HERAKLES

For a, uh, man?

DIONYSOS

Shush shush shush.

HERAKLES

Well, what about you
and Kleisthenes?

DIONYSOS

Don't laugh at me, brother dear. Truly I am in a bad
way. I've got this craving. It's demoralizing me.

HERAKLES

What kind of craving, little brother?

DIONYSOS

I don't know how
to explain. I'll paraphrase it by a parable.
Did you ever feel a sudden longing for baked beans?

HERAKLES

Baked beans? Gosh yes, that's happened to me a million
times.

DIONYSOS

Shall I give you another illustration? Expound this one?

HERAKLES

Don't need to expound baked beans to me. I get the point.

DIONYSOS

Well, that's the kind of craving that's been eating me: a craving for Euripides.

HERAKLES

You mean, dead and all?

DIONYSOS

And nobody's going to persuade me to give up my plan of going after him.

HERAKLES

Way to Hades', down below?

DIONYSOS

Absolutely. Belower than that, if there's anything there.

HERAKLES

What do you want?

DIONYSOS

What I want is a clever poet
*For some of them are gone. The ones who're left are bad.**

HERAKLES

What? Isn't Iophon* living?

DIONYSOS

He's the one good thing
that's left—that is, if he really is any good.
I don't quite altogether just know about that.

HERAKLES

But if you *got* to resurrect somebody, why
not Sophocles instead of Euripides?

DIONYSOS

No. First I want to get Iophon all by himself
without Sophocles, take him apart, see how he does.
Anyway, Euripides is a slippery character
who'd like to make a jailbreak and come back with me.
Sophocles behaved himself up here. He would down
there.

HERAKLES

What happened to Agathon?*

DIONYSOS

Oh, he's left me, gone away.
And he was a good poet, too. His friends miss him.

HERAKLES

Too bad. Where did he go?

DIONYSOS

To join the saints. For dinner.

HERAKLES

What about Xenokles?

DIONYSOS

I only wish he *would* die.

HERAKLES

Pythangelos?

XANTHIAS

And nobody ever thinks of me,
and look at me standing here with my shoulder dropping
off.

HERAKLES

Look here, there still are a million and one young guys
   around.
You know, Tragic Poets
who can outgabble Euripides by a country mile.

DIONYSOS

A lot of morning-glories talking to themselves,
just twitterbirds and free-verse writers, sloppy craftsmen.
One performance, and you never hear of them again.
They sprinkle Drama in passing like a dog at a pump.
You tell me where there's still an honest-to-god poet
to bark me out one good round solid tragic line.

HERAKLES

Honest-to-god like what?

DIONYSOS

Honest-to-god like this,
someone with an adventurous style, as who should say:
*Bright upper air, Zeus' penthouse** or *the foot of Time,*
or *heart that would not swear upon the holy things*
or *tongue that was forsworn when the heart knew it not.*

HERAKLES

You like that stuff?

DIONYSOS

It's absolutely dreamy, man.

HERAKLES

It's bilge. It's awful. Nobody knows it better than you.

DIONYSOS

*Rule not my mind. Thine own is thy mind. Rule thou it.**

HERAKLES

No, really, it does seem the most awful slop to me.

DIONYSOS

You stick to food.

XANTHIAS

And nobody ever thinks of me.

DIONYSOS

Now, let me tell you why I'm here, wearing all this stuff
that makes me look like you. It's so you can tell me
about your friends who put you up when you went *there*
to fetch the Kerberos dog. Well, I could use some
friends, so tell me about them. Tell me the ports, the
bakery shops, whorehouses, parks and roadside rests,
highways and springs, the cities, boarding houses, and
the best hotels scarcest in bedbugs.

XANTHIAS

Nobody ever thinks of me.

HERAKLES

You poor idiot. You're really going to try and get there?

DIONYSOS

No more of that stuff, please, just tell me about the
roads, and what's the quickest way to Hades' under-
house, and don't make it a hot one. Not too cold either.

HERAKLES

Hm. What's my first recommendation? What indeed?
Well, here's a way. You need a footstool and a rope.
Go hang yourself.

DIONYSOS

Stop stop. That's a stifling sort of way.

HERAKLES

Well, there's a short well-beaten path. *Well-beaten*,
I say, via mortar-and-pestle.

DIONYSOS

That's hemlock you're talking about?

HERAKLES

Nothing else but.

DIONYSOS

A chilly way. It makes me shiver.
Your shins go numb.

HERAKLES

Shall I tell you about a downhill road? It's good and
quick.

DIONYSOS

That's what I'd like. I'm somebody who hates to walk.

HERAKLES

Well, take just a little walk down to the Potters' Quarter.

DIONYSOS

Yes.

HERAKLES

Climb up the tower, the high one.

DIONYSOS

What do I do then?

HERAKLES

Watch for the drop of the signal torch that starts the
race, and when they drop it, all the spectators around
will say "go!" You go, too.

DIONYSOS

Go where?

HERAKLES

Over the edge.

DIONYSOS

I'd smash my twin croquettes of brains.
No, I won't go that way of yours.

HERAKLES

What *do* you want?

DIONYSOS

The way you went, the deathless way.*

HERAKLES

It's a long voyage.

The first thing that you'll come to is a great swampy
lake. It's bottomless.

DIONYSQS

Well, then, how do I get across?

HERAKLES

There's an ancient mariner with a little tiny boat.
He'll take you across. And you'll give him two bits*
    for it.

DIONYSOS

Oh, gee.
Those two bits. You can't ever get away from them.
How did they ever get here?

HERAKLES

Theseus* brought them along from
Athens. After that, you'll see snakes, and armies of wild
animals, monsters.

DIONYSOS

Stop trying to scare me out of this.
You'll never stop me.

HERAKLES

Next comes a great sea of mud
and shitten springs eternal, and people stuck therein,
whoever did an injury to his guest or host,
debauched some child and picked its pockets in the
process, or beat his mother up, or broke his father's jaw,
or swore an oath and broke it,
or copied out a tragic speech of Morsimos.*

DIONYSOS

Don't stop. I've got another one to add to those.
Whoever learned the war-dance by Kinesias.*

HERAKLES

Next a sweet sound of flutes will come upon your ears,
and you'll see a lovely light like the sunlight here above,
myrtles, and solemn troops and sweet societies
of men and women, and an endless clapping of hands

DIONYSOS

And who are they?

HERAKLES

The blessed, the Initiates.*

XANTHIAS

And I'm the donkey carrying mystic properties,
but I don't mean to keep them for the rest of time

HERAKLES

Ask them. They'll tell you everything else you need,
for they live closest to the road you have to go.
Their habitation is by Pluto's doors.
So, good luck, little brother.

Herakles disappears, shutting the door.

DIONYSOS

Oh, the same to you!
Keep healthy. You there, Xanthias, pick the bundles up.

XANTHIAS

You mean, before I've put them down?

DIONYSOS

Get a move on.

XANTHIAS

Oh please, please don't make me do it. Why don't you

hire one of these stiffs they're carrying out? There'll
be one soon.

DIONYSOS

What if I can't get one?

XANTHIAS

Then I'll do it.

DIONYSOS

Fair enough.
Look, here comes a corpse now being carried out.

Corpse is brought in on a stretcher.

Hey! Hey, you there, the dead one. I'm talking to you.
Want to carry some luggage to Hades?

Corpse sits up.

CORPSE

How much?

DIONYSOS

Showing his hand.

That much.

CORPSE

Give me two bucks*?

DIONYSOS

My god no, that's too much.

Corpse lies down again.

CORPSE

Keep carrying me, you guys.

DIONYSOS

Hey, what's the matter, wait, we've got to work this out.

CORPSE

Two bucks. Put up or shut up.

DIONYSOS

Make it one and a half.

CORPSE

                              I'd sooner come to life again.

Corpse is carried off.

XANTHIAS

Stuck up bastard, isn't he? The hell with him!
I'll take the baggage.

DIONYSOS

                    You are nature's nobleman.
Let's go catch a boat.

CHARON

Off stage.

                    Woo-oop! Coming alongside!

XANTHIAS

What's going on here?

DIONYSOS

                    What indeed. Oh here, it's the lake
right where he said it would be, and now here comes
the boat.

Charon, in a little boat (on wheels) is pushed in.

XANTHIAS

So help me Poseidon, so it is, and Charon too.

DIONYSOS

O carry me Charon o sweet chariot carry me home.*

CHARON

Who wants a cruise? Relaxation from business worries?
The Meadows of Forgetting, or Horsefeatherland?
To go to the Dogs? To go to the Birds? To go to Hell?

DIONYSOS

Me.

CHARON

  Get aboard and shake a leg.

DIONYSOS

                  Where d'you think we're bound?
Strictly for the Birds?

CHARON

                  We sure are, with you aboard.
Get on, get on.

DIONYSOS

        Here, boy!

CHARON

                  No, I won't take a slave.
Only a veteran of our hide-saving sea battle.*

XANTHIAS

I would have made it but I was sick. I had the pinkeye.

CHARON

Then you can just take a little walk around the lake.

XANTHIAS

Where shall I wait for you?

CHARON

                    By the Stone of Parching Thirst,*
at the pull-off.

DIONYSOS

          Got it?

XANTHIAS

                Oh, I've got it. Wish I were dead.
What kind of bad-luck-sign did I run into this morning?

Xanthias trudges off, carrying the bundles. Dionysos climbs, awkwardly, into the boat.

CHARON

You, sit to your oar.

Dionysos sits on his oar.

               Anyone else going? Hurry it up.

A few Extras (the ones who carried the corpse), get into the boat, each taking an oar.

Hey, *you* there. What d'you think you're doing?

DIONYSOS

With dignity.

                    I am sitting
to my oar. Exactly what you told me to do.

CHARON

Rearranging him.

Well, sit *here*, fatso. Sit like this. Got it?

DIONYSOS

                                                        Okay.

CHARON

Now get your hands away and bring them back.

DIONYSOS

                                                        Okay.

CHARON

Stop being such an ass, will you? Bring your weight
forward. Get your back into it.

DIONYSOS

                        What do you want? I never rowed before.
I'm no Old Navy Man. I didn't make the First Crew.*
How'm I supposed to row?

CHARON

                                Easily. Just begin to do it.
and you'll get a pretty song to give you the time.

DIONYSOS

                                                Who's singing?

CHARON

It's a swan song, but the swans are lovely frogs.

DIONYSOS

                                        Go ahead.
Give me the stroke.

CHARON

OO-pah, oo-pah.

If he cares to, Charon can go on doing this all during the following chorus.
The Chorus appears, in green masks and tights, as Frogs. They are Frogs only in this rowing-scene. They dance around the boat.

CHORUS

Brekekekex ko-ax ko-ax,
Brekekekex ko-ax ko-ax,
children of freshwater ponds and springs,
gather we all together now
and swell our lofty well-becroaken chorus,
ko-ax ko-ax

Dionysos' Nysos-song
we sing to the son of Zeus,
Dionysos-in-the-marshes,
when with morning-frog-in-the-throat
the hangover-haggard procession
staggers to the holy Pot-Feast through my dominion,
brekekekex ko-ax ko-ax.

DIONYSOS

I think that I'm beginning to fail,
I'm raising blisters on my tail,
ko-ax ko-ax, I think I am,
but possibly you don't care a damn.

CHORUS

Brekekekex ko-ax ko-ax.

DIONYSOS

I can't hear anything but ko-ax,
go 'way, I'd like to give you the axe.

CHORUS

Of course, you fool, you can't hear anything else,
for the sweet Muses have gifted me with their lyres,
and Pan the horned walker, voice of reed in the woods.
and lyric Apollo himself goes glad for my singing
when with the music of piping my lyrical
song is heard in the pondy waters.
Brekekekex ko-ax ko-ax.

DIONYSOS

My bloody blisters refuse to heal.
My anguished bottom's beginning to squeal.
When I bend over it joins the attack.

CHORUS

Brekekekex ko-ax ko-*ak*.

DIONYSOS

Oh ah ye songful tribe, will you
shut up?

CHORUS

Exactly what we won't do.
Longer stronger
sing in the sunny daytime
as we wriggle and dive in the marsh-
flowers blithe on the lily pads
and dive and duck as we sing,
and when Zeus makes it rain
in green escape to the deep
water our song still pulses
and bubbles up from below.

DIONYSOS

Brepepepeps ko-aps ko-aps
I'm picking the rhythm up from you chaps.

CHORUS

We're sorry for us if *you* join in.

DIONYSOS

I'm sorry for *me* if I begin
to split in two from bottom to chin.

CHORUS

Brekekekex ko-ax ko-ax.

DIONYSOS

And the hell with you. I don't *care* what you do

CHORUS

Whatever you say we'll croak all day
as long as we're stout
and our throats hold out.

DIONYSOS

Brekekekex ko-ax ko-ax.
There, I can do it better than you.

CHORUS

No, *we* can do it better than *you*.

DIONYSOS

No, *I* can do it better than *you*.
I'll croak away
if it takes all day,
brekekekex ko-ax ko-ax,
and I'll croak you down in the grand climax
brekekekex ko-ax ko-ax

Frogs slink away. Silence.

Ha ha. I knew I could beat you. You and your ko-ax!

CHARON

Easy. easy Ship oars now. Coming alongside.
Everybody off Pay your fare.

DIONYSOS

Two bits for you. my good man

Charon with his boat is wheeled off.

Xanthias! Hey. Xanthias! Now where's he got to?
Xanthias'

XANTHIAS

Off

Yoo hoo'

DIONYSOS

This way Over here

Xanthias appears

XANTHIAS

Why. hello. master.

DIONYSOS

What's over there'

XANTHIAS

A lot of mud and darkness.

DIONYSOS

Well. did you see those criminal types he was talking
about. the murderers and swindlers?

XANTHIAS

Haven't *you* seen them?

Dionysos stares at the audience and points rudely.

DIONYSOS

Oh, sure, now I know where to look. They're all out
there. Well, what do we do next?

XANTHIAS

                                   I think we'd better get out of here.
This is the place he said the wild animals would be,
you know, those monsters he was talking about.

DIONYSOS

                                                 Oh, him.
He was just laying it on thick, trying to frighten me.
He knows what a fighting man I am, and it makes him
jealous. There's nobody who's quite as vain as Herakles.
I wish we could have met some terrifying thing,
you know, some ghastly struggle, to make the trip
worth while.

XANTHIAS

You know, I think I do hear something moving around.

DIONYSOS

Wh wh which direction?

XANTHIAS

                        Right behind us.

DIONYSOS

                                      Get behind.

XANTHIAS

No, it's in front of us now.

DIONYSOS

You better stay in front.

XANTHIAS

I see it. It's an animal—an enormous thing.

DIONYSOS

What does it look like?

XANTHIAS

Monster. It keeps changing shape.
Now it's a cow. Now it's a mule Oh. now it's a girl.
whee-whew, what a beauty!

DIONYSOS

Let me at her Where'd she go?

XANTHIAS

Too late No girl any longer. She turned into a bitch

DIONYSOS

It's Empousa. *

XANTHIAS

Whoever she is. she done caught fire
Her face is burning

DIONYSOS

Does she have one brazen leg?

XANTHIAS

She does, she does The other one is made of dung.
I'm not lying.

DIONYSOS

Where can I run to"

XANTHIAS

Where can I"

DIONYSOS

To the priest of Dionysos sitting in the front row

Save me. your reverence' We belong to the same lodge

XANTHIAS

Lord Herakles. we're lost

DIONYSOS

Dumb-bell. don't call me that
Don't give away my name *Please*

XANTHIAS

Lord Dionysos then

DIONYSOS

No no. that's even worse
Go on the way you were going.

XANTHIAS

Here. master. over here

DIONYSOS

Got something?

XANTHIAS

Don't be frightened. we've come out all right
and I can speak the line now that Hegelochos spoke:

The storm is over, and the clam has stilled the waves.*
Empousa's gone.

DIONYSOS

You swear it's true?

XANTHIAS

So help me Zeus.

DIONYSOS

Swear it again.

XANTHIAS

So help me Zeus.

DIONYSOS

Swear.

XANTHIAS

Help me Zeus

DIONYSOS

What a fright. I lost my pretty color when I saw her.

XANTHIAS

Our donkey got a fright too, so you're all in yellow.*

DIONYSOS

Now what did I ever do to have this happen to me?

Looking upward.

Which one of you gods must I hold responsible for this?

XANTHIAS

Bright upper air Zeus penthouse' Or the foot of Time"
Flute within

DIONYSOS

Hey. you

XANTHIAS

                    What is it?

DIONYSOS

                                    Did you hear'

XANTHIAS

                                                Did I hear what''

DIONYSOS

Flutes being blown

XANTHIAS

                            I heard them too. and there's a crackle
and smell of torches Seems like it's mysteries going on

DIONYSOS

Let's just quietly squat where we are. and listen in

CHORUS

Off

Iacchos Iacchos*
Iacchos o Iacchos

XANTHIAS

That's what I tnought it was. master. The Initiates.
Remember. he told us. their playground's hereabouts

They sing the Iacchos song by that noted theologian,
Diagoras.*

DIONYSOS

I think you're right. but still we'd better sit quiet here
until we find out just exactly what goes on.

CHORUS

In white, as Initiates.

Iacchos! Well beloved in these pastures o indwelling
Iacchos o Iacchos
come to me come with dance steps down the meadow
to your worshipping companions
with the fruited, the lifebursting,
the enmyrtled and enwreathed garland on your brows,
and bold-footed stamp out the sprightly measure
of the dancing full of graces, full of light and sweet and
sacred for your dedicated chosen ones.

XANTHIAS

Demeter's daughter, Persephone, holy lady and queen,
ineffable fragrance wafts upon me. Roasting pigs!*

DIONYSOS

If I promise you a handful of tripes, will you shut up?

CHORUS

Let flames fly as the torch tosses in hand's hold
Iacchos o Iacchos
star of fire in the high rites of the night time.
And the field shines in the torch light,
and the old men's knees are limber,
and they shake off aches and miseries
and the years of their antiquity drop from them
in the magical measure.
Oh, torch-in-hand-shining.

Iacchos go before us to the marsh flowers and the
  meadow
and the blest revel of dances.

*Parabasis. The Chorus advances down stage and the leader
addresses the audience directly.*

LEADER

All now must observe the sacred silence: we ban from
  our choruses any
whose brain cannot fathom the gist of our wit: whose
  hearts and feelings are dirty;
who never has witnessed and never partaken in genuine
  cult of the Muses,
who knows not the speech of bullgobble Kratinos,* who
  knows not the Bacchic fraternity,
who laughs at cheap jokes that should not have been
  made, who writes such stuff at the wrong time,
who stirs up sedition dissension and hate, who does not
  like the Athenians,
who hopes to make money out of our quarrels and
  lights them and fans them to fury,
who holds high office and then takes bribes when the
  city is tossed in the tempest,
who sells out a ship or a fort to the enemy, smuggling
  our secret intelligence
from Aigina over to Epidauros, like any goddam tax-
  collecting
Thorykion,* with the oarpads and sails and pitch that
  was meant for our navy,
who goes on his rounds and collects contributions to
  finance the enemy's war fleet,
who, humming his cyclical verses the while, uses
  Hekate's shrine as a backhouse,*
who gets up to speak in the public assembly and nibbles
  at the fees of the poets
just because they once made a fool of him in the plays
  that our fathers established.
Such men I forbid, and again I forbid, and again I
  forbid them a third time,

let them get up and go from our choral mysteries.

                                All others, strike
  up the singing
and dance of our holy and nightlong revels befitting
  this solemn occasion.

CHORUS

Slowly.

Advance all now, firmly
into the flower strewn hollows
of meadow fields. Stamp strongly
and jeer and sneer
and mock and be outrageous.
For all are well stuffed full with food.

Advance advance, sing strongly
our Lady of Salvation
and march to match your singing.
She promises
to save our land in season
for all Thorykion can do.

LEADER

Come now and alter the tune of the song for the queen
  of the bountiful seasons;
sing loud, sing long, and dance to the song for Demeter
  our lady and goddess.

CHORUS

Demeter, mistress of grave and gay,
stand by now and help me win.
Protect this chorus. It is your own.
Let me in safety all this day
play on and do my dances.
Help me say what will make them grin.
Help me say what will make them think.
Help me say what will make me win

in your own festival today
and wear the victor's garland.

LEADER

Change the tune.
Sing to the pretty god of the time   summon him to
  join us.
We have a sacred way to go   and he goes with us.

CHORUS

Iacchos, well-beloved spirit of song, o be
my leader and march along with me
this holy way.
Bring me to Eleusis swift and musically.
To you I pray.
Iacchos lover of dancing help me on my way.

You split my shirt to make them laugh and boo.
You cut my cheap little shoes in two.
My rags flap on me.
You know how to make do.
Wartime economy.
Iacchos lover of dancing help me on my way.

I saw a sweet little girl in the crowd down there.
As she leaned forward, her dress, I swear,
bust open a trifle
and I was happy to stare
at a bosomy eyeful.
Iacchos lover of dancing help me on my way.

DIONYSOS

I've always been a fellow who's good
at follow-my-leader; I gladly would
go down and help you play with her.

XANTHIAS

                    I would if I could.

CHORUS

Shall we now, all together
make fun of Archedemos?*
Seven years he tries to naturalize and still he hasn't
    made it.

Now he's a leading citizen
among the upworld corpses.
Nobody up there can claim a similar fame—for being
    a bastard.

And Kleisthenes,* they tell me,
sits mourning among the tombstones,
and tears the hair from his you-know-where, and
    batters his jawbones.

He was seen, in his usual posture
in tears for his vanished sweetheart—
the dear little friend (of his after-end) Sebinos of
    Anaphlystos.

And Kallias,* they say,
the son of Ponyplay,
wears a panoply and has gone to sea and the ships with
    a lionskin over his hips.

DIONYSOS

Can any of you guys tell
me where Pluto happens to dwell?
We're visiting firemen. Never been here before.

CHORUS

Stop bothering me so.
You haven't got far to go.
He lives right here. Walk up and knock at the door.

DIONYSOS

Boy! Pick up the stuff again.

The Frogs   513

XANTHIAS

What's the matter with this guy?
Pick up, pick up, it's nothing but pick up bundles.

CHORUS

Forward, now
to the goddess' sacred circle-dance to the grove that's in
    blossom
and play on the way for we belong to the company of
    the elect,
and I shall go where the girls go and I shall go with
    the women
who keep the nightlong rite of the goddess and carry
    their sacred torch.

Let us go where roses grow
and fields are in flower,
in the way that is ours alone,
playing our blessed play
which the prosperous Fates today
ordain for our playing.

On us alone the sun shines here
and the happy daylight,
for we are Initiates, we
treat honorably
all strangers who are here
and our own people.

The white-robed Chorus file off.

DIONYSOS

Well, tell me, how am I supposed to knock on the door?
How do the natives knock on doors in these here parts?

XANTHIAS

Stop dithering around. Take a good whack at it.
You wear the gear and spirit of Herakles. Act
according.

DIONYSOS

Knocking.

Boy! Hey, boy.

AIAKOS*

Inside.

Who's out there?

DIONYSOS

The mighty Herakles.

AIAKOS

Still inside but he will appear later on.

You hoodlum; did you ever have a nerve,
you bastard, bastard plus, and bastard double-plus.
You were the one who dragged our Kerberos-dog away.
You choked him by the collar and made off with him,
and *I* was on duty. We've got a scissors-hold on *you.*
We've got the cliffs of blackheart Styx* all ready
    for you,
the blood-dripping rocks of Acheron to shove you off—
or maybe the bloodhounds sniff your trail by Kokytos.
Echidna, our pet hundred-headed viper, waits
to chew your gizzard, and Muraina, eel of hell
shall have your lungs to gnaw on, while your kidneys go
with all the rest of your innards and the bleeding bowels
to the Teithrasian gorgons. Oh, they'll rip you up.
They're straining at the leash. I'll let them loose on you.

Dionysos collapses, doubled up.

XANTHIAS

What's the matter?

DIONYSOS

I can't hold it. Is there a god in the house?

XANTHIAS

You clown. Don't disgrace us. Alley oop! On your feet
before somebody sees you.

DIONYSOS

But I feel so faint.
Be a good chap, put a wet sponge over my heart.

XANTHIAS

Here it is, you put it.

DIONYSOS

Where are we?

Takes it, searches, and claps it over his lower anatomy.

XANTHIAS

O ye golden gods,
is that where you keep your heart?

DIONYSOS

You see, the poor little thing
got awfully frightened, so she crept down there to hide.

XANTHIAS

You're the worst coward of all gods and men.

DIONYSOS

Who, *me?*
Call *me* a coward? Didn't I ask you for a sponge?
Nobody else would have dared do that.

XANTHIAS

What would they have done?

DIONYSOS

Laid there and stunk, that's what a good coward would have done. I got to my feet again. What's more, united I stand.

XANTHIAS

That's manliness, by Poseidon.

DIONYSOS

Goodness gracious yes.

Long pause.

He talked so loud and said such awful things. Weren't you a little scared?

XANTHIAS

Hell no, I never gave it a thought.

DIONYSOS

Well, tell you what. You win. I guess you're the hero-boy. So you be me. Here you are. Here's the club, here's the lion's skin.

Exchange going on.

You're the guy with the fearless guts. I'll be you, and take my turn with the duffel bags.

XANTHIAS

*I cannot but obey thee.** Gimme. Hurry it up.

Exchange completed. Xanthias parades the stage.

Hey, look at me, everybody. I'm Xanthierakles. Now see if I'm a sissy, like you.

DIONYSOS

                    You look like someone
who came from the same ward—but got rode out on
a rail. Well, there's the baggage. Suppose I've got to
carry it.

A maid comes out of the door, and squeals with joy.

MAID

Why, *He*rakles! Darling, it's you! Come on inside.
When the Mistress* heard you might be around, she put
the buns in the oven, and lit the stove, and put the
pot of beans to cook, and, oh yes, barbecued you a
steer, whole, and there'll be cakes and cookies.
So come on in.

XANTHIAS

Thanks, it's awfully kind of you, but . . .

MAID

                    Here me, Apollo,
I simply won't let you go away. Let's see, we were fixing
some roast chickens, and she was toasting the salted nuts
and mixing the wine—vintage stuff. Here, take my hand
and follow me in.

XANTHIAS

                Awfully nice, but . . .

MAID

                    Don't be so silly.
It's all yours, and I won't let you go. Oh, there's a flute-
player-girl waiting for you inside, she's lovely, and
two or three dancers, too, I believe.

XANTHIAS

What did you say? Dancing girls"

MAID

Pretty, just come to flower, all bathed and plucked for
you. Come on, come on, they were just putting the tables
out, and the cook was taking the hot dishes off the stove

XANTHIAS

*Danc*ing girls! Dancing *girls!* Run on ahead, will you
please and tell those dancing girls of yours I'm coming
right in

Maid disappears

Boy, you pick up the baggage there, and follow me

DIONYSOS

Hey, wait a minute. You didn't think I was serious,
did you, when I got you up as Herakles, for fun?
Xanthias, will you kindly stop being such an ass?
Here's your baggage again Take it It's all yours

*During the following dialogue, the Chorus come back on
They are no longer Initiates specifically, but simply represent
an ideal audience, the population of Hades.*

XANTHIAS

What is this, anyway? Are you thinking of taking back
What you gave me?

DIONYSOS

I'm not thinking of it, I'm doing it
Give me that lionskin

XANTHIAS

           Witnesses! Make a note! I'll sue!
I'm putting this in the hands of my—uh—gods.

DIONYSOS

                    What gods,
you stupid clown, thinking you could be Herakles,
Alkmene's son, when you're human, and a slave at that.

XANTHIAS

Oh, the hell with it. Here, take it, take it.

Re-exchange.

                    Maybe, though,
if God so wills, you'll find you need me after all.

CHORUS

There's an *adaptable* guy.
Must have been in the navy.
He's been around. He'll never get drowned.
Always knows where the gravy
is. The ships on her beam,
he's on the side that's dry.
He's got supersensory vision
like our glorious politician
Theramenes.* Just call him galosh
or any old boot you can easily put
on either your right- or your left-hand foot.

DIONYSOS

Here's what would have been funny.
Picture it like this.
Here's Xanthias and his honey
ready to kiss.
But he needs to go. Here's me,
and I hold the pot for him, see?
I make a pass at the girl's—well

anyway. he's on to me,
so he hauls off and socks
me one in the teeth, and knocks
the spots out of Attic Tragedy

Hostess comes out the door.

HOSTESS

Plathane! Plathane! Come out, come out. Here's that
awful man! Remember the one who came to our hotel
one time and ate up sixteen loaves of our bread?

Plathane the maid. emerges

PLATHANE

                                                            Heavens yes
it's him. it's him

XANTHIAS

                        Somebody's going to be sor-ry

HOSTESS

That's wasn't all. He made away with twenty pounds
of roast beef too

XANTHIAS

                        Somebody's going to get hu-urt.

HOSTESS

And a lot of garlic

DIONYSOS

                        Woman, you're crazy in the head.
You don't know what you're talking about

HOSTESS

                                            I don't, don't I?

You thought I wouldn't know you in your tragic boots'?
Well. what about it? I didn't even mention the herrings

PLATHANE

You didn't even mention our poor white feta cheese
He ate the lot. boxes and all.

HOSTESS

Then, when I asked him please if he would pay for it
he just glared at me. fighting mad. He bellowed at me

XANTHIAS

Yes, that's exactly like him. He always does like that

HOSTESS

Pretended he was out of his mind, and pulled a sword

PLATHANE

You poor thing, so he did.

HOSTESS

                He frightened us girls so
we had to run away upstairs and hide.
He charged away Took our rush mats along with him

XANTHIAS

Yes. that's him all the way.

PLATHANE

                Let's do something about it

HOSTESS

Run and get us a dead Politician Kleon* will do.

PLATHANE

Bring the whole subcommittee. Bring Hyperbolos.
We'll fix him, once for all.

HOSTESS

You horrid gourmet, you,
I'd like to take a rock to you and break those teeth
you ate me out of house and home with.

PLATHANE

And I'd like
to throw you in the ditch they bury criminals in.

HOSTESS

I'd like to find that carving knife you used
to cut our sausages up—and carve your neck with it.

PLATHANE

I'll go get Kleon. If we ask him he'll come today
and pull the stuffings out of this guy, bit by bit.

Women rush off. Long pause.

DIONYSOS

Dear Xanthias. How I love him. Wonder if he knows it.

XANTHIAS

I know what you're thinking about. You stop right there.
I will *not* be Herakles again.

DIONYSOS

Sweet little Xanthias
say not so.

XANTHIAS

Tell me, how can I be Herakles,
Alkmene's son, when I'm human, and a slave at that?

DIONYSOS

I know you're cross, my Xanthias. I don't blame you a
  bit.
You can even hit me if you want, I won't say a thing
I tell you: If I ever make you change again
I hope to die, with my whole family: my wife:*
my kiddies:* throw in bleary Archedemos too.

XANTHIAS

I note your oath, and on these terms I will accept

Re-exchange going on. Xanthias becoming Herakles

CHORUS

Now you've got his costume on you.
Now you've got a reputation
to live up to. Better do
a transformation.
Remember the kind of god*
you're supposed to be.
Act accordingly
with masculinity.
Be rough and tough
or you'll be reduced to the bottom roost
and have to carry the stuff.

XANTHIAS

Gentlemen, you are not so
far off the mark, but, you know,
I thought of that too.
If it's anything bad this lovely lad
hands it to me: anything good
he'd take it back if he could.
I'll chew brave herbs* and I won't take fright,
so fight fight fight
for Xanthias. Yeah!
And it's time for it, boys. I hear a noise.
The doors! Trouble coming this way

Aiakos rushes out, followed by two unprepossessing assistants.

AIAKOS

There's the dog-stealer. Get him, fellows, tie him up
and take him away. We'll fix him.

DIONYSOS

Somebody's going to be sor-ry.

Xanthias waves the club of Herakles and holds them off.

XANTHIAS

The hell with you. Keep away from me.

AIAKOS

So you'll fight, will you?
Hey Ditylas hey Skeblyas hey Pardokos,
out here. Fight going on! Come along, give us a hand.

The reinforcements rush on.

DIONYSOS

Tut tut. Shocking, isn't it, the way this fellow
steals from you, then assaults you?

AIAKOS

He's too big for his boots.

DIONYSOS

Outrageous, shouldn't be allowed.

XANTHIAS

So help me Zeus
and hope to die if I ever was in this place before
or ever stole a hair's worth of goods that belonged to you.

Here, I'll make you a gentlemanly* proposition, my man.
Here's my slave-boy. Take him, put him to the torture;
then kill me, if you find I did anything wrong.

AIAKOS

What tortures?

XANTHIAS

Oh, try them all. Tie him on the ladder,
hang him up, beat him with a whip of bristles, take his
skin off, twist him on the rack, pour vinegar up his nose,
pile bricks on him. Just give him the works—only please
excuse him from anything gentle, like soft onion-whips,
or leeks.*

AIAKOS

Why, fair enough. And if I hit your slave too hard
and cripple him—the damages will be paid to you.

XANTHIAS

Never mind paying me. Take him away and work on
him.

AIAKOS

I'll do it right here, so he'll confess before your eyes.
Here, put that luggage down. Be quick about it. See that
you don't tell me any lies.

DIONYSOS

I protest. I'm warning everybody
not to torture me. I'm a god. If you touch me
you'll have yourself to blame.

AIAKOS

What are you talking about?

DIONYSOS

I am immortal Dionysos, son of Zeus.

Pointing to Xanthias.

And *he*'s the slave.

AIAKOS

You hear that?

XANTHIAS

Oh, I hear it. Sure.
That's all the better reason for him to get a whipping.
If he's really a god, he won't feel anything.

DIONYSOS

Well, you're claiming you're a god too. So what about it?
Shouldn't you get the same number of strokes as me?

XANTHIAS

That's fair enough too. Whip us both, and if you see
either of us paying any attention, or crying in pain
at what you're doing, you'll know that one isn't a god.

AIAKOS

You must be a gentleman. Can't be any doubt about it,
the way you love a trial scene. Well, strip, both of you.

Xanthias and Dionysos bare their backs.

XANTHIAS

How are you going to make this even?

AIAKOS

Picking up a whip.

Easy.
Hit one of you first and then the other, and so on.

XANTHIAS

Okay.

AIAKOS

Hitting him.
There!

XANTHIAS

And when you hit me, see if I move.

AIAKOS

I did hit you.

XANTHIAS

Like hell you did.

AIAKOS

Hm. Must have missed him.
Well, here goes for the other one.

Hits Dionysos.

DIONYSOS

When are you going to hit me?

AIAKOS

I did hit you already.

DIONYSOS

Oh? Why didn't I sneeze?
I do when I'm tickled.

AIAKOS

Dunno. Let's try this one again.

XANTHIAS

You supposed to be doing something?

Aiakos hits him.

Oh my gosh!

AIAKOS

My gosh?

That hurt, did it?

XANTHIAS

Nyet. Just thought of something. Time for my feast at Diomeia,* and the enemy won't let us hold it.

AIAKOS

The man's too religious. Can't get to him. Try the other one.

Hits Dionysos.

DIONYSOS

Wahoo!

AIAKOS

What's the matter?

DIONYSOS

There go the cavalry. That's their call.

AIAKOS

But there're tears in your eyes.

DIONYSOS

Got a whiff of their onion rations.

AIAKOS

Didn't feel anything?

DIONYSOS

Nothing that would bother me.

Aiakos goes back to Xanthias

AIAKOS

I'd better go back to this one and try again.

Hits Xanthias.

XANTHIAS

Owoo!

AIAKOS

What's the matter?

Xanthias holds up his foot.

XANTHIAS

Take this thing out. will you? Thorn.

AIAKOS

Where am I getting to? Try this other one again.

Hits Dionysos.

DIONYSOS

*Apollo who art lord of Delos and Pytho.**

XANTHIAS

That hurt him! Didn't you hear?

DIONYSOS

It did not. I was
simply going over a line of verse by Hipponax.

XANTHIAS

You aren't trying. Give him a good hard whack in the
ribs.

AIAKOS

Thanks. Good idea. Here, turn your belly. That's the
way.

Hits Dionysos in the belly.

DIONYSOS

Owoo Poseidon . . .

XANTHIAS

Somebody did get hurt that time.

DIONYSOS

Singing.

Who dost hold sway
over Aigaion's promontories.
or in the depths of the sea's green waters.*

AIAKOS

Demeter. I can't tell
which of you two is a god. You'd better go on in.
The master will know who you are, anyway,
and Persephone the mistress. They're real gods, those
    two.

DIONYSOS

Struck.

You're absolutely right, only I wish you'd thought
of that first. Then you wouldn't have had to whack me.

*The principals enter the door, leaving the stage to the
Chorus.*

CHORUS

Muse of the holy choruses come to us, come, make all
    enjoy my music,
cast your eyes on this multitude of wits here seated
sharper than Kleophon,* that sharper, on whose no-spik-
    Athenian beak
mutters bad pidgin-Attic,
Thracian swallowbird he
perched on a barberry blackball bush
singing his mournful nightingale threnody, how he must
    hang, though the votes come out equal.

LEADER

It's the right and duty of our sacred chorus to determine
better courses for our city. Here's the first text of our
    sermon.
All the citizens should be equal, and their fears be taken
    away.*
All who once were tricked by Phrynichos, caught and
    held and led astray,
ought to be allowed to join the rest of us, who slipped
    away.
Amnesty. Let's all forgive them for mistakes made long
    ago.
Nobody in our community ought to lose his civic rights.
Isn't it unfair that, just for having been in one sea fight,
slaves should have Plataian status,* and be over men
    once free?
Please, I'm not against their freedom in itself. I quite
    agree.

They deserve it. That's the only thing you've done in-
    telligently.
Still, there are those others, men who also often fought
    at sea,
by your side, whose fathers fought for us, akin by blood
    to you.
Let their one fault be forgotten. Let them know your
    mercy, too.
Oh, Athenians, wise beyond all other men, forget your
    rage;
any man who fights at sea beside us, let him be our
    friend,
take him as a citizen, honored kinsmen; let all hatred
    end.
Now our city fights the storm and struggles in the grip of
    the waves,
surely this is not the time for your old hard exclusive
    pride.
Some day, you'll regret it, if you leave unsaid the word
    that saves.

CHORUS

If I have true discrimination to judge a man and his sor-
    rows to come,
not long will our current baboon be here to bother us.
That is little Kleigenes,*
cheapest of all the lords of the babble-whirlpool-bath
    where soap's without soda.
What they really use
is the clay of Kimolos.
He won't be around very long, and he knows it,
but he carries a club against robbers whenever he goes
    on one of his drunken strolls.

LEADER

We've been thinking much of late about the way the city
    treats
all the choicest souls among its citizens: it seems to be

like the recent coinage as compared with the old currency.*

We still have the ancient money: finest coins, I think, in Greece,

better than the coins of Asia; clink them, and they ring the bell,

truly fashioned, never phony, round and honest every piece.

Do we ever use it? We do not. We use this wretched brass,

last week's issue, badly minted, light and cheap and looks like hell.

Now compare the citizens. We have some stately gentlemen,

modest, anciently descended, proud and educated well

on the wrestling ground, men of distinction who have been to school.

These we outrage and reject, preferring any foreign fool,

redhead slave, or brassy clown or shyster. This is what we choose

to direct our city—immigrants. Once our city would not use

one of these as public scapegoat.* That was in the former days.

Now we love them. Think, you idiots. Turn about and change your ways.

Use our useful men. That will look best, in case of victory.

Hang we must, if we must hang; but let's hang from a handsome tree.

Cultured gentlemen should bear their sufferings with dignity.

Aiakos and Xanthias come out of the door. Xanthias is in his slave's costume.

AIAKOS

This master of yours, by Zeus the savior, he's a man of parts, a gentleman.

XANTHIAS

That's a logical conclusion
if trencherman plus wencherman means gentleman

AIAKOS

But he didn't have you on the mat and beat you up
even when you said you were the master and he was the
slave.

XANTHIAS

He'd have been sorry if he had.

AIAKOS

Good slavemanship
that. Well played. Exactly the way I like to do it

XANTHIAS

Come again, please. You like what?

AIAKOS

Seeing myself in action
when *I* get off where he can't hear, and curse my master

XANTHIAS

What about sneaking out of doors after a good beating
and muttering at your master?

AIAKOS

I enjoy that too

XANTHIAS

And poking into his business?

AIAKOS

Can you think of anything nicer?

XANTHIAS

My brother, by Zeus! How about listening at the keyhole
when masters are gossiping?

AIAKOS

Just about sends me crazy, man.

XANTHIAS

And spreading secrets you listened in on? Like that?

AIAKOS

Who, me?
That's more than crazy, bud, that's super crazy plus.

XANTHIAS

Phoebus Apollo! You're one of us. Give me the grip,
and kiss me, and let me kiss you, and then tell me, please,
in the name of Zeus-of-the-slaves, who wears his stripes
with us, what's all this racket and yelling and screaming? What goes on inside?

AIAKOS

One's Aeschylus and one's Euripides.

XANTHIAS

Aha!

AIAKOS

Oh, it's a big business, it's a big business:
great fight among the corpses: this high argument.

XANTHIAS

What's it all about?

AIAKOS

We have a local custom here.
sort of award for literature and humanities.
and the one who wins top rating in the work he does
gets to eat dinner in the capitol and sits
in a chair next to Pluto. see?

XANTHIAS

I see

AIAKOS

That's until somebody else comes along who's better
at it than he is. Then he has to move over

XANTHIAS

I don't see
Aeschylus having anything to worry about

AIAKOS

He held the Chair of Tragedy
He was the best at writing them

XANTHIAS

So who is now?

AIAKOS

Well. when Euripides came down. he exhibited
before the toughs. the sneak-thieves. and the pickpockets
and the safecrackers and the juvenile delinquents.
and there's a lot of that in Hades. and they listened
to his disputations and his wrigglings and his twists
and went crazy. and thought he was the cleverest writer
That all went to his head. so he challenged for the chair
where Aeschylus was sitting

XANTHIAS

                              Didn't they throw him out?

AIAKOS

They did not. The public cried out for a contest
to see which one really was better than the other.

XANTHIAS

You mean, the criminal public.

AIAKOS

                              Sure. They yelled to heaven.

XANTHIAS

But wasn't there anyone on the side of Aeschylus?

AIAKOS

Honesty's scarce. The same down here; the same up
there.

XANTHIAS

Well, what's Pluto getting ready to do about it?

AIAKOS

He's going to hold a contest, an event, that's what,
and judge their skills against each other.

XANTHIAS

                              But how come
Sophocles didn't make a bid for the Tragic Chair?

AIAKOS

He never even tried to. When he came down here,
he walked up to Aeschylus, kissed him, and shook hands
with him, and gave up his claim on the chair, in favor

of Aeschylus. His idea, Kleidemidas* was telling me,
was to sit on the bench as substitute. If Aeschylus wins,
he'll stay where he is: if Aeschylus loses, then he means
to fight for his own art against Euripides.

XANTHIAS

So the thing's coming off?

AIAKOS

                    Zeus, yes, in just a little while,
and all the terrors of tragedy will be let loose.
They're going to have a scale to weigh the music on.

XANTHIAS

What's the idea of that? Short-changing tragedy?

AIAKOS

And they'll bring out their rulers and their angled rods,
and T-squares, the kind you fold.

XANTHIAS

                    Bricklayers' reunion?

AIAKOS

Wedges and calipers. You see, Euripides says
you have to wring the gist from tragedy, word by word.

XANTHIAS

I guess all this is making Aeschylus pretty mad.

AIAKOS

He lowered his head and glared, like a bull on the
charge.

XANTHIAS

Who's going to judge this?

AIAKOS

> That was sort of difficult.
They found the intellectuals pretty hard to find.
Aeschylus didn't go down so well with the Athenians.

XANTHIAS

Maybe he noticed most of them were bank robbers.

AIAKOS

Besides, he thought it was pretty silly for anyone
but poets to judge poets. Then your master came
along, and they handed it to him. He knows technique.
We'd better go inside. When the masters get excited,
you know what happens: screams and yells of pain—
from us.

Aiakos and Xanthias go in the door.

CHORUS

Fearful shall be the spleen now of Thundermutter within-
  side.
when the riptooth-sharpening he sees of his multi-
  loquacious
antagonist to encounter him. Then shall ensue dread
eyewhirl of fury.

Horse-encrested phrases shall shock in helmtossing combat,
chariots collide in whelm of wreckage and splinter-flown
  action,
warrior beating off brain-crafted warrior's
cavalried speeches.

Bristling the hairy mane of his neck of self-grown horse-
  hair
bellowing he shall blast the bolts from compacted joinery
banging plank by plank nailed sections of verse in
stormburst gigantic.

Next, mouthforged tormenter of versification, the slim-
    shaped
tongue unraveling to champ on the bit of malignance
wickedly shall chip and chop at its tropes, much
labor of lungwork.

*Enter from the door Aeschylus and Euripides, Dionysos (in
his proper costume, without the gear of Herakles or Xanthias),
and Pluto. The poets stand one on each side of the stage.
Three chairs are placed. Pluto sits in the middle, Dionysos
on his right, and the chair on his left is empty.*

EURIPIDES

I won't give up the chair, so stop trying to tell me to,
I tell you, I'm a better poet than he is.

DIONYSOS

You heard him, Aeschylus. Don't you have anything to
    say?

EURIPIDES

He's always started with the line of scornful silence.
He used to do it in his plays, to mystify us.

DIONYSOS

Now take care, Aeschylus. Don't be overconfident.

EURIPIDES

I know this man. I've studied him for a long time.
His verse is fiercely made, all full of sound and fury,
language unbridled uncontrolled ungated-in
untalkable-around, bundles of blast and boast.

AESCHYLUS

Is that so, child of the goddess of the cabbage patch?*
You, you jabber-compiler, you dead-beat poet,

you rag-stitcher-together. you say this to me?
Say it again   You'll be sorry

DIONYSOS

Now, Aeschylus. stop it.
Don't in your passion boil your mortal coils in oil.

AESCHYLUS

I won't stop. until I've demonstrated in detail
what kind of one-legged poet this is who talks so big.

DIONYSOS

Black rams, black rams, boys. run and bring us black
rams. quick. Sacrifice to the hurricane   It's on the way

AESCHYLUS

Why, you compiler of Cretan solo-arias.
you fouled our art by staging indecent marriages

DIONYSOS

Most honorable Aeschylus, please stop right there
And as for you, my poor Euripides, if you
have any sense, you'll take yourself out of the storm's
way before the hail breaks on your head in lines of
wrath and knocks it open, and your—*Telephos* oozes out
—your brains, you know. Now, gently, gently, Aeschylus, criticize, don't yell. It's not becoming for two poets
and gentlemen to squabble like two bakers' wives. You're
crackling like an oak log that's been set ablaze

EURIPIDES

I'm ready for him. Don't try to make me back down
I'll bite before I'm bitten. if that's what he wants.
with lines, with music. the gut-strings of tragedy.
with my best plays. with *Peleus* and with *Aiolos*.
with *Meleagros*. best of all. with *Telephos*

DIONYSOS

All right, Aeschylus, tell us what you want to do.

AESCHYLUS

I would have preferred not to have the match down here.
It isn't fair. We don't start even.

DIONYSOS

                              What do you mean?

AESCHYLUS

I mean my poetry didn't die with me, but his
did die with him; so he'll have it here to quote. Still,
if this is your decision, then we'll have to do it.

DIONYSOS

All right, bring on the incense and the fire, while I
in the presence of these great intelligences pray
that I may judge this match most literarily.
You, chorus, meanwhile, sing an anthem to the Muses.

CHORUS

Daughters of Zeus, nine maidens immaculate,
Muses, patronesses of subtly spoken acute brains
of men, forgers of idiom, when to the contest they
hasten, with care-sharpened wrestling-hooks
and holds for their disputations,
come, o Muses, to watch and bestow
potency on these mouths of magnificence,
figures and jigsaw patterns of words.
Now the great test of artistic ability goes into action.

DIONYSOS

Both of you two pray also, before you speak your lines.

AESCHYLUS

Putting incense on the fire.

Demeter. mistress. nurse of my intelligence.
grant me that I be worthy of my mysteries

DIONYSIS

Now you put your incense on. too

EURIPIDES

                              Excuse me. please
Quite other are the gods to whom I sacrifice

DIONYSOS

You mean. you have private gods? New currency'

EURIPIDES

                                        Yes. I have

DIONYSOS

Go ahead. then. sacrifice to your private gods.

EURIPIDES

Bright upper air. my foodage! Socket of the tongue!
Oh. comprehension. sensitory nostrils. oh
grant I be critical in all my arguments

CHORUS

We're all eager to listen
to the two great wits debating
and stating
the luminous course of their wissen-
schaft. Speech bitter and wild.
tough hearts. nothing mild
Neither is dull
From one we'll get witty designs

polished and filed.
The other can pull
up trees by the roots for his use.
goes wild, cuts loose
stampedes of lines.

DIONYSOS

Get on with it, get on with it, and put your finest wit
   in all
you say, and be concrete. and be exact; and, be original.

EURIPIDES

I'll make my self-analysis a later ceremony
after having demonstrated that my rival is a phony.
His audience was a lot of louts and Phrynichus* was all
   they knew.
He gypped and cheated them with ease, and here's one
   thing he used to do.
He'd start with one veiled bundled muffled character
   plunked down in place.
Achilleus,* like, or Niobe, but nobody could see its face.
It looked like drama, sure, but not one syllable would
   it mutter.

DIONYSOS

By Jove, they didn't and that's a fact.

EURIPIDES

                     The chorus then would utter
four huge concatenations of verse. The characters just
   sat there mum.

DIONYSOS

You know, I liked them quiet like that. I'd rather have
   them deaf and dumb
than yak yak yak the way they do.

EURIPIDES

That's because you're an idiot too.

DIONYSOS

Oh, by all means, and to be sure, and what was
  Aeschylus trying to do?

EURIPIDES

Phony effects. The audience sat and watched the
  panorama
breathlessly. *"When will Niobe speak?"* And that was
  half the drama.

DIONYSOS

It's the old shell game. I've been had. Aeschylus, why
  this agitation?
You're looking cross and at a loss.

EURIPIDES

He doesn't like investigation.
Then after a lot of stuff like this, and now the play was
  half-way through,
the character would grunt and moo a dozen cow-sized
  lines or two,
with beetling brows and hairy crests like voodoo goblins
  all got up,
incomprehensible, of course.

AESCHYLUS

You're killing me.

DIONYSOS

Will you shut up?

EURIPIDES

Not one word you could understand . . .

DIONYSOS

No, Aeschylus.
don't grind your teeth . . .

EURIPIDES

. . . but battles of Skamandros, barbicans with ditches
    underneath,
and hooknosed eagles bronze-enwrought on shields,
    verse armed like infantry,
not altogether easy to make out the sense.

DIONYSOS

You're telling me?
Many a night I've lain awake and puzzled on a single
    word.
A fulvid roosterhorse is please exactly just what kind
    of bird?

AESCHYLUS

It was a symbol painted on the galleys, you illiterate
    block.

DIONYSOS

I thought it was Eryxis, or Philoxenos's fighting-cock.

EURIPIDES

Well, should a rooster—vulgah bird!—get into tragedy
    at all?

AESCHYLUS

Tell me of *your* creations, you free-thinker. if you have
    the gall.

EURIPIDES

No roosterhorses, bullmoosegoats, nor any of the
    millions

of monsters that the Medes and Persians paint on their
    pavilions.
When I took over our craft from you, I instantly became
    aware
that she was gassy from being stuffed with heavy text
    and noisy air,
so I eased her aches and reduced the swelling and took
    away the weights and heats
with neat conceits and tripping feets, with parsnips,
    radishes, and beets.
I gave her mashed and predigested baby-food strained
    from my books,
then fed her on solo-arias.

DIONYSOS

                Kephisophon* had you in his hooks.

EURIPIDES

My openings were never confused or pitched at random.
    They were not
difficult. My first character would give the background
    of the plot at once.

DIONYSOS

           That's better than giving away your personal
background, eh, what, what?

EURIPIDES

Then, from the opening lines, no person ever was left
    with nothing to do.
They all stepped up to speak their piece, the mistress
    spoke, the slave spoke too,
the master spoke, the daughter spoke, and grandma
    spoke.

AESCHYLUS

                      And tell me

> why
> you shouldn't be hanged for daring that.

EURIPIDES

> No, cross my heart and hope
> to die,
> *I* made the drama *democratic.*

DIONYSOS

To Aeschylus.

> You'd better let that one pass, old sport;
> you never were such a shining light in that particular line
> of thought.*

EURIPIDES

> Then I taught natural conversational dialogue.

AESCHYLUS

> I'll say you did.
> And before you ever taught them that, I wish you could
> have split in middle.

EURIPIDES

Going right on.

> Taught them delicate tests and verbalized
>   commensuration,
> and squint and fraud and guess and god and loving
>   application,
> and always how to think the worst of everything.

AESCHYLUS

> So I believe.

EURIPIDES

> I staged the life of everyday, the way we live. I couldn't
>   deceive

my audience with the sort of stuff they knew as much
    about as I.
They would have spotted me right away. I played it
    straight and didn't try
to bind a verbal spell and hypnotize and lead them by
    the nose
with Memmons and with Kyknoses with rings on their
    fingers and bells on their toes.
Judge both of us by our influence on followers. Give
    him Manes,
Phormisios* and Megainetos and sundry creeps and
    zanies,
the big moustachio bugleboys, the pinetreebenders
    twelve feet high,
but Kleitophon is mine, and so's Theramenes, a clever
    guy.

DIONYSOS

I'll grant your Theramenes. Falls in a puddle and comes
    out dry.
The man is quick and very slick, a true Euripidean.
When Chians are in trouble he's no Chian, he's a Keian

EURIPIDES

So that's what my plays are about,
and these are my contributions,
and I turn everything inside out
looking for new solutions
to the problems of today,
always critical, giving
suggestions for gracious living,
and they come away from seeing a play
in a questioning mood, with "where are we at?"
and "who's got my this?" and "who's took my that?"

DIONYSOS

So now the Athenian hears a pome
of yours, and watch him come stomping home

to yell at his servants every one:
"where oh where are my pitchers gone?—
where is the maid who hath betrayed
my heads of fish to the garbage trade?
Where are the pots of yesteryear?
Where's the garlic of yesterday?
Who hath ravished my oil away?"
Formerly they sat like hicks
fresh out of the sticks
with their jaws hung down in a witless way.

CHORUS

To Aeschylus.

See you this, glorious
*Achilleus?** What have you got to say?
Don't let your rage
sweep you away,
or you'll never be victorious.
This cynical sage
hits hard. Mind the controls.
Don't lead with your chin.
Take skysails in.
Scud under bare poles.
Easy now. Keep him full in your sights.
When the wind falls, watch him,
then catch him
dead to rights.

DIONYSOS

O mighty-mouthed inventor of harmonies, grand old
   bulwark of balderdash,
frontispiece of Hellenic tragedy, open the faucets and
   let 'er splash.

AESCHYLUS

The whole business gives me a pain in the middle, my
   rage and resentment are heated

at the idea of having to argue with *him*. But so he can't
    say I'm defeated,
here, answer me, you. What's the poet's duty, and why is
    the poet respected?

EURIPIDES

Because he can write, and because he can think, but
    mostly because he's injected
some virtue into the body politic.

AESCHYLUS

                    What if you've broken your trust,
and corrupted good sound right-thinking people and
    filled them with treacherous lust?
If poets do that, what reward should they get?

DIONYSOS

                            The axe. That's what
we should do with 'em.

AESCHYLUS

Then think of the people *I* gave him, and think of the
    people when he got through with 'em.
I left him a lot of heroic six-footers, a grand generation
    of heroes,
unlike our new crop of street-corner loafers and
    gangsters and decadent queer-os.
Mine snorted the spirit of spears and splendor, of white-
    plumed helmets and stricken fields,
of warrior heroes in shining armor and greaves and
    sevenfold-oxhide shields.

DIONYSOS

And that's a disease that never dies out. The munition-
    makers will kill me.

EURIPIDES

Just what did you do to make them so noble? Is that
what you're trying to tell me?

DIONYSOS

Well, answer him. Aeschylus, don't withdraw into
injured dignity.
That don't go.

AESCHYLUS

I made them a martial drama.

DIONYSOS

Which?

AESCHYLUS

Seven Against Thebes, if you
want to know.
Any man in an audience sitting through that would
aspire to heroic endeavor.

DIONYSOS

That was a mistake, man. Why did you make the
Thebans more warlike than ever
and harder to fight with? By every right it should mean a
good beating for you.

AESCHYLUS

To the audience.

Well, *you* could have practiced austerity too. It's exactly
what *you* wouldn't *do*.
Then I put on my *Persians*,* and anyone witnessing that
would promptly be smitten
with longing for victory over the enemy. Best play I ever
have written.

DIONYSOS

Oh, yes, I loved that, and I thrilled where I sat when I
     heard old Dareios was dead
and the chorus cried "wahoo" and clapped with their
     hands. I tell you, it went to my head.

AESCHYLUS

There, there is work for poets who also are MEN From
     the earliest times
incitement to virtue and useful knowledge have come
     from the makers of rhymes
There was Orpheus first. He preached against murder,
     and showed us the heavenly way.
Musaeus taught divination and medicine; Hesiod, the
     day-after-day
cultivation of fields, the seasons, and plowings. Then
     Homer, divinely inspired,
is a source of indoctrination to virtue. Why else is he
     justly admired
than for teaching how heroes armed them for battle?

DIONYSOS

                                        He didn't teach
     Pantakles, though.
He can't get it right. I watched him last night. He was
     called to parade, don't you know,
and he put on his helmet and tried to tie on the plume
     when the helm was on top of his head.

AESCHYLUS

Ah, many have been my heroic disciples; the last of
     them, Lamachos (recently dead).
The man in the street simply has to catch something
     from all my heroics and braveries.
My Teucers and lion-hearted Patrokloses lift him right
     out of his knaveries
and make him thrill to the glory of war and spring to the
     sound of the trumpet.

But I never regaled you with Phaidra* the floozie—or
Sthenoboia* the strumpet.
I think I can say that a lovesick woman has never been
pictured by me.

EURIPIDES

Aphrodite never did notice you much.

AESHYLUS

                Aphrodite can go climb a tree.
But you'll never have to complain that she didn't bestow
her attentions on you.
She got you in person, didn't she?

DIONYSOS

             Yes, she did, and your stories came
true.
The fictitious chickens came home to roost.

EURIPIDES

             But tell me, o man with-
out pity:
suppose I would write about Sthenoboia. What harm has
she done to our city?

AESCHYLUS

Bellerophon-intrigues, as given by you, have caused the
respectable wives
of respectable men, in shame and confusion, to do away
with their lives.

EURIPIDES

But isn't my story of Phaidra a story that really has
happened?

AESCHYLUS

      So be it.

It's true. But the poet should cover up scandal. and not
    let anyone see it.
He shouldn't exhibit it out on the stage. For the little boys
    have their teachers
to show them example, but when they grow up we poets
    must act as their preachers.
and what we preach should be useful and good.

EURIPIDES

                      But you, with your
    massive construction,
huge words and mountainous phrases. is that what you
    call useful instruction?
You ought to make people talk like people.

AESCHYLUS

                      You folksy style's for the
    birds.
For magnificent thoughts and magnificent fancies. we
    must have magnificent words.
It's appropriate too for the demigods of heroic times to
    talk bigger
than we. It goes with their representation as grander in
    costumed and figure.
I set them a standard of purity You've corrupted it

EURIPIDES

                      How did I do it?

AESCHYLUS

By showing a royal man in a costume of rags. with his
    skin showing through it.
You played on emotions

EURIPIDES

                But why should it be so wrong to awaken
    their pity?

AESCHYLUS

The rich men won't contribute for warships.* You can't
    find one in the city
who's willing to give. He appears in his rags, and howls,
    and complains that he's broke.

DIONYSOS

But he always has soft and expensive underwear under
    the beggarman's cloak.
The liar's so rich and he eats so much that he has to feed
    some to the fishes.

AESCHYLUS

You've taught the young man to be disputatious. Each
    argues as long as he wishes.
You've emptied the wrestling yards of wrestlers. They
    all sit around on their fannies
and listen to adolescent debates. The sailormen gossip
    like grannies
and question their officers' orders. In my time, all that
    they knew how to do
was to holler for rations, and sing "yeo-ho," and row,
    with the rest of the crew.

DIONYSOS

And blast in the face of the man behind, that's another
    thing too that they knew how to do.
And how to steal from the mess at sea, and how to be
    robbers ashore.
But now they argue their orders. We just can't send them
    to sea any more.

AESCHYLUS

That's what he's begun. What hasn't he done?
His nurses go propositioning others.
His heroines have their babies in church
or sleep with their brothers

or go around murming: "*Is* life life?"*
So our city is rife
with the clerk and the jerk,
the altar-baboon, the political ape,
and our physical fitness is now a disgrace
with nobody in shape
to carry a torch in a race.

DIONYSOS

Be Zeus, you're right. I laughed till I cried
at the Panathenaia* a while ago,
as the torch-relay-runners went by.
Here comes this guy;
he was puffed, he was slow,
he was white, he was fat,
he was left behind,
and he didn't know where he was at,
and the pottery works gang
stood at the gates to give him a bang
in the gut and the groin and the ribs and the rump
till the poor fellow, harried
by one cruel thump
exploded his inward air
and blew out the flare that he carried.

CHORUS

Great is this action, bitter the spite, the situation is ripe
    for war.
How shall the onlooker judge between them?
One is a wrestler strong and rough;
quick the other one, deft in defensive throws and the
    back-heel stuff.
Up from your places! Into the ring again!
Wit must wrestle wit once more in fall upon fall.
Fight him, wrestle him, throw the book at him,
talk to him, sit on him, skin him alive,
old tricks, new tricks, give him the works.
This is the great debate for the championship. Hazard
    all.

Never hold back any attack for fear you may not be
   understood.
You have an audience who can follow you,
don't be afraid of being too difficult.
That could once have happened, but now we've changed
   all that. They're good
and they're armed for action. Everyone's holding
his little book, so he can follow the subtle allusions.*
Athenian playgoers, best in the world,
bright and sharp and ready for games
waiting for you to begin.
Here's your sophisticated audience. Play it to win.

EURIPIDES

All right, I'll work on your prologues first of all, because
they come at the beginning of every tragedy.
I'll analyse this great man's prologues. Did you know
how murky you were in getting your action under way?

DIONYSOS

How are you going to analyse them?

EURIPIDES

                                        Lots of ways.
First, read me the beginning of your *Oresteia.**

DIONYSOS

Silence all. Let no man speak. Aeschylus, read.

AESCHYLUS

*Hermes, lord of the dead, who watch over the powers of
my father, be my savior and stand by my claim. I have
come back to my own soil. I have returned.**

DIONYSOS

Find any mistakes there?

EURIPIDES

Yes, a dozen. Maybe more.

DIONYSOS

Why, man the whole passage is only three lines.

EURIPIDES

But each of them has twenty things wrong with it.

Aeschylus growls

DIONYSOS

Aeschylus, as counsel I advise you: keep quiet,
or you'll be mulcted, three lines of blank verse, plus
costs.

AESCHYLUS

I have to keep quiet for *him?*

DIONYSOS

That's my advice to you.

EURIPIDES

He made one colossal howler, right at the beginning.

AESCHYLUS

To Dionysos

Hear that? *You're* crazy.

DIONYSOS

Fact has never bothered me much.

AESCHYLUS

What kind of mistake?

EURIPIDES

Take it from the beginning.

AESCHYLUS

Hermes, lord of the dead, who watch over the powers

EURIPIDES

Well, look, you've got Orestes saying this over the tomb
of his father, and his father's dead. That right?

AESCHYLUS

That's right.

EURIPIDES

Let's get this straight. Here is where his father was killed,
murdered in fact, by his own wife, in a treacherous plot.
You make him say Hermes is *watching over* this.

AESCHYLUS

I don't mean the Hermes you mean. He was talking to
the Kindly Hermes of the world below. He made that
clear when he said he was keeping his inheritance for
him.

EURIPIDES

Why that's a bigger and better blunder than I hoped.
It makes his inheritance an underworld property.

DIONYSOS

Orestes then would have to rob his father's grave?

AESCHYLUS

Dionysos, the wine you're drinking has bouquet. It
stinks.

DIONYSOS

Read the next line. Watch for errors, Euripides.

AESCHYLUS

of my father, be my savior and stand by my claim.
I have come back to my own soil. I have returned.

EURIPIDES

Ha! The great Aeschylus has said the same thing twice.

DIONYSOS

Twice, how?

EURIPIDES

        Look at this sentence. Or better, I'll show you.
I have come back, he says, but also *I have returned.*
I have come back means the same as *I have returned.*

DIONYSOS

You're right, by golly. It's like saying to your neighbor:
"Lend me your kneading-trough, your trough to knead
things in."

AESCHYLUS

You two jabberwocks, it is not the same thing at all.
The diction's excellent.

EURIPIDES

Show me. Tell me what you mean, will you, please.

AESCHYLUS

Come back just means getting back home again, arrival
without further context. If he gets there, he arrives.
The exile arriving *comes back*; but he also *returns.*

DIONYSOS

That's good, by god. What do you say, Euripides?

EURIPIDES

I say Orestes didn't *return*, if *returned* means
restored. It wasn't formal. He sneaked past the guards.

DIONYSOS

By god, that's good. (Except I don't know what you
mean.)

EURIPIDES

Go on. Next line.

DIONYSOS

Yes, Aeschylus, better go on.
Keep at it. You, keep watching for anything wrong.

AESCHYLUS

*And by this mounded gravebank I invoked my sire
to hear, to listen. . . .*

EURIPIDES

Saying the same thing twice again.
To hear, to listen. Same thing twice. Perfectly clear.

DIONYSOS

Of course, you fool, he has to; he's talking to the dead.
We call to them three times,* and still we don't get
through.

AESCHYLUS

How do you make *your* prologues, then?

EURIPIDES

                              I'll give you some,
and if you catch me saying the same thing twice, or
padding my lines, without adding to the sense—spit in
my eye.

DIONYSOS

Speak us some lines then, speak them. There's nothing
else for it than to listen to your prologues and criticize
the verse.

EURIPIDES

Oedipus at the outset was a fortunate man . . .*

AESCHYLUS

By god, he was not. He was most *un*fortunate
from birth. Before birth, since Apollo prophesied
before he was even begotten, that he would kill his
father. How could he have been, at the outset, *fortunate?*

EURIPIDES

. . . But then he became the wretched of humankind.

AESCHYLUS

He didn't *become* the wretchedest. He never stopped.
Look here. First thing that happened after he was born
they put him in a broken pot and laid him out in the
snow so he'd never grow up to be his father's murderer.
Then he went to Polybus, with sore feet, wasn't that luck?
and then he married an old lady, though he was young,
and also the old lady turned out to be his mother,
and then he blinded himself . . .

DIONYSOS

                              That would have saved his life
if he'd been a general along with Erasinides.*

EURIPIDES

You're crazy. The prologues that I write are very fine.

AESCHYLUS

By Zeus! I'm not going to savor you, word by word
and line by line, like you, but, with the help of the gods.
I'll ruin your prologues with a little bottle of oil.

EURIPIDES

Ruin my prologues with a bottle of oil?

AESCHYLUS

                                        Just one
bundle of fleece or *bottle of oil* or *packet of goods*.
The way you write iambics, always there's just room
for a phrase the length of one of those. I'll demonstrate

EURIPIDES

Demonstrate? Poof.

AESCHYLUS

                    I say I can.

DIONYSOS

                              Read us a line.

EURIPIDES

Aigyptos, as the common tale disseminates
with all his sea-armada and his fifty sons
*coming to Argos**

AESCHYLUS

                    lost his little bottle of oil.*

DIONYSOS

A naughty little bottle. It'll be spanked for that.
Give us another line, I want to see what happens.

EURIPIDES

Dionysos, who, with thrysos and in hides of fawns
appareled on Parnassos up among the pines
*dances on light feet**

AESCHYLUS

              lost his little bottle of oil.

DIONYSOS

*Ah me, again, I am struck again,** with a bottle of oil.

EURIPIDES

He hasn't done much to me; here's another prologue
I'll give him, where he can't tag on his bottle of oil.
There's been no man who's had good fortune all his days.
For one was born to fortune, but his goods are gone.
*One, born unhappy**

AESCHYLUS

              lost his little bottle of oil.

DIONYSOS

Euripides.

EURIPIDES

     What?

DIONYSOS

            Maybe you'd better strike your sails.
That little bottle of oil is blowing up a storm.

EURIPIDES

Demeter be my witness, it doesn't mean a thing.
Here comes a line to smash his little—uh—property.

DIONYSOS

Go ahead, read another, but look out for that bottle.

EURIPIDES

*Kadmos, son of Agenor, once upon a time
sailing from Sidon**

AESCHYLUS

                    lost his little bottle of oil.

DIONYSOS

My poor dear friend, you'd better buy that bottle of oil
or it'll chew up all our prologues

EURIPIDES

                              You mean that?
You're saying *I* should buy from *him?*

DIONYSOS

                              That's my advice

EURIPIDES

I refuse to do it. I have lots of prologues left
where he can't tag on any little bottle of oil.
*Pelops the son of Tantalos reaching Pisa plain
with his swift horses**

AESCHYLUS

                    lost his little bottle of oil

DIONYSOS

You see? Once more he makes the little bottle fit.
Now be a good fellow. It isn't too late yet, buy one quick
For only a quarter you can get one, nice and new.

EURIPIDES

Not yet, by god, not yet. I still have plenty left.
*Oineus, from his land**

AESCHYLUS

          lost his little bottle of oil.

EURIPIDES

Hey, wait a minute. Let me get a whole line out.
Oineus from his land choosing out a store of grain
and sacrificing

AESCHYLUS

         lost his little bottle of oil.

DIONYSOS

In the middle of his sacrifice? Who found it for him?

EURIPIDES

Let me alone, please. See what he can say to this:
*Zeus, as the most authentic version hath maintained . . .**

DIONYSOS

He'll do you in. Zeus lost his little bottle of oil.
That bottle of oil is in your prologues everywhere
and multiplies like scabs of sickness in the eyes.
For god's sake, change the subject to his lyric lines.

EURIPIDES

Good idea. I've plenty of material to show
he's a bad lyric poet. It all sounds alike.

ARISTOPHANES

CHORUS

What can be the meaning of that?
Think as I will, I can not concieve
any thing he can say
against the man who can boast
the loveliest lyrics and the most
of any until today.
Much I wonder, what charge he can make
good against the great master
of tragic verse. He courts disaster.
I fear for his sake.

EURIPIDES

Wonder is right, if you mean his prosody. You'll see.
One little cut, and his metres all come out the same.

DIONYSOS

The same? Give me a handful of pebbles. I'll keep count.

Flute music off.

EURIPIDES

> *Phthian A - chilleus as you hear in the slaughter of
> heroes
> oho what a stroke come you not to the
> rescue?**
> *Hermes ances - tral, oh how we honor you, we of the
> lakeside**
> *oho what a stroke come you not to the
> rescue?`*

DIONYSOS

There's two strokes scored against you, Aeschylus.

EURIPIDES

*Greatest Achaian. At - reus son who art lord over mul-
titudes hear me**

> *oho what a stroke come you not*
> *to the rescue?*

DIONYSOS

Another stroke. dear Aeschylus. That makes the third

EURIPIDES

> *Quiet. all O bee-keepers   now open the temple of*
> *Artemis nearby**
> *oho what a stroke come*
> *you not to the rescue?*
> *I am enabled   to sing of the prodigy shown*
> *at the wayside**
> *oho what a stroke come you*
> *not to the rescue?*

DIONYSOS

Oh what a mess of strokes, lord Zeus. I'm on the ropes
Stroke upon stroke has got my kidneys black and blue
I think I'd better go and take a soothing bath

EURIPIDES

Wait till you've listened to my next melodic line-up
We will now take up the music written for the lyre

DIONYSOS

Go ahead. But leave the strokes out, will you please

EURIPIDES

> *How the twin-throned—power of Achaia and manhood*
> *of Hela**
> *di tum di tum di tum di tum*
> *Sends forth the—sphinx who is princess of om·*
> *inous hellhounds**
> *di tum di tum di tum di tum*
> *hand on the—spear and embattled. the bird*
> *of encounter**

> di tum di tum di tum di tum
> *giving assault—there to the hovering hounds*
> *of the airways**
> di tum di tum di tum di tum

DIONYSOS

Where did you get this tum diddy stuff? From
   Marathon?*
It sounds like water-pulling-from-the-well-up music.

AESCHYLUS

My source is excellent, if that's what you mean, the
result excellent too. I only tried not to be seen reaping
the same Muse-meadow Phrynichos had reaped. But
this man draws from every kind of source, burlesque,
Meletos'* drinking-ditties, all that Karian jazz,
dirges, folksongs. Here, let me show you. Bring me a lyre
somebody. Wait! No, don't. What's the use of a lyre
for this stuff? Where's that girl who uses oyster shells
for castanets? Hither, Euripidean Muse.

*A scantily clad girl comes on. Aeschylus bows to her with
mock ceremony.*

To thee, onlie begetter of these melodies.

DIONYSOS

So that's the Tenth Muse is it? Well, she ain't no
Sappho. That's a man's woman if I ever saw one.*

AESCHYLUS

*Halycon-birds who in the sea's ever-streaming**
billows twittering
dabble wings in the flying spray
dipping and ducking feathery forms:
you in the angles under the roof
finger-wee-hee-heeving embattled
handiwork of your woof-warp-webs,

singing shuttle`s endeavor
where the flute-loving dolphin leaps
next the cutwater`s darkened edge
oracular in her pastures.
gleam and joy of the grapevine
where clusters of heart's ease curl and cling.
Circle me in your arms. o my child

Breaking off in disgust

Just look at that line

DIONYSOS

I'm looking

AESCHYLUS

And look at *that* one

DIONYSOS

I'm looking

AESCHYLUS

And you the writer of lines like that
dare to say that verse is bad.
Yours is made like a whore displayed
in all the amorous postures

So much for your choral metres Now I'll demonstrate
the composition of your lyric monodies *

O darkness of night. shining
in gloom. what vision of dream
bring you poor me
fished from the occult depths.
envoy of Hades
spiritless spirit possessing.
child of the sable night.
ghastly grim apparition
in dark trappings of death

and bloodily bloodily glaring,
and her nails were long they were long.
Help me, my handmaidens, light up the lanterns and
run with your pitchers and fetch from the river and heat
    up the water
that I may wash this vision from me.

O spirit of the sea
that was it. Heigh-ho housemates
behold, here are portents.
Glyke has stolen my rooster away,
and lo, she is gone.
O ye nymphs of the mountains,
Mania, arrest her.

Soft you now. I was sitting
plying my humble tasks
at the loom filled with its flax
wee-hee-hee-hee-hee-hee-heeving
with my hands, spinning a veil
so I could take it at dawn
to market to market it there,
and he fluttered he fluttered away
on gossamer wings to the air
and sorrows sorrows he left me
and tears tears from my eyes
I shed I shed. Poor me.

But o Kretans, nurselings of Ida,
seize your bows and come to aid me, .
prithee, shake your leaping legs and surround me the
    house,
with you Diktynna, and Artemis—pretty child—
holding her puppies in leash let her search the premises,
and you, Zeus' daughter, in both hands upholding
your brightest twin torches, appear, o Hekate.
at Glyke's house, that I may
get her with the gods. (My ravishéd rooster.)

DIONYSOS

That will be all for the lyric verse.

AESCHYLUS

I've had enough.
I want to bring him out and put him to the scales,
for that alone will show our poetry's true weight.
Weigh phrase with phrase, for their specific gravity.

DIONYSOS

Bring out the scales then, if my duty is to judge
two master poets like a grocer selling cheese.

CHORUS

Devious is the great intellect.
Here is a portent of poetry
beyond what anyone could expect.
Who could have thought of this, but he?
Had anyone else proceeded
to such invention
I would have said he needed
medical attention.

*Scales are brought. As each poet speaks one of the lines of
verse, he drops, I think, a scrap of papyrus into the scale
pan.*

DIONYSOS

Now take your places by the weighing pans.

AESCHYLUS AND EURIPIDES

Ready.

DIONYSOS

Each of you hold his line while he is speaking it.
Don't drop it in the pan until I say "cuckoo."

AESCHYLUS AND EURIPIDES

We have them.

DIONYSOS

Say and lay a line upon the scale.

EURIPIDES

I wish the Argo's hull had never winged her way. *

AESCHYLUS

River Spercheios with your cattle-pastures near. *

DIONYSOS

Cuckoo! Let go.

The slips drop, and the scale of Aeschylus descends.

Aha. The scale of Aeschylus
is far the heavier.

EURIPIDES

What can be the cause of that?

DINOYSOS

He put a river in it, the wool-merchant's trick,
and soaked his words in water as they do their wool.
But you put in a winged word, a feathery line.

EURIPIDES

Have him speak another one. Match us again.

DIONYSOS

Take your next lines.

AESCHYLUS AND EURIPIDES

We're ready.

DIONYSOS

Speak them.

Same business as before.

EURIPIDES

*Persuasion has no shrine except within the word.**

AESCHYLUS

*Death is the only god who is not moved by gifts.**

DIONYSOS

Let go, let go. Aeschylus has the weight again.
He put Death in. There's nothing more *depressing* than
that.

EURIPIDES

But I put in Persuasion. That's a handsome word.

DIONYSOS

Persuasion she's a scatterbrain, a featherweight.
Better see if you can't turn up a heavier line,
something massive and bulky, that will give you heft.

*Euripides frantically rummages through a pile of papers,
muttering to himself.*

EURIPIDES

Now where on earth did I put my lines like that?

DIONYSOS

                                    Here's one.
"Achilleus threw the dice, and shot a deuce and a four."
All right, ready with your lines. This is the final test.

EURIPIDES

*His right hand seized the spear heavily shod with steel.**

AESCHYLUS

*Chariot piled on chariot and corpse on corpse.**

DIONYSOS

Aeschylus fooled you again.

EURIPIDES

How?

DIONYSOS

Threw in a couple of chariots and two dead men.
A hundred Egyptian coolies couldn't lift that load.

AESCHYLUS

Don't do it line by line, now. Let him climb in the scale
with his children and his wife, I mean Kephisophon,
and all his books, and hold them in his lap. I'll speak
only two lines of verse, and still I'll sink the scale.

DIONYSOS

Gentlemen, my friends. I can not judge them any more.
I must not lose the love of either one of them.
One of them's a great poet. I like the other one.

PLUTO

You mean, you won't do what you came down here
to do?

DIONYSOS

And if I do decide?

PLUTO

Then take the one you want
and go; we must not let your journey be in vain.

DIONYSOS

To Pluto.

Bless your heart.

To the poets.

          Very well, then. Answer me this.
I came down here to get a poet. Why? To help
our city survive, so it can stage my choruses.
The one of you who has the best advice to give
for saving the city is the one that I'll take back.
Alkibiades is a baby who's giving
our state delivery-pains. What shall we do with him?
That's the first question.

EURIPIDES

          How does the state feel about him?

DIONYSOS

It longs for him, it hates him, and it wants him back.
Speak your minds both, and tell us what we are to do.

EURIPIDES

I hate the citizen who, by nature well endowed,
is slow to help his city, swift to do her harm,
to himself useful, useless to the community.

DIONYSOS

Good answer, by Poseidon.

To Aeschylus.

          Now, what about you?

AESCHYLUS

We should not rear a lion's cub within the state.

[Lions are lords. We should not have them here at all.]*
But if we rear one, we must do as it desires.

DIONYSOS

By Zeus the savior, I still can't make up my mind.
One answer was so clever. The other was so clear.
Give me one more opinion, each of you.
How can we save the city?

EURIPIDES

Give Kleokritos Kinesias* to serve as wings;
let him be airborne over the vast sea's expanse.

DIONYSOS

Well, that would be amusing. Would there be some
point?

EURIPIDES

They could be armed with vinegar-jars, and bomb
the enemy at sea with vinegar in their eyes.

Embarrassed pause.

No, really, I do know what to do. Let me speak.

DIONYSOS

                                              Speak.

EURIPIDES

When that we trust not now, we trust, and trust no more
what now we do trust—we shall win.

DIONYSOS

                                    How's that again?
Please be a bit more stupid, so I'll understand.

EURIPIDES

If we mistrust those citizens whom now we trust,
and use those citizens whom we do not use now,
we might be saved.
If we are losing using what we use, will it
not follow we might win by doing the opposite?

DIONYSOS

Ingenious, o my Palamedes, soul of wit.
Did you think that up yourself, or was it Kephisophon?

EURIPIDES

All by myself. The vinegar was Kephisophon.

DIONYSOS

Well, Aeschylus, what is your view?

AESCHYLUS

                          First tell me this.
Which men *is* Athens using? Her best?

DIONYSOS

                      Her best? Where've *you* been?
She hates them like poison.

AESCHYLUS

                    Does she really like her worst men?

DIONYSOS

She doesn't *like* them. Uses them because she has to.

AESCHYLUS

How can you pull a city like that out of the water
When neither the fine mantle nor coarse cloak will
serve?*

DIONYSOS

Better find something, or she'll sink and never come up.

AESCHYLUS

I'd rather tell you up there. I don't want to down here.

DIONYSOS

Oh please, yes. Send your blessings up from underground.

AESCHYLUS

They shall win—
when they think of their land as if it were their enemies',
and think of their enemies' land as if it were their own,
that ships are all their wealth, and all their wealth, de-
    spair.

DIONYSOS

Good! But the jurymen will eat up all that wealth.

PLUTO

Decide.

DIONYSOS

        Out of their own mouths have they spoken it.
For I shall choose the poet that my soul desires.

EURIPIDES

Do not forget the vows you swore by all the gods,
to take me home with you. Choose him who loves you
best.

DIONYSOS

My tongue swore, not my heart.* I'm taking Aeschylus.

EURIPIDES

Can you do this, and look me in the face for shame?

DIONYSOS

What's shameful?—unless it seems so to the audience?*

EURIPIDES

And wilt thou leave me thus for dead? Say nay, say nay.

DIONYSOS

Who knows if life be death indeed or death be life,*
or breath be breakfast, sleep in fleece be comforter?

PLUTO

Go all inside now, Dionysos.

DIONYSOS

                Why, what for?

PLUTO

So I can feast you before you sail away.

DIONYSOS

                        Good news.
I am not discontented with my morning's work.

CHORUS

Blessed he
who has such wisdom and wit.
Many can learn from it.
Through good counsel he won the right
to return home again
for the good of the cause and state,
for the good of his fellow men,
to help them fight the good fight
with his great brain.

Better not to sit at the feet
of Sokrates* and chatter,
nor cast out of the heart
the high serious matter
of tragic art.
Better not to compete
in the no-good lazy
Sokratic dialogue
Man, that *is* crazy.

PLUTO

Go forth rejoicing, Aeschylus, go,
save us our city
by your good sense and integrity
Instruct the foolish majority.
Here is a rope to give Kleophon,
here's one for the revenuers,
Myrmex and Nikomachos,
this for Archenomos.*
tell them their hour
has come; they are waited for here, today,
and if they delay
I, in person, will go brand them, sting them,
sling them each in a thong
and bring them
here to Hades', where they belong

AESCHYLUS

All this I will do. Here is my Chair
of Tragedy. Give it to Sophocles there
to keep for me until I come down
once more, for I judge him to be
the greatest of poets—after me.
But mind; never give My Chair
over to the vile uses
of this pseudo-poet, this lying clown
Not even if he refuses

PLUTO

Torches, this way.
With holy illumination light him
and with his own songs and dances delight him
as you escort him away.

CHORUS

First, o divinities under the ground indwelling, we pray
    you,
grant fair journey to the poet as he goes back to the
    daylight:
grant him success in all the thoughts that will prosper
    our city.
So at last may we find surcease from sorrows we suffer
through war's encounters. Let Kleophon and all similar
    aliens
who love to fight go home and fight—in the lands of
    their fathers.

Notes

page 481. *Phrynichos, Lykis, Ameipsias:* Comic poets, rivals of Aristophanes.

482. *sea battle:* The battle of Arginousai, fought in 406 B.C., the summer before this play. Slaves were then used in the Athenian navy for the first time, and these slaves were set free after the victory.

484. *Kleisthenes:* Aristophanes makes him a synonym for effeminacy and homosexuality throughout his plays (see also page 512 in this play) and uses him as a character in *The Thesmophoriazusae.*

484. *Molon:* An actor apparently, who was either very little or very large.

486. *For some . . . are bad:* From the lost *Oeneus* of Euripides.

486. *Iophon:* The son of Sophocles. The point here and in the following lines was that the younger man had been helped by his father.

487. *Agathon:* A tragic poet whose works are lost but who had a good reputation as a poet and seems to have been personally very well liked. There are portraits of him in Plato's *Symposium* and Aristophanes' *Thesmophoriazusae,* and though the latter

teases him for a ladylike manner and appearance, the teasing is done without Aristophane's usual cruelty. The reader would think Agathon had died. He had not. At some time not long before this play, he left Athens and joined a group of celebrities at the court of King Archelaos in Macedonia. The thought is, that for Athenian audiences he might just as well have quitted this world for the Islands of the Blest at the end of the world. Little is known about Xenocles and nothing about Pythangelos.

page 488. *Bright upper air, Zeus' penthouse:* All these lines are Euripidean. "Bright upper air, Zeus' penthouse" seems to be adapted from a phrase in the lost *Clever Melanippe.* "The foot of Time" is from the lost *Alexander.* The *heart that would . . .* and *Tongue that was . . .* are an adaptation from *Hippolytus* 612.

489. *Rule thou it:* This line is Euripidean, but the scholiast's ascription of it to *Andromache* is wrong.

491. *the deathless way:* As the Greeks conceived it, death is the separation of the soul or *psyche* (life, breath, ghost, or image) from the body. The body decays. The soul, such as it is, goes to the house or realm of Hades, or to Hades (Hades is Plouton or Pluto, a person rather than a place). Usually, *but not always,* Hades is imagined to be under the ground. An alternate thought is to put the land of the dead, sometimes of the blessed dead only, at the end of the world. So certain special heroes pass to the other world merely by going further than natural means could have taken anyone: they do not go underground, their psyche is not torn out of their body, *they do not die.* Odysseus makes a long voyage and returns. Herakles went, and came baċk alive, so he must have gone by the roundabout way (Tainaron, land's end of the Peloponnese, the jumping-off place). In *The Metamorphoses* (*The Golden Ass*) of Apuleius (6. 17-18), Psyche must do an errand in Hades and return. She climbs a

high tower and is about to jump. But the tower tells her not to, for if her spirit is broken out of her body she will go to the deepest place and never come back. Instead, she should go the long way, via Tainaron. Apuleius wrote in the second century A.D., but he helps to show what Dionysos is here talking about. In this play, the ferryboat on the Styx is combined perhaps with the far-voyaging ship, such a one as carried Odysseus. But one should not go too far in quest of intelligibility, since this is a funny play, not theology.

page 492. *two bits:* Literally, two obols. The *diobelia* or "two-obol payment" was a notorious but mysterious payment, probably some kind of dole, instituted by the demagogue Kleophon.

492. *Theseus:* The Athenian hero also made the trip to Hades and back.

492. *Morsimos:* A tragic poet, great-nephew of Aeschylus.

492. *Kinesias:* A writer of dithyrambs.

493. *Initiates:* Those initiated in the Eleusinian Mysteries expected a blissful life after death.

494. *bucks:* Literally, drachmas.

496. *carry me home:* The Greek here has a punning sequence only a little less idiotic than the translation.

496. *sea battle:* See the note to page 482.

497. *Stone of Parching Thirst:* (*Auainou lithos*). This would be a landmark in the country of the dead. Refreshing *water* from the Well of Memory stands for immortality ("may Isis give you cold water" on many Greek-Egyptian epitaphs): so being dried out would be a preliminary torment.

498. *First Crew:* Literally "I am asalaminious." This could mean, "I am not a Salamis man," that is, "I didn't fight at the battle of Salamis." But it could also mean "I am not a Salaminia man." The "Salaminia" was a consecrated ship, used for sacred and special missions. Its crew would doubtless be picked men. Since the sea fight of seventy-five years earlier is quite remote from this part of the play's action, I prefer the second interpretation

page 504. *Empousa:* A bogey to frighten children with.

506. *the clam has stilled the waves:* In Euripides *Orestes* 279 the line runs:

ἐκ κυμάτων γὰρ αὖθις αὖ γαλήν(a) ὁρῶ.

The storm is over and the *calm* has stilled the waves.

But the actor, Hegelochos, spoke it:

ἐκ κυμάτων γὰρ αὖθις αὖ γαλήν ὁρῶ.

The storm is over and the *cat* has stilled the waves. Since "cat" (or "weasel"?) makes no plausible confusion in English, I have taken a slight liberty. In this, I find I have been anticipated by Mr. Dudley Fitts.

506. *all in yellow:* This seems the likeliest interpretation, though it is difficult to have the donkey on stage for so long.

507. *Iacchos: Both* Dionysos *and* the companion of Demeter and Persephone (that the god is eavesdropping on his own rituals is part of the fun). In the choral passage to come, and in the parabasis, the features of the Mysteries are combined with the worship of the Muses—which is drama.

508. *Diagoras:* A poet notorious for his atheism.

508. *Roasting pigs!:* Pigs were sacrificed at the Mysteries.

509. *Kratinos:* A distinguished comic poet, older contemporary (no longer living at the time of this play) of Aristophanes.

509. *Thorykion:* A tax-collector, evidently. Nothing is known about him except what is alleged here.

509. *shrine as a blackhouse:* This seems to mean Kinesias. See page 492.

512. *Archedemos:* The demagogue who instituted proceedings against the generals after the battle of Arginousai (see the note on page 519). Non-Athenian birth is a frequent charge brought against demagogues by the comic poets.

512. *Kleisthenes:* See page 484. He is supposed to be mourning for a lost boy friend, like a wife for a husband killed in the war. Mourners tore out their hair (from their heads) and beat their faces.

page 512. *Kallias:* Member of a very rich family in Athens. Then as now only the rich raced horses.

514. *Aiakos:* In epic and saga a great hero, grandfather of Achilleus, head of that heroic line, the Aiakidai, so dear to the Aiginetans and Pindar and, according to some, made for his uprightness a judge of the dead in the underworld. Here he is a slave, plainly the janitor or porter.

514. *Styx, Acheron, Kokytos:* The rivers of the underworld. But Styx, often personified, is here hinted at in her true and ancient form, a waterfall dribbling off a huge black cliff on the northern face of Mount Chelmos, between Arkadia and Achaia.

516. *I cannot but obey thee:* This sounds like a tragic tag, but I cannot place it.

517. *Mistress:* Persephone.

519. *Theramenes:* A well-known politician of the time. Having in mind his own schemes for reform, he would join whatever party seemed temporarily to be most likely to further them, and then change sides at discretion. He showed the same kind of "adaptability" after the victory at Arginousai (see page 482). Bad weather prevented the victorious Athenians from picking up many survivors and floating corpses after the battle. The assembly was out of blood, and things looked bad for the captains of the ships, of whom Theramenes was one. He saved himself by adding his voice to the clamor, but putting the blame on the admirals of the fleet, who were condemned to death. Such maneuvers won Theramenes the nickname *kothornos,* which means "tragic buckskin," or a military boot, or, more important for our purpose here, any boot which would fit either foot. The nickname is attested by Xenophon *Hellenica* 2. 3. 31. It does not appear in our text. I apologize for crowding it in; it seemed to me to make clear the well-known character of the man Aristophanes was attacking.

521. *Kleon:* If you have read the early plays, especially

The Knights, you know all about Kleon. Hyperbolos was his successor, and of the same sort

page 523. *my wife:* He hasn't any.

523. *my kiddies:* He hasn't any.

523. *the kind of god:* Herakles, as brother of Dionysos, is treated mostly as a god in this play.

523. *braver herbs:* Oregano. It was supposed to put one in a fighting mood.

525. *gentlemanly:* Athenian law permitted the torture of slaves in order to make them give evidence. This could not be done to free men, or "gentlemen," so it is a "generous" and "gentlemanly" gesture on the part of Xanthias when he offers his *slave* to be tortured for evidence concerning *himself.*

525. *or leeks:* A master might ask that his slave be excused for tortures too injurious or painful, either for the slave's own sake, or with thoughts of his future uses.

528. *Diomeia:* This feast of Herakles was held outside the walls and could not be celebrated while the enemy occupied Attica.

529. *Apollo . . . Pytho:* A line of verse by Hipponax, the iambic poet.

530. *Who . . . green waters:* The lyric is said to be from the lost *Laocoön* of Sophocles.

531. *Kleophon:* Politician, leader of the popular party, which was also the war party, detested by the comic poets, and attacked as being of non-Athenian (Thracian) birth. See the last lines of this play. Swallow and nightingale (Philomela and Prokne) are associated with Thrace (see *The Birds*), and the twittering of birds is often used to describe barbarian speech. The point is apparently something like this: Kleophon must stand trial at some time, and though in Attic law even ballots mean acquittal, Kleophon is so awful that an exception ought to be made.

531. *fears be taken away:* What follows is a plea for amnesty, and the restoration of full citizens' rights to all those who had lost them for political reasons,

particularly for supporting Phrynichos in the revolution of 411 B.C.

page 531. *Plataian status:* Plataia, a city of Boiotia, had been the most steadfast and devoted of the allies of Athens. When in 427 B.C. the city was destroyed by the Spartans and Thebans, the survivors were granted Athenian citizenship (with a few limitations).

532. *Kleigenes:* This bathman was doubtless also a politician but we know nothing more about him.

533. *currency:* The Spartan occupation of part of Attica had cut off access to the silver mines at Laurion. This resulted in a debasing of the coinage.

533. *scapegoat:* Or *pharmakos*. This was a condemned criminal on whom was loaded all the accumulated guilt of the city. His execution, therefore, amounted to an act of public sacrifice and expiation.

538. *Kleidemidas:* Perhaps a son of Sophocles, perhaps only a friend.

540. *cabbage patch:* Aristophanes is fond of saying that Euripides' mother maintained a truck garden.

544. *Phrynichus:* The earliest of the great tragic poets, active in the first decades of the fifth century (not to be confused with the comic poet mentioned on page 481).

544. *Achilleus:* References are to lost plays, *The Phrygians* (or *The Ransoming of Hector*) and *Niobe*.

547. *Kephisophon:* Euripides' secretary, supposed, here, to have done some ghostwriting for him.

548. *line of thought:* Aristophanes portrays Aeschylus as a haughty patrician who disliked the common people. See the Introduction.

549. *Phormisios:* A "reactionary" politician. Of Megainetos and Manes (this may be a nickname) nothing is known. Kleitophon, who appears in the dialogue of Plato which bears his name, seems to have belonged with Phormisios, as does Theramenes (see note 515 on page 585). Euripides' disciples seem to be distinguished from those of Aeschylus not so much for their views as for their character and methods.

page 550. *See you . . . Achilleus?:* The opening of the lost *Myrmidons* of Aeschylus.

552. *Persians:* This seems to be a slip of memory on the part of Aristophanes. *The Persians* is reliably dated 472 B.C., *The Seven Against Thebes* 467 B.C.

554. *Phaidra:* See Euripides, *Hippolytus.*

554. *Sthenoboia:* The heroine of a lost play named after her. Her story is similar to that of Phaidra, insofar as she made advances to Bellerophon, her husband's guest, was refused, and told her husband that Bellerophon had tried to seduce her.

556. *warships:* No one is willing to be a *trierarch.* The *trierarchy*, a special duty of liturgy imposed on rich citizens, involved the outfitting and upkeep of *trireme* (war galley), as well as the nominal command of the vessel on active service.

556. *His nurses . . . life?:* The nurse-procuress could be Phaidra's nurse in *Hippolytus.* In *Auge*, the heroine gave birth in the temple of Athene. In *Aeolus*, Makareus and Kanake, brother and sister, are involved in a love affair. For musings on life, see the fragment from the lost *Polyeidus:*

> Who knows if life be not thought death, or death
> be life in the world below?

There is a similar thought in the lost *Phrixus.*

557. *Panathenaia:* The pan-Athenian festival.

558. *subtle allusions:* We are told that *The Frogs* was so well received that a second performance was given during the poet's lifetime. This stanza may conceivably have been written for this second performance, when "the book was out." But an annotated edition, by which the audience could identify allusions, is something absolutely unexampled for this date.

558. *Oresteia:* The title is here used for the play we call *The Choephori*, or *The Libation Bearers.*

558. *Hermes, . . . I have returned:* These lines are missing from our mss. of Aeschylus. I have discarded my previous translation for a more literal one, in

order to make the use of synonymous phrases, real or apparent, more obvious.

page 562. *three times:* At the last rites for the dead, the name was called three times.

563. *Oedipus . . . man:* This and the fifth line below are the first two lines of Euripides' lost *Antigone*.

563. *Erasinides:* A general at the time of the battle of Arginousai. Had one of these generals lost his sight, he would have been excused from military service, and so would have escaped the fate that befell Erasinides and his colleagues. See the note on Theramenes on page 589.

564. *Aigyptos . . . Argos:* Said to have been the first lines of the lost *Archelaus*, but the opening of this play is also given in another form.

564. *little bottle of oil:* The *lekythion*, or little oil bottle, was part of the traveler's regular luggage.

565. *Dionysos . . . feet:* Opening of the lost *Hypsipyle*.

565. *Ah me, . . . again:* This line combines the two death cries of Agamemnon, Aeschylus *Agamemnon*, 1343, 1345.

565. *There's been . . . born unhappy:* Opening of the lost *Sthenoboia*.

566. *Kadmos . . . Sidon:* Opening of the lost *Phrixus*.

566. *Pelops . . . horses:* Opening of *Iphigeneia in Tauris*.

567. *Oineus, from his land:* Opening of the lost *Meleager*.

567. *Zeus . . . maintained:* Opening of the lost *Clever Melanippe*.

568. *Phthian . . . rescue?:* Two lines from the lost *Myrmidons*, the second repeated as a refrain by Aristophanes.

568. *Hermes . . . lakeside:* From the lost *Psychagogi*.

568. *Greatest Achaian . . . hear me:* From either *Telephus* or *Iphigeneia* (both lost).

569. *Quiet, all . . . nearby:* From *The Priestesses* (lost).

569. *I am . . . at the wayside: Agamemnon* 104.

569. *How the . . . of Hellas: Agamemnon* 108.

569. *Sends forth . . . hellhounds:* From the lost *Sphinx*.

569. *hand on . . . of encounter: Agamemnon* 111.

570. *giving assault . . . airways:* Provenance unknown.

page 570. *From Marathon:* The next Aeschylean line, *which leaning on Aias,* is meaningless here, since unmetrical, and I have omitted it.

570. *Meletos':* A poet of indifferent reputation, better known as the accuser of Socrates.

570. *That's a man's woman . . . one:* Literally, Dionysos says: "This Muse was never a Lesbian, not at all." Rogers, reading the Greek so as to obtain "The Muse herself" instead of "This Muse," translates: "The Muse herself can't be a wanton? No!" I do not find this convincing. Outraged indignation does not suit Dionysos, and the expression "be a Lesbian" should not mean "be a wanton" in any general sense. If Sappho had ever, at this time, been called "The tenth Muse," the point would be perfect. She was so called, but I do not find it earlier than *Palatine Anthology* 9. 506. This is attributed to Plato, and therefore could, by an exceedingly strenuous stretch of the imagination, have been current before *The Frogs* was written. But attributions in the *Anthology* are frequently suspect, and this epigram does not sound Platonic to me. Still, "Tenth Muse" could have been a tag already applied to Sappho, and the allusion to Lesbos ought to be accounted for in the translation.

570. *sea's ever-streaming:* This sequence seems to be a patchwork of Euripidean passages, but not all can be identified. The first four lines are said to be from *Iphigeneia,* but do not appear in our extant texts for either of the plays so called. Other identifications are: the eighth line, *Meleager;* ninth and tenth, *Electra;* eleventh to fourteenth, *Hypsipyle.*

571. *monodies:* The monody is a solo for the female character (played of course by a male actor). Unlike the patchwork demonstration of "Euripidean lyric" above, this is a true parody, done "in the manner of Euripides" but without (apparently) direct quotations.

574. *I wish . . . her way:* The opening line of *Medea.*

574. *River . . . near:* From the lost *Philoctetes.*

page 575. *Persuasion . . . the word:* From the lost *Antigone.*
575. *Death . . . by fits:* From the lost *Niobe.*
575. *His right hand . . . steel:* From the lost *Meleager*
576. *Chariot . . . on corpse:* From the lost *Glaucus.*
578. *[Lions . . . all]:* The authenticity of this line, omitted by two good mss., is highly doubtful, so I have left it in square brackets. The allusion to the lion's cub may be to *Agamemnon* 716-36, but there is no direct quotation. Lions are constantly associated with kingship. There would be a hint at Alkibiades' suspected ambitions toward tyranny. I have read this thought into my translation. To the question, what shall we do about Alkibiades, the answers may be paraphrased thus: Euripides: He is selfish and therefore unreliable: Aeschylus: True, but he is our only promising leader, and we should put ourselves in his hands.
578. *Kleokritos* and *Kinesias:* see *The Birds* 877, 1372.
579. *will serve?:* I hope I am right this interpretation. Neither the mantle of the rich nor the sack-cloth of the poor is satisfactory. These articles of clothing are, I believe, thought of as emergency life preservers. Cf. *Odyssey* 5. 346-50.
580. *My tongue . . . heart:* See *Hippolytus* 612.
581. *What's shameful? . . . audience?:* Adapted from the lost *Aeolus.* It should read: "What's shameful, unless it seems so to those who do it?"
581. *Who knows . . . life:* See note 556 on page 592.
582. *Sokrates:* The word *sophia* stands sometimes for literary skill, sometimes for wisdom. The ambiguity shows that the Greeks did not always distinguish between the two as sharply as we do. Aristophanes, acknowledging perhaps that the clever Sokrates does possess some kind of *sophia*, rejects it as the wrong kind. The objection is based, clearly, on certain antiliterary views of Sokrates which are attested again and again in the works of Plato.
582. *Archenomos:* They were involved in the collection of taxes.

Glossary

Glossary

ACHARNAI: Largest of the rural demes of Attika, located about seven miles north of the city of Athens.

ADONIS: Mythical youth of marvelous beauty, beloved of Aphrodite, early cut off by a boar. His death was regularly bewailed by women of Greece and the East at summer festivals.

AESCHYLUS, AISCHYLOS: The great Athenian tragedian (525-456 B.C.).

AESOP, AISOPOS: A writer of fables, perhaps legendary himself. He was reputed a native of Samos who flourished in the sixth century B.C

AGAMEMNON: In mythology, commander-in-chief of the Greek forces at the siege of Troy.

AISCHINES: An indigent Athenian braggart, much given to boasting about his fabulous estates, as imaginary as Cloud-cuckooland.

AJAX, AIAS: Greek hero of the Trojan War, son of Telamon of Salamis.

AKADEME, ACADEMY: Originally a precinct sacred to the hero Akademos and afterward used as a gymnasium and recreation area. The general Kimon planted it with groves of olives and plane trees. Only in the fourth century, after becoming the haunt of the philosopher Plato and his followers, did the once athletic Academy become academic in the modern sense of the word.

AKESTOR: An Athenian tragic poet. See SAKAS.

AKROPOLIS, ACROPOLIS: The citadel of Athens.

ALKIBIADES: An Athenian politician (*ca.* 450-404) of great ability and brilliance. Of aristocratic Alkmaionid descent, he was related to Perikles and was, for some time, a devoted disciple of Sokrates. Distinguished by wealth, birth, and spectacular personal beauty, he spent his youth in lavish display and debauchery (Pheidippides in *The Clouds* has been thought to be a caricature of Alkibiades). After the death of Kleon in 422, Alkibiades became chief of the belligerent anti-Spartan party in Athens in opposition to the more conservative Nikias and was one of the primary advocates of the disastrous Sicilian expedition.

ALKMEME: Wife of Amphitryon and mistress of Zeus by whom she became the mother of Herakles.

ALOPE: Mortal woman beloved by Poseidon.

AMAZONS: The mythical race of warrior-women, said to have invaded Attika in heroic times to avenge the theft of their queen's sister, Antiope, by Theseus of Athens.

AMMON: A celebrated shrine and oracle of Zeus and Libya.

AMPHION: Musician and husband of Niobe; at the touch of his lyre the stones rose from the ground and formed themselves together to make the ramparts of Thebes.

AMYKLAI: A Lakedaimonian town, traditional birthplace of Kastor (q.v.) and Pollux, site of a temple of Apollo

AMYNIAS: Son of Pronapes and one of Strepsiades' creditors in *The Clouds*. He was not, however, a professional moneylender but a notorious effeminate and wastrel, probably addicted to gambling.

ANTIMACHOS: A homosexual on a prodigious scale.

APHRODITE: Goddess of beauty and sexual love.

APOLLO: God of prophecy, music, healing, and light; his two chief shrines were at Delphoi (q.v.) and Delos (q.v.)

ARES: God of War.

ARISTOGEITON: Athenian hero who, with Harmodios, assassinated the tyrant Hipparchos in 514 and was put to death. With the expulsion of Hipparchos' brother Hippias four years later, the tyranny of the Peisistratids came to an end. Statues to Harmodios and Aristogeiton were erected in the Athenian Agora.

ARISTOKRATES: Son of Skellias; a prominent Athenian politician of conservative persuasion. In 421 B.C. he was one of the signers of the Peace of Nikias between Athens and Sparta. In 411 he joined the moderate conservative Theramenes in setting up the government of the Four Hundred, but later withdrew.

ARTEMIS: Goddess of chastity, childbirth, and the hunt; sister of Apollo.

ARTEMISIA: Queen of Halikarnassos, who, as an ally of the Persian King Xerxes in his invasion of Greece, fought with particular distinction at the sea battle of Salamis in 480.

ARTEMISION: Site on the northern coast of Euboia, off which the Athenians defeated the Persians in a sea battle in 480.

ATHAMAS: King of Orchomenos and the legendary subject of a (lost) play by Sophokles. Having attempted to murder his son Phrixos (q.v.), Athamas was sentenced to be sacrificed. He was crowned with a sacrificial wreath and dragged before the altar, but just before being dispatched, was saved by the sudden intervention of Herakles.

ATHENA, ATHENE: Goddess of wisdom and war and patroness of Athens. On her breast she wore the aegis, a goatshin plated with scales and a Gorgon's head in the center.

BABYLON: Ancient capital of Mesopotamia, situated on the Euphrates River. It was one of the largest cities of the ancient world, and among its wonders were its great brick walls, described by the historian Herodotos.

BACCHOS: Dionysos, the god of vineyards, wine and dramatic poetry, celebrated at Athens in a series of festivals, among them the Lenaia (January–February) and the City Dionysia (March–April).

BAKIS: A famous prophet of Boiotia, whose oracles were delivered in hexameter verse. In Aristophanes' comedies, the seers who cite Bakis are usually charlatans.

BASILEIA: The personification of Empire and Sovereign Power; in the present version she appears as Miss Universe.

BOIOTIA: A plentifully supplied state directly northeast of Attika, allied with Sparta during the Peloponnesian War.

BYZANTION: A city on the Bosporos and a subject-city of the Athenian Empire. Its siege by the Athenians under Kimon in 469 was celebrated.

CHAIREPHON: Friend and disciple of the philosopher Sokrates. His utter devotion to philosophy and the studious life and his striking pallor and emaciation made him a popular image of The Philosopher. Hence his nickname, The Bat or The Vampire.

CHAOS: The nothingness or vacancy which existed before the creation of the world. In mythology Chaos was the mother of Erebos and Night.

CHARON: A minor deity in charge of ferrying the souls of the dead to Hades.

CHIANS: Inhabitants of the island of Chios, a state closely allied to Athens during the early Peloponnesian War and whose fidelity to the Athenian cause was rewarded by inclusion in the Athenian prayers for prosperity and success.

DARIUS, DAREIOS: King of Persia (ruled 521-486 B.C.).

DELOS: Small Aegean island sacred to Apollo.

DELPHOI, DELPHI: A town in Phokis, celebrated for its great temple and oracle of Apollo.

DEMETER: The Earth Mother; goddess of grain, agriculture, and the harvest, worshipped at her shrine at Eleusis in Attika.

DEMOSTRATOS: A choleric Athenian demagogue, first to propose the disastrous Sicilian Expedition of 415-413.

DIAGORAS: Poet and philosopher of Melos. Charged with atheism in Athens and condemned to death, he fled the city.

DIEITREPHES: A notorious social climber. Of doubtful Athenian origin, he began his public career as a worker in wicker and a basketmaker, and gradually made his way upward in the military hierarchy. In 413 a detachment of Thracians under his command went amok and massacred a school full of children at Mykalessos.

DIONYSOS: God of vineyards, wine, and dramatic poetry: also called Bacchos, Evios, Bromios, etc.

DODONA: An ancient oracle of Zeus in the mountains of Epiros.

ELEKTRA: Daughter of Agamemnon and Klytaimnestra; with her brother Orestes she murdered her mother for having killed her father. In the *parabasis* of *The Clouds*, Aristophanes alludes to the famous scene in Aischylos' *Choephoroe*. when Elektra recognized that her brother Orestes had returned to Argos from the lock of hair left on Agamemnon's tomb.

EPHESOS: A city in Asia Minor (Ionia). site of a famous temple of Artemis.

EPOPS: The Hoopoe, Tereus (q.v.).

EROS: God of sensual love, son of Aphrodite.

ETNA, AITNA: A city situated on a spur of the Sicilian mountain of the same name, founded by Hiero of Syracuse.

EUBOIA: A large and fertile island northeast of Attica. In 457 Perikles planted an Athenian colony on the island and otherwise exploited it. As a result the island revolted in 445 and had to be resubjugated. This time, however, Perikles' treatment of the island was so severe that it was commonly said (at least by his enemies) that he had "stretched Euboia on the rack of torture."

EUPOLIS: An Athenian poet of the Old Comedy and a rival of Aristophanes. Eupolis claimed that Aristophanes had imitated him in *The Knights,* and Aristophanes countered by charging the Eupolis' *Marikas* was a plagiarism of his own *The Knights.*

EURIPIDES: Athenian tragedian (480-406 B.C.) whose character and plays were constantly ridiculed by Aristophanes. Euripides' mother may have been (though this is uncertain) a marketwoman who sold chervil, and Aristophanes never tires of twitting the tragedian about his mother's vegetables.

EUROTAS: A river in Laconia, on which is located the city of Sparta.

EXEKESTIDES: Evidently a foreign slave of Karian extraction who succeeded in passing himself off as an Athenian citizen, i.e., the sort of man who would be at home anywhere.

GORGIAS: Of Leontini, a noted sophist and teacher of rhetoric.

HARMODIOS: Athenian hero; assassin, with Aristogeiton (q.v.), of the tyrant Hipparchos.

HEBROS: A river of Thrace.

HEKATE: Goddess of the moon, night, childbirth, and the underworld.

HELEN: Daughter of Leda and Tyndaros, wife of Menelaos

of Sparta. Her abduction by Paris of Troy furnished a *casus belli* for the Trojan War.

HERA: Consort of Zeus

HERAKLES: Hero and demigod, son of Zeus and Alkmene. renowned for his great labors. prodigious strength. and equally prodigious appetite. Because Herakles is *par excellence* the monster-killer, it is particularly appropriate to swear by him when confronted by the monstrous, prodigious. freakish. or strange

HERMES: God of messengers and thieves; in Athens in every doorway stood a statue of Hermes (i.e., a *herm*, usually a bust of the god surmounting an ithyphallic pillar), protector of the door and guardian against thieves—it takes one to know one. The wholesale mutilation of these statues by persons unknown, just before the sailing of the Sicilian expedition in 415, led to the recall of Alkibiades—and thus, perhaps. to the loss of the expedition and ultimately of the war.

HESTIA: Goddess of the hearth (and among Birds. goddess of the nest).

HIERO: Famous tyrant of Syracuse in Sicily. celebrated by the poet Pindar.

HIERONYMOS: A dithyrambic poet and tragedian, notorious for his extraordinary shagginess. bestial appearance. and pederasty.

HIPPOKRATES: Athenian general and nephew of Perikles; his three sons, it seems, were all distinguished for their stupidity and were popularly nicknamed "The Pigs."

HIPPONAX: A satirical iambic poet of Ephesos (fl. 540 B.C.). noted for his limping meter and his touchy temper.

HIPPONIKOS: A common name in a wealthy and aristocratic Athenian family.

HOMER: The great epic poet of Greece. author of the *Iliad* and *Odyssey*.

HYPERBOLOS: An Athenian demagogue, successor to Kleon on the latter's death in 422. Of servile origins, he seems to have been a peddler of lamps and then to have studied with the Sophists in order to advance himself politically. (At least these are the charges made against him by Aristophanes.) He was later ostracized and finally murdered by the oligarchical leaders in Samos.

HYMEN: God of marriage.

IKAROS: Son of the craftsman Daidalos, who escaped from Krete with his father by means of homemade wings of wax and feathers. But when Ikaros flew too high, the sun melted the wax, his wings dissolved, and he fell to his death in the sea.

IRIS: Messenger of the gods; in the earlier poets represented as a virgin.

ITYS   The son of Tereus and Prokne (q.v.), murdered by his mother in revenge for Tereus' rape and mutilation of Philomela. To the Greek ear, the name Itys seemed to form part of the refrain of the mourning nightingale.

KALLIAS: Common name in a wealthy and aristocratic Athenian family. The Kallias singled out here was a notorious profligate and spendthrift.

KARKINOS: An Athenian tragic poet whose poetry and three sons are all ridiculed by Aristophanes. Karkinos' name means "Crab."

KARYSTIAN: From Karystos, a town in Euboia allied to Athens, whose male inhabitants enjoyed a seemingly deserved reputation for lechery.

KASTOR: Divinity, son of Leda and Tyndaros, or of Leda and Zeus; twins of Polydeukes (Pollux), with whom he constitutes the Dioskouroi. These twin gods were particularly honored by their native state of Sparta.

KEKROPS, CECROPS: Legendary first king of Attika and reputed founder of Athens. Hence "country of Kekrops" is equivalent to "Athens" and "son of Kekrops" to "Athenian." He is usually represented as twi-form, i.e., with the head and upper trunk of a man, but serpent-shaped below (symbolizing this earthborn origin).

KIKYNNA: An Athenian deme of the tribe of Akamantis.

KIMON: One of Athens' greatest generals (died 449 B.C.); in the years following the Persian Wars, principal architect of the Athenian Empire—an activity abruptly interrupted by his ostracism in 461.

KINESIAS: A clubfooted dithyrambic poet of great pretensions but little ability.

KLEISTHENES: A notorious homosexual; on that account, one of Aristophanes' favorite targets for at least twenty years.

KLEOMENES: Sixth-century king of Sparta, whose two Athenian expeditions had rather different results: The first, in 510, materially assisted in the expulsion of the tyrant Hippias; the second, in 508, failed to establish the power of the aristocratic party led by Isagoras

KLEON: Son of Kleainetos; the most notorious and powerful of all Athenian demagogues After the death of Perikles in 429 B.C., Kleon became. until his own death in 422. the leader of the radical democracy and the anti-Spartan extremists in Athens An impressive speaker and a thoroughly unscrupulous and venal politician, he was bitterly loathed and attacked by Aristophanes In 424 B.C., thanks to his coup in capturing the Spartan hoplites at Sphakteria. he reached the height of his power; so unchallengeable was his position that he was able to persuade the Athenians not to accept the handsome terms offered by Sparta in an attempt to recover her imprisoned hoplites. Filled with confidence in his military ability and tempted by the hope of further glory, Kleon took command of an Athenian army in Thrace, where, in 422. he was defeated and killed by the Spartan forces under Brasidas.

In Aristophanes' *The Knights*. Kleon is only slightly masked under the name of Paphlagon (q.v.).

KLEONYMOS: A corpulent glutton and part-time informer; Aristophanes' commonest butt for cowardice (i.e., throwing one's shield away).

KOLONOS: Small town on a hill near Athens; here the astronomer Meton (q.v.) had evidently constructed a complicated piece of engineering or clockwork.

KORDAX: A salacious dance commonly used in Athenian Old Comedy.

KORINTH: Greek city allied to Sparta during the Peloponnesian War; situated on the strategic Isthmus of Korinth.

KORKYRA: Modern Corfu, a large island off the western coast of Greece. "Korkyrean wings" means "whip."

KRONOS: Father of Zeus, Hera, and Poseidon. Deprived of his rule by Zeus. Synonymous with "old fogy."

KYBELE: A Phrygian Mother Goddess, worshipped as The Great Mother, "mother of gods and men."

KYNTHOS: A mountain on the island of Delos, sacred to Apollo.

KYPROS: A large Greek island in the eastern Mediterranean, especially associated with the goddess Aphrodite, said to have stepped ashore there after her birth from the sea-foam.

LAKONIA: The southernmost state on the Greek mainland, Athens' principal opponent in the Peloponnesian War. Its capital city is Sparta.

LAURIUM, LAUREION: In southeastern Attika, famous for its silver mines. Athenian silver coins, stamped with the owl of Athena, were commonly called "owls of Laureion."

LENAIA: An Athenian Dionysiac festival, celebrated in January–February.

LEOGORAS: A wealthy Athenian gourmet, addicted to horse raising (or possibly to pheasant-breeding). Father of the orator Andokides.

LEONIDAS: Spartan king and general, who led his 300 troops against Xerxes' Persian army at Thermopylae in Thessaly (480).

LEOTROPHIDES: An extremely fragile, delicate, and·unsubstantial poet.

LEPREUS, LEPREUM: A town in Elis; it recovered its independence from Elis during the Peloponnesian War.

LETO: Mother of Artemis and Apollo.

LYDIA: A district of Asia Minor; under its greatest king, Kroisos (Croesus), it included almost all of Asia Minor from the river Halys to the Ionian coast. Its wealth and effeminacy were proverbial among Greeks.

LYKOURGOS: An Athenian of sufficient distinction and/or oddity of appearance to have won the nickname of The Ibis. In this translation, however, he appears as The Lame Duck.

MAENADS: The frenzied female worshippers (Bacchantes) of Dionysos (q.v.).

MAIOTIS: An inland sea (the modern Sea of Azov), northern arm of the Black Sea.

MANES: A lazy slave.

MANODOROS: A slave.

MARATHON: A plain in the eastern part of Attika; site of the famous battle (490 B.C.) in which the Athenian forces under Miltiades crushingly defeated the first Persian invasion of Hellas.

MEGAKLES: A name belonging to the Alkmaionid family, one of the proudest and most distinguished families of Athens.

MEGARA: The Greek state immediately to the west of Attika; also, its capital city.

MEIDIAS: A venal and corrupt Athenian informer, evidently also a quail-breeder in his own right, whence his nickname, The Quail. For Aristophanes the propriety of the name is confirmed by Meidias' habitually dazed expression, like that of a freshly stunned quail.

MELANION: A mighty hunter, evidently proverbial for his chastity. Probably not to be identified with Meilanion (Milanion), victorious suitor of the huntress Atalante.

MELANTHIOS: Son of Philokles and, like his father, an atrocious tragedian. Afflicted with leprosy, he seems to have been also a noted glutton (cf. *Peace*, 804).

MEMNON: Famous hero, son of Tithonos and Eos (Dawn); killed in the Trojan War at the hands of Achilleus.

MENELAOS: Mythological king of Sparta and brother of Agamemnon; husband of Helen.

MENIPPOS: An Athenian horse-raiser, nicknamed The Swallow (from a pun on the word *chelidon* which means both "swallow" and the tender "hollow" in a horse's hoof).

MESSENIA: The western half of Lakedaimon in the Peloponnese; in spite of revolutions, held by Sparta from ca. 730 B.C. until her defeat by Thebes at Leuktra in 371 B.C.

METON: An Athenian astronomer, geometrician, and city-planner of considerable notoriety (see KOLONOS). According to Plutarch, Meton objected to the Sicilian expedition and pretended madness in order to keep his son at home.

MIKON: A famous Athenian painter of murals, who flourished between the Persian and Peloponnesian Wars.

MILESIAN: From Miletos, a city in Karia in Asia Minor, which had broken off its alliance with Athens in mid-412, following the Sicilian disaster.

MIMAS: A mountain on the coast of Ionia.

MYRONIDES: Athenian general in the period between the Wars; his best-known victory was over the Boiotians at Oinophyta (456).

NESTOR: King of Pylos and a hero of the Trojan War, famous for his wisdom and eloquence.

NIKIAS: Prominent Athenian general during the Peloponnesian War. Enormously respected at Athens during his lifetime.

Nikias' caution, slowness to move, stiffness, and superstitious piety were among the chief causes for the defeat
of the Sicilian expedition. But as a cautious strategist
and tactician, he had no equal among the Athenian
generals.

ODYSSEUS: Hero of the *Odyssey* of Homer.

OLOPHYXIANS: Inhabitants of Olophyxos, a small town on the
peninsula of Akte in Thrace.

OLYMPOS: Mountain (app. 9700 feet, alt.) in Thessaly, covered at the summit with perpetual snow and reputed by the
Greeks to be the abode of the gods.

OPOUNTIOS: A notorious one-eyed sycophant nicknamed The
Crow.

OPOUS: A town in Lokris, whose inhabitants were called the
Opuntian Lokrians.

ORESTES: A notorious burglar and highwayman; not to be
confused with the heroic son of Agamemnon.

PAIAN: Manifestation of Apollo as god of healing.

PALLAS: The goddess Athena (Pallus Athene).

PAN: Rural Arkadian god of the flocks and woodlands; his
cult at Athens was instituted by way of thanks for his help
to the Athenians at the battle of Marathon.

PANATHENAIA: The great Athenian festival in honor of Athena.

PANDALETOS: A professional informer.

PANDORA: Mother Earth, the giver of all gifts (*pan*, all;
dora, gifts); not to be confused with the mythological
mischief-maker and her box of human troubles.

PAPHLAGON: Aristophanes' (and presumably Athens') nickname for the demagogue Kleon (q.v.). The name is intended to suggest: (1) that Kleon came of slavish and
foreign stock—i.e., was not an Athenian but a Paphlagonian—
and (2) the sheer volume and violence of Kleon's rhetorical
assaults (from Greek *paphlazein*, to froth, bluster, storm).

PARIS: Prince of Troy; in the famous judgment of Paris, he was offered the most beautiful woman in the world by Aphrodite in return for awarding her the prize for beauty.

PARNASSOS: A high mountain to the north of Delphoi (q.v.); one of the chief haunts of Apollo and the Muses, but frequented also by Dionysos.

PARNES: A mountain in the northeast of Attika, forming part of the boundary between Attika and Boiotia. Near its foot was situated the deme of Acharnai.

PASIAS: One of Strepsiades' creditors; evidently a grotesquely fat man and probably a drunkard to boot.

PEGASOS: The famous winged horse of mythology.

PEISANDROS: Engineer of the oligarchic revolt which overthrew the Athenian constitution in May 411 and set up the Council of Four Hundred.

PEISIAS: Otherwise unknown, but evidently a noted traitor in his day.

PELEUS: Hero of mythology, husband of Thetis and father of Achilleus. According to legend, Astydamia, wife of Akastos, fell in love with Peleus but was rejected by him. Angered, she denounced him to her husband for having attempted to seduce her. Akastos thereupon invited Peleus to a hunting expedition on Mt. Pelion, stripped him of his weapons, and left him to be torn to pieces by the wild animals. When Peleus was almost on the point of death, however, the god Hermes brought him a sword.

PERIKLEIDAS: The ambassador sent by Sparta to beg Athenian aid in putting down the Messenian revolt of 464.

PERIKLES: Greatest of Athenian statesmen of the fifth century, and from 461 B.C. until his death in 429, the almost unchallenged leader of the radical Athenian democracy. Of one of Athens' most aristocratic families (the Alkmaionids), he was nonetheless the politician most responsible for the creation of the extreme democracy of the late fifth century. To Aristophanes' critical and conservative eyes, it was Perikles who was responsible for the corruption of Athens, and Aristophanes never tires of contrasting the Athens of the Persian War period with the Athens of Perikles—corrupt, effete, cruelly imperialistic, avaricious, at the mercy of Sophists, clever orators, and impostors, cursed with a system (e.g., the law courts) which practically guaranteed further excesses and injustices. Worst of all in Aristophanes' eyes was Perikles' belligerent war policies (e.g., the famous Megarian Decree of 432) and the fact that, after 429, Athens was left to the mercies of men like Kleon and Hyperbolos who lacked Perikles' restraint and political genius. Like almost all the comic dramatists, Aristophanes was a conservative (*not* an oligarch), and although he distinguishes clearly between Perikles and his corrupt successors, he nonetheless holds Perikles responsible for creating the political system in which men like Kleon could thrive.

PHILOKLES: Athenian tragic poet and nephew of Aischylos; among his lost plays was one which treated the story of Tereus and was evidently plagiarized from Sophokles' play of the same name. His nickname was The Lark because, according to the Scholiast, his head tapered like the pointed crest of that bird.

PHILOKRATES: An Athenian bird-seller.

PHLEGRA: A plain in Thrace said to have been the site of the great battle between the Gods and the Giants.

PHOIBOS: Apollo (q.v.).

PHORMION: Athenian admiral, noted for his victory over the Korinthians at Naupaktos in 429.

PHRIXOS: Son of Athamas (q.v.); on the point of being sacrificed to Zeus, he was rescued by his mother Nephele.

PHRYGIA: A country in central Asia Minor.

PHRYNICHOS: The famous early Athenian tragedian.

PHRYNIS: Of Mytilene, a famous citharist and musician of the fifth century; his innovations shocked and angered contemporary conservatives.

PINDAR: Great lyric poet of Thebes (518-438 B.C.).

PORPHYRION: Name of one of the Titans who fought against Zeus in the Battle of the Gods and the Giants; it is also the name of a bird, the Purple Waterhen.

POSEIDON: Brother of Zeus and god of the sea. As god of the sea, he girdles the earth and has it in his power, as Poseidon the Earthshaker, to cause earthquakes. In still another manifestation, he is Poseidon Hippios, patron god of horses and horsemen.

PRIAM: King of Troy.

PRODIKOS: Of Keos, the famous Sophist and friend of Sokrates.

PROKNE: The nightingale, wife of Tereus (q.v.).

PROMETHEUS: The great Titan who championed the cause of mankind against Zeus. Because he stole fire from heaven and gave it to men, he was regarded by the gods as a traitor to Olympos. His name means Foresight and his cleverness and philanthropy were both proverbial.

PROXENIDES: An Athenian braggart and blowhard.

PYLOS: Town of the southwestern coast of Messina whose siege and capture, along with the neighboring island of Sphakteria in 425-24, became a *cause célèbre* of the Peloponnesian War and the major source of Kleon's prestige and power in Athens. As a result of their defeat at Pylos and the capture of their hoplites, the Spartans were forced to sue for peace; every overture, however, was met by the determined refusal of Kleon, eager for the war to continue.

SAKAS: The nickname of the Athenian tragic poet Akestor (q.v.). The word Sakas seems to be a pejorative for "Skyth" and presumably Akestor, like Exekestides, was a foreigner who had managed, or was reputed to have managed, to get his name entered on the citizenship rolls of Athens.

SALAMIS: An island in the Saronic Gulf, between Megara and Attika. Subject to Athens, it is divided from the shore by a narrow strait, site of the famous sea battle of 480 which saw the defeat of Xerxes' Persians by Themistokles' Athenians.

SAMOS: A large Aegean island lying off the coast of Ionia. At the beginning of 411, the effective headquarters of the Athenian forces, who had just aided a democratic revolution there. Other Athenians, especially Peisandros, were already fomenting an oligarchic counterrevolution.

SARPEDON: Legendary hero, son of Zeus and Europa; killed by Patroklos during the Trojan War.

SEMELE: Daughter of Kadmos of Thebes and mistress of Zeus, by whom she became the mother of Dionysos.

SICILY: Scene of Athens' most disastrous undertaking during the war, the Sicilian Expedition of 415-413, which ended in the annihilation of the Athenian forces.

SIKYON: Greek city situated on the northeast of the Peloponnesos, adjacent to Korinth.

SIMON: A swindler, the details of whose peculations are unknown.

SIMONIDES: Of Keos, a lyric and elegiac poet (ca. 556-468 B.C.).

SKYTHIANS: Barbarians who lived in the region northeast of Thrace. Skythian archers were imported to Athens for use as police.

SOKRATES: (*Ca.* 469-399 B.C.) The great Athenian philosopher and teacher of Plato. In appearance he was almost grotesquely ugly; with his bulging eyes, fat lips, and a round paunch, he looked like nothing so much as a Satyr or

Silenos. This, combined with his practice of strolling about the marketplace and accosting citizens with questions about truth, justice, beauty, etc., made him an apt target for ridicule, all the more since it is doubtful whether the majority of Athenians could, in fact, distinguish between Sokrates and the average Sophist. That this is the case can be inferred from *The Clouds* and Aristophanes' extremely sophistic presentation of Sokrates.

SOPHOKLES: The Athenian tragedian (495-404 B.C.).

SOLON: Famous Athenian legislator (*ca.* 638-588 B.C.), whose achievement it was to have ended debt-slavery in Athens.

SPARTA: Capital city of Lakonia, principal opponent of Athens during the Peloponnesian War.

SYRAKOSIOS: An extremely garrulous Athenian orator whose loquacity earned him the sobriquet of The Jaybird.

TARTAROS: The great abyss which opened underneath Hades in the classical underworld.

TAŸGETOS: A high mountain in central Lakedaimon that separates Lakonia from Messenia.

TELAMON: Legendary king of Salamis; father of Aias.

TELEAS: Flighty and irresponsible Athenian bureaucrat; secretary to the Committee in charge of the Parthenon treasury.

TELEPHOS: Legendary king of Mysia and the subject of tragedies by Aischylos, Sophokles, and Euripides. Wounded by Achilleus while defending his country, Telephos was informed by an oracle that only the weapons which had given him his wound would cure him. Thereupon, disguised as a beggar, he made his way to Argos where, with the connivance of Klytaimnestra, he covertly took the young Orestes hostage. When the gathered Greeks were condemning Telephos for his hostility to their cause, the disguised hero made a speech in his own defense, but with such warmth and eloquence that the Greeks recognized him. When

Achilleus demanded his death. Telephos threatened to kill the infant Orestes. Finally, Achilleus relented and agreed to give Telephos the weapon which had wounded him and which would cure him

TEREUS: In mythology, a son of Ares and king of the Daulians in Thrace. According to the legend, Pandion, king of Athens, had two daughters, Prokne and Philomela. Prokne was married to Tereus, by whom she became the mother of a son, Itys. Tereus, however, became infatuated with Prokne's sister Philomela, raped her, and cut out her tongue to keep her from informing Prokne But Philomela managed to embroider her story in needlework and sent it to Prokne who, in retaliation against her husband, murdered her son Itys and served him up to Tereus for dinner When he discovered the truth, Tereus pursued Prokne and Philomela but, before he could catch them, he was transformed into a Hoopoe, Prokne into a Nightingale, and Philomela into the Swallow. (In the better known but less appropriate Latin version of the myth, Philomela is the nightingale and Prokne the swallow).

The story of Tereus was tragically treated by both Sophokles and Philokles.

THALES: Of Miletos, one of the Seven Sages of antiquity, renowned for his scientific genius and for having predicted an eclipse of the sun (ca. 636-546 B.C.)

THASIAN: From Thasos, a volcanic island in the northern Aegean, celebrated for the dark, fragrant wine produced by its vineyards.

THEBES: The principal city of Boiotia; during the Peloponnesian War an ally of Sparta.

THEOGENES: An Athenian braggart; probably took part with Kleon in the blockade of Sphakteria and was one of the signers of the Peace of Nikias in 421 B.C

THEOROS: Flatterer, perjurer, sycophant of Kleon

THESSALY: A large district in northern Greece. renowned throughout antiquity for its abundant supply of witches

THETIS: The sea nymph, mother of Achilleus by Peleus (q.v.). Courted against her wishes by Peleus, she changed herself successfully into a bird, a tree, and a tigress. But Peleus, acting on the instructions of the centaur Cheiron, countered by holding her fast until she assumed human form and consented to marry him.

THRACE: The eastern half of the Balkan peninsula.

TIMON: The famous Athenian misanthrope, a contemporary of Aristophanes; a legend during his own lifetime.

TITANS: The race of pre-Olympian deities, born of Heaven and Earth. After the coming of the Olympians, the Titans rebelled against Zeus and were vanquished in the Battle of the Gods and the Giants at Phlegra.

TLEPOLEMOS: Hero and son of Herakles, the subject of a tragedy by the dramatist Xenokles, one of the sons of Karkinos (q.v.). In the play one of the characters describes how his brother was killed by Tlepolemos.

TRIBALLOI: A savage people of Thrace. The name Triballos is merely an eponym of this people.

TROPHONIOS: King of Orchomenos, worshipped as a hero after his death. His oracle in a cave in Boiotia was celebrated throughout Hellas, and those who consulted him made it their practice to take honeycakes with which to appease the snakes who frequented the cavern.

TYPHO, TYPHON: A fire-breathing giant, frequently represented as a hurricane.

XANTHIAS: A common servile name.

XENOKLES: An Athenian tragedian, son of Karkinos (q.v.).

XENOPHANTES: Father of Hieronymos (q.v.).

ZAKYNTHOS: A large island in the Ionian Sea, south of Kephallenia and west of Elis; during the Peloponnesian War, an ally of Athens.

ZEUS: Chief god of the Olympian pantheon: son of Kronos, brother of Poseidon, father of Athene. As supreme ruler of the world, he is armed with thunder and lightning and creates storms and tempests